COLLECTED ECONOMIC ESSAYS
by Nicholas Kaldor

1. Essays on Value and Distribution
2. Essays on Economic Stability and Growth
3. Essays on Economic Policy I
4. Essays on Economic Policy II
5. Essays on Economic Theory
6. Essays on Applied Economics
7. Reports on Taxation I
8. Reports on Taxation II

COLLECTED ECONOMIC ESSAYS

Volume 8

REPORTS ON TAXATION II

REPORTS TO FOREIGN GOVERNMENTS

REPORTS ON
TAXATION II

REPORTS TO FOREIGN GOVERNMENTS

NICHOLAS KALDOR

DUCKWORTH

First published in 1980 by
Gerald Duckworth & Co. Ltd.
The Old Piano Factory
43 Gloucester Crescent
London NW1

ISBN 0 7156 0911 4

British Library Cataloguing in Publication Data

Kaldor, Nicholas
  Reports on taxation.
  2: Reports to foreign governments. – (Kaldor,
  Nicholas. Collected economic essays; 8).
  1. Taxation
  I. Title
  336.2'008   HJ2305
  ISBN 0-7156-0911-4

Printed in Great Britain by The Anchor Press Ltd
and bound by Wm Brendon & Son Ltd
both of Tiptree, Essex

CONTENTS

INTRODUCTION

The present volume assembles for the record a number of reports written at the request of foreign Governments or Governmental agencies at various times. These are predominantly concerned with taxation problems—in the context of various stages of economic development, and in differing socio-political settings. Except for two of the reports (on India and Ceylon) they have not been published before. Most of these reports relate to under-developed countries: the underlying problems which these encountered, and the reactions to which they gave rise, have already been described in the Introduction to Volume 3 of these Essays (pp. xviii–xx), as well as in a paper written at the request of the American periodical *Foreign Affairs* in 1962, also reproduced in Volume 3.[1] The present introduction is therefore largely confined to a brief explanation of the circumstances in which they came to be written.

The first paper reproduced here (in a much abridged form[2]) was written in Paris, in the office of the Comissariat du Plan. This was then headed by Jean Monnet, the real author and architect of the post-war reconstruction of France, which was based on the modernisation and expansion of a limited number of "key" industries under State guidance, with the aid of State finance, and which proved an unqualified success in the light of France's subsequent industrial development. My work for him was due to Robert Marjolin whom I had known as a colleague-economist from pre-war days, and who was familiar with my work on the fiscal and monetary implications of full employment policies written for Beveridge during the War.[3] When I met him in London

---

[1] "Will Underdeveloped Countries Learn to Tax?", Vol. 3 of these Essays, pp. 255–65.

[2] The original paper contained a fairly detailed analysis of social security provisions and their finance; it was not thought worthwhile to reprint these.

[3] Reproduced in Vol. 3 of these Essays, pp. 23–82.

in December 1946, the main work in connection with the first 5-year plan was already completed; Monnet was chiefly worried as to whether the state of the finances of France would permit the creation and mobilisation of savings for the plan, or whether continued inflation and financial disorder would prevent its implementation.

My work consisted in applying Keynesian methods of analysis to assess the size of the "gap" that would need to be closed and the methods by which this could be achieved, partly from domestic revenues and partly by mobilising external assistance or reserves. Tax reform was an essential part of the solution; and the main suggestions already under discussion—the introduction of a comprehensive and progressive income tax and of the value added tax—were duly carried out subsequently. There was, of course, also the Marshall Plan but when I wrote this report it was not yet conceived (though it rapidly took shape not many months later).

The experience gained in writing this report—particularly on the importance of agricultural prices, taxation and incentives in dealing with inflation—proved highly fruitful in much of my subsequent work in various countries.

All other reports in this volume date from after 1955—that is to say, after the publication of the minority report of the Royal Commission and my book on *An Expenditure Tax*. The first of these, relating to India, was written in New Delhi in January–March 1956, in the offices of the Income Tax department and with the assistance of officials of that department.[1] "Indian Tax Reform" is probably the most noteworthy of these reports and contains ideas which were newly developed in the course of writing it. It proposed a system of direct personal taxation based on the simultaneous application of a number of criteria or "yardsticks" (such as income, disposable wealth, capital gains, gifts and bequests received, personal expenditure) to be administered jointly on the basis of a single comprehensive return, which would

---

[1] Detailed acknowledgments of assistance received from local officials or experts accompanied the original Letters of Transmittal of these reports to the Ministers of Finance or other Ministers, but these are omitted from this volume.

have had (together with an automatic reporting system on capital transactions) important self-checking features for countering tax evasion. The joint return and the reporting system were essential parts of this plan, and so was the recommendation that the *rates* of taxation under the new system should be relatively moderate (with the highest band of income tax at 45 per cent).

A year after I left India, the then Minister of Finance, Mr. T. T. Krishnamachari, made a grandiose attempt to put these proposals into effect. But, from the start, the essential *props* of the system (the comprehensive return, the reporting system and the large reduction in the existing rate schedules) were missing; and in the course of a turbulent passage through Lok Sabha (the Indian Parliament) the various tax proposals became heavily riddled with exceptions and loopholes so that, in the end, the various taxes bore only a superficial resemblance to the taxes proposed.[1]

In the following year I received a request from Mr. Solomon Bandaranaike, the Prime Minister of Ceylon, to carry out an inquiry on tax reform in Ceylon; this was suggested to him, as I learnt from him later, by Pandit Nehru during a visit to Colombo.

I visited Ceylon twice, prepared a report in close collaboration with the Commissioner of Income Tax and also helped with drafting the legislation.

In the event, neither in India or Ceylon were the new taxes really "enforced"—they hardly yielded any revenue; and the particular tax on which the main hopes were based, the Expenditure Tax, was withdrawn in each country after a relatively short period. I have never found out whether the true cause of non-enforcement was the corruption of the officials or the connivance of Ministers. However, the experience gained in these two cases served as a warning which I invariably repeated on subsequent occasions when I received similar requests from other countries— i.e. that passing laws aiming at income redistribution through taxation is not likely to succeed in its object unless there is a genuine will and ability to carry the laws into execution. In

---

[1] My view of the shortcomings of the reform as it reached the Statute Book is given in an address to members of the Lok Sabha on "Tax reform in India" reproduced in Vol. 3 of these Essays, pp. 216–21.

countries (such as Mexico) where the institution of permanent civil servants is virtually non-existent (the tradition is that a fresh set of officials is appointed with each new President) or in countries like India or Turkey, where a career civil service exists but the revenue officers in charge of administering the tax laws are generally comparatively low-grade officials on very low salaries, it is too much to expect that the assessment of millionaires will not be affected by the scope for huge rewards to be gained through bribery.[1]

The invitation to me from Mr. Ortiz-Mena, the Finance Minister, to visit Mexico and report on tax reform in the summer of 1960, was prompted by my report on India, a copy of which seems to have reached him. I found it difficult to believe that Mexico was politically ready for a major change in the system of taxation in a progressive direction; but the Minister insisted that he was very keen on my doing this work and promised every assistance as well as freedom to publish my report, subject to the usual safeguards.[2] In the end my report was not released for publication in Mexico but given to a succession of "committees" for consideration (and I had no wish, of course, to interfere with their work by a premature publication of my report). I thought that, after a time, the recommendations of the report had been quietly buried; but when I was last in Mexico two years ago, to attend a Conference, I gathered from various economists working for the Government that quite a number of the recommendations concerning a simplified system of income tax had, in fact, been carried out and others were under consideration.

[1] The one aspect of my report on India, on the publication of which Ministers had serious misgivings, concerned the estimate of tax evasion (printed on pp. 156–7 below). However, since I was not given any reason why my estimate was biased, I insisted on publishing the figures, particularly since the method by which they were derived was fully shown, so that anyone would be able to amend them in the light of further information or more detailed estimates concerning the amount of incomes and their distribution. (Partly as a result of the publicity which these estimates received in India, the Government appointed a Commission of Inquiry composed of Members of Parliament, lawyers, etc., to recommend ways of improving the administration of direct taxes. The Commission invited me to Delhi to give evidence and my main suggestion was that they should look on the history of the Chinese Maritime Customs as a model in establishing a *corps d'élite* of financial inspectors, which effectively ended bribery in the administration of taxes in a country where corruption was as deeply ingrained as Imperial China. However, the suggestion that this required the institution of a corps of highly-paid officials, selected by competitive examinations, appointed for life and protected from interference by Ministers or politicians, found very little favour among the members of the Commission.)

[2] These concern confidential information or the premature disclosure of recommendations while these are still under consideration by the Government.

During 1961, I was pressed to examine and advise urgently on the budgetary position and tax system in two developing countries heading for economic crisis: first in Ghana and then in British Guiana. My report on British Guiana is reproduced in this volume (pp. 272–309). Though I made several short visits to Ghana after the first in May, beguiled by the magic charm of Dr. Nkrumah's personality to become deeply involved in Ghana's economic and financial problems, and collaborated closely with officials in the preparation of the Budget Statement and Finance Bill of that year, there was nothing in the nature of a report which could be reproduced here.

In both countries, the basic fiscal measures immediately required to avoid balance of payments crises and enable sound development were similar; and so, especially with benefit of hindsight, was the frailty of the existing power base for bringing into operation the requisite restraints and reforms. The nature and style of the two governments, and of their respective leaders who had called for my advice—President Dr. Nkrumah and Prime Minister Dr. Jagan—could hardly have been in stronger contrast, however; and the political settings, which in each case delayed or frustrated some urgent economic measures, were quite different. In both countries there was a clear need for a fairer contribution to local revenue by great international companies, from profits all too easily concealed by syphoning these off to tax havens through the device of "transfer pricing" between subsidiaries, as well as for generation of savings from the locally employed population with earnings above a certain level. It is a matter for speculation, in both countries, what unholy alliance of capitalist interests and organised labour may have underpinned popular disturbances which followed government proposals to advance on both these fiscal fronts.

In Ghana, at that time, the ambience of government was that of a mediaeval court, flamboyant, extravagant and corrupt. An initially strong financial position, based on Ghana's rapidly expanding cocoa output and the high world price of cocoa, had been dissipated in a grasshopper's summer of waste, extravagance, corruption and prestige projects recklessly undertaken, on the basis of short and medium term export credit financing, on the blandishments of European (mainly British) business interests.[1] While the President was personally convinced that disaster, threatened by a large budgetary deficit, a balance of payments gap and rapidly dwindling reserves, could only be averted by radical measures to restore balance to the budget, discourage luxury imports, stem extravagance and fight corruption, events proved that he lacked the power to deal with corrupt ministers and the strength to eschew, at least for a three year period, the adoption of additional prestige projects. His Budget did introduce provisions whereby the profits arising in Ghana of expatriate companies would be deemed to be no lower, in relation to their local turnover, than the ratio of their consolidated world profits to their consolidated world sales to third parties—which resulted in the event in a manifold increase in revenue from company taxation. A scheme of compulsory savings (equivalent to 5 per cent. of income above a certain exemption limit) in the form of non-negotiable bonds intended for transfer to a contributory old-age pension scheme in due course, was also introduced but subsequently abandoned as a result of agitation against this "anti-social" measure. Some effect was also given to my recommendation that high import duties should be imposed on luxury imports (the alternative of a licensing system I dismissed as inevitably leading to a new source of corruption). At the President's personal request, I had also worked out a scheme to deal with corruption amongst ministers and party bosses but, in the course of putting this into execution, Nkrumah found himself confronted with a minor revolt of ministers and their collaborators. This resulted in a last-minute abandonment of the scheme, bar some face-saving trivialities; it also brought a sudden end to my association with Dr. Nkrumah.[2]

The contrast in atmosphere when I visited British Guiana later

[1] Unlike the Volta River Dam Project, which was thoroughly justified in terms of long-run development and financed by long-term loan from the World Bank.

[2] By no means was all lost, however: in 1965 the former Commissioner of Income Tax in Ghana (a Canadian, who served in Ghana under United Nations technical assistance) wrote to me from the International Monetary Fund, Washington, that the principles for taxation and its administration which I set forth in 1961 in Ghana were, after the initial shock, singularly successful. The tax yield, in the Central Revenue Department, rose from £9 million in 1960–61 to approximately £29 million in the financial year ended September 30, 1964. The gains from purchase tax and customs duties were also very considerable.

in the year was extreme. Here the Cabinet of Dr. Jagan brought
to mind the Elders of some Scottish Presbyterian Church: a group
of men of strong, puritanical convictions and honesty, though
with little political experience or sagacity in wielding power. The
latter was in any case insecurely based, in that they lacked an
absolute majority of votes, depending almost entirely on the support of the Indian population (descended from indentured labour
brought over from India in the nineteenth century to work on the
sugar plantations), as against the negro population (brought over
from Africa as slaves in the eighteenth century and earlier) of
approximately equal number. Forbes Burnham, the political
leader who enjoyed the support of the urban negro population,
had but to make common cause with Mr. d'Aguiar, the leader of
the white minority, to shake the party in power. This constellation
of forces and population structure paved the way for a constitutional reform of the electoral system to one of proportional repre-
sentation (urged by the United States) a few years later, with the
result that Dr. Jagan's party fell from power to be replaced by a
coalition government in 1964.

Meanwhile, the Budget Speech of January 1962, which embraced all my recommendations, led to rioting in Georgetown,
severe enough to involve calling in the British military; and, as
in Ghana, an attempt by the unions to bring the Government
down through strike action. Whether or not this reaction was
fomented by wider tensions or particular interests, implementation of the Budget provisions was delayed and modified, though
substantial reforms (some cancelled later following the change of
Government) were put through to the benefit of the critical
financial situation and future development.[1]

The invitation to Turkey in 1962 came through the U.K.
Ministry of Overseas Development. It appeared that the Turkish
Government had asked for my services under a scheme of British
technical assistance; and though there was natural reluctance at
first among Conservative Ministers (who would have preferred
to send a less "controversial" economist) they finally agreed when

---

[1] In the Introduction to volume 3 in this series, pages xix–xx, there is some discussion
of the political agitations which followed presentation of the budgets drawing on my
advice in Ghana and British Guiana, with references given to the published official
post-mortems on the disturbances in both countries.

the Turks refused to accept any substitute. The overriding problem in Turkey was (and, as far as I know, still is) agricultural stagnation, which is the main cause of inflation and of the chronic balance of payments crisis. My main suggestion was to force the large land-owners through a progressive land tax (reminiscent of the famous land tax introduced in Japan after the Meiji restoration, which was the foundation of Japan's economic development) to increase the production of cash crops or, failing that, to sell off part of their land. This agreed very much with the State Planning Organis-ation's ideas of the primary economic needs of Turkey. The Turkish cabinet (which at that time was of the relatively pro-gressive Republican Party, following the removal of the Govern-ment of the Justice Party of Mr. Menderes by a military coup two years earlier) refused its approval, however, despite the personal support of the Prime Minister, Ismet Inonü, the G.O.M. of Turkey. As a result the whole leadership of the State Planning Organisation offered its resignation; but their resignation was accepted without strain, and this seems to have been the end, not only of my tax plans, but of any radical land reform in Turkey.

After the experience in Turkey I was not anxious to accept any further assignments from "developing" or "peripheral" countries; and with the return of a Labour Government in 1964 I became fully preoccupied with British public finance. However, three years later, in 1967, a deputation of Iranians called on me at the Treasury saying that their Prime Minister, Mr. Hoveyda, was anxious for my advice on a number of matters—having been told by a British visitor (who might well have had mixed motives) that I was the best economist in Britain to call on for such advice. I explained that it would not be possible for me to come to Teheran for more than a short period, and even that would depend on my political and official chiefs (Mr. Callaghan and Sir William Armstrong) giving their approval.

However, this approval was granted and I visited Iran in July 1967 and left behind the report which is reprinted on pp. 336–55. The most intriguing part of that report is in the third section on taxation issues. In commenting on the new Income Tax Bill then before Parliament, after showing that the existing income tax of

Iran cost a great deal to collect while yielding very little revenue to the State, I made clear my view that the main outcome of the proposed reforms would be to increase the efficiency of an instrument of extortion by the bureaucracy—that the uncertain taxes and the wide discretionary powers given to tax inspectors would have the effect not only of encouraging corruption but of forcing taxpayers into paying bribes to avoid ruinous assessments. Indeed my brief visit to Iran convinced me that corruption played a distinctive role in Iran: that while in countries like India it was an undesirable by-product of the system, in Iran it constituted the cement which held the system together—complicated regulations were made or taxes enacted in order to enable a body of privileged officials to extort bribes from the business community; and it was the very system of extorting bribes which gave coherence and solidity to the ruling regime. As subsequent events have proved, the very same system set up centrifugal forces which in the end proved stronger than the cohesion enforced by the universal spread of extortionate bribery and corruption.

The last and most recent of the papers printed here was written in Caracas at the invitation of Mr. Gunesaldo Rodriguez, the Minister of Co-ordination and Planning of the Government. The purpose of this assignment was rather a different one from that of the earlier reports—it was to review and assess the merits of a tax reform plan which had already been submitted to the Congress of Venezuela by Mr. Hurtado, the Minister of Finance. The circumstances of Venezuela were rather different from those in the other countries I visited—it is a country where the operations of the Government have been largely financed by oil revenues; the payment of *direct* taxes was virtually unknown. The problem was to make the tax revenues cover at least the current expenditure of the Government and to ease the transition to a future period when oil revenues would no longer be adequate to finance both current and capital expenditures—without at the same time slowing down the rate of economic development in the country. Mr. Hurtado's carefully thought out reform plan seemed to me to promise reasonable advance towards these ends.

The purpose of publishing these reports is chiefly to provide a record. It was essential therefore to refrain from "editing" solely to avoid repetition. While each report is tailored to the particular time and place, there was naturally an underlying general philosophy which was set out in each case in a manner appropriate to the recommendations. This does mean, however, that reading the papers consecutively a reader would find particular arguments recurring in various reports.

NICHOLAS KALDOR

King's College
Cambridge
May 1980

1

A PLAN FOR THE FINANCIAL
STABILISATION OF FRANCE[1]

SINCE the end of 1946, the economic situation of France shows
a period of comparative tranquillity. Prices have, on the whole,
been stabilised, and even show a slight reduction. The value of
gold in the black market, and Stock Exchange prices, have shown
a spectacular fall. There are even signs of a mild deflation in
certain consumers' goods markets, particularly in the luxury
trades. All this followed a period of comparatively rapid inflation
in the second half of 1946, and can be dated from the time of the
first price-reduction decree of the Blum Government.

Any analysis of the present position and prospects in France must
start with an explanation of the reasons for the present stability;
how, and why the inflation of the previous year was brought
(perhaps only temporarily) to an end. A simple orthodox explanation would not suffice, since the main factor that is generally
looked for as the basic cause of an inflationary process, the rate of
Government expenditure in excess of tax receipts, has not—
apparently—been sensibly diminished, if both ordinary and
extraordinary expenditures are taken into account.

To explain the situation, one must, first of all, bear in mind
that an inflationary process has two separate consequences:

(1) It creates a re-distribution of income from the rentiers,
shareholders, and owners of immobile capital (and to a lesser
extent, from wage and salary earners including civil servants) in
favour of the profits of enterprise;

(2) It creates an expectation of a continued rise in prices, and
thus increases the monetary profitability of real investment—i.e.,
it raises the "marginal efficiency of capital" of Keynes.

To the extent that the first effect is operative, an inflationary

<hr />

[1] Extract from a report prepared for the *Commissariat Général du Plan* in Paris, March–
May 1947. Not hitherto published.

process tends to bring about its own cure; since the process of income re-distribution is likely to reduce the pressure of excessive demand. The reason for this is that the standards of consumption of all classes of society are imperfectly elastic; the reduced consumption of the classes whose incomes are wiped out by the inflation is not fully replaced by the increased consumption of the classes which gain (this process is further assisted if in the course of inflation—as actually happened in France—the prices of consumers' goods rise faster than the prices of investment goods so that a smaller proportion of income saved may suffice to finance a given volume of real investment).

If, nevertheless, historical inflations so often become progressive, instead of degressive, this is to be accounted for by the second factor: the expectation of rising prices created by the inflation itself, assisted by the vicious spiral of rising wages and prices. This is the reason why a purely psychological change—such as a belief in a coming monetary stabilisation—is sometimes sufficient to halt, or reverse the process, without any major change in the basic factors of the situation. In such cases, the basic factors which originally caused the inflation must have ceased to be operative; and the inflationary process was fed mainly by the psychological factor.

This appears to have been the situation in France towards the end of 1946. Table 1 shows the manner in which the inflationary process has altered the distribution of incomes. This table shows the total value of production at market prices, and how this value was divided between the different elements of cost that enter into prices. It can be looked upon as the "make-up" of a composite commodity which is representative of the whole national output of goods and services. The item "profits" is residual, and it contains both depreciation, distributed (both in dividends and in other forms) and undistributed profits. (The division of profits between these elements in the different sectors of the economy is shown in Table 2.) As shown in Table 1, the share of work (wages and salaries, but excluding the salaries of the officials, has fallen, between 1938 and the second half of 1946, from 32·5 per cent. to 26·5 per cent.[1] Even if the employers' contributions to

[1] These percentages refer to gross output at *market prices*, i.e. without deducting indirect taxes.

Table 1

DISTRIBUTION OF NATIONAL PRODUCT BY CLASSES OF
RECIPIENTS

milliards of francs

	1938	%	2nd half 1946 (current prices)	%
Income from work	130	32·5	840	26·5
Social insurance	3 ⎫		64 ⎫	
Family allowances	3 ⎬ 7	1·7	52 ⎬ 136	4·3
Pensions	1 ⎭		20 ⎭	
Investment income: loan interest	9	2·2	16	0·5
Property income	35	8·7	99	3·1
Profits (including depreciation):				
Agriculture	61 ⎫	15·2 ⎫	626 ⎫	19·8 ⎫
Manufacturing	69 ⎪	17·5 ⎪	570 ⎪	18·0 ⎪
Transport	11·5 ⎬ 192	2·9 ⎬ 48·2	90 ⎬ 1872	2·8 ⎬ 59·2
Commerce	37·5 ⎪	9·4 ⎪	464 ⎪	14·7 ⎪
Services	13 ⎭	3·2 ⎭	122 ⎭	3·9 ⎭
Gross product at factor cost	373	93·2	2963	3·6
Indirect taxes less subsidies	27	6·8	202	6·4
Gross national product at market prices	400	100·0	3165	100·0

Note: Columns may not add precisely to given totals, because of rounding.

social insurance, etc. are added to the cost of labour, there is
still a percentage diminution from 34·2 per cent. to 30·8 per cent.
The share of loan interest and rents (both on houses and land
property) has fallen from 10·9 per cent. to 3·6 per cent. (If the
dividends of joint stock companies were added to this group—as
logically they should be—the fall is from 12·4 per cent. to just
under 4 per cent.) On the other hand, the gross profits had
increased from 48 per cent. to 59 per cent., while the weight of
indirect taxes had remained unchanged.

The shift in income distribution is even larger if the weight of
direct taxation falling on the different types of income is also taken
into account. As will be shown later on, in the section on taxation,
the amount of taxes (in real terms) paid out of wages and salaries

Table 2

ALLOCATION OF PROFITS AMONG DIFFERENT SECTORS

1938, milliards of francs

	Agriculture	Manufacturing	Transport	Commerce	Services	Total
Distributed profits:						
dividends	–	4	1	–	1	6
other	52	37	3	33·5	11·5	137
Undistributed profits	–	14	–	1.5	0·5	16
Depreciation	9	14	7·5	2·5	–	33
Total	61	69	11·5	37·5	13	192

1946 (2nd half at annual rates) in current prices, milliards of francs

	Agriculture	Manufacturing	Transport	Commerce	Services	Total
Profits (distributed and undistributed)						
dividends	–	8	2	1	1	12
all other profits	573	477	40	447	119	1656
Depreciation	53	85	48	16	2	204
Total	626	570	90	464	122	1872

has risen, while those paid out of profits have considerably fallen, as compared with the pre-war situation.

If prices in the first four months of 1947 remained roughly stable, and the pressure of excess demand, as evidenced by black market prices, had diminished, this indicates that the proportion of incomes not spent on consumption during these months must have been sufficient to offset the budgetary deficits of the Government accounts (including, here, the extraordinary budget) and of private investments. The latter, of course, must have sensibly diminished since 1946, as a result of the reduced investment in stocks—both of speculative stocks, and of the replenishment of stocks of a non-speculative character.

Tables 3 and 4 show the total amount of credit granted through the monetary and financial system in the first and second halves of 1946 and the first quarter of 1947 to the State and local authorities and to private industries (including the nationalised industries)

Table 3

FINANCING OF EXPENDITURES OF PRIVATE AND NATIONALISED COMPANIES
(excluding self-financing)

milliards of francs

	1st half 1946	2nd half 1946	1st quarter 1947[1]
Savings invested on the market	33	28	28
Bank credit	39	98	30
Movements in public bond portfolios of companies	−22	22	−26
Banque de France	13	40	−18
Total	63	188	14

[1] At half-yearly rates.

Table 4

FINANCING OF THE DEFICIT OF THE STATE AND LOCAL AUTHORITIES

milliards of francs

	1st half 1946	2nd half 1946	1st quarter 1947[1]
Franc equivalent of gold and foreign exchange	50	50	50
Savings invested on the market through the intermediation of the Casse des Dépôts	28	15	8
Short-term bonds:			
subscribed by the banks	35	−46	−
subscribed by private individuals	22	−22	26
Current postal accounts	10	10	16
Banque de France	30	73	92
Total	175	80	192

[1] At half-yearly rates.

respectively. The interest of these tables is that while there was no diminution in the credit requirements of the State, as between the first three months of the present year and the previous year (in fact, on a six months' basis, 192 milliards of francs were required by the State in the first three months of 1947 as against 175 milliards in the first six months of 1946), the credit granted to private industries has shown a remarkable fall: from 178 milliards in the second half of 1946 to 14 milliards. The explanation of this fall must be due to a reduction in the investments in stocks by private industry and thus tends to support the explanation of the situation that was suggested above. It must be borne in mind that not all investment in stocks is financed by bank credit. To a certain extent (that cannot be quantitatively measured) investment in stocks is financed directly out of current profits. Assuming that the trends of these investments was the same as those financed through bank credit, the change in private investment (taking into account both fixed investments and working capital) must have been even larger than these figures suggest.

There is no very reliable estimate as to the division of private investments between investments in fixed capital and working capital. The total fixed investment in private industries and the nationalised corporations was estimated at the rate of 125 milliards in 1948 and at the annual rate of 150 milliards at present. Of this sum, about 50 milliards per annum can be regarded as being provided by self-financing. On the basis of this calculation, the fixed investments through the financial and banking system in private industries and the nationalised companies can be put at 40 milliards for the second half of 1946 and 50 milliards for the first half of 1947. Thus, of the 165 milliards taken up by this sector in the second half of 1946, no less than 125 milliards must have represented increases in stocks. On the same calculation in the first quarter of 1947, there must have been a net dishoarding of stocks, which, expressed on a six months' basis, amounts to 35 milliards. In other words, there was a reduction of investment in working capital of 160 milliards on a six months' basis, or 320 milliards on an annual basis. This must have been cause of the relief from inflationary pressure: and we must again remember that to the extent that investments in stocks are financed directly out of profits, these figures must understate the magnitude of the change.

While the increase in stocks in 1946 must have been exceptionally large, partly because of the rapid increase of productive activities and partly owing to the speculative hoarding of stocks engendered by the inflation, it is obvious that the *negative* investment in stocks in the first months of the present year must have been due to a dishoarding of speculative stocks and is therefore purely temporary in character. Although there are no statistics in France as to a normal movement in stocks in relation to the movement of productive activities, on the basis of the experience of other countries the normal investment in stocks can be put at some 100 milliards of francs a year.[1]

It follows from this analysis that the relief from inflationary pressure which France has experienced since the end of 1946 must be purely temporary, and that, unless new measures are taken, the process of inflation will be resumed. The relief must have been due to changing expectations as regards the movement of prices which led to a reversal of speculative investments—a cessation of the hoarding of stocks and a certain net dishoarding. This may have been due to a change of expectations, as a result of the success of the first price reduction decree of the Blum Government, coupled with the expectation that further similar decrees will succeed in the future; it may have been linked also with the fall of the price of gold which can be partly attributed to the action of the Swiss Government. On the other hand, it may have been due also to the new measures of credit control introduced towards the end of 1946, which make it more difficult for traders to borrow for speculative purposes. To the extent that it was mainly caused by the first factor, the situation is essentially volatile: the mere resumption of the normal investment in stocks would be sufficient to renew the inflationary pressure, and this, in turn, by renewing the expectation of rising prices, would further accelerate the investments in stocks as well. Expectation of rising prices could also be created as the result of price adjustments in the economy

---

[1] This is based on the assumption that the gross value of production at current prices increases by 200 milliards a year, and that for the economic system as a whole, stocks represent an average of six months' turnover.

which we shall discuss later (such as rises in the price of wheat, and in the prices of coal, gas, or electricity) quite apart from additional pressure coming from the side of demand.

THE REQUIREMENTS OF MONETARY STABILISATION

We are now in a position to make some tentative estimates as to what would be required to ensure monetary stabilisation without sacrificing the level of real investment envisaged in the Plan. As Table 5 shows, the amount of State deficit for 1947 can be put at

Table 5

ORDER OF MAGNITUDE OF STATE EXPENDITURES AND EFFECTIVE RECEIPTS
(based on budget estimates)

milliards of francs

	1946			1947	
	1st half	2nd half	Total	1st quarter[1]	Year
Non-productive expenditures	250	302	552	320	640
Investment expenditures[2]	80	115	195	140	320
Total	330	417	747	460	960
Budgetary receipts	193	260	453	280	590
Difference	137	157	294	180	370

[1] At half-yearly rates.
[2] Includes military investments and excludes investment by the nationalised corporations.

360 milliards, as against some 300 milliards in 1946. This includes both the deficit of the ordinary budget, the expenditures of the Treasury in connection with the deficit of State enterprises, etc. and the share of the State in the financing of the investment plan. The deficit of the ordinary budget can be put at 50 milliards while another 50 milliards represent non-productive expenses outside the budget.

Table 6 is an attempt to put together all the expenditures which must be financed out of savings of some kind or another, in order

Table 6

ESTIMATES OF GROSS INVESTMENT AND OF OTHER
FINANCING NEEDS OF THE STATE AND ENTERPRISES

milliards of francs

	Total	To be financed by the State	To be financed by industries, nation-alised and private
Deficit of the State and Local Authorities	120	120	–
Investment envisaged in the Plan	400	250[1]	150
Maintenance of capital:			
Plant and equipment (including transport) Buildings	135 ⎫ 210 75 ⎭	–	210
Increment of stocks (at normal rates)	100	–	100
Total investment and deficit	830	370[1]	460[2]
of which externally financed (by excess of imports)	150[3]	150	–
Remainder	680	220	460
Self-financing:			
Maintenance of capital Investment in new equipment	210 ⎫ 260 50 ⎭	–	260
Remainder: to be financed by the financial and banking system	420	220[1]	200[2]

[1] Not including 70 milliards of investment by nationalised industries.
[2] Including 70 milliards of "basic investments" by nationalised industries.
[3] Estimate based on the possibilities of reductions in the import programme.

that inflation should be avoided. It includes the effective maintenance of capital and makes a corresponding allowance for this in the figures of self-financing. It shows that the total call on resources for the main requirements for non-productive deficit, investments, maintenance of capital and increase of stocks will be 830 milliards, out of which 370 must be financed by State funds, and 460 by private funds (this includes 70 milliards investment by the nationalised corporations under private financing. If this is also to be debited to the State, the respective amounts are 440 by the State, and 390 by private industries).

A certain proportion of the total is financed from abroad in the form of an excess of imports over exports; this is put at 150 milliards and it reduces by an equivalent amount, the amount required to be raised internally for stocks financing. (This item should be credited to the State, to whom it accrues either as the franc equivalent of gold and exchanged foreign currency or else, in so far as it covers goods and services bought abroad directly for the use of the State, by reducing the expenditure of the State in francs by a corresponding amount.) A further 260 milliards is covered by self-financing (including of course the maintenance of capital) which leaves 420 milliards to be financed internally, 220 by the State and 200 by private industries. We must envisage that this allows only for the normal increase of stocks. In so far as there is speculative hoarding in stocks engendered by inflation, the total investment and the amount to be financed through the banking system are raised correspondingly.

Although available statistics do not permit any close estimates to be made, it appears that this amount of 400 milliards is just about double the sum that could, while preserving the conditions of monetary stability, be safely financed through the monetary and banking system. The flow of savings in the market may perhaps be put at some hundred milliards per annum while a further hundred milliards might be put as the amount saved in the form of bank deposit or hoarding in cash. These are of course extremely tentative figures, but they are not unreasonable and could be supported to a certain extent by the figures of the distribution of national income that were given in Table 1. It was there shown that the total gross profit of agriculture, industry, etc. amounts to some 1,890 milliards at the prices in the second half of 1946; if we assume that these sectors consume in real terms the same amount as before the war (the consumption in the agricultural sector is known to be considerably more, but the consumption out of this revenue in the rest of the economy might well be less on balance), and if we deduct the direct taxes falling on this income, this leaves some 400 to 500 milliards for the purpose of maintenance, direct investment and monetary savings. Since the self-financing shown in Table 5 takes up 250 milliards, this would leave some 200 milliards as monetary savings.

On this basis, it will be necessary, in order to secure monetary stability without reducing the contemplated level of real investment, to reduce potential consumption by some 200 milliards per annum, either through additional taxation or compulsory loans, or other special measures intended to discourage consumption (more extensive and effective rationing system, and/or special measures taken to prevent luxury consumption). The problem of taxation and of other means of reducing consumption will be discussed below. But, before we come to that, it is necessary to deal with the other great problem endangering both the stability of the currency and the efficient working of the economic system, namely the problem of relative prices.

THE RELATION OF PRICES

Owing to the unusual degree of effectiveness with which measures of control could be applied in the economic system, and partly also on account of the increased relative scarcity of certain commodities, the present price system shows considerable alterations as compared with before the war.

These are shown by a comparison of the percentage distribution of the "produit national brut" (G.N.P.) and the "disponibilités nationales" (Disposable National Product) in terms of 1938 prices and current prices, which is given in Table 7.

(1) The reduced shares in the total "disponibilités" of importation (and also of exportation) in terms of current prices as compared with 1938 prices is evidence of the over-valuation of the franc at the current official rate of exchange. This does not necessarily indicate the desirability of a devaluation of the franc. But it suggests that, unless special measures are going to be taken to subsidise exports (by means of tax remissions, for example), the envisaged increase in exports in future years may be difficult to bring about.

(2) More important are the changes in relative prices in the sphere of the home economy itself. As Table 7 shows, industrial

Table 7
DISTRIBUTION OF NATIONAL INCOME AT CURRENT AND 1938 PRICES

In Percentage of disposable National Product

	1938	2nd half 1946	2nd half 1946
		(1938 prices)	(1946 prices)
Gross National Product	98	95	97
Imports	+11	+10	+7
Exports	−9	−5	−4
Disposable National Product	100	100	100
Gross Product of Government services	6	9	7
Food products	37	32	48
Other non durable goods	20	21	16
Lodgings	6	5	1
Clothing, textiles and leather	9	9	9
Other durable goods	6	6	6
Total consumption goods	78	73	80
Mechanical equipment	5	6	4
Transport equipment	3	5	3
Buildings and public works	6	6	5
Armaments	2	1	1
Total capital goods	16	18	13

consumption goods (clothing, textiles and leather, and other durable goods) show a price increase that is equal to the average. Food products, on the other hand, show a very large relative increase, the percentage of this group in the G.N.P. being 48 in terms of current prices, and only 32 per cent. in terms of 1938 prices. On the other hand, the group "other non-durable goods" which includes coal, electricity, gas, railway transportation, P.T.T., as well as newspapers, books, pharmacy and medicine, cinema and other entertainments, shows a considerable relative fall in prices, because, in this group, measures of price control could be made relatively more effective. The same distortion is apparent among capital goods, particularly the mechanical equipment and transport material groups. The greatest relative fall is however shown in the case of lodgings, which makes up 5 per cent. of the disposable product in terms of 1938 francs, and only 1 per cent. in terms of 1946 francs.

In some cases, these present artificially low prices may not have very detrimental effects on the working of the economy apart from causing a deficit in the industries supplying these goods and services, and thus compelling the State to subsidise them and hence raising the requirements of taxation. In other cases, however, the existence of these unduly low prices indirectly impedes the mechanism of adjustment; in the case of lodgings, for example, the low level of rents undoubtedly increases the housing shortage by making it more difficult for people to move and, in some cases, forcing them to maintain a larger establishment than they would find suitable. It must also be borne in mind that the low prices of lodgings and of public utilities like gas, electricity, transports, etc. directly contribute to the high level of food prices. The reason for this is that, owing to the ineffectiveness of price control (apart from particular commodities like wheat), the level of food prices depends predominantly on the purchasing power of the town population. Owing to the scarcity of foodstuffs, the town population is willing to devote most of its free income to the purchase of food, after covering the essential requirements of the household. A rise in rents and of the prices of public services, by reducing the available purchasing power for food, would, therefore, as will be argued below, tend to decrease the price of foodstuffs to the town population.

(3) The most detrimental maladjustment in the field of relative prices is, however, within the agricultural sector: the low price of wheat in relation to other cereals and meat. This endangers essential supplies owing to the high elasticity of substitution between different agricultural goods. This problem will be discussed in connection with agriculture below.

The removal of these maladjustments in relative prices will certainly become necessary sooner or later. The danger is that, when made, the adjustments will on each occasion cause a certain increase in the cost of living (because it is much easier to adjust low prices upward than to secure a reduction in high prices) and thus risk destabilising the money-wage system. In the present situation, moreover, an increase in money wages will automatically tend to raise food prices and to recreate the same kind of maladjustment in the realm of relative prices as existed before. Hence, so long as adequate measures cannot be taken to insure that price increases in certain sectors of the economic system have previously been offset through decreases in others, it is far better to maintain the low prices in the controlled sector, even though this means a continuation of State subsidies.

The solution of the problem will really require a scheme for an overall adjustment in the whole price system, in other words a scheme by which the total effects of the necessary adjustments in the cost of living could be calculated beforehand, and their effect on the system of wages could be initially determined and agreed upon with the representatives of the trade unions. An overall adjustment of this kind would of course be rendered very much easier if the problem of controlling food prices could be solved beforehand. This, in my opinion, is the key to the solution of the problem of monetary stability from the point of view of prices and also to any successful attempt to increase the real wages of the working classes. We shall, therefore, consider next the special problem presented by agriculture.

THE SPECIAL PROBLEM OF AGRICULTURE

As between 1938–9 and 1946–7 the total output of agriculture is estimated to have fallen by 16·6 per cent. The proportion of the final product which is consumed on the farm is estimated to have risen from 20 to 30 per cent. and, in addition, there is an increase of agricultural stocks (including livestocks) in the later years which is estimated at 50 milliard francs. As a result of these changes, the supply of food (apart from imported food) available to the non-agricultural population appears to have been reduced by 33 per cent. as compared with pre-war. (This does not take into account any net increase in the importation of foodstuffs from abroad, as compared with pre-war.)

Table 8
AGRICULTURE

(a) Disposition of farm output   milliards of francs

	1938–9	1946–7 at 1938 prices	1946–7 at current prices
Final agricultural product	90	75	750
Percentage	100	83·3	
Total consumed on farms (including farm workers)	18	22·5	225
Percentage	20	30	
Increase of stocks	–	5	50
Total marketed product	72	47·5	475

(b) Allocation of receipts from marketed product   milliards of francs

	1938	1946
Purchase of means of production	20	150
Purchase of food products	8	50
Purchase of industrial consumer goods	(30)	225
Savings and direct taxes	(14)	50
Total	72	475

(c) Population and food consumption

	1938	1946
Agricultural population (millions)	10 to 10½	9 to 9½
As percentage of total population	25	23
Food consumption per head, 1938=100:		
Agricultural population	100	138
Non-agricultural population	100	66

The consumption per head of the agricultural population on the other hand (taking the fall in the agricultural population into account) must have risen by no less than 38 per cent. (these figures are set out in Table 8); hence, if the agricultural population could be made to consume only the same amount of food per head as before the war, this would make it possible to increase the food supply to the urban population without increasing total production by some 15 per cent.

This, in brief, is the essence of the agricultural problem. Its causes are:

(1) That the prices of agricultural products have increased

relatively to the industrial products; which in turn is to be explained by the fact that, owing to the control of prices of certain goods and services which enter into the urban cost of living, the proportion of urban incomes which are available to the purchase of food has increased.

(2) That owing to the non-availability of many industrial products, the desire of the agricultural population for monetary purchasing power has diminished (although the figures appear to show that the real consumption of industrial products by the agricultural population is no less than it was before the war).

(3) The fact that the weight of direct taxation on agriculture has also diminished as compared with pre-war, thus further lessening the farmers' need for money.

A further problem, indicated above, is that while the price of wheat has risen five times, that of meat and lard is up 14 times, that of eggs and milk about 9 times, and other prices about 11 times as compared with before the war. The result is that the production of wheat is discouraged, and the proportion of cereal production used for cattle breeding and egg production is greatly enhanced.

The solution of these problems could be sought along four alternative lines:

(1) The introduction of effective methods of control, which would reduce the present prices of meat, lard, etc. to a level comparable to that of wheat. This presupposes that for these commodities, distribution is taken over by Government agencies, similarly to wheat. The introduction of effective control of distribution, if practicable, would present far the best solution, as it would, at the same time, remove the discord in relative prices and also reduce the monetary receipts of the farmers, and thus compel them to sell a higher proportion of their produce. It would also reduce the cost of living of the urban population and thus enable price adjustments in other sectors without necessitating an increase of wages. The danger is, however, that if the measures of control could not be effectively carried out, the re-introduction of these policies would serve to delay the adoption of other means of solution.

(2) Increase in industrial prices of those groups of commodities which the farmers need to buy; this could be achieved by in-

creasing the sales tax on those commodities. It would be difficult, however, to delimit this increase in such a way that it would not affect significantly the cost of living of the urban population; and politically, it would be bound to meet with resistance, especially since in order to make an effective contribution to the problem, the price increases might have to be fairly large.

(3) Special schemes could be devised to divert additional supplies of industrial goods to the farmers by giving them priority in the purchase of motor-cars, tyres, rubber boots, etc. The priorities could be made dependent on the farmers selling additional products; or else it could be coupled with subscriptions to Government loans which would syphon off purchasing power. Further commodities which are at present scarce could be sold for future deliveries at a guaranteed price if payment were made immediately, or else the guarantee extended only to that proportion of the price for which advance cash payment was made. At the same time, the supply of coupons to which they are now entitled (for things like tyres, rubber boots and items of agricultural equipment) could be made dependent on satisfactory delivery.

(4) Finally the problem could be greatly alleviated if agriculture could be subjected to an adequate measure of direct taxation. In the campaign-year 1946–7, the net income of agriculture, i.e., the value of its production (after deducting the purchase of material, amortisation, salaries, and rents) is estimated to be 455 milliards. In 1946, the total payment of direct taxes of all kinds was 8 milliards, or less than 2 per cent. of the net income. For 1947 (when in some cases it is possible that a certain number higher rates of taxation will apply) payments in respect of all kinds of direct taxes are estimated at 19 milliards (excluding the new social security contribution now imposed in connection with the extension of the social security system). An adequate system of taxation, on the other hand, that would impose on agriculture its proper share in the expenses of the State, would have to yield 60 to 80 milliards. If an amount of this order could really be extracted from the agricultural sector, this would have much the same effect in compelling the farmers to sell a higher proportion of their produce as a fall in agricultural prices or a rise in industrial prices.

B

It would not be sufficient in itself, however, to remedy the discrepancy between the price of wheat and of other agricultural prices. It would have to be imposed therefore in conjunction with an increase in the official wheat price of the order of 50 per cent. To avoid the inflationary effect of this increase on the level of wages, it might be preferable to offset the effects of the higher wheat price on the price of bread by means of a subsidy. The cost of this might be of the order of 20 milliards, which, to that extent, would offset the withdrawal of the purchasing power from the agricultural sector by means of new taxation.

The question is how much could agricultural taxation be raised? The ultimate remedy must be sought in a radical revision of the system of assessment which would force farmers to declare their true revenue for taxation purposes, including their self-consumption. This, however, would even in the best of circumstances take a considerable time. To obtain an immediate result, it would be necessary to impose a temporary tax based on a much rougher method of assessment, as, for example, an emergency contribution of 2,000 frs. per hectare per annum. If it were made clear that it was a purely temporary levy introduced in order to cover the period until a proper system of assessment applying to agriculture could be worked out, it could perhaps be made politically more acceptable.

The basic difficulty in agriculture is that the present situation represents an unsound mixture of a controlled and a free system. Partially effective control led to a maladjustment of production and distribution. The ideal solution would be to extend the efficiency of control so that it should cover the great bulk of agricultural products; failing that, it is necessary to introduce some method of global control of agricultural purchasing power that would remove the present large disparity in the real incomes of town and country.

TAXATION

1. *The need for fundamental reform*

Apart from the question of prices discussed above, the main problem of monetary stability and of ensuring the envisaged level of investment for purposes of reconstruction is that of raising a sufficient revenue by taxation. As compared with other countries, the level of budgetary expenditures of France, or the total amount raised in taxation, is not large.

For 1947, the total tax revenue could hardly exceed 20 per cent. of the net national income. The total receipts from taxation in Britain, on a comparable definition, amounted in 1944 to 44 per cent. Yet, as regards nominal rates, the taxes in force in France were fully comparable, and in many cases exceeded, those of Britain. If the French tax revenue is insufficient in relation to needs (that are themselves relatively smaller), this must be due to the relative inefficiency of the French system of taxation. Apart from its relative inefficiency, the French system is also iniquitous:

(a) because the share of regressive indirect taxes is too large in total taxation;

(b) because an undue proportion of direct taxation is raised from wages and salaries.

This emerges clearly from a comparison of the yield and the burden of direct taxation on different kinds of income in the two countries which is shown in Table 9. While in Britain, the burden of direct taxation amounted to 12 per cent. of the total wages and salaries, 38 per cent. of the property income and 43 per cent. of that of profits and interest, in France, in the same year, the burden was 9 per cent. on wages and salaries, 38 per cent. on property income, and only 3 per cent. on profits and interest. It is interesting to note that where the French system does not permit evasion of tax, as in the case of property income, the burden is the same in both countries. In the case of the large proportion of income earned as profits and mixed income, the burden in France is only one fifteenth of that in Britain.[1] Moreover, while the percentage tax burden on the category profits and interest has doubled in Britain as compared with 1938, in France, it has actually fallen to half of its pre-war level. Even if exceptional taxes like the "impôt de solidarité" and the "taxe sur les profits illicites" (which are not properly chargeable to the income of one particular year)

---

[1] The category "profits and interest" had to be taken together, because the figures cannot be separated in the French statistics. Actually, in France, (a) the item "interest" is heavily taxed, to a comparable extent to the property income; (b) the item "intérêt" is small, relatively to "profits", as shown in Table 1.

Table 9

PERSONAL TAXES BY CATEGORIES OF INCOME

These two tables compare direct taxes in Great Britain and France. For France conveyancing duty and stamp duty have been excluded as have exceptional taxes (i.e. the "impôt de solidarité" and the "taxe sur les profits illicites"), the receipts from which are shown separately; included however are workers' social security contributions, and family allowance contributions of owners of businesses and the self-employed. The data are thus made comparable to those for Great Britain.

I GREAT BRITAIN

	1938					1946				
	Income		Taxes		Effective Tax Rates	Income		Taxes		Effective Tax Rates
	£ million	%	£ million	%	%	£ million	%	£ million	%	%
Wages and salaries	2865	60	108	21	4	4695	59	588	30	12
Property income	380	8	76	15	20	386	5	146	7·5	38
Profits and interest	1534	32	355	64	23	2840	36	1222	62·5	43
Total	4779	100	519	100	11	7921	100	1956	100	25

Table 9—continued
II FRANCE

	1938						1946					
	Income		Taxes		Effective Tax Rates		Income		Taxes		Effective Tax Rates	
	milliards of francs	%	milliards of francs	%	%		milliards of francs	%	milliards of francs	%	%	
Wages and salaries	163	43	6	25	3·5		982	36	81	54	8	
Property income[1]	20	5	5·8	24	29		48	2	18	12	38	
Profits and interest	198	52	12·3	51	6		1723	62	52	34	3	
Total	381	100	24·1	100	6		2753	100	151	100	5·5	
Taxes not considered:												
"Impôts de solidarité"									50·3			
"Taxe sur les profits illicites"									18·4			
Others			2						10·4			

[1] Net income, arrived at by deducting 50% from gross income in the case of built-on property, and 20% for undeveloped property, in accordance with the fiscal schedules.

are included, the percentage burden of the taxation on profits and interest still hardly exceeds the pre-war level.

The basic cause for all this is the inability of the tax administration with its complexity of different income taxes to have a proper system of assessment on mixed incomes. The evasion of taxation appears to be greatest in the case of agricultural and professional income, but it must be substantial in the case of industry as well, especially small industry. The only satisfactory permanent remedy seems to be a reform of taxation along the lines suggested by the C.G.T., of which a note is appended at the end of this report[1]. The main features of this reform are:

(1) a uniform income tax, in place of the various existing income taxes;

(2) an annual tax on capital as the sole means of differentiation between earned and unearned income;

(3) a tax on capital gains other than that secured through saving or changes in the value of money;

(4) a uniform tax on business in the form of a tax on value added instead of the present multiplicity of taxes on sales or turnover;

(5) a merger of tax administrations and a strengthening of the system of controls and penalties.

The main merit of this scheme is that it offers a system of self-checking taxes, where the administration of any one tax makes it more difficult to practice evasion in the others. Thus, the capital tax provides a check on income and the tax on value added provides a check on purchases and sales and also on income. It also avoids a unique stage of collection which is a source of evasion of the present turnover taxes. But the most important feature, apart from the great simplification of the tax system, consists in the particular suggestions for obtaining correct returns on income and discouraging evasion by a very heavy system of penalties; as against that the existing system, by giving legal recognition to evasion through the differentiation of tax rates on different types of income, penalises honesty and leads to a vicious circle of an ever increasing difference between actual and nominal rates of taxation.

It is estimated that if a reform of this kind were adopted in the near future the tax revenue of France could be raised by 50 to

[1] Not reproduced.

60 per cent. in two years, without increasing the nominal rates of taxation and in many cases reducing them. But the reform could of course be carried out in such a way that some of its benefit would accrue in a much shorter period.

II. *The immediate problem*

The adoption of this basic reform in the tax system appears to be by far the most satisfactory method of dealing with the taxation problem and the only one that could ensure stability and at the same time satisfy the criteria of social justice. Without it, additional taxation is bound to be of a character that will aggravate still further the existing disparity of burden between different classes of society. This is because, without an efficient system of taxing profits directly, all other levies are bound to be passed on to the final consumer. This is true, apart from taxes on commodities, also of taxes to be paid by the entrepreneur such as the contribution to the social insurance.

Nevertheless, the question arises whether it may not be necessary to resort to measures of more or less temporary character which secure more immediate results. The case for such a special tax in connection with agriculture has already been discussed above. We should here like to discuss: (1) the case for special measures to be taken to discourage luxury spending; (2) the case for a special levy as an explicit contribution for the financing of the investment plan.

(1) It must be evident, from the discussion at the beginning of this paper, that with the present distribution of income, and until a reform of direct taxation makes it possible to tax profit income substantially, it is necessary to rely on profits to provide the main source of saving. If it is not possible to reduce the available income from profits substantially, an attempt could at any rate be made to discourage the beneficiaries of this income from spending it. The main channels of luxury spending are:

(a) through maintaining a large household or a number of households;

(b) through keeping one or more large motor-cars;

(c) through luxury eating in restaurants;

(d) through luxury spending in elegant resorts, etc.

All this could be stopped, or at least severely discouraged through special taxation or total prohibition. This could take the form of punitive taxes imposed on the owner of large dwellings in relation to the size of his family, on secondary or tertiary dwellings, on persons employing several domestic servants, on the owners of large cars or of several cars, on the prolonged residence in luxury hotels, etc. The luxury spending in restaurants could be prevented by putting an effective ceiling to the total amount spent on any one meal in a similar manner to the system in force in Britain. In the case of clothing, a similar effect could be secured through increasing the proportion of materials allocated to utility goods.

The well-known objection to such measures is that it would discourage tourists' expenditure. It is doubtful how far this would in fact be the case: in Britain, where a much more rigid system of restrictions is in force than in France, a considerable flow of American tourists is nevertheless expected for the summer.

Apart from this, it would not be difficult to exempt tourists from some of the measures proposed.

Apart from measures taken to discourage unnecessary spending, it would be equally necessary to take measures to prevent or discourage socially unnecessary investments that are outside the scope of the investment plan. This is above all a matter of controlling building activities. The existing means of control are not applied effectively at present. To prevent unnecessary building, the system of building permits and of the allocation of building material would have to be greatly tightened up.

It would equally be necessary to prevent an unnecessary holding of stocks. To the extent that this is financed by bank credit, the most suitable means to do this is credit control. To the extent however that it takes place by means of the reinvestment of current profits by businesses, other means of control have to be devised. This implies exercising some control on the volume of stocks held in relation to turnover; and an effective scheme could only be thought of in connection with a business tax on value added which has already been discussed.

(2) The attraction of a special levy for the financing of the investment plan is that it would secure for the plan a direct

claim on the financial resources of the State. Although this could theoretically also be achieved by legally setting aside certain of the existing revenues of the State which would thus be paid into a special investment fund, the advantage of a special levy is that —as it serves a purpose of investment—it need not take the form of a tax for which no direct "quid pro quo" is given; it could take the form of a compulsory loan, which differs from a tax in that it is taken in exchange for Government paper on which either immediately, or from some future specified date, onwards, interest is paid. To secure the economic purpose of the levy (i.e. of reducing expenditure on consumption), the security issued in connection with the loan would have to be non-negotiable. To prevent its being paid out of capital instead of income, it would have to be a monthly or annual contribution, and not a once-for-all payment. Although the loan would have to be a compulsory contribution to ensure the desired effect of reducing consumption expenditure (and also, in order to obtain a sufficient yield); and although it would have to take the form of a non-negotiable security (to prevent or to minimise, the danger of its being substituted for the holding of other securities), it would nevertheless make a considerable difference in its psychological effect if the levy took the form of a compulsory loan for which a security was issued rather than an outright tax. Further, the compulsory loan could be made considerably more attractive, if in place of a fixed payment of interest, it carried something in the nature of a "national dividend", the amount of which would vary with the size of the national income. In this way, the community would have a direct stake in the success of the national reconstruction plan, for the sake of which they are asked to undertake this additional sacrifice.

The national income, in terms of money value, increases with a rise in the level of production, or a general rise in prices, or both. Hence, a security, the yield of which varies with the national income, would, in fact, offer a virtual guarantee against the devaluation of the currency, and thus, from this point of view, be greatly superior to ordinary loans which carry no such guarantee. It would only fail to protect the holder against the dangers of a rise in prices in so far as the latter were associated with a reduction in output and hence not reflected in the national income figures This is reasonable; on the other hand, the holder of these bonds might be offered a larger increase in dividends, when the increase in the national income is due to a rise in production (which may be associated with constant or even falling prices), than in the case when it is merely due to a fall in the value of money. The initial rate of interest might be very low (of the order of 1–1·5 per cent. per annum), the rate increasing proportionately with the increase in the national income, and (perhaps) more than proportionately with the increase in the national income at constant prices; the Government retaining the option of repaying the loan, or converting it into an ordinary loan after, say, 15 years.

The main problem of such a scheme is that of finding the right method of assessment and ensuring, as far as possible, that the incidence of the loan does not fall on those classes who are already unjustly treated both from the point of view of the distribution of the national income and from the point of view of the distribution of taxation. We have already discussed above (p. 18) the need for a levy on agricultural incomes that would syphon off surplus agricultural purchasing power and thus compel the farmers to sell a higher proportion of their produce. This could suitably be linked (as far as agriculture is concerned) with the compulsory loan. To be effective, the contribution would have to be assessed on the size of holdings (i.e., according to the number of hectares) with exemptions varying with the number of people dependent on the farm, with special exemptions for wheat fields to encourage wheat production and regional variations in the scale of contributions per hectare to take account of the differences in yield.

As far as the rest of the economy is concerned, the most suitable basis of assessment is a levy on business profits, varying with the number of people employed in each business (including the employer himself), the contribution per person varying according to the nature of the business, being highest in those sectors (i.e., the wholesale trade) where the profit per person engaged is the largest. To satisfy the criteria of justice, the whole contribution raised from each sector of the economy would have to be approximately proportional to the contribution of each sector to the total national output.

It is probably unavoidable that the burden of the contribution of the non-agricultural sectors should be passed on in the form of higher prices, particularly in those sectors where price control is ineffective. Until the basic reform of taxation makes it possible to raise a substantial levy which is a direct charge on profits, the only practical alternative would be a contribution assessed on the value of capital; and this, again, would be unjust in its incidence on account of the facts:

(a) that the owners of immobile property, as is shown in Table 8, are already heavily taxed;

(b) that the really large profits at present appear to be made in commerce, agriculture, services and small industries: in those sectors therefore where the earning of large profits does not give rise to correspondingly large tangible capital value.

It was argued above that the re-establishment of monetary stability, at the envisaged levels of State expenditures and of investment, requires additional revenue from compulsory contributions of the order of 200 milliard francs per annum. If the measures proposed relating to the discouragement of luxury consumption and the control of investment expenditures were put into effect, it might be sufficient to fix the scale of contributions to the compulsory loan in such a way as to collect some 150 milliard francs per annum. This would, at the same time, ensure the financing of the investment plans in the basic industries, and would probably suffice for the State-financed investments in complementary industries as well.

SUMMARY OF THE ARGUMENT

It may be convenient to summarise the conclusions that have emerged from our analysis:

(1) The present monetary stability appears to be the consequence of a very considerable change in the investment in stocks by private industries; whereas, in the latter part of 1946, there was a considerable increase in the volume of stocks held, in the early

months of the current year there appears to have been a net dishoarding of stocks. This may have been due to:

(a) the system of credit control imposed at the end of last year; or

(b) a change in the expectations of private traders as to the future trend of prices.

In so far as it was due to the latter, the present relief from inflationary pressure may be purely temporary and a result of accidental events. The inflationary process might be suddenly renewed. In so far, however, as the change in the investment in stocks was mainly brought about through credit control, the present stability might be of a more lasting character. Even though the present stability appears to have been achieved only by a net dishoarding of stocks, there is no reason why this should not continue for a longer period, if the system of credit control gradually succeeds in forcing traders to dishoard the stocks in those particular sectors of the economic system where they are relatively large. Experience of other countries seems to suggest that the dishoarding of stocks may be carried to fairly great lengths without serious interference with the technical efficiency of the productive system. (In France, of course, it is not generally true to say that the stocks held at present are unnecessarily large; in the case of commodities like coal, the stocks are probably near a minimum.)

(2) The past inflation has left behind the legacy of an ill-adjusted price system. Three types of adjustments appear to be necessary:

(a) a rise in the wheat price in relation to other agricultural prices (to be secured preferably through a fall in the money prices of other agricultural produce brought about by extension of control);

(b) a reduction of the whole level of agricultural prices in relation to industrial prices (in order to secure that a higher proportion of agricultural produce should be sold);

(c) a rise in "unduly depressed prices", in particular rents of lodgings, and some of the public utility services.

(b) and (c) are to a certain extent interconnected in that the level of agricultural prices depends on the proportion of urban income available for the purchase of goods while the latter is artificially kept up through (c). There is a grave danger, however, that piecemeal and sporadic adjustments as regards (c) will lead to renewal of inflationary expectations, and, through the mechanism of wage-increase, will tend to re-establish the same kind of maladjustment in relative prices as existed before. Hence, it is desirable to postpone adjustment of unduly depressed industrial prices until it can be made certain that the repercussions in the field of wages can be avoided; and that in turn, presupposes that the problem of (b) is simultaneously dealt with. Thus the adjustment of agricultural prices, in one of the various ways proposed, is the key to, and, at the same time, the most difficult part of, economic adjustment.

(3) The carrying out of the investment plan, even in its present reduced dimensions, is not in the long run compatible with monetary stability unless tax revenues are raised above the present level. Assuming the "normal" increase of stocks in proportion to the rise of the national production, and assuming the present level of Government expenditures (including the subsidy of the deficit paid to enterprises at the prevailing low prices), it would be necessary to increase aggregate tax revenue by some 200 milliards above the level currently envisaged for 1947. This, of course, is not a firm figure, as available statistics only permit a broad indication of the probable order of magnitude of the sum. Not that it is to be supposed that in the absence of this increase in tax revenue the inflation will necessarily be renewed in the near future. In so far as the dishoarding of stocks by means of credit control mentioned under (1) can be made to continue and the prices adjustment mentioned under (a) can be postponed, or the danger of related increase in the level of wages can be prevented, the present stability might continue for a longer period—perhaps for long enough for the necessary increase in tax revenue to be secured by basically sound measures.

(4) The increase in taxation is best achieved by a fundamental reform in the tax system which simplifies existing taxes and prevents, or at any rate, reduces, evasion, rather than by the imposing of additional taxes. This tax reform would rectify the social injustice of the present system, and thus contribute to social

stability as well as create a powerful instrument of control for the direction of the economic system.

(5) It appears therefore, that from a long-run point of view, it is most important to concentrate on the fundamental reform of the tax system; since however this could not yield its fruits immediately it is necessary to have recourse to a number of intermediary measures such as:

(a) strict control of credit;

(b) discouragement of luxury spending by means of control and taxes;

(c) control of building acitivity and, if possible, the size of stocks held in relation to turnover.

(6) It is desirable, further, to impose a compulsory loan, to be paid in annual investments, and assessed on the size of holdings in the case of agriculture, and on the number of people engaged in the case of other kinds of businesses. This should be fixed on a scale as to yield some 150 milliards per annum, to be given in exchange for non-negotiable securities with a minimum rate of interest of 1–1·5 per cent., the actual payments to be adjusted with the movements of the national income. It would serve the purpose of (a) ensuring general monetary stability; (b) of eliminating surplus purchasing power in agriculture; (c) of creating a special fund for the investment plan, which would create general confidence in the ability of the country to execute the plan, and would enable firm orders to be given to industries for long-term execution.

2

INDIAN TAX REFORM
REPORT OF A SURVEY[1]

TABLE OF CONTENTS

[1] Prepared in New Delhi in January–March 1956 and published by the Department of Economic Affairs of the Indian Ministry of Finance in June 1956. Introductory Preface and letter of transmittal have been omitted.

INTRODUCTION AND SUMMARY

A MORE efficient and equitable tax system is one of the most important requirements for the fulfilment of India's national aspirations. At present the total revenue raised in taxation by the Centre and the States is a little over 7 per cent. of national income; and on the record of the last five or six years, the tax revenue does not exhibit that natural buoyancy—i.e. the automatic rise in yields with the increase in national production and income—which is a common feature of the tax systems of Western countries.

The Second Five Year Plan envisages additional tax revenue (by the Centre and the States) of Rs. 450 crores for the five-year period, a deficit expenditure of Rs. 1,200 crores and a "gap" of a further Rs. 400 crores. In my view (and this, I think, would be shared by most economists) the amount of deficit expenditure which the economy can absorb is not likely to exceed Rs. 150 crores a year, or, say, Rs. 800 crores in the five-year period. Hence, if the targets of the Second Five Year Plan are to be ful-filled the additional taxation required is more of the order of Rs. 1,250 crores for the five years (or Rs. 250 crores a year) than of Rs. 450 crores.

There is nothing impossible about these targets, provided the problem is tackled on bold lines and the tax system is subjected to a thorough and comprehensive reform. It is essential that the additional burden that will inevitably be imposed (either through taxation or through an inflationary rise in prices) on the broad masses of population should be complemented by an efficient system of progressive taxation on the small minority of the well-to-do who in India number only about one per cent. of the population. Without that, the rise in expenditure during the Plan will inevitably increase the wealth of the richest classes disproportionately, and the distribution of the burden imposed on the community at large will be contrary to the sense of justice and equity of a democratic society.

The present system of direct taxation in India is both inefficient and inequitable. It is inequitable because the present base of taxation, "income" as statutorily defined is defective and biased as a measure of taxable capacity and is capable of being manipulated by certain classes of taxpayers. It is inefficient because the limited character of the information furnished by taxpayers, and the absence of any comprehensive reporting system on property transactions and property income makes large-scale evasion through concealment or under-statement of profits and property income relatively easy.

The proposals outlined in this Report aim at broadening the tax base through the introduction of an annual tax on wealth; the taxation of capital gains; a general gift tax; and a personal expenditure tax (the last in partial substitution of the present super tax on income). They also aim at the elimination of (or at least a considerable reduction in the scope of) tax evasion through the institution of a comprehensive return, and the introduction of a comprehensive reporting system on all property transfers and other transactions of a capital nature.

The five taxes—income tax, capital gains tax, annual wealth tax, personal expenditure tax and the general gift tax—would all be assessed simultaneously, on the basis of a single comprehensive return; and they are "self checking" in character, both in the sense that concealment or under-statement of items in order to minimise liability to some of the taxes may involve an added liability with regard to others, and in the sense that the information furnished by a taxpayer in the interest of preventing over-assessment with regard to his own liabilities automatically brings to light the receipts and gains made by other taxpayers.

The introduction of a personal expenditure tax and an annual tax on wealth serves the purpose also of mitigating the severe disincentive effects on work, saving, and enterprise of a heavy progressive tax levied on *income*. At present these disincentive effects are avoided through the exemption of capital gains from taxation, through over-liberal provisions concerning deductible expenses, and through straightforward tax evasion—all of which make the incidence of taxation between different classes of income-earners absurdly inequitable. When the marginal rate of income tax is 90 per cent., the net profit on any particular concealment is 900 per cent. of the post-tax income. It is suggested that from every point of view it is far better to have a fool-proof system of taxation with a modest rate schedule, than a system which has the appearance of high progressivity, but which cannot be effectively or impartially administered.

It is suggested that the maximum rate of tax on income should not exceed 45 per cent. (as against the present 92 per cent.), the maximum rate of an annual wealth tax $1\frac{1}{2}$ per cent. (on the excess of capital value over Rs. 15 lakhs), the maximum rate of the personal expenditure tax 300 per cent. (on a net personal expenditure per head of over Rs. 50,000 per annum) and the maximum rate of gift tax 80 per cent. (on gifts received by persons whose total estate, including the gift, exceeds 40 lakhs). It is suggested that all realised capital gains should be taxed at the same rate as income (i.e., subject to the maximum rate of 45 per cent.).

With regard to the taxation of business profits it is suggested that if the rule as regards deductible expenses were modified so as to comprise only such expenses as have been "unavoidably incurred in earning the profits of the year" the tax would be fairer and less arbitrary in incidence, and at the same time far simpler and easier to administer than the present system. It would also avoid the distorting effects of the present income tax on the allocation of resources of the community, since it would avoid the payment of a subsidy for unnecessary outlays of doubtful social value. It is also suggested that in place of the various kinds of allowances for capital expenditure given at present (normal depreciation, additional depreciation, and the development rebate) there should be a single capital allowance granted simultaneously with the capital expenditure and amounting to a proportion of the total outlay; the proportion varying with the lifetime of the capital asset. Unabsorbed capital allowances carried forward to future years should be augmented by an annual interest allowance. The right to offset losses from any one source against income from any other source (whether in the same year or in the subsequent year) should be limited to a trading loss in the strict sense representing an excess of unavoidable current outlays over current receipts. Other losses should only be capable of being carried forward against future income from the same source, provided there is no change of ownership of the source.

Finally, in place of all the present taxes on company profits, it is suggested that a single uniform tax of 7 annas in the rupee should be levied on the whole income of the companies—this rate to be reduced to 6 annas, if capital allowances were rationalised on the lines recommended. The whole of the tax should be non-refundable; but income tax at the rate of 7 annas in the rupee should be deducted from all dividends etc., paid out, and credited to the account of the recipient. Dividends received by companies from other companies subject to the company tax, should not be treated as part of the recipient companies' income for purposes of company tax.

With regard to the control of evasion of business income, it is suggested that there should be a compulsory auditing of accounts of incomes in excess of Rs. 50,000 in the case of business income and Rs. 1,00,000 in the case of other personal income; that auditors should be under a statutory obligation to certify that accounts submitted for tax purposes were drawn up in a manner to show the true income assessable to tax; that the scale of remuneration of auditors should be laid down by public regulation; and that 50 per cent. of the fees of auditors should be payable by the State, and the approval of the Controller of Public Accounts should be required to the appointment of auditors in all cases in which the law prescribes the compulsory auditing of accounts for tax purposes. It is also suggested that additional measures should be taken to facilitate the scrutiny of accounts by I.T.O.s; the penalties for income tax evasion should be considerably raised and the policy of abstaining from criminal prosecution in fraudulent cases abandoned. Finally, it is suggested that to ensure high standards of administration in the Revenue Department there should be an adequate increase in the range of salaries payable to Income Tax Officers.[1]

[1] It is also suggested that the efficiency and uniformity of income tax administration could be greatly enhanced through the establishment of a central register of income tax returns.

Rough calculations suggest that the net yield of the suggested reforms of personal taxation (taking into account both the revenue from the new taxes and the additional yield due to greater efficiency of assessment and collection) would be of the order of Rs. 100 crores a year or more—though it may take some years before the full benefit is reaped. It is not possible to make any proper estimate of the effects of the various changes suggested in the taxation of business profits. The combined effect of the narrower definition of deductible expenses and of the various measures suggested for the control of evasion, might yield at least a further Rs. 20–30 crores a year.

These proposals should thus provide the greater part of the requirements necessary to ensure the success of the Second Five Year Plan. The remainder of the additional revenue (which may be of the order of Rs. 100 crores a year) would have to be raised from land taxation and excise duties which are outside the scope of the present Report. The land revenue at present (at around Rs. 50 crores) amounts to only 1 per cent of the net product of agriculture. Even if the yield were doubled (whether by revision of rates or by the long overdue re-assessment of annual land values) it would clearly not represent an excessive burden. Any residual financial need could be met by excise duties on a limited number of commodities of mass consumption. This last should be regarded as the "marginal source" of taxation to be resorted to only when, and to the extent that, the total yield from direct taxes falls short of the requirements. The adoption of the proposals outlined here will have an immediate effect in releasing resources for public purposes which will not be adequately reflected (in the initial years) by the additional yield of taxation. In terms of actual yield it may take some years before the full benefit of the proposed changes is reaped. In terms of their restraining influence on private expenditure the new taxes will begin to take effect from the moment the liabilities are imposed.

The proposals thus aim at broadening the base of taxation through bringing into charge many forms of wealth accrual that are now exempt from taxation and by excluding many concessions of an anomalous character. Instead of placing the main weight of progressive taxation on a single tax—the income tax—it is proposed that progressive taxation should be levied on a number of "yard-sticks" of taxable capacity like total wealth, income, expenditure, etc. At the same time it is proposed that the schedule of rates should be far more moderate than at present. The maximum rate of income tax at 45 per cent. would be lower than the maximum rate imposed in those countries (such as Sweden) which levy progressive annual taxes on wealth as well as taxes on income. The schedule of rates suggested for the progressive annual tax on wealth (as is shown in the calculations in Appendix C of this Report) is only about one-half as heavy as the schedule of rates now in force in Sweden. For the progressive expenditure tax, the proposed exemption limit exempts reasonable middle-class living standards from liability to this tax altogether.

I realise that these moderate rates (especially when set against the high nominal rates in force at present) may arouse opposition in political quarters for being unduly lenient in appearance. Nonetheless, I am strongly of the opinion that India should not at the present stage impose taxation on capital and income at heavier rates than I have suggested here. There is very much to be said for making the tax base a comprehensive one—for closing the enormous loop-holes in the present system by embracing capital and capital gains in the scope of taxation and by introducing a broader definition of business income—but there is also a great deal to be said for keeping the rates of taxation low, both in the interests of economic development (so as to maintain economic incentives) and also to lessen the temptation on taxpayers to sabotage the tax laws by all available means. India, like most Western countries, has been in the grip of a vicious circle as far as progressive taxation is concerned—evasion and avoidance, by cutting down potential revenue, led to higher nominal rates of taxation and this in turn to further evasion and avoidance and still higher rates. It is a vicious circle of charging more and more on less and less. The prime requirement is to break that vicious circle. The adoption of a comprehensive tax-base would be a great deal easier—imposing fewer strains on the social fabric and on the administration of the tax system—if it were introduced with a moderate rate schedule; and this would nevertheless inaugurate a more truly equitable and progressive tax system, as well as bringing in a great deal of additional revenue.

Although I cannot claim expert knowledge of the economic and social customs of India, I feel I ought not to close this Report without dealing with two objections that have been raised (and are likely to be raised more vociferously when this Report reaches a wider public) against the proposals put forward here, considered as a practical and integrated programme for immediate adoption. One is that India, being an under-developed country, ought not to be more ambitious in its system of progressive taxation than the countries of the West—whereas the proposals explained here suggest a system of personal taxation that is more "advanced" in character than that of even the most "developed" countries of the West. The second is that under Indian conditions, any system which aims at making tax avoidance and evasion more difficult is bound to make the economic consequences of any remaining amount of evasion far more serious, since it will cause the hoarding of gold for purposes of concealing tax liability.

With regard to the first point, I believe it is a fallacy to suggest that because India is an under-developed country it ought to have an under-developed tax system. Indeed, the existing system of personal taxation of India—very largely an imitation of the British system—is certainly not any the less complex in its definitions or its mode of administration than the systems in force in Britain or America. The difference between the requirements of a developed country and an under-developed country lies not in the nature of the direct taxes that are to be imposed, but in the proportion of the population (and of total incomes) that is embraced by these taxes. In Britain the number of income-tax payers amounts to over 16 million, or some 70 per cent. of a total 23 million income earners. In India the number of persons liable to income tax is probably less than 1 million, or a little over 1 per cent. of income earners. (The actual numbers assessed to tax is less than $\frac{1}{2}$ million.) The top 1 per cent. of income receivers in India are as fully capable of filling up complicated income-tax returns and of preparing accounts, as the average income-tax payer in Britain or America.

With regard to gold hoarding, I believe, for reasons analysed at the end of Section IX of this Report (p. 172) that both the danger of an increased propensity to hoard and the economic ill-consequences of this may be very greatly exaggerated. To the extent, however, that the argument has validity it constitutes a case in favour of a moderate schedule of rates for progressive taxation and not an objection against the introduction of an equitable system of personal taxation. The incentive to evade taxes depends on the marginal rates of taxation, since these govern the gains from evasion as a percentage of the sums so evaded. The actual extent of evasion depends on these incentives, as well as on the ease with which evasion can be accomplished. Since different tax-payers are very differently situated as regards facilities for evading taxation, anything that makes tax evasion easy is bound to be the source of great social inequities. There is no point, however, in having a system of progressive personal taxation at all—which is far more complicated and difficult to administer than indirect taxation of various kinds—unless it is to secure a more equitable distribution of wealth in the country than would obtain without it. (In Communist countries the State relies very largely on turn-over taxes for the necessary revenue, and personal taxation plays only a negligible role.) If the system fails to secure equity—whether on account of the legal loop-holes tolerated, or the failure to enforce the strict statutory provisions of the tax laws—it is better to abandon it altogether or to reduce it to the level a which it can be efficiently administered, than to allow it to continue in a form in which its redistributive effects on wealth are only formidable on paper but ineffective in reality; and as a result of which some unfortunate minorities in the community (who are unable to make use of the facilities for evasion and avoidance) are both unjustly, and from a social point of view most harmfully, penalised. The danger of gold hoarding, therefore, while it may reinforce the case for moderate schedules of tax rates, cannot justify the continued toleration of wide loop-holes in the tax system, or constitute an argument against the introduction of more effective antidotes to tax evasion.

I. THE CASE FOR A COMPREHENSIVE REFORM OF PERSONAL TAXATION

A. INTRODUCTION

1. The purpose of personal (or "direct") taxation is to provide equity and fairness in the distribution of the tax burden in the community. Looking at the problem from the revenue aspect alone, it might be administratively simpler to collect any given total of revenue by taxes on transactions such as sales taxes, excise duties, etc.—or *ad rem* taxes of various kinds—rather than by taxes levied on persons assessed according to some overall criterion (or criteria) of "ability to pay", on a graduated scale. But in a developing economy, where privately owned wealth grows rapidly and unevenly, a situation in which the burden imposed on the broad masses of population is not complemented by an efficient system of progressive taxation on the minority of wealth-owners would become socially intolerable. The question of the necessity of reforms in the scope, comprehensiveness, and efficiency of administration of personal taxation should not be judged, therefore, from a narrow revenue point of view alone. Certain reforms may be essential even if the immediate revenue prospect is small, if they can be shown to be a necessary precondition for imposing higher burdens on the community at large, in a manner consistent with the prevailing sense of justice and equity of the community.

2. This problem is a particularly important one for India which is on the threshold of a period of accelerated economic development, and whose people desire to strike a "middle road" between Western capitalism and Eastern Socialism. In India the great bulk of the national wealth is, and will continue to be, privately owned—industries or landed property that may be taken over by

the State will not fundamentally alter this state of affairs if due compensation is paid to the owners, so that the growth in public property will be offset by the growth in public indebtedness[1]—it appears inevitable, therefore, that both the amount of privately owned wealth, and (in the absence of effective tax measures) the skewness of the distribution of ownership of that wealth should increase *pari passu* with economic growth. Owing to the fact that the savings of the community are more unevenly distributed than income, there is an inevitable tendency, unless effectively counteracted by the tax system or other instruments of public policy, for the wealth of the largest property owners to grow at a faster rate than wealth in general. The more income and wealth grow, therefore, the more the inequality of wealth between individuals increases.

3. All politically "advanced" democracies possess some form of progressive personal taxation, generally based on "income". But with the possible exception of Sweden, none have succeeded in bringing about the degree of redistribution of wealth and income the attainment of which has been the avowed objective of their taxation policies. Thus in the United Kingdom, though the combined income and surtax rates for the last 15 years have exceeded 90 per cent. in the top brackets, and estate duties reached a maximum of 80 per cent., vast new fortunes are still being made, and the degree of concentration in the ownership of wealth—as measured, e.g., by the percentage of persons owning one-third of the national wealth, etc.—has not been reduced. The same is true, I believe, of the United States and other Western countries. The reasons are to be sought in the fact that owing to the numerous loop-holes of one sort or another that are tolerated (and in some cases deliberately nurtured) by the legislatures, as well as the failure of the tax administration to force a full disclosure of income or wealth, the true burden of taxation on the owners of property is far below that indicated by the nominal rates of taxation on "income". On incomes derived from office, employment, or pension, on the other hand, i.e., on salaries and wages, the comprehensive reporting systems introduced during

---

[1] Deficit financing or public loan-expenditure equally imply, of course, a corresponding increase in privately owned wealth.

and after the war ensure practically 100 per cent. coverage; nor does the definition of "taxable income" permit the same kind of manipulation here as with the profits of business or of income derived from the ownership of capital. The only important loop-holes in the case of salary-incomes are expense allowances and benefits in kind provided by the employer; and these can be, and are being, plugged by means of special legislative provisions such as those recently introduced in the United Kingdom, India, and some other countries. Public employees, like judges or high civil servants, who do not receive such "perks" from their employer, and have no tax loop-holes to fall back on, are exposed to the full blast of punitive rates that are only nominally applicable to the other sectors of the community.

4. So far from attaining its avowed objectives of mitigating economic and social inequality, progressive taxation in most Western countries has thus served to create new inequities by imposing an altogether disproportionate burden on the professional classes, on intellectuals and administrators, and in particular, on leading public servants of all kinds. The strongest disincentive effects have been on the quality of entrants in the public service, and on the level of ability of the administrative personnel of public enterprises of all kinds. There is no need to stress the disadvantages and dangers of this in a society which will be increasingly dependent on the quality and initiative of its public service.

5. In my view, the main factors responsible for the failure of progressive taxation to attain its objectives are the following (the relative importance of these factors varies, of course, for different countries):

(a) Absence of a clear and comprehensive notion of what constitutes "income" for tax purposes; and the consequent exclusion of numerous kinds of beneficial receipts (of which capital gains and capital profits of all kinds are the most important); and the consequent impossibility of preventing manipulations of innumerable kinds which aim at making the accrual of benefits from the ownership of property or business activity appear as non-taxable capital profits or gains, rather than as taxable receipts.

(b) Failure to recognise that the ownership of disposable assets confers a benefit on the owner over and above the income which the property yields; and the failure to supplement taxes on income with taxes on net worth.

(c) The elastic definition of expenses as permissible deductions to be set against receipts in the calculation of trading profits, together with over-generous recognition of the notion of, and over-generous provision for the relief of, "losses", which bring it about that a trader can manufacture "losses" for tax purposes and thereby build up assets at the cost of the Revenue, without his consequent gains being brought into charge.

(d) Failure to secure the true aggregation of a man's (or a family's) total property or income for tax purposes, due (in part) to defective provisions concerning the compulsory aggregation of family income, and to provisions concerning the transfer of income or property into trusts and settlements, etc. (quite apart from any illegal concealment of income).

(e) Failure to secure the full reporting of income, or of property, due (i) to the absence of any automatic reporting systems for property income and property transactions analogous to that existing for incomes from employment; (ii) to the failure to make the return required of the taxpayer comprehensive enough to ensure that it is self-checking in character; (iii) to the facilities afforded in common law for the concealment of income and property through the registration of property in bogus names (*benami* holdings) or through anonymous holdings (like bearer bonds, or the system of blank transfers in the case of shares).

6. Points (a) to (d) above provide the sources of (legal) tax avoidance, while (e) the facilities for (illegal) tax evasion. The difference between the situation in India and majority of Western countries is only that in the case of India (e) is probably more prominent, and in consequence (a) to (d) relatively less important, than for the countries of the West.

7. I am convinced that it would be technically feasible so to

reform the tax system as to eliminate altogether, or at least greatly to diminish, both the legal avenues for tax avoidance and the scope for large-scale tax evasion. For reasons explained below, the administrative feasibility of doing so is far more promising in the case of a comprehensive reform than in the case of the adoption of partial or piecemeal remedial measures. Neither in the case of countries like the United Kingdom or the United States of America, nor in the case of India, is large-scale tax avoidance and evasion an ineluctable consequence of human or administrative imperfections or folly, or of the private enterprise system, or any other ineradicable feature of society. The factor which has so far prevented the establishment of an effective system of taxation on profits and capital in the Western democracies or in India is the opposition of vested interests, not the "technical" impossibility of devising an equitable and foolproof system.

B. THE THREE MAJOR CONSIDERATIONS

8. The three prime considerations that should be taken into account in framing an effective tax system are equity, economic effects, and administrative efficiency.

9. From the point of view of equity, the most important consideration is that the tax system should not contain a systematic bias in favour of particular groups of taxpayers and against others. For reasons which I analysed in some detail in my book[1] and which it is unnecessary to repeat here, equity in taxation between income from work and income from property cannot be secured unless (i) the concept of "income" is made sufficiently comprehensive to embrace *all* beneficial receipts which increase the taxpayers' spending power, and not merely the conventional forms of income; (ii) the tax on income is supplemented by an annual tax on capital wealth in recognition of the fact that taxable capacity cannot be adequately measured either by income alone, or by capital wealth alone, but can be approximated through a mixture of both; (iii) in the calculation of taxable income, profit or gain, permissible deductions should proceed on uniform and non-discriminatory principles as between different kinds and

[1] *An Expenditure Tax.* Ch. I, pp. 25–42.

forms of income. This means, in effect, that only such expenses should be chargeable against the receipts as can be shown to have been necessarily involved in producing the receipts of the year in question.

10. From the point of view of the economic effects of taxation the major consideration is to prevent the tax system from becoming too much of a disincentive on effort, initiative or enterprise. Taxes on income make it less attractive to undertake work or to risk capital in productive enterprise; and through the factor of "double taxation" of savings, penalise savings and put a premium on spending. The importance of all these effects depends on the marginal rates of taxation. I am strongly of the view that the developments of the last 15–20 years which imposed (nominally) fantastically high marginal rates of tax, while permitting the continuance of wide loop-holes for tax avoidance, are highly pernicious in character. As Henry Simons said before the War[1] the whole procedure smacks of a "subtle kind of moral and intellectual dishonesty". "One senses here a grand scheme of deception whereby enormous surtaxes are voted in exchange for promises that they will not be made effective. Thus the politicians may point with pride to the rates, while quietly reminding their wealthy constituents of the loop-holes."

11. These high marginal rates, amounting to 80 to 90 per cent. (in the U.K. at one stage they amounted to 97·5 per cent.) could never have been imposed had they really been what they pretended to be, a tax on the genuine accrual of wealth. As it is, these confiscatory tax rates truly apply only to a small minority of people who cannot avoid their incidence, and their long-run effect is bound to be wholly pernicious, both in penalising the prospects of certain careers which are vital from the national point of view, and in undermining public morality.[2]

---

[1] *Personal Income Taxation* (Chicago 1938), pp. 219.
[2] I feel bound to say that I regard the current proposals in India for a "ceiling" on income as carrying these trends to their ultimate logical absurdity. The authors behind these proposals never stop to inquire just what is the meaning and definition of the term "income" which they so light-heartedly wish to be subject to an absolute upper limit; and how such proposals could serve to reduce social inequality so long as wealth continues to be privately owned. In the sense in which (in the U.K., for instance) the marginal tax on income had already reached 97·5 per cent. in 1946–51, this marginal tax could clearly be raised to 100 per cent. without making any radical difference. But can anyone seriously believe that this instrument could be made to

12. Assuming a comprehensive tax-base, the marginal rate of income tax ought never to exceed, in my view, something of the order of 40–50 per cent. for income that is both earned and saved. (For spent income, the effective rate could, of course, be made considerably higher, if income tax were supplemented by a progressive spendings tax, in replacement of the higher brackets of super tax.) For unearned income (income from business or property) a differential tax should be imposed in the form of an annual tax on wealth (in addition to the tax on income) which has not the same disincentive effects on the productive employ-

---

serve the elimination of anything but desirable social incentives? The extremes of wealth and poverty will not be eliminated thereby—for the simple reason that as far as capitalists are concerned, the benefits accruing from capital will not be lost, merely that they will take on some other form than "income". (As it is said in England, heavy taxation makes taxable income into a luxury which "the rich can no longer afford to have".)

This is not meant to suggest that the current agitation for a "ceiling on income" droceeds from any but the highest moral and social motives; and I am sure that their authors meant them to apply to the true benefits derived from the ownership of property just as much as to incomes derived from work. They were wrong, however, in thinking that a ceiling on "income" was an appropriate instrument for giving effect to these aspirations—unless the notion of "income" were broadened considerably in relation to the current legal definition of this term and the "ceiling" were meant to comprise a ceiling on the ownership of wealth, and not only on annual accruals. Interpreted in this comprehensive sense, however, the proposal is not one which a country like India could adopt, without seriously compromising her prospects of growth and improvement or even the maintenance of existing standards. Soviet Russia discovered to her cost that economic incentives cannot be eliminated without perilous consequences—except perhaps at a stage of economic well-being which is far above that of even the richest nation (like the U.S.A.), let alone India.

There is, no doubt, a strong case in India for reducing the prevailing degree of economic inequality. But the way to do this is by making the tax system comprehensive and administratively effective, not by introducing absolute "ceilings". (There may be a case for a ceiling on land holdings, but in my view this provides no analogy for ceilings on income and capital. Since the effective size of farms in India is relatively small, land ownership above a certain amount serves no economic purpose and is merely a method of exploiting the peasantry, and often a positive impediment to improvements in productivity on the land. This is certainly not true of the high incomes earned through a successful business or professional career, or of the accumulation of fortunes through successful enterprise.)

I am fairly confident that the proposals for an "income ceiling" will not eventuate either in the introduction of 100 per cent. marginal tax rates or in any legal prohibition for the payment of income above a certain maximum. Yet the agitation will have done considerable harm if it led to low top-salary scales being paid to the top executive personnel in the newly established State enterprises. I think it is essential to the success of India's current approach to her future development—"the Socialist pattern of society"—that the important enterprises in the public sector should be able to attract the best available talent; and this means that they should be able to pay remuneration on a scale that is fully competitive with that offered by private industry. I do feel, therefore, that it would serve important national interests if public pronouncements on this subject could, as early as possible, be veered round towards the objective of a reduction in the inequalities of wealth through comprehensive and effective taxes on wealth, instead of the spectacular but meaningless (and indirectly harmful) notion of an "income-ceiling".

ment of capital (i.e. on the assumption of risks) as a tax on income. This tax, however, has a similarly discouraging effect on savings as income tax, and for that reason, an annual tax on wealth, conceived as a progressive tax, ought not to exceed a top marginal rate of 1–1½ per cent. per annum.

13. From the point of view of administrative efficiency the main requirements are:

(i) *Simplicity*. The taxes should be based on simple definitions, avoiding, as far as possible, exemptions of various kinds or the special treatment of special categories, since all such complications lend themselves to manipulations (e.g., the existing difference in tax treatment between different kinds of companies, or as between companies and individuals, or as between the "profits" of business and "capital profits").

(ii) *Comprehensiveness*. Taxes on income should embrace all forms of beneficial receipts, taxes on capital wealth all forms of property. Exceptions to this should only be made on strictly administrative grounds (e.g., exemption limits for the sake of limiting the number of cases to be dealt with).

(iii) *A single, comprehensive return; a self-checking system of taxation; and an automatic reporting system*. These, I consider, are the most important requirements from the point of view of administrative efficiency:

(a) A Comprehensive Return

At the moment the tax-payer is only asked to return his income; and since the question whether a particular receipt falls into the category of "income" or not, is often a highly doubtful matter, the taxpayer is left, in effect, to decide for himself whether particular receipts are returnable or not. The Revenue authorities have power to ask for a return of capital assets and other details, but these powers are sparingly used— as it is indeed not possible to compel taxpayers to supply information on matters that are not directly relevant to the assessment of their tax liabilities. If a complete set of accounts is to be furnished, i.e., a statement of total wealth at the beginning of the year, all accruals during the year—by way of gifts, bequests, winnings, etc., as well as all forms of taxable income

C

and gains; the application of these to personal expenses and investments—as well as the resulting asset-position at the end of the year, the concealment of particular items of income or property, or the falsification of accounts, would obviously become far more difficult. (This is not to suggest that it is impossible to keep a complete duplicate set of books or to make out a "phoney" set of comprehensive accounts. But it is obviously a more difficult thing to do than to conceal receipts when only a partial return is called for.)

(b) A Self-checking System of Taxation

The present system of taxation already contains, of course, some self-checking elements. But owing to gaps in the legislation, the vagueness of the distinction between taxable and non-taxable receipts, and other factors, the efficiency of this is limited and it only works in certain directions. Assuming, however, that in addition to the present taxes on income, all realised capital gains are brought into charge (the transfer of assets by way of gifts, bequest and legacy counting as "realisation" in the same way as transfer by way of sale), a gift tax is imposed alongside of (and ultimately in replacement of) estate duties, and finally a personal expenditure tax is introduced, the system becomes completely self-checking in the sense that A's attempt to ensure that he is not over-assessed with regard to his own tax liabilities automatically brings to light the receipts and gains made by B, and so on. If the present taxes on income were extended to capital gains and other receipts of a capital nature, and were supplemented by an annual tax on wealth and a gift tax, if a super tax were levied on an expenditure-base (see below), and if all these taxes were assessed at the same time, by the same authority, and on the basis of a single comprehensive account submitted by the tax-payer (containing all receipts in the year, all tax-exempt outlays, a record of all capital transactions, and a full statement of all property owned) evasion and concealment would become more difficult, not only on account of the difficulty of the individual taxpayer to conceal consistently particular receipts or items of property but owing to the fact that the evidence furnished by one taxpayer (in the interests of minimising his own liability) directly serves as a check on the return furnished by others. Thus in computing A's liability for a personal expenditure tax all "exempt outlays" must be returned, and such exempt outlays represent taxable receipts of one kind or another (i.e., profit, capital gain, gift, etc.) to B. Similarly, since under this system all gains or losses on capital transactions are brought into the account, there is an automatic check on all new purchases of capital assets through the record of sales, and it is in the interest of the purchaser not to allow an under-statement of the price at which an asset was acquired since this enhances his future liability for a capital gains tax, as well as his liability to the personal expenditure tax.

(c) An Automatic Reporting System Extending to All Property

A system extending to all property transactions and all cash payments over a certain sum is outlined in Section VI. As indicated there, by means of a system of code numbers and tax vouchers, it would be relatively simple (administratively) to introduce an automatic reporting system for all property transactions requiring registration and attracting stamp duty. As suggested, the system can be extended to various other types of transactions if taxes were levied on personal expenditure, as well as on income.

C. OUTLINE OF MAIN PROPOSALS

14. An effective system on the above lines requires taxes on (a) income; (b) capital gains; (c) net wealth; (d) personal expenditure; and (e) gifts. All these can be assessed as a single operation, and on the basis of a single comprehensive return provided by the tax-payer.

(a) Income Tax

In place of the present income tax and super tax there should be a single income tax which, for individuals and partnerships, etc., is progressive up to an annual income of Rs. 25,000 and at a flat rate of 7 annas in the rupee for all income above that level.

The top marginal rate on income, therefore, becomes 43½ per cent. (or, say, 45 per cent. including the sur-charge) above that level. Companies should not be required to pay income tax but should pay a non-refundable tax of 7 annas in the rupee on their whole income (in place of the present income and corporation taxes). Income tax should be deducted at the maximum of 7 annas in the case of all interest and dividend payments as a matter of collection at source and credited to the recipients' income tax account.

(b) Capital Gains Tax

All capital gains on realisation and all casual gains and capital receipts not chargeable at present (such as the sale of terminable rights, premium on leases etc.) should be charged to income tax which means a flat rate charge of 7 annas in the rupee once the combined income (including capital gains) exceeds Rs. 25,000. Capital gains of companies should be chargeable to tax in the same way as trading profits.

This means that all beneficial receipts (whether trading or capital profits, other kinds of income, individual or company income, or the income of public or of private companies) are charged at a single uniform rate of 7 annas in the rupee (in the place of the present multiplicity of rates and exemptions), except that individuals are charged at reduced rates when their aggregate beneficial receipts are less than Rs. 25,000. The tremendous advantage of this, both as regards administrative simplicity and the prevention of evasion and manipulation of all kinds, cannot be over-emphasised.

(c) Annual Tax on Wealth

Payable by individuals, H.U.F.s,[1] partnerships etc. Suggested scale, ⅓ per cent. per annum on personal net worth of, say, Rs. 1,00,000–4,00,000; ½ per cent. per annum on 4,00,000–7,00,000; ¾ per cent. per annum on 7,00,000–10,00,000; 1 per cent. on capital value of Rs. 10,00,000–15,00,000 and 1½ per cent. in excess of Rs. 15 lakhs (tax liability to be calculated on the slab system).

[1] Hindu Undivided Families.

(d) Personal Expenditure Tax

Payable on a per head basis, on personal outlay in excess of Rs. 10,000 per annum per adult (infants counting as one half adult for the purpose) on a progressive scale, calculated on the slab system, rising from 25 per cent. for expenditure between Rs. 10,000–12,500 to 300 per cent. on expenditure in excess of Rs. 50,000 per annum per adult. (Example: A family of four, father, mother, two children, incurs an expenditure of Rs. 40,000 a year. As the family consists of three adult units, the expenditure is Rs. 13,333 per adult, and the tax liability is three times the tax on the first Rs. 3,333 of taxable expenditure.)[1]

(e) General Gift Tax

Payable on gifts in excess of Rs. 10,000 for any single recipient of gifts (the donee) and taxed at a rate depending on the total net worth of the recipient (as ascertained for annual wealth tax) at the rate of 10 per cent. if the net worth is below Rs. 1,00,000 and at double the current corresponding estate duty rates for correspondingly higher amounts of net worth, i.e., at the rate of 15 to 80 per cent., depending on the net worth of the recipient. (Examples: (i) A receives a gift of Rs. 50,000 from his parent; possesses no property; his tax liability is Rs. 4,000. (ii) B receives a bequest of Rs. 50,000 and possesses net worth (before the bequest) valued at Rs. 2,50,000; B's liability is 25 per cent. on 40,000, i.e., Rs. 10,000. (iii) C inherits from his father Rs. 2,00,000; has no other property; his liability is Rs. 26,500. (iv) D owns property valued at Rs. 5,00,000; receives a gift of Rs. 50,000; his liability is 40 per cent. of Rs. 40,000, i.e., Rs. 16,000.) It is suggested that once the annual wealth tax is in operation, and adequate returns are obtained on annual net worth, the above tax should replace

[1] These suggested scales for the expenditure tax were so chosen as to cause the tax to come into operation only when the net expenditure of a typical family unit exceeds the net income remaining on a taxable income of Rs. 40,000 a year—the level at which the present combined income and super tax rate begins to exceed the marginal rate of 7 annas in the rupee at present—so that the tax becomes a substitute for the loss of the present super tax on slabs above 3 annas in the rupee. It would be possible, of course, to fix lower exemption limits that would be more consonant with the standards of living and the expenditure scales of the top income groups of India.

the present estate duty altogether. The latter is based on an antiquated conception. The true incidence of inheritance taxes falls on the recipients of the inheritance, and not on the deceased. Also, there is no justification in equity for a difference in treatment as between gifts *inter vivos* and the receipt of legacies or bequests. Hence a single progressive tax on gifts should take the place of the estate duty, as well as serving as a tax on all other gratuitous or quasi-gratuitous property transfers.[1] (The exemption of Rs. 10,000 should apply, of course, only to the initial gift received by a particular donee.)

D. PROBABLE EFFECTS ON REVENUE

Income Tax

15. The elimination of super tax above 3 annas will mean, on the basis of 1953–54 assessments, a loss of revenue of Rs. 18·3 crores, of which Rs. 14·2 crores represent the loss of super-tax on individuals, Rs. 2·3 crores on the H.U.F.s and Rs. 1·8 crores on unregistered firms. A uniform tax of 7 annas in the rupee (plus sur-charge) levied on companies would bring in the same yield as the income and corporation taxes do at present.

Capital Gains Tax

16. A tax on realised capital gains has a long gestation period (of, say 5–15 years) but ultimately the average annual assessment of realised gains should correspond to the average annual accrual of gains. Capital gains mainly arise on ordinary shares, on the sale of individual business (as goodwill), on urban property, and on jewellery and valuables. The value of ordinary share capital in India may be put at the order of Rs. 800–1,000 crores,[2] and the total value of property of the "appreciating" kind, including shares, at say Rs. 1,800–2,000 crores. The long-run rate of appreciation in value may be put at 3–5 per cent. per annum corresponding to the rate of growth of the national income. This would give a long-run annual rate of accrual of the order of

---

[1] The level of rates and the degree of progression needs, of course, to be higher than with the estate duty, since the rates vary with the size of the individual gift or bequest, and not the size of the total estate of the donor; hence the suggestion that the rates should be double the current estate duty rates.

[2] Reached by capitalising annual dividend payments to individuals etc., of Rs. 40 crores.

Rs. 60–100 crores,[1] on which the tax revenue might be of the order of Rs. 25–40 crores. (These are, of course, meant as "long-run" average figures; the yield of any particular year would show wide variations.)

Annual Wealth Tax

17. A computation based on current income tax assessments, reproduced in Section II, indicates that the yield of this, on the scales suggested above, would be of the order of Rs. 15–25 crores.

Personal Expenditure Tax

18. Assuming that the personal expenditure of the upper classes (those with taxable incomes above Rs. 40,000) corresponds, for the group as a whole, to their net income after tax, the yield of this tax would roughly offset the loss on super tax. In fact, however, the upper income groups save considerable amounts, but whether they do so in relation to their taxed incomes or only out of capital gains, it is impossible to say. It might be safe to assume that spendings are less than the net incomes after tax (to the exclusion of capital gains) and hence the revenue from this tax, on the scale suggested above, might be less than the equivalent of, say, Rs. 10–15 crores.

General Gift Tax

19. The yield of this can only be estimated on present data on broad lines. Assuming the total value of non-agricultural property in the hands of owners possessing Rs. 1 lakh or over is Rs. 4,000 crores (a figure derived from the calculations in Section II and based on income tax assessments), 1/25th of this may be assumed to be transferred (by way of gifts, dowry, legacy, etc.) annually.[2] Assuming the average rate of duty to be 20 per cent., the yield of this tax should come to Rs. 30 crores.

[1] Another method of calculation based on the net ploughed-back profits of companies yields even higher estimates. Net company savings after tax amount to around Rs. 70 crores a year; and since in the long run the market values of shares must be at least equal to the accumulated share capital and reserves (otherwise companies would go into liquidation sooner or later) the long-run appreciation of share values should alone amount to some Rs. 70 crores a year, giving a total appreciation of, say, Rs. 120–150 crores.

[2] The figure of 1/25th is derived from the assumption that the average length of a generation of property owners in India is 25 years.

20. Hence the "long run" yield of the above suggestions—i.e. allowing for the time necessary for the smooth and efficient administrative operation of the proposed system, and for the "gestation period" in the case of the capital gains tax, but on the basis of the present level of the National Income—should come to a net additional revenue of Rs. 60–100 crores per annum.

21. These estimates do not take into account the additional yield of income tax that would follow from the checking of evasion or avoidance or the additional yield of the property tax on such property the income from which is concealed at present.

22. In the following chapters the proposals outlined above are discussed in detail and specific problems relating to the suggested new taxes and system of comprehensive reporting and compulsory registration of property transfers examined.

II. AN ANNUAL TAX ON NET WEALTH

A. INTRODUCTION

23. The purpose of this chapter is to examine the case for an annual tax on net wealth owned by individual taxpayers alongside of, or in partial substitution of, the present tax on income. Though annual taxes on property form part of the tax legislation of over a dozen countries, only a few of them (chiefly the Scandinavian countries) possess a tax on the lines recommended here.

24. An annual tax on wealth, though it is levied on the value of the principal, is really a tax on accrual and not a tax on the principal itself—as, for example, estate duties or a capital levy are. If all property yielded the same percentage of income, an income tax and an annual wealth tax would amount to the same thing. The two differ precisely because some property yields a large money income, other property a small income (or no money income at all) in relation to its current market value.

25. The tax, similarly to income tax, should be conceived as a progressive one, and levied at rates (i) which are well within the total accrual from property—whether in the form of money

income, expected appreciation, or psychic income; and (ii) which take into account the other taxes on accruals, in particular, the income tax. In the light of this, it would seem reasonable to levy a tax at the rate of 0·3 per cent. per annum on the lowest slab (i.e., from Rs. 1,00,000 to Rs. 4,00,000) rising to 1·5 per cent. per annum on the highest slab (i.e., on the value of property in excess of Rs. 15,00,000). The exemption limit of Rs. 1,00,000 is recommended solely for administrative considerations—i.e., until more experience is gained with the administration of the tax. For ultimately there is something to be said for a rather low exemption limit regarding this particular tax—an exemption limit low enough for encompassing those sections of the community which are not touched by the existing tax on income. In a country like India, a tax based on capital ownership should prove administratively easier to assess and collect in the lower reaches of the income scales than a tax based on current earnings.

26. For the sake of equity, as well as administrative efficiency, it is essential that the tax should be comprehensive—i.e. extending to all forms of property. The inclusion of agricultural property in this connection may require a constitutional amendment, unless the procedure adopted in the case of estate duties of the States delegating the powers to the Centre could be repeated here.[1] Property in the form of bank balances, jewels and valuables above a certain exemption limit of, say, Rs. 5,000, as well as real estate of all kinds, assignable rights with a market value, the ownership of stocks and shares etc., should all be comprised in it. Personal effects like household furniture and clothing should be exempted up to a certain limit per family member. (In Sweden, motor cars and motor boats are exempted as well as personal effects, works of art and art collections; ornaments only if their total value is below Rs. 1,000.)

B. THE GENERAL CASE FOR AN ANNUAL TAX ON WEALTH

27. The arguments can be grouped under three heads, equity, economic effects, and administrative efficiency.

---

[1] In the meanwhile, the tax could be made chargeable only on non-agricultural property with a provision that agricultural property would be aggregable with the rest of the property for determining the rate at which the tax would become payable.

(a) The main argument in equity for the tax is that income taken by itself is an inadequate yardstick of taxable capacity as between incomes from work and incomes from property, and also as between the different property owners. The basic reason for this is that the ownership of property in the form of disposable assets endows the property owner with a taxable capacity as such, quite apart from the money income which that property yields. This is best shown if you compare the position of a beggar who has neither income nor property with the position of a man who keeps the whole of his wealth of, say, Rs. 10,00,000 in the form of jewellery and gold. Judging their capacities by the test of income alone, the taxable capacity of both is nil. Quite apart from such an extreme case, it should be evident that as between people who possess property and income in different proportions, income alone is not an adequate test of capacity to pay; nor can that capacity be adequately assessed by a tax based on property alone. Suppose two individuals, A and B, have the same income of, say, Rs. 50,000, but one of them derives it from the property worth Rs. 2,00,000 and the other derives it from the property worth Rs. 5,00,000. It would clearly be wrong to suggest that the taxable capacities of the two men are identical and they should be called upon to pay the same amount of tax (which is what happens if only income is used as the tax base). It would be equally wrong to regard the taxable capacity of B as being $2\frac{1}{2}$ times as great as that of A, which would be the case if they were assessed on the basis of property alone. A man who derives Rs. 50,000 a year from property of Rs. 5,00,000 is clearly better off than a man who derives Rs. 50,000 a year from property of only Rs. 2,00,000, but he is evidently not as well off as a third man who possesses the same capital of Rs. 5,00,000 and has an income of Rs. 1,25,000. Hence, only a combination of income and property taxes can give an approximation to taxation in accordance with ability to pay. (The existing earned income relief is intended to give some recognition to the higher taxable capacity of incomes derived from property as against similar incomes derived from work, but precisely because the relation between income and property value varies so much as between one individual and another the problem could never be adequately dealt with by the technique of earned income relief, even if that relief were extended to all income ranges and made far more substantial than at present.)

(*b*) From the point of view of economic effects, the great advantage of taxes assessed on property value as against taxes assessed on income is that a property tax does not discriminate against the risky employments of capital in the same way as an income tax. If a man can get a "safe" return by putting his money in Government bonds yielding 3 per cent., whereas he could expect 10 per cent. on his money if he employed it in productive business, the difference of 7 per cent. may be taken to measure the investor's subjective estimate of the risks associated with the productive employment of capital. An income tax by taxing the additional income obtained through risk bearing in the same way as if it were "safe" income discriminates against risk bearing. Under the property tax, the same property value would bear the same tax, whether it is invested in Government bonds yielding 3 per cent., in productive employments yielding 10 per cent. or held in cash or in jewellery etc., yielding no money income at all.

It is true that under the present system of income tax which exempts capital gains or capital profits from taxation altogether a great part of the additional reward of risk bearing does not, in effect, bear any tax, since it takes the form of capital gains rather than of taxable income. A property tax on the other hand, would automatically bring into charge the increase in value resulting from capital appreciation. Even so, an annual capital tax provides a smaller disincentive on the productive employment of capital than even the present restricted income tax, for while the latter exempts capital gains it also provides complete tax exemption for the socially unproductive hoarding of wealth in the form of gold and jewellery etc., whereas the property tax would make these a less attractive form of holding wealth.

(*c*) From the point of view of administrative efficiency, it must be borne in mind that while property value is something distinct from annual profit or income, the two, in fact, are closely related in the sense that profits and property incomes of all kinds (other than the profits associated with professional and vocational activities) have always some tangible assets behind them; and similarly, most forms of property, though not all, yield money income or profit of some kind. Hence if taxes were assessed both on income and on property, by the same taxing authority, the administrative efficiency of the system is bound to be improved in consequence. For the examination of a man's property ownership is bound to lead to the discovery of his concealed income, and similarly the examination of his income receipts is bound to lead to the discovery of concealed property. A tax on both, therefore, should provide a better check on evasion and concealment than a tax on either.

C. ARGUMENTS AGAINST AN ANNUAL TAX ON WEALTH

28. Despite its great advantages, a progressive annual tax on wealth has so far only been adopted in a few countries. Its exclusion from the scope of taxation in others has been defended on numerous grounds, few of which stand up to serious examination. The arguments against the tax can again be grouped under the heads of equity, economic effects and administrative efficiency.

29. It has been suggested (occasionally by no less an economist than Prof. Pigou) that an annual tax on property is inequitable, because not all property yields an income, and a tax on property may force a man to make payments "even if he has no income to pay it with". These arguments wholly beg the question of what is meant by "income". All property which has a positive market value (which can be bought and sold currently or exchanged for other forms of property) must yield a benefit to the owner at least comparable to the benefit obtained from other forms of property which he could buy—otherwise he would sell it and exchange it for something else (the only exception to this is the case of entailed property which the owner cannot alienate). If a property does not yield money income, it must either yield an equivalent psychic income to the owner or it must be held in the expectation of a certain appreciation in value which makes it at least as attractive to the holder as other property on which a current money return is obtained.[1] So far, therefore, from this constituting an argument

---

[1] If a man holds shares in, say, a developing gold mine, and the shares are expected to, and do, appreciate in value year by year, can we really distinguish between this benefit (which takes the form of a capital profit) and the benefit which takes the form of a dividend paid on them?

against the property tax, it shows the inherent defect of income tax which concentrates on one particular form of accrual from property, namely money income, to the exclusion of other forms.

30. The economic arguments against the wealth tax sometimes refer to the alleged discouraging effect of the tax on productive enterprise and sometimes to the possibility of its incidence being shifted from the taxpayer to the ultimate consumer.

(a) As far as the discouraging effects on enterprise are concerned, it is true, of course, that a tax on wealth has a discouraging effect as compared with no taxation at all. But as we have shown, it has a lesser discouraging effect than an equivalent amount of tax collected from the taxpayer in the form of an income tax. (The argument that capitalists can now evade income tax through the conversion of income into capital gains, while there are no equivalent evasion possibilities in the case of property tax, could hardly be construed as a respectable reason against the property tax and in favour of the income tax.)

(b) The idea that the incidence of a property tax can be shifted in an analogous manner to commodity taxes is mistaken. Precisely because the tax is on the value of capital irrespective of the use to which the capital is put, the tax lacks the discriminatory effect by which alone a shifting of the incidence could take place. In fact, the possibility of shifting the incidence of an annual tax on property is far smaller than that of an equivalent tax on income.

31. From the administrative point of view, it is often suggested that an annual property tax presents special problems of assessment on account of (a) the difficulties of "discovering" the true owners of property; and (b) the difficulties of valuation. I propose to deal with each of these aspects at some length.

The Problem of "Discovery"

32. As regards the problem of under-statement and concealment, it should, of course, be borne in mind that the "discovery" of a man's property is intimately linked with the "discovery" of his income. If property is concealed so is the income: if the income is known the property behind the income can be traced. Introducing an annual property tax does not, therefore, really raise formidable additional problems, from the point of view of discovery, to those

that already have to be faced on account of the income tax. On the contrary, the obligation on a taxpayer to return annually his total net wealth as well as his income should help considerably in checking the evasion of income tax, just as the existence of income tax should help in checking the evasion of an annual property tax. As set out in Section I, if the individual taxpayer is asked to supply a comprehensive account of his personal affairs—his asset position at the beginning and at the end of the year; his total accruals and their application as between personal expenses and investments—concealment of any one item becomes far more difficult, since it requires a consistent falsification of the accounts. The essential requirement is that the assessment and administration of the two taxes should be closely linked with one another, the work of assessment being done on the basis of a single comprehensive return, and by the same tax officials.

33. This is not meant to suggest that an annual wealth tax (any more than the income tax) could be administered efficiently (i.e., with only a limited amount of fraudulent evasion) without a considerable tightening up in the present methods of registration and control over the ownership of property. The most important reforms in this connection may be described as follows:

(a) As the present municipal records of urban property are admittedly defective and incomplete it would be advisable to set up a Central Records Office for the listing and valuation of urban property on an all-India basis as recommended by the Local Finance Enquiry Committee.

(b) Ultimately something analogous would also be advisable in the case of rural and agricultural property. This, however, will undoubtedly take far more time and in the meantime reliance must be placed on village records which I understand are fairly detailed, at least in the non-zamindari areas, and make a distinction between land used for cultivation and land used for building. (It should also be remembered that the great bulk of rural property is probably held by owners whose total property is well under the exemption limits suggested for the tax.)

(c) With regard to investments in stocks and shares of companies there is a strong case for the abolition of the existing Indian practice of buying and selling shares by means of "blank transfer" certificates. This system does not exist either in the U.K., or the U.S.A., and it would be difficult to maintain that its preservation in India is an important prerequisite of economic development. As is suggested later on in Section VI, if the system of taxation code numbers were introduced, the share registers of companies could be made to include the code numbers of beneficial owners as well as nominal holders in whose names the shares are registered.

(*d*) In the case of Government securities it would be advisable to adopt the same system as in the U.K., by which the owners of all Government securities are registered at the Reserve Bank, and changes in ownership have to be registered in the same way as changes in other property. In India interest on Government securities is payable by means of coupons and transfers take place by mere endorsement on the back of securities. It would be perfectly simple to exchange the present securities against securities of a registered type when the coupons are presented for encashment.[1]

(*e*) With regard to stock-in-trade, machinery and plant the problems involved are not different from those already faced in the administration of income tax.

(*f*) For property of all types, as I suggest in Section VI, the compulsory disclosure of beneficial ownership in the case of benami holdings or holdings in the names of trustees or nominees is essential for the efficient administration of both income tax and wealth tax. This could best be ensured by the nominal holder being asked to sign a declaration to the effect that he is the beneficial owner, or only a benamidar, etc., such declaration having full legal force from the point of view of any subsequent civil action concerning the property.

The Problem of Valuation

34. I think that the best method or procedure is to follow

---

[1] In the U.K., transfers of stocks and shares of companies and of Government securities require a transfer deed in much the same way as transfers of real property. In the case of share transfers, this also serves the purpose of ensuring payment of stamp duty. I understand that in India only the transfer of immovable property requires completion of a transfer deed. I cannot see any fundamental reason why this system should not be extended to stocks and shares, and to Government securities generally, in the same way as in the U.K.

ordinary accounting rules and to value each particular item of property at its "book value" until it is sold. This means, in effect, that when an account is initially set up, all items of property are valued at current value which forms the cost at which they are entered into the accounts and they will continue to be valued at that cost (apart from cases in which the Revenue Department allows depreciation and they are valued at cost less accrued depreciation) until such time as the property passes out of the account through a sale, gift, or bequest. Property, therefore, only has to be valued (*a*) initially when the tax is introduced and the personal accounts are set up; and (*b*) subsequently when the property is transferred to a different owner otherwise than by sale.

35. The responsibility for the initial valuation of property would rest on the taxpayer who would be asked to value all items at current market value. If the Revenue Department disputes a particular item of valuation, it should have the right to ask the taxpayer to name his own reserve price for the disputed item of property and to substitute that reserve price for the market value, for purposes of the tax. If the Revenue Department is of the opinion that the reserve price as stated by the taxpayer is still below the true current market value of the property, it can so advise the Central P.W.D.[1] who can then acquire the property at the taxpayer's own reserve price. Thus taxpayers who purposely under-value properties in their returns would run the risk of having to substitute their own reserve price for the market value and thereby incur the penalty of being taxed on a higher value than the current market value; and if their reserve price is also an under-statement of the true market value they run the risk of having the property "bought out" at that price by the State.[2]

36. The establishment of a Central Valuation Department under the C.B.R., with regional and sub-regional valuation

---

[1] Or any other department which may be entrusted with the job of looking after government properties.

[2] I do not know whether there is any country where this system is actually in force; but it has often been suggested (e.g., in connection with the discussion of a capital levy in U.K., after the First World War) that the problem of valuation of properties for the purpose of taxation could be effectively solved if the responsibility of valuing the property was put squarely on the taxpayer, with the Government retaining the right of acquiring the property at the taxpayers' own valuation in cases of dispute.

offices will be necessary in order to be able to check the valuations of properties given by the taxpayers. (This does not present a problem with stocks and shares quoted on the Stock Exchange but mainly with immovable property.) This will be necessary mainly to check the initial valuation of properties and the valuation in case of a gratuitous or quasi-gratuitous transfer (gift, inheritence, etc.) where the valuation will be necessary both for the purposes of the gift tax and the capital gains tax, as well as for the revision of the value of the property for the annual wealth tax[1] in the hands of the new owners. Under the system here proposed, a capital gains tax is charged every time property passes hands, and in addition a gift tax is charged in the hands of the recipient in case of all gratuitous transfers. For the purposes of the annual tax on property the capital value will be the same as the valuations accepted for the purpose of capital gains tax and the gift tax in case of gratuitous transfers, and the actual proceeds of sale and purchase cost in case of other transactions.[2]

D. PROBABLE YIELD OF THE TAX

37. In the absence of any direct statistics bearing on the value of various forms of property in India, and its distribution according to size-groups, any estimate of the yield of the wealth tax can only be undertaken by the rough method of "working backwards" from income. By capitalising the profits of firms, partnerships and individual businesses and the dividend income of companies, a rough estimate of the total value of wealth and its size distribution

---

[1] In the U.K., the Central Valuation Office under the Board of Inland Revenue evaluates properties for both estate duty and stamp duty purposes, and has now also been entrusted with the listing and valuation of all land and buildings for the purposes of local rates.

[2] Valuing all property by "book values" instead of by current market values will mean that the valuation of property for the purposes of the annual tax will lag 8 to 10 years behind the current market valuation of property. Assuming that property appreciated in the long run at the average compound rate of 3 per cent. it will mean that the tax will be levied on a basis which in the average of cases, and over a run of years, will correspond to about two-thirds of the current market value. This should, of course, be taken into account in fixing the appropriate schedule of rates. (The gap of 8–10 years is estimated in the following manner. If no property were to change hands except through decease the average book value of properties at any one time would be equal to the current values of half a generation earlier; since a generation is 25 years, this means an average lag of 12·5 years. This needs to be further reduced on account of transfers of properties of all kinds through purchases and sales and through *inter vivos* gifts.)

(excluding agricultural property) can be obtained. Assuming an average yield of 5 per cent. from shares and 10 per cent. from other property, the total of privately owned wealth in estates over one lakh works out at Rs. 3,350 crores, while assuming an average of 4 per cent. on shares and 8 per cent. on other property, the total is Rs. 4,200 crores. A minimum addition of 10 per cent. may be made to those figures for cash, bank balances and all other forms of property which do not yield a money income. On the scale of the tax rates suggested, the estimated yield of the tax comes out at Rs. 17–25 crores. The details are shown in Table 1.

38. Sweden possesses very detailed statistics relating to both income and property and it is possible to make estimates of the relationship for different property groups and make inferences from these as to the likely value of these ratios in India and the consequent yield of the annual tax. These estimates are given in Appendix C. The net result is that under the proposed schedule of rates the estimate of initial revenue from the wealth tax can be placed at Rs. 20 crores a year.

39. Since the above estimates are based on disclosed income, they are almost certainly too low, both as a measure of the true value of non-agricultural property and of the probable yield of the tax, once the administration is made more water-tight through the system of comprehensive returns and the institution of an automatic reporting system.

E. CONCLUDING REMARKS

40. An annual tax on wealth is recommended both on account of its merits taken by itself and because it is an essential element in the institution of a comprehensive and evasion-proof system of taxation. Although its operation cannot be expected to become fully efficient until the existing rules concerning the registration of property are tightened up, and an efficient staff of valuers is evolved within the Revenue Department, these are not to be regarded as adequate reasons for postponing the introduction of the tax. There is no reason why the obligation to submit comprehensive income and capital returns, on the lines outlined in Section I, should not be introduced immediately. As has been

Table 1

ESTIMATED YIELD OF AN ANNUAL TAX ON WEALTH BASED ON INCOME TAX ASSESSMENTS FOR 1954–55

(Rupees in lakhs)

Size of estate	Assessed income	Number of assessees	Alternative I[1] Capital value	Alternative I[1] Tax[3] rate%	Alternative I[1] Tax yield	Alternative II[2] Capital value	Alternative II[2] Tax[3] rate%	Alternative II[2] Tax yield
1. Company share capital								
1– 4,00,000	11,95		2,39,00	$\frac{1}{3}$	80	2,98,75	$\frac{1}{2}$	1,00
4– 7,00,000	5,75		1,15,02	$\frac{1}{2}$	58	1,43,77	$\frac{3}{4}$	72
7–10,00,000	3,60		71,98	$\frac{3}{4}$	54	89,98	$\frac{3}{4}$	67
10–15,00,000	3,52		70,44	1	70	88,06	1	88
above 15,00,000	10,62		2,12,36	$1\frac{1}{2}$	3,19	2,65,45	$1\frac{1}{2}$	3,98
Total	35,44		7,08,80		5,81	8,86,01		7,25
2. Other capital								
1– 4,00,000	1,57,03	1,02,224	15,70,30	$\frac{1}{3}$	1,83	19,62,88	$\frac{1}{2}$	3,14
4– 7,00,000	34,31	7,874	3,43,10	$\frac{1}{2}$	93	4,28,88	$\frac{3}{4}$	1,36
7–10,00,000	15,96	2,173	1,59,60	$\frac{3}{4}$	60	1,99,50	$\frac{3}{4}$	90
10–15,00,000	14,03	1,295	1,40,30	1	73	1,75,38	1	1,08
above 15,00,000	43,67	1,354	4,36,70	$1\frac{1}{2}$	4,82	5,45,87	$1\frac{1}{2}$	6,46
Total	2,65,00	1,14,920	26,50,00		8,91	33,12,31		12,94
3. Addition of 10% for non-income yielding capital			3,35,88	$\frac{4}{5}$[4]	2,69	4,19,83	$\frac{4}{5}$[4]	3,36
Total		1,14,920	36,94,68		17,41	46,18,15		23,55

1 Dividend income is capitalised at 5% and other profits at 10%.
2 Dividend income is capitalised at 4% and other profits at 8%.
3 Tax rates are assumed to apply on a slab system and yield is calculated accordingly.
4 Stands for the effective rate of tax on the total chargeable capital value.

suggested in paragraph 35 above, the Revenue could initially assess the tax on the basis of the taxpayers' own declared values.

III. THE TAXATION OF CAPITAL GAINS

A. GENERAL CONSIDERATIONS[1]

41. The exclusion of capital gains from the scope of income taxation is quite indefensible on grounds of equity (since it involves the privileged treatment of a particular class of tax-payers as against others), or of administrative efficiency (since it enables taxpayers to camouflage income as tax-exempt gains and to conceal gains). It can only be supported on grounds of economic expediency, in that it reduces the ill-effects of the taxation of income on savings and on risk bearing, i.e. on accumulation and enterprise. It does this precisely because it exempts certain kinds of income from taxation; any other device which enables people to avoid taxation to a similar extent (as, e.g., a rule that every third taxpayer chosen at random should be immune from income tax altogether) would have an equally desirable economic effect.

42. If capital gains were treated in the same way as other forms of income, which means (since the gains are concentrated in the top income and capital brackets) taxing them at the rate of 90 per cent., the economic effects would undoubtedly be serious. But the moral of this is that it is useless to push the marginal rates of income taxation to levels at which the tax can only be endured because it can be so largely evaded or avoided. The disincentive effects of taxation depend on the *marginal* rates of taxation; and if these are kept down to reasonable levels, there is no need to resort to inequity and dishonesty in order to keep the system going. It is far better to forgo the *appearance* of high progressiveness in the schedule of taxation than to choose a definition of "income" for the tax base which is neither consistent,

---

[1] Only a cursory statement of the case can be given here. My own views on the concept of "income" appropriate to income taxation, and on the taxation of capital gains, are set out in detail in the Memorandum of Dissent to the Final Report of the Royal Commission on the Taxation of Profits and Income (Cmd. 9474), paras 2–18, and 34–72 (reprinted in *Reports on Taxation,* vol. I).

nor impartial, nor unambiguous in its application to different taxpayers.

43. The preferential treatment of capital gains (if not their complete exemption from tax) is sometimes defended on the ground that the taxable capacity inherent in any given amount of capital gain is less than that of other kinds of income of an identical amount, either because the gains may be "illusory", if they merely represented money appreciation, and not real appreciation, or they reflected a fall in interest rates and not a rise in the expected income of assets, or because they are casual or isolated rather than regularly recurrent. None of these arguments really provide any justification for the preferential or privileged treatment of capital gains as such. For not only capital gains, but any kind of savings may be "illusory" in varying degrees and for much the same reasons; the argument, therefore, has some validity against the choice of income (rather than consumption, or net worth) as the base of taxation, but not against the inclusion of capital profits in the concept of income. Similarly while it is true that non-recurrent or casual gains do not give rise to the same taxable capacity (in a given period) as recurrent gains of the same magnitude, it is certainly not true to suggest that all non-recurrent or casual gains are capital gains, or even that capital gains are necessarily more irregular in their occurrence than some other forms of profit which are not immune from taxation. So long as, and to the extent that, taxation is based on "income" the only impartial concept of income is that which treats all realised gains equally.

44. The present concept of taxable profits (which is taken over in Indian law from the British law) leaves the distinction between taxable and non-taxable receipts extremely vague and ambiguous. This constitutes a further source of inequity as between different taxpayers, since identical (or substantially identical) circumstances may involve widely differing tax treatment according to the whims or energy of particular revenue officers, the attitude of the courts, or the extent to which the Revenue is apprised of the existence of receipts of a disputable character. For the very approach which treats the taxability of particular forms of receipts as a matter to be decided "on the facts of the case"

(without specifying what particular "facts" are relevant to the matter) naturally opens the door to the widest possible differences of interpretation as between taxable and non-taxable profits; and taxpayers can hardly be blamed for preferring the interpretation most favourable to themselves and making their returns accordingly.

45. It may be that the Indian Revenue authorities have been more successful than the British in "roping in" profits of a speculative or casual character into the tax net, but I doubt it. The fact that the Revenue in both countries has succeeded in obtaining favourable decisions in the courts in a few spectacular cases must not be taken to mean that the range of cases covered by these decisions are now effectively within the tax net. In England, court decisions since 1920 established that casual profits in transactions of an unusual character (like the purchase and sale of farms by a motor engineer, or the sale of bonded whisky by a woodcutter, etc.) are within the range of taxable profits. But not more than a minute fraction of such speculative transactions are effectively taxed partly because each case is to some extent distinct from every other, and hence legal precedents are inadequate for establishing it as a transaction "in the nature of trade"; partly also because gains with an adumbra of doubt are not brought to the knowledge of the Revenue. Despite Reynold's Executors v. Bennet (25 T.C. 401, 1943)[1] land speculation goes on unhindered by the tax officer. As regards Stock Exchange transactions, the taxability of speculative profits by people other than registered professional dealers or by professional dealers operating on their "personal" rather than their "business" account has never been tested in the courts in Britain and it is generally admitted that none of these, in practice, come within the tax net. Equally, I understand, in India the factors distinguishing a speculative profit from mere realisation of investment are so vague as to make it impossible in practice to bring gains by other than professional speculators within the tax net.

[1] In this case the High Court in the U.K., held that the profits made on the sale of two farms by a motor engineer were liable to be taxed despite the fact that evidence was produced (and accepted by the Crown) that (a) the motor engineer bought the farms for the purpose of farming them and not for the purpose of resale, and (b) he was only persuaded to sell them with great reluctance when a man came and offered him a good price for them.

46. The fact moreover that some taxpayers (the professional dealers in securities, finance houses, etc.) are taxed on their capital gains and correspondingly relieved of capital losses, whilst other taxpayers are not, makes it possible to extract money from the Treasury by fictitious transactions of all kinds, the common feature of which is that the party which is exempt from capital gains exchanges a taxable object (e.g., a dividend) for tax-free gain, whilst the other party off-sets its taxable income against the manufactured loss on capital transactions. In this way the tax-exemption of capital gains to some sections of the community reduces the yield of ordinary income tax below the amount it would have had if everybody's gains had been uniformly taxed or uniformly exempted from taxation.[1]

47. The taxation of capital gains is sometimes opposed by the curious argument that its introduction would actually stimulate tax avoidance instead of reducing it. Thus the Taxation Enquiry Commission in their report say:[2] "If a capital gains tax were to be introduced now—and is bound to be levied at rates lower than the ordinary income and supertax on account of its casual or irregular character—there is a danger of tax avoidance being stimulated by attempts to pass off as capital gains what may otherwise have been treated as part of taxable income". This view overlooks the fact that the complete exemption of capital gains must necessarily afford a much stronger stimulus to tax avoidance than the reduction of liability arising out of differential treatment. In fact, as we have argued above, under the present system the Revenue has the worst of both worlds. It can neither prevent income masquerading as tax-exempt capital gains, nor capital losses being offset against current income, either of a special or an ordinary kind, for tax purposes.

---

[1] Existing anti-avoidance provisions prevent such transactions in case the sale and subsequent re-purchase was undertaken "by the same or any collateral agreement". But there is nothing illegal in buying and selling securities through two separate and unrelated transactions, and it would indeed be impossible to frame anti-avoidance provisions, which prevented a man from selling one day and buying the next day, especially since he need not even buy back the identical security to accomplish his object. Nor is it at all easy for the Revenue to establish that a set of transactions was the result of a single or collateral agreement.

[2] Volume 1, Chapter VIII, para. 56 (p. 163).

48. The legal position in India differs from that of Britain in that provisions relating to the taxation of capital gains are actually on the Statute Book (Section 12 B of the Income Tax Act). As far as I understand the position, while the operation of this Section is suspended at present, it could at any time be re-activated by a simple clause in the Finance Act.

49. I have not been able to discover whether any detailed consideration of the problem preceded the abolition of the tax, after only two years of its operation, in the Finance Act of 1949. The reasons given by the Finance Minister in the Budget speech were:

   (i) the yield was expected to be comparatively small, about Rs. one crore;

  (ii) the psychological effect of the tax on investment was bad; and

 (iii) the tax operated to hinder the free movement of securities in the capital market, which was a necessary pre-requisite of industrial development.

None of these reasons appear to me adequate to justify the abandonment of the experiment after only two years of operation. The actual yield of the tax for these two years amounted to over Rs. 6 crores; and since the yield in the initial years could obviously have only represented a fraction of the ultimate yield it is not clear how the surprisingly low estimate of Rs. one crore was arrived at. It is well known that no complicated new tax can be expected to work satisfactorily or to show its full yield in the first few years of its operation; the Rs. 6 crores collected in the years 1947/48 to 1952/53, in respect of the financial years 1947/48 and 1948/49, were based on a total of 1,814 assessments only. Nor is it clear how the Government could have had the information or experience at its disposal to be able to conclude that the tax had important adverse effects on investment, or hindered the free inter-change of securities.[1] There is also a logical contradiction

[1] Various studies in the United States (such as Seltzer's) concluded that in the U.S.A., the tax had no significant effect on the volume of Stock Exchange transactions.

involved in arguing both that the tax has only a negligible yield, and at the same time has important adverse repercussions on the economy.[1]

50. The Central Board of Revenue, in their evidence submitted before the Taxation Enquiry Commission came down unhesitatingly in favour of the tax, but they felt doubtful "whether its reintroduction at the present time (December 1953) is likely to lead to any considerable revenue". According to the Board's statement, "the general tendency seems to be for profits and prices falling rather than rising; transactions in capital assets are also much less frequent than they were a few years ago". The Taxation Enquiry Commission in their Report took up a more ambiguous position and gave only a very cursory treatment (half a page) to the whole problem.

51. In my opinion it would be a great mistake to treat the question of the taxation of capital gains mainly on short-term revenue considerations, and to put the tax off and on according as the immediate revenue expected in the light of the prospective economic situation was small or large. Quite apart from the fact that the basic and most important reason for the tax lies in the field of equity, and not just revenue, the revenue potential of a capital gains tax can only be gauged on a long-term basis. It is common knowledge that in general, realised capital gains reflect accrued capital gains with a time-lag of a number of years. This time-lag, moreover, is by no means uniform so that it is more correct to regard the average yield of the tax over a period, of, say, five years as reflecting the average rate of accrual of capital gains of a five-year period which elapsed 10–15 years previously. Hence the full yield potential of the tax should only become apparent after it has been in operation for 10–20 years.

52. It seems to me, therefore, that the tax ought to be reintroduced as soon as possible, and quite irrespective of the immediate prospects of rising or falling prices, or of the immediate expectation of the yield. But apart from this, in view of the greatly accelerated rate of capital expenditure under the Second Five

---

[1] Opponents of the taxation of capital gains in England also frequently argue both that the tax would be ruinous on industry and that it would yield practically nothing, without realising that the two assertions are not compatible with one another.

Year Plan, I do not think that the Board's view expressed in December 1953 that "the general tendency seems to be for profits and prices falling rather than rising" could be supported in the present circumstances.

C. SUGGESTED CHANGES IN EXISTING LEGISLATION

53. Assuming the re-introduction of the tax, the provisions laid down in Section 12B seem to me to be on the right lines. In fact the scheme propounded last year by the Minority of the British Royal Commission on the Taxation of Profits and Income, subject to one important difference, is essentially similar—though the Minority of the Royal Commission were quite oblivious of the Indian law on the subject. The important difference relates to the exemptions from the scope of the tax introduced in the third proviso of sub-section (1) of Section 12B. This proviso exempts such transfers of capital assets as result from compulsory acquisition by public authorities, or from a scheme of partition of H.U.F.s, the liquidation of a firm or a company, or transfers under a deed of gift or will, or to an irrevocable trust. These exemptions are in accord with the existing American law on the subject, but do not, in the opinion of many, conform to the correct principles of taxation.[1] While a tax on realised gains is the only feasible method of taxing capital gains, it must be borne in mind, of course, that the realisation criterion serves mainly administrative considerations and there should be no basic difference of principle between the concepts of "realised" and "accrued" gains. The tax should, therefore, be so framed that all capital gains should come under the tax net sooner or later—i.e. that over a long period, the tax charged on realised gains should come to the same as the charge on accrued gains. This will be the case if transfers of assets of all kinds (by way of gift or inheritance, as well as by sale, etc.) are treated as realisation for tax purposes.

[1] This is shown by the extent of criticism in the U.S.A. concerning these exemptions in the writings of American authorities on public finance, etc. These exemptions were also opposed by the Board of Inland Revenue of the U.K. in discussing a scheme for the taxation of capital gains in their evidence to the Royal Commission on Taxation. (Cf., U.S. Treasury Study on the Taxation of Capital Gains, and Memorandum by the Board of Inland Revenue, reprinted in the Final Report of the Royal Commission on Taxation, pp. 425–470).

On this conception the accumulated total of realised capital gains over a taxpayer's whole life necessarily comes to the same as the accumulated total of accrued capital gains. If on the other hand, transfers by way of gifts, bequests, etc., are exempted, not only will a considerable part of capital gains escape from taxation, but the taxpayer will be given an unhealthy incentive so to manipulate his asset holdings as to make net unrealised gains as large as possible, since all unrealised gains are wiped out for tax purposes when the property passes hands on decease. These exemptions may easily cut the potential long-term yield of the tax by two-thirds or three-quarters and they do not seem to be justified on any principle of equity.

54. Nor does it seem to me that the compulsory acquisition of property by public authorities forms any genuine ground for exemption from the tax. If the exemption is to be justified on the ground that the compensation paid by public authorities does not correspond to the full economic value of the property, the tax-payer is automatically relieved from the capital gains tax to a corresponding extent. There is no case, therefore, for complete exemption.

55. If the tax were re-introduced now there would be a case, also, for amending the provision in Section 12B concerning the determination of the cost of the capital assets to the assessee. As it is, the Section provides for the fair value on the 1st of January 1939, to be substituted for the actual cost, at the tax-payer's option, if the assets were held prior to that date. I think there is something to be said in equity, as well as on administrative considerations, for choosing a post-war date, such as the 1st of January 1948, for such an option in place of the pre-war date mentioned in the Section.

56. The provisions of Section 12B exempt agricultural land, personal effects including jewellery, as well as the stock in trade, etc., of a business, profession, or vocation. The last exemption is certainly correct since the capital gains on stock-in-trade get automatically taxed as ordinary profits as and when the stock is realised. Exemption of agricultural land will perhaps be retained so long as the existing constitutional provisions concerning agricultural income remain unmodified. The exemption of

jewellery, however, was presumably introduced mainly on administrative considerations. Jewellery, etc., above a certain value represent a form of investment, and ought certainly to be brought within the scope of the tax. If a personal expenditure tax and an annual tax on net wealth were introduced as suggested in this Report, coupled with an automatic reporting system suggested in Section VI, the Revenue would be capable of checking transactions in jewellery in almost the same way as transactions in other forms of property.

57. The schedule of rates in operation in the years 1947–49 reflected the right principle also in putting a relatively low ceiling rate of 5 annas in the rupee though the schedule was unduly lenient in the scale of progression leading up to that rate. If the suggestions made in Section I concerning income tax were accepted and the present income tax and super tax were replaced by a single income tax with a ceiling rate of 7 annas in the rupee, I do not believe that the separate tax treatment of capital gains would continue to be justified. A ceiling rate of 7 annas, or say 45 per cent., does not appear to me unduly high from the point of view of economic expediency, nor is the difference between a ceiling rate of 5 annas and 7 annas of sufficient importance to offset the great advantages of having the same rates of taxation applicable both to capital gains and ordinary income. For administrative reasons, a higher exemption limit (such as the Rs. 15,000 under the 1947 Act) may be justified for capital gains than in the case of ordinary income, but I do not see why the rise in rates through the successive slabs should proceed at such a leisurely pace once the exemption limit is passed. Under the 1947 Act the tax began at a rate of one anna in the rupee up to Rs. 50,000 and the top rate of 5 annas in the rupee was only reached when the gains exceeded Rs. 10 lakhs, whereas in the case of ordinary income, the rate of 7 annas in the rupee is reached for income over Rs. 25,000. These differences provide a strong incentive for tax avoidance and it cannot be emphasised too strongly that they lack any justification in equity.

58. The recommendation in Section I that income tax should be subject to a ceiling rate of 7 annas in the rupee was, of course, part of the wider reform which envisaged the replacement of the

present super tax by a progressive personal expenditure tax and the introduction of an annual tax on net wealth. Assuming, however, that the introduction of an annual tax on net wealth or a personal expenditure tax are not considered for immediate adoption, it would be well worth to examine whether the present relationship between income tax and the supertax should not be so altered as to raise the ceiling rate on income tax from 4 to 7 annas in the rupee and to make super tax begin at an income of Rs. 40,000 per annum, i.e. starting from the present third super-tax slab. In that case, capital gains could be made liable to income tax but not to super tax, with the result that the rate of tax deducted at source from interest and dividend payments, etc., would become identical with the rate of taxation on capital gains, thus obviating the possibility of gaining from manipulations of all kinds by converting income into capital gains.[1]

D. THE LONG-TERM YIELD OF THE TAX

59. As indicated above, if the suggestions made in paragraphs 53 and 54 were accepted, the assessment of realised capital gains should correspond in the long run to the average rate of accrual of capital gains. The question is, therefore, what long-run rate of capital appreciation should be taken as the basis for the purpose of calculating the tax yield. It can safely be assumed that the value of privately owned property increases at least as fast as the national income measured at current prices. This means that if the rate of progress envisaged in the Second Plan is attained, the total value of property should rise by at least 3–5 per cent. per annum. The total privately owned property in India (in estates of over Rs. 1 lakh and excluding agricultural land) can be put at a minimum of Rs. 3,500–4,500 crores. Of this about Rs. 1,000 crores takes the form of ordinary share capital while another Rs. 1,000 crores may

---

[1] Quite apart from the question of the taxation of capital gains, the rise in ceiling rate of income tax from 4 to 7 annas and a corresponding increase in the exemption limit of, and the rates of, super tax, would have considerable other advantages. Just because the ceiling rate of income tax governs the deduction at source on interest and dividend payments etc., income tax evasion will be far less common than super tax evasion. If more weight were thus put on income tax and less on super tax (as is, in fact, the case in the U.K., where the ceiling rate of income tax is 42½ per cent.), the scope for tax evasion would automatically be narrowed down.

be assumed to represent the value of urban property and of other property with an inherent tendency to capital appreciation (such as business goodwill).[1] Hence the average annual accrual of capital gains can be put at Rs. 60–100 crores, and the effective rate of tax, on the schedule of rates suggested above, may be as high as 40 per cent.[2] The long-term yield of the tax, on these assumptions, would come to Rs. 25–40 crores.

60. These figures may appear surprisingly high in the light of the two years' experience with the tax, and an attempt ought certainly to be made to reconcile them with the actual yield for the years 1947–49 (which averaged just over Rs. 3 crores a year). (a) A part of the difference can be accounted for by the difference in the schedule of assumed tax rates. The effective rate in the case of the assessments for 1947–49 was 23 per cent., or somewhat under 4 annas in the rupee. With an effective rate of 40 per cent. the corresponding yield would have been Rs. 5 crores a year. (b) The major difference, however, is due to the fact that the total gains assessed for the years 1947–49 averaged only Rs. 13 crores a year, as against the Rs. 60–100 crores suggested above. This difference is partly to be accounted for by the exemptions, under Section 12B, to transfers by way of gift, inheritance, etc., and partly by the incomplete coverage of the assessments. Although no figures are available, American data tend to suggest that the exemption of transfers through inheritance, etc., alone causes two-thirds or more of all capital gains to be relieved. Hence, the inclusion of the exempt categories might have raised the total gains assessed from the actual figure of Rs. 13 crores to Rs. 40–50 crores. (c) Finally, the assessments by no means covered the full extent of the cases liable. During the six years up to 1952–53, only 1,814 assessments were made in respect of capital gains for both years together. Since the number of major shareholders (with shareholdings of Rs. one lakh and over) is over 40,000, and the number of property owners (with estates over Rs. 1 lakh)

[1] In the case of individual businesses and partnerships, normally only the goodwill of the business (i.e., the excess of the value of business when sold as a going concern over the written down value of the tangible assets) gives rise to capital gains.
[2] The figure of 40 per cent. is based on the schedule of rates suggested above and size-distribution according to capital gains assessments in the years 1947–53 and it assumes that the present 5 per cent. surcharge will continue to be added to the standard rate of 7 annas.

more than 1,00,000, the figure of 1,814 is not likely to represent more than a fraction of the cases (though probably a somewhat larger fraction of larger cases than of smaller cases).

61. The greater part of capital gains over a longer period probably arises on ordinary shares.[1] I personally do not think it excessive to put the long-run rate of appreciation of share capital in India of the order of 10 per cent. per year, rather than 3–5 per cent. My reasons for this are that the expansion in production in the organised private sector the economy can be assumed to proceed at a rate of 10 per cent. per annum for many years to come. This was the rate of growth attained for the last five or six years, and there is no reason why it should not be maintained for the next 10–20 years. It is true that the expansion of industrial production has not carried with it during the last five years an equivalent percentage increase in company profits. I think, however, that this was due to special circumstances. It is much more likely that in the future, over longer periods, the rise in company profits will be fully proportionate to the rise in production; the rise in dividends to the rise in profits; and the rise in share values to the rise in dividends. During the last five years, according to the figures given by the Taxation Enquiry Commission,[2] the rise in industrial production of over 40 per cent. coincided with a fall in profit margins (on gross sales) from around 17 to around 10 per cent. If these figures are correct, they can only be interpreted in terms of a changeover from "inflationary" to "normal" conditions, which coincided with the expansion in production since the war. There is no reason to suppose, however, that this tendency will continue. Profit margins are unlikely to fall below 10 per cent. over longer periods; while the rise in expenditures under the Second Five Year Plan should, if anything, cause a revival of inflationary tendencies and a renewed rise of profit margins. If profit margins were maintained (let alone increased), the rise in profits will be as great as, or greater

[1] American experience suggests that more than two-thirds of net reported capital gains arise on transactions in ordinary shares. This corresponds also with the limited Indian experience where during the two years that the tax was in operation some 70 per cent. of the total assessed gains were in transactions other than immovable property, machinery and plant, and which, therefore, largely reflected transactions in ordinary shares.
[2] Vol. I, Table 15.

than, the rise in production.[1] It should also be borne in mind that the net ploughed-back profits of companies (after taxation and depreciation) amount to Rs. 70 crores per year (on the evidence of the income tax assessments), and this would normally be regarded as the minimum amount by which the market valuation of companies should increase annually over a run of years.

IV. A PERSONAL EXPENDITURE TAX

62. In Section I it was proposed that a progressive tax on personal expenditure (with a relatively high exemption limit) should be imposed along with other suggested reforms, and the maximum rate of income tax should, at the same time, be lowered to 7 annas in the rupee (or 45 per cent. including sur-charge). The effect of these proposals would thus be the replacement of the higher ranges of super tax on personal income with a super tax on personal expenditure. The purpose of this section is to explain these proposals in more detail, and at the same time to deal with some of the objections that have been raised against the introduction of a personal expenditure tax in India.

A. GENERAL CONSIDERATIONS

63. In my book,[2] I argued the case in favour of a personal expenditure tax on grounds of both equity and economic expediency in some detail and, therefore, do not wish to repeat the general arguments here. The main arguments which have been put forward against the proposals made in my book, in the particular context of India, may be listed as follows:

(a) It would not be practicable to impose an expenditure tax on top of the present taxes on income, since this would make taxation altogether too severe.

---

[1] It is impossible to say how far the fall in margin, over the last five years was a genuine phenomenon, or merely a consequence of increasing concealment of profits by companies (through under-valuation of stock-in-trade, the masquerading of capital expenditure under current expenditure, etc.).

[2] *An Expenditure Tax* (London, Allen & Unwin, 1955).

(b) Taxation of expenditure in replacement of taxation of income means the exemption of savings; this would greatly stimulate accumulation by the wealthier classes and would lead to an even greater concentration of property ownership. If property taxes were imposed to counter the tendency to concentration of property, this, in turn, would cancel the advantages of the expenditure tax in regard to the incentive to save.

(c) The expenditure tax would be administratively more difficult to handle than the income tax.

(d) As expenditure met out of agricultural income would have to be exempted from taxation, it would encourage people to debit the maximum part of their expenditure against their agricultural income.

64. I think it ought to be made clear that while an expenditure tax is superior to income tax, both because "expenditure" is more strictly definable than "income" as the basis of taxation and because "expenditure" is a better index of taxable capacity than "income", there is nothing inherently wrong in having both a tax on expenditure and a tax on income side by side. Even if it could be argued that the present taxation of income at the high rates of income and super taxes is being applied effectively, one could still justify the introduction of an expenditure tax if economic considerations require a restriction of personal spending and if that restriction could not be attained by a further increase in income and property taxes. If income and property are taxed too severely, while expenditure out of accumulated wealth is not taxed or restricted, the effect would merely be to encourage the capitalists to dissipate their wealth rather than to reduce their living standards.[1] I argued in earlier chapters that the present high marginal rates of taxation on income would have far more deleterious effects on the behaviour of wealth-owners (i.e. on their incentives to save or to invest) if these taxes were applied effectively. The fact that these effects are largely avoided because

[1] Moreover, such dissipatory spending, by increasing profits, would offset the effect of high taxation in reducing the income and the savings of the capitalist classes; if the community's investment expenditure is given, the true incidence of taxes on income and property can only fall on the capitalist classes to the extent that their propensity to spend is reduced in consequence. By encouraging spending, the tax system thus unwittingly causes the burden of taxes to be shifted from the profit-earning classes (taken as a whole) to other sections of the community.

D

the tax system contains large enough loop-holes to permit the owners of risk capital to make tax-free gains and to accumulate capital out of tax-free savings, is an argument against the present system of taxation, and not against the expenditure tax. For if these loop-holes were closed (i.e., all capital gains, etc., were brought into charge in the same way as other income) it would soon become evident that these high marginal rates on income could not be maintained. Hence progressive taxation, if it is to be both effective and impartial, cannot be levied beyond a certain point on an income-base, but only on an expenditure-base.

65. It would also be incorrect to say that imposition of taxes on property (whether in the form of an annual tax on wealth, estate duties, or the general gift tax) would cancel the advantages of an expenditure tax in restricting spending. On the contrary, the imposition of a personal expenditure tax would counter the disincentive effects of these property taxes on the spending and saving habits of the rich. A progressive expenditure tax taken by itself would effectively reduce the standard of living of the upper classes, though it might augment the rate of accumulation of large fortunes. Property taxes cut down the rate of accumulation but encourage spending. A combination of the two types of taxes, therefore, far from cancelling the good effects of either, makes it possible to restrict effectively the living standards of the rich without sacrificing the long-run egalitarian objective of a more even distribution of property.

66. While an expenditure tax would be administratively more difficult to handle than the present income tax, it is not more difficult to handle than a comprehensive and effective system of income taxation. On the contrary, the incorporation of an expenditure tax in a system of personal taxation which includes both taxes on income (including capital gains) and on property would ease considerably the prevention of evasion—partly because it would introduce an opposition of interests between the different parties as regards the concealment of particular transactions (whereas under the present system both parties to a transaction may have an identical interest in concealing altogether or in understating the value of a particular transaction), and partly also because the necessity to account for the amounts

spent on personal purposes over a particular period together with the obligation to produce a balance-sheet of personal net wealth at the beginning and at the end of the period forces the taxpayer into a full disclosure of receipts; just as the need to make a full return of current receipts and expenditure forces the taxpayer into a full disclosure of capital assets.

67. It should also be remembered that the problem of personal expenses being met out of business expenditure accounts or benefits given in kind rather than in cash already arises under an income tax. The obligation on a taxpayer to return his personal expenditure as well as his income would make it easier to detect such cases of income tax evasion since they would automatically be reflected in an unduly low figure being returned for personal expenditure. The plain fact is that the incorporation of an expenditure tax would make the administration of the income tax a great deal more effective as well. It is possible for a man to conceal some part of his expenditure effectively by concealing a corresponding part of his receipts, or by getting some part of his own expenses paid by someone else (his business employer or some friend or relation in a lower tax bracket), but the important point is that such concealments could not be carried to the point at which the taxpayer's own returned figure for his expenditure becomes apparently inconsistent with his mode of living. I think the experience of income tax officers would confirm that while it is not possible to estimate from external criteria a man's expenditure with any great precision, it is certainly possible to do so with a fair margin of approximation.[1] A man who keeps several houses, a large number of servants, and several cars and entertains frequently, might well manage to understate his true expenditure by a few thousand rupees a year, but he could not possibly return a figure of, say, Rs. 10,000 when, in fact, he spent Rs. 50,000 or Rs. 1,00,000. Yet under the present system, there is no limit to the extent to which he could understate his income through fraudulent concealments or the extent to which he can economise on having a taxable income by converting

[1] In fact, obvious inconsistencies between a man's disclosure of income and his mode of living are already being used in India and in other countries as a means of detecting income tax evasion.

income into capital gains or economise on super tax by transferring property into trusts and settlements.

68. With regard to the point concerning agricultural income, the constitutional position seems to be rather in favour of the expenditure tax. The Constitution does not assign specifically a tax on expenditure either to the Centre or to the States, nor does it state anywhere that expenditure out of agricultural income (as distinct from the agricultural income itself) should not be taxable by the Centre. I believe, therefore, that a tax on personal expenditure would be constitutional irrespective of the sources from which the expenditure was drawn; and the revenue from it could be taken as belonging exclusively to the Centre under item 97 of List I of the 7th Schedule to the Constitution.

69. The one contention which no one has called into question is that a progressive personal tax on expenditure is a most potent weapon for inducing economies in personal spending among the well-to-do classes. It is also beyond dispute that an accelerated rate of economic growth requires a higher proportion (and not merely a higher amount) of investment expenditure to total expenditure—i.e. a higher proportion of savings in the national income. Resources for such additional savings can only come from a reduction in consumption in relation to current income. As the consumption standards of the masses of the population in India are so near to the bare minimum level, the reduction in the propensity to consume of the well-to-do classes appears to me as an indispensable requirement for sustaining a higher rate of economic growth. Luxury consumption is, in fact, the only part of the national expenditure that could be compressed for the sake of releasing resources for a higher rate of capital accumulation; and a graduated progressive tax on personal consumption is undoubtedly the ideal instrument for attaining this end.

B. DEFINITION OF EXPENDITURE AND MODE OF ASSESSMENT AND GRADUATION

The Real Basis of the Charge

70. Although, as explained further below, the taxpayer would not normally be required to give any detailed account of his

outlays on consumption (but only a statement of his total outlay
as part of a comprehensive return showing all his receipts,
investments, etc., and all the items for which he claims exemption)
the legal basis of the charge ought to be a reasonable everyday
conception of personal consumption (or expenditure), including
not only items met by expenditure out of the taxpayer's own
spending but also consumption out of benefits and gifts received
in kind, expenses met by the employer, friend or relation, subject
to an annual exemption limit of, say, Rs. 2,000 a year per head
for such gifts or benefits received. If the charge is based on
personal consumption thus defined, attempts to avoid tax by
making gifts to persons of low spending power, etc. (in return for
such persons meeting part of the taxpayer's expenses), or by
getting employers or businesses to meet one's personal bills would
all be unavailable. The taxpayers would, in fact, be chargeable
on the value of all goods and services received for personal consumption irrespective of how and by whom these were financed.

Definition of Personal Consumption
71. Personal consumption excludes outlays on the following
items:

(*a*) Business expenses in the strictest sense; the question of
adequacy of the present legal definition of such expenses as
expenses "wholly or exclusively incurred for the purposes of a
trade or business" will be further discussed in Chapter 7.

(*b*) All investment outlays, i.e. sums devoted to the purchase of
income-yielding property (like land, stocks and shares, securities
of all kinds) or non-income-yielding "stores of wealth" (like
bank deposits, bar gold, current deposits, bank notes and coins);[1]
loans of all kind and sums devoted to the repayment of past
indebtedness.

(*c*) Capital expenditures for personal use, only the annual
benefits from which, and not the outlay itself, enters into "consumption". The purchase of a dwelling house for owner-occupa-
tion, works of art, jewellery and ornaments above a certain value
(say, Rs. 10,000) fall into this category.

[1] The latter require to be deposited with the banks or other institutions to qualify
for exemption.

(*d*) Gifts made to other persons above a certain amount (say, Rs. 2,000) including settlements made on children, dowries,[1] etc.

Claims for exemption under items (*a*) to (*d*) would have to be supported by duly certified tax vouchers as described in Section VI but whilst outlays under items (*a*), (*b*) and (*d*) carry complete exemption, outlays under (*c*) would carry a notional addition to personal consumption in the year of purchase and subsequent years (until the items are sold), based on, say, 5 per cent. of the purchase price.[2]

Chargeable and Exempt Consumption Expenditure

72. Outlays not falling within categories (*a*) to (*d*) above may be defined as personal expenditure but not all such expenditure would be charged to tax. Certain categories of necessitous items should be exempted and the range of such items would vary with the particular customs and modes of living. Items which I would regard as falling reasonably within the "necessitous" categories and deserving exemption in addition to all personal taxes paid are: (i) funeral and birth expenses; (ii) medical expenses up to a certain amount per head; (iii) any additional expenses incurred as a result of severe physical disabilities up to a certain amount per year; (iv) fines, etc., imposed by courts; and (v) expenses incurred as a result of fire, burglary, theft, flood, damage, etc. (Since all such outlays represent insurable risks, it would be administratively convenient to restrict such exemptions to payments received under the insurance policies rather than to the outlays themselves.)

Treatment of Chargeable Consumption Expenditure

73. The residual left after deduction of exempted items constitutes chargeable consumption expenditure; not all of which, however, is fully chargeable in the year of purchase. Expenditure on durable goods of all kinds like furniture, motor cars, house

---

[1] These gifts may be subject to gift tax in the hands of the recipient.

[2] It is thus proposed that the purchase of works of art, jewellery and ornaments should be treated as capital expenditure and thus exempted from the personal expenditure tax but an annual charge should be imposed in all cases where the taxpayers claim exemption under this head. It is not proposed, however, that such a notional charge should be made with respect to any existing possessions of jewellery, ornaments or works of art.

repairs, etc., or on unusual outlays like weddings, can be spread at the taxpayer's option over, say, a five-year or possibly a ten-year period. Since under a progressive system any tax relief obtained on account of such unusual expenditure would automatically swell the taxpayer's chargeable expenditure in the following and subsequent years, spreading would be against the taxpayer's interest except in so far as it genuinely assisted to even out his rate of expenditure over time. There would be no need, therefore, in these categories to require the same kind of proof to be furnished as would be necessary for claiming exemption under categories (a) to (d) in paragraph 71 above.[1]

Mode of Assessment and Graduation

74. Since the purpose of the tax is to discourage high-level spending by steeply rising marginal rates on expenditure, it is far more necessary in the case of this tax than in the case of income tax to take into account differences in needs arising out of differences in the size of the family which the taxpayer has to support. Hence unlike the income tax (where only a very small difference is introduced in the tax liability through a variation of the amount of initial exemption), the rates of taxation in the case of expenditure tax ought to vary with the scale of expenditure per head rather than the total expenditure of the whole family unit. This means the adoption of the so-called quotient system, which is already applied in France for income tax purposes, according to which the income (or expenditure) of all members of the family is first aggregated and then divided into a number of parts, depending on the number of persons in each family, and the tax is charged separately on each part. Children may count as one-half unit each (though the fraction could be varied with their age and number).[2] Apart from wife and children it may be permitted to add other family members living in a joint household to the conception of the "family", provided only that their receipts,

---

[1] An alternative method would be to permit the spreading of all expenditure for tax purposes and to calculate the tax on a moving average of the expenditure of the last five years rather than the actual expenditure in a particular year.

[2] This means that two adults comprising a family would pay twice the tax of a single person with half that expenditure, a married couple with two children would pay three times the tax payable by a single person with one-third of the joint family expenditure and so on.

income and property are effectively aggregated with the family for tax purposes. It would be reasonable, however, to count such additional members in the same way as children as a fractional rather than full unit each. This is because the aggregate family expenditure, assuming a given living standard, rises less than in proportion to the increase in the numbers in the household. I would, therefore, suggest that additional family members should be converted to adult units on a tapering-off scale so that a family of say four members would count as three adult units, a family of seven members as four adult units and that five should be the maximum number of adult units for a family. That means that the minimum liability to tax in case of a large family is as on the total family expenditure divided by five, this liability being multiplied five times.

75. The pre-condition of this method of charging, as already stated, is the effective aggregation of all receipts, income and property of the family members. Although, in principle, such aggregation could be adopted for purposes of the expenditure tax only without being applied for income and property taxes, from an administrative point of view, it would clearly be far more convenient if the rules of aggregation applied equally to all types of personal taxation. In India, unlike in England, the income of husband and wife is not automatically aggregated for tax purposes, though there are special anti-avoidance provisions which enforce aggregation in case of partnership shares, etc., and cause income and property transfers between family members to be ignored for tax purposes. It would, however, be far more equitable as between different taxpayers if a general rule of aggregation were adopted for purposes of income and property taxes as well as for purposes of expenditure tax as between husband and wife and minor children (excepting in the case of a legal separation). In the case of other family members aggregation for income and property tax purposes would be optional but a necessary pre-condition for aggregation for expenditure tax purposes.

C. SUGGESTED SCHEDULE OF RATES

76. In Section I, it was suggested that there should be an

exemption limit of Rs. 10,000 per adult and expenditure in excess of this amount should be charged according to the slab system of graduation, starting from 25 per cent. on the lowest slab (i.e., on expenditure between Rs. 10,000 and Rs. 12,500) and rising gradually up to a maximum of 300 per cent. on expenditures in excess of Rs. 50,000 per head. An exemption limit and schedule of rates of this character seem to me appropriate for replacing the present super tax on personal incomes on the slabs above 7 annas in the rupee—i.e. in excess of gross income of Rs. 40,000 and a net family income, after income tax, of Rs. 30,000. Since the typical family may be assumed to comprise at least three adult units, a net expenditure of Rs. 10,000 per head corresponds to a net family expenditure of Rs. 30,000. Assuming that personal expenditure corresponds to net income after tax, the substitution of an expenditure tax on this scale for the higher brackets of super tax would not change appreciably the total burden of taxation. There would, of course, be a considerable shift in the tax burden as between relatively high spending and relatively high saving taxpayers.

77. It could be argued, however, that in the present conditions of India a stronger deterrent to spending and a stronger stimulus to personal saving would be justified, and, therefore, the exemption limits ought to be put lower and the scale of graduation made stiffer than the scale which is the nearest equivalent to the present super tax. If the exemption limit were put at Rs. 6,000 per head and the maximum slab of 300 per cent. were imposed on expenditures in excess of Rs. 30,000 per head the liability to tax would extend to a considerably larger segment of the population and it would have a more powerful effect in restraining spending. It might, therefore, be more appropriate in the present situation of India even though it would probably imply considerable increase of the present tax burden of a typical family in the higher income groups.

78. There are unfortunately no statistics available in India, even on a sample survey basis, of the consumption expenditure of the top income groups. Some of the cases investigated by the Taxation Investigation Commission, I understand, suggest that personal expenditure might be rather low in relation to true income. In

these particular cases, however, the amount of concealed income was probably very large in relation to declared income and it is quite possible that such concealed income is saved to a far greater extent than declared income precisely because the spending of concealed income would cause suspicion and might lead to detection. There might be a large number of cases where the level of expenditure is greatly in excess of the taxable income and where the difference is financed not out of concealed income, but out of capital gains that are exempted from taxation or simply out of accumulated wealth. Some observers put the expenditure of the upper classes in India at over Rs. 500 crores a year—an amount which is considerably in excess of the total of net incomes after tax of all income recipients with incomes of over Rs. 10,000. It is possible, therefore, that total yield of the tax would prove to be very much greater than the present yield of that part of the present super tax which it replaces. It is, however, impossible in this case to make even a rough guess of the magnitude of the probable yield.

D. ADMINISTRATION

79. The tax would be administered in much the same way as the present super tax on the basis of individual assessments relating to the previous year and paid around 18 months in arrear. The mode of administration of the tax could perhaps best be illustrated by showing in a simplified form the type of comprehensive return which, it has been suggested should replace the present tax return and which would provide the material for assessment for the other proposed taxes, the annual wealth tax, the capital gains tax and the gift tax, as well as the expenditure tax.

80. It will be evident from the sample comprehensive return reproduced in Appendix A to this Report that the taxpayer would not be asked to give a direct account of his personal expenses, the amount chargeable for the expenditure tax being arrived at as a residual after deduction of various items from the receipts. The need to make the various items and parts of this return consistent with one another, together with the requirement that a duly certified voucher should be submitted in support of each particular claim for exemption, provides the check on the

accuracy of the computed figure of expenditure. The taxpayer would, however, also be required to make a formal declaration that to the best of his knowledge and belief the computed expenditure tallied with his true personal expenditure for the period in question. The Revenue would, of course, have the power to ask for details concerning particular items of expenditure (such as the amount paid for electricity or other public utility services, the rents paid for the year, the amounts spent on the children's education, etc.), as well as details concerning his mode of living (e.g., the number of servants kept, the number of rooms, furniture and fittings, motor cars and travels made during the year) which would enable the tax officer to check the accuracy of the computed figure and the consistency of the whole return.

V. A GENERAL GIFT TAX

81. The purpose of this section is to put forth a proposal for a single integrated tax on gifts of all kinds (including under this term accession to property through bequest and inheritance) which should replace the present estate duty, as well as bring into charge other gratuitous transfers of property which are not now taxable. The case is argued on grounds of equity, expediency and administrative efficiency.

A. GENERAL CONSIDERATIONS

82. Property is passed on from generation to generation either through inheritance or bequest or through *inter vivos* gifts and settlements. The basic justification for taxes on inheritance is that the community has the right to limit each individual's freedom to pass on his property intact to his successors just as it has the right to circumscribe the power of control and disposition exercised through the legal institution of ownership in numerous other ways. Progressive taxes on estates can, in fact, only be justified as a graduated limitation of the right to pass on ownership rights to others. If this is so there is no reason in equity for differentiating

between the right to pass on property through gifts and the right to pass on property by bequest. There is, therefore, a *prima facie* case for supplementing estate duties with taxes on gifts made *inter vivos*; and as far as possible, the incidence of taxes on gratuitous transfers of property should be made independent of the mode in which, or the form through which, property is transferred.

83. An additional reason for the taxation of *inter vivos* gifts is that the imposition of estate duty itself stimulates the *inter vivos* transfer of property to heirs and successors so as to avoid tax; even though the motive of tax avoidance is not the sole or even the main reason for a general tax on gifts. *Inter vivos* gifts are made on many occasions, as for example on the marriage of children or grand-children, or when children reach maturity and set up a separate household or business. Again there is no *a priori* reason why such gifts should be differently rated for tax purposes than gifts received through inheritance.

84. An attempt is usually made to limit the scope of tax avoidance through *inter vivos* settlements by providing that gifts made within a limited period prior to death should be aggregated with the estate for estate duty purposes. In India the period is six months for gifts made to a charity and two years for other gifts. These provisions are questionable devices from an equity point of view (*a*) since they carry the presumption that all gifts made within the prescribed period prior to death were made with the dominant motive of tax avoidance (which certainly cannot be true of all cases), and (*b*) because they make the taxability of gifts entirely dependent on the fortuitous circumstance of the donor surviving or not surviving the prescribed period.[1]

85. The attempt to give away a part of one's estate with a view to reducing the liability to estate duty is particularly strong when taxes are levied on a progressive scale, since in that case tax is saved not only through a portion of the estate being passed on *inter vivos*, but also through a lower rate of duty becoming applic-

---

[1] If the principle that gifts made in contemplation of death (and/or with a view of avoiding death duties) should be brought within the tax net, while other gifts should be exempt, were correct, the proper method to give effect to it would be to compound the potential death duty liability in respect of chargeable gifts on an actuarial basis, rather than rely on some purely arbitrary rule by which gifts made at a particular date prior to death or earlier are entirely exempt and gifts made after that date are fully taxable.

able to the remainder. The more the State attempts to limit the scope for such tax avoidance by extending the period prior to death during which gifts are made taxable, the more arbitrary the incidence of the duty becomes, and the greater the element of luck or ill-fortune in determining the liability to the tax.

86. Some countries such as the U.S.A., Sweden, Canada, Australia and others have introduced separate taxes on *inter vivos* gifts to supplement the death duties. Since, however, in most cases the two taxes are not properly integrated with one another, loop-holes for tax avoidance remain. Thus in the United States, the gift tax is charged at three-fourths of the normal estate duty rates, and successive gifts by a donor are aggregated for tax purposes. There is, however, an annual exemption of $3,000 (in addition to an initial exemption of $30,000) so that if gifts are made in regular annual instalments of $3,000 or less, the gifts still escape the tax. It is usual, moreover, in the tax laws relating to gifts to regard the gift tax as a liability payable by the donor, with the result that whereas estate duties are levied gross (i.e. the tax is paid out of the assessed estate), gift taxes are levied net (i.e. on the net amount transferred). This reduces the tax liability in two ways; partly because the tax is levied on a smaller base, and partly because the rate of tax (and not only the amount payable) applicable to the smaller base may be smaller.

87. There is also the question whether the whole conception of an estate duty which taxes the property of the deceased on a progressive scale depending only on the size of the estate, and irrespective of whether it is passed on to one person or a number of different hands is correct from an equity point of view or not. The presumption of an estate duty is that the incidence of the tax falls on the deceased person. In fact, the true incidence falls on the heir or legatee and not on the deceased. The fact that a man's property will be reduced through death duties after his decease does not reduce his economic power but only of the people who inherit the property. It seems to me, therefore, that from the point of view of equity, the rate of progression should vary with the amount *received* by a particular person (the principle underlying the so-called legacy or succession duties) and not with the total amount of property *left* by a man. Apart from reasons of equity,

considerations of economic expediency also argue in favour of the principle of the legacy duty as against the principle of the estate duty. For the main justification for levying a steeply progressive tax whenever property passes from one generation to the next is to counter the tendency towards the increasing concentration of wealth which is an inevitable consequence of economic progress in society. If a rich man leaves his estate, not to a single heir, but to a large number of beneficiaries, he is, thereby, doing something himself to counteract that tendency by spreading his property among several persons. Moreover, when the rates of estate duty are very stiff (and they have to be very stiff in the higher brackets to provide an effective antidote to the tendency of increasing concentration of wealth) the temptation on the rich to dissipate their capital during their lifetime—a temptation held in check at present by the loophole of tax-exempt transfers *inter vivos*—must be pretty strong. This temptation would undoubtedly be less if a man of property could reduce the extent to which his estate will be taxed at death by spreading it among a large number of potential beneficiaries.

B. PROPOSAL FOR A GENERAL TAX ON GIFTS

88. The above considerations argue in favour of a uniform tax on all gratuitous transfers, irrespective of whether the transfers were made *inter vivos* or by way of legacy or bequest. The legal liability for this tax should be placed squarely on the donee (and not on the donor) on whom the ultimate incidence of tax must in any case fall. It is necessary moreover that the rate of progression of the tax should not be dependent on the size of any particular gift or legacy—otherwise the taxation could be defeated by a fragmentation of gifts. It is for this reason that existing legal provisions generally aggregate successive gifts by a donor for tax purposes. I do not believe that this method of aggregation (by donors) is the ideal solution. The ideal method appears to be to make the rate of taxation dependent neither on the size of the gift nor on the wealth of the donor but on the total wealth of the recipient, i.e., his net worth including the gift. A man who owns Rs. 10 lakhs and receives another Rs. 1,00,000 as a gift ought

surely to be more heavily taxed on that than another man who receives an identical gift but owns nothing else. The most reasonable principle, therefore, seems, to be to apply a slab system of graduation to a man's total estate, and to tax the gifts received in any one year according to the additions they make to his net wealth and at the rate applicable in the relevant zone (or zones). Assuming that an annual tax on wealth is introduced so that the property of an individual, above the exemption limit, is in any case returned annually for the purpose of the annual tax, the introduction of a general gift tax on these lines would not cause any additional administrative problem.

89. In Section I, I suggested that there should be an exemption limit of Rs. 10,000 for any single recipient and that gifts over and above this should be taxed at the rate of 10 per cent. if the net wealth of the recipient is below Rs. 1 lakh, and at double the present estate duty rates applicable in the case of individuals—i.e., 15 per cent. between Rs. 1,00,000 and Rs. 1,50,000, 20 per cent. between Rs. 1,50,000 and Rs. 2,00,000, 25 per cent. between Rs. 2,00,000 and Rs. 3,00,000, and so on, the rate becoming 80 per cent. if the total estate of the donee exceeds Rs. 20 lakhs. I think this should be subject to the proviso—in order to prevent small and regular allowances from becoming subject to an excessive duty—that the taxpayer should have the option to have the gifts of any one year treated as ordinary income for tax purposes (i.e., aggregated with his other income).

90. The suggestion that the schedule of estate duty rates should be doubled when the tax is levied on the above lines may be thought as harsh. It should, however, be borne in mind that (a) the rates of estate duty in India are rather low at present in comparison to other countries,[1] and (b) since the typical estate is inherited by several heirs and not a single heir, the changeover from the estate duty principle to the legacy duty principle would mean a considerable reduction in the effective burden of taxation unless the rates are made considerably higher. Suppose a man dies possessing Rs. 10,00,000. Under the existing estate duty law he would be

[1] Compared with the United Kingdom, the Indian rates appear remarkably low in medium ranges as well as the top brackets. An estate of Rs. 10 lakhs bears 40 per cent. in the U.K. but only 15 per cent. in India, at Rs. 20 lakhs the ratios are 50 per cent. and 20 per cent., and at Rs. 1 crore 70 per cent. and 34 per cent., respectively.

subject to a tax of Rs. 1,51,250. If he left his estate in equal parts to three of his surviving children, the liability to gift tax according to the estate duty rate schedule would be three times Rs. 26,250, or Rs. 78,750 altogether, meaning a reduction of nearly 50 per cent. But under the schedule of rates suggested here (assuming the children possess no other property) the liability of each heir would amount to Rs. 61,500 or a total of Rs. 1,84,500 which exceeds the liability under the present estate duty by just under 22 per cent.—an increase which certainly cannot be regarded as excessive when compared with the rates obtaining elsewhere in the world.

91. A further considerable advantage of these proposals is that it makes tax evasion far more difficult than the existing system of estate duty. The experience with the latter in India so far tends to suggest that under Indian conditions, it is difficult to discover what a man's property is after his decease. The new system relies on the *recipient* of gifts and bequests as well as on information supplied by the donor or legator, and assumes that the system of comprehensive returns recommended in Section IV is adopted in which case the transfer of property through gifts or inheritance is bound to be revealed.

C. PROBABLE YIELD OF THE TAX

92. Assuming that the system of comprehensive returns on all receipts and property and the comprehensive reporting system on all property transactions, etc., are adopted (and are functioning satisfactorily) the net yield from this tax would be considerable. Private property in India in estates of say, Rs. 25,000 or over is not likely to be below Rs. 4,000 crores, whilst the annual transfer of property through death or *inter vivos* gifts cannot be much less than one twenty-fifth of the total.[1] This makes the amount annually assessable to the gift tax something of the order of Rs. 150 crores. On the rate schedule suggested above, the average rate of duty could not be put at less than 20 per cent. which makes the yield of the tax of the order of Rs. 30 crores a year. The

---

[1] Since the average period of a "generation" in India (which is equal to the average age of the father when the children are born) cannot be put at more than 25 years.

consequential loss from estate duty is estimated at present at only Rs. 2 crores a year.

VI. A COMPREHENSIVE REPORTING SYSTEM

A. THE PROPOSAL

93. The existing evasion of income tax, super tax, and estate duty, as well as the administrative difficulties in connection with the taxation of capital gains, an annual tax on wealth and a personal expenditure tax, could be overcome through the institution of an automatic reporting system of all capital transactions, etc., with the aid of a simple system of code numbers. The idea can be briefly described as follows:

(a) Every income-tax payer is supplied with a code number by the Income Tax Officer who handles his case. Any other person who so desires, can register his name in the Income Tax Department of his home district and can get a code number even if he is not so far assessed or liable. The code number should indicate the State/District/Income Tax Circle No. and can be of the form 1/2/5/348 indicating West Bengal/Calcutta/I.T. Distt. Ward No. V-2/ and GIR No. 348.

(b) It should be obligatory in the case of all property transfers registerable under the Transfer of Properties Act to disclose the code numbers of the transferor and the transferee. The transferee at the same time must sign a declaration stating whether he is the beneficial owner or merely a trustee, nominee or benamidar. In the latter case there is an obligation on him to disclose the code number of the beneficial owner. Failing such declaration, the transferee is deemed to be the beneficial owner in law and any claim of benami on property purchased after the "appointed day" would fail, even though the transferee may not be in possession of the transfer deed. This would stop evasion through benami holdings.

(c) It should be obligatory to produce these declarations when transfer deeds are handed in to the Registration Offices for purposes of registration. The most convenient form is a duplicate perforated voucher, consisting of two copies, A and B. The suggested forms of this tax voucher are reproduced in Appendix B. The recipient of cash (or the seller of property) should have an obligation to fill out the part of these vouchers relevant to him and hand it to the buyer (transferee). The transferee having completed the rest of the form hands it over to the Registration Office together with the transfer deed. The Registration Office transmits it to the Revenue Department who route the two slips to the tax officers of the transferor and the beneficial owner (or transferee, if the transferee is himself the beneficial owner), respectively.

(d) In case the system of taxation comprises an expenditure tax (as one of the taxes) it would be administratively convenient to make the voucher in triplicate, one of which (copy C) is retained by the transferee who hands it to his I.T.O. as a supporting voucher for tax-exempt outlays. Under an expenditure tax, the taxpayer's interest is to under-state his receipts and to over-state his tax-exempt outlays; the latter should, therefore, be required to be supported with vouchers, furnished by the tax-payer himself; whereas the under-statement of receipts can be checked by the vouchers produced by the other parties and accumulating in his file with the tax office.

(e) In this manner, the Revenue Department would be able without any cumbrous investigation of individual cases, to obtain a full record of the capital transactions of taxpayers during the year. There is no need to stress the importance of this for efficient administration, not only of an expenditure tax but of income tax, a capital gains tax, an annual tax on wealth, and of a general gift tax as well. Concealments of gains for income tax purposes are revealed through the investment of such gains, if such investments are automatically notified to the tax authorities. At present large-scale concealments can only be unearthed through the detailed investigation of capital transactions. The adoption of the above system would ensure that the I.T.O.s have immediate information on all capital transactions whereas at present any such information can only be obtained subsequent to the filing of the annual returns and in some cases only some years after that.

(*f*) Moreover, if the system of taxation includes an expenditure tax as well as taxes on income and capital, the economic interest of taxpayers would ensure the completion and surrender of these vouchers even in the case of such transactions which do not involve compulsory registration. Thus in the case of Stock Exchange transactions where no actual delivery of shares takes place, but where only the balance of a large number of transactions gives rise to cash receipts or payments (differences), the payer can be asked to surrender a voucher, filled out by the payee, in support of his claim. In this case, the departure from the already existing practice will mainly consist in the disclosure of the code number of the recipient on the voucher.

(*g*) Further, in the case of all payments above a certain sum (say, Rs. 10,000) which are not payments for goods and services rendered of non-exempt categories, the completion of a receipt in the form of voucher described above, and its surrender by the payer could be made a statutory requirement. Given an expenditure tax, there is a strong incentive on the payer to insist on the proper completion of such a voucher since otherwise he might involve himself in added tax liabilities. Thus the lender in the case of a loan, the debtor in the case of a repayment of a debt, the depositor in the case of a bank deposit, donor (or his executors) in the case of a gift, bequest, or legacy, the purchaser of such jewellery or other valuables as are treated as exempt categories of expenditure, could all be relied on to produce the appropriate voucher in connection with their tax returns.

(*h*) Equally, the code number of the beneficial owners, if included in the companies' share registers along with the names of the nominal holders would produce an automatic check on interest and dividend income (as well as on secret holdings out of concealed profits of the past). Copies of dividend vouchers issued by companies to shareholders would also be routed to the tax officers through the code number system.

(*i*) The amount of clerical work involved in the routing and filing of vouchers for the whole of India would be no larger than the clerical work which was involved in the administration of the rationing system during the war in a single large city. At the moment, the number of assessees on the General Index Register

is of the order of one million and the code numbers that may have
to be allotted may be of the order of two millions or so for the
whole of India. In other words, it will mean that each of the
1,000 I.T.O.s will have on their Registers on an average about
2,000 names each, and this is obviously not a very difficult problem
to manage. In fact, the Sales Tax authorities are working on the
system of Sales Tax Registration Nos. which is essentially similar.
The routing of the tax vouchers to the local tax offices can be done
on a continuing basis without undue additional expenditure. Each
Registration Office would post every evening the vouchers
accumulated during the day to the Central Collating Agency at
Madras who would send them on to the local offices. The collection, filing and utilisation of vouchers by the Income Tax Officers
could be most conveniently done through a card index filing
system.

B. THE SWEDISH PRECEDENT

94. I obtained from Sweden copies of some of the tax vouchers
in connection with the comprehensive reporting system in that
country which in some ways is essentially similar to the one I
have outlined. Rough translations of Forms 18A and 17 are given
in Appendix B to this Report. These forms relate to the receipt
of interest and dividend payments. I understand, however, that
analogous forms have to be completed in connection with the
receipt of cash resulting from the sale of capital assets and perhaps
other types of transactions as well.

95. The Swedish tax vouchers are analogous to the system
suggested by me in the two important respects. First, the obligation to fill up the vouchers rests always on the person who receives
money (the payee) whereas the obligation to ensure that the form
is duly completed and surrendered to the appropriate tax authorities rests on the payor. Secondly, the declaration by the payee
contains, in addition to the sum received, the nature of the
dividend, the amount of the payment etc., a declaration by the
recipient whether he is the beneficial owner or not; and in case
he is not the beneficial owner (or if the beneficial owner is not a
Swedish resident), another form, Form 18B must be completed.
The forms, while they ask for details concerning the name and

address of the payee and of the payor, do not contain any reference to code numbers.

96. The system proposed here would be a great deal simpler to operate, for several reasons. The universal use of code numbers must greatly facilitate the routing of the tax vouchers to the appropriate tax officers. The completion of such vouchers would not be required in connection with the dividend and interest payable in so far as payments are rendered to registered holders and not to holders of "bearer" securities in exchange for the surrender of a coupon. Instead the company or corporation which pays the dividend or interest and deducts income tax at the source at the maximum rate would be asked to supply duplicate copies of the income tax vouchers now issued in connection with such payments to the Revenue Department. The only change involved would be that in addition to the name and address of nominal holder, the code number of the beneficial owner would also figure on the tax vouchers. There would be no obligation, however, on recipients of dividend and interest payments to complete a voucher every time they receive a payment (as is the case in Sweden). On the other hand, our proposal is to extend the system to all kinds of transactions whereas the Swedish Law (as far as I am aware of it) does not require the completion of tax vouchers in connection with payments representing lending or the repayment of a past loan, the sale of jewellery, gold or valuables above a certain value and other kinds of payments with respect to which the payer (in the system proposed) would claim exemption from the personal expenditure tax.

97. Nevertheless, the operation of the Swedish system does, I believe, afford strong evidence that the adoption of the kind of system I propose for India would not create difficult administrative problems. It is true that Sweden is a small country; on the other hand, the number of taxpayers of all kinds is $3\frac{3}{4}$ million, i.e. eight times the number of Indian income tax payers and almost four times the number of names in the G.I.R. The number of assessments for the Annual Property Tax in Sweden amounts to 1,80,000 which again is a somewhat larger number (certainly not a smaller number) than the number of cases likely to be involved in India. I am quite certain also that this system would be

perfectly feasible for large income tax paying countries, such as
the U.K. or the U.S.A. The absence of any automatic reporting
system on dividend and interest income or on capital transactions
in these countries cannot be explained either by technical difficulties (the introduction of P.A.Y.E. in case of salary and wage
incomes raised far more complex technical problems), or by the
lack of need for it, but mainly on account of the opposition of
vested interests which its introduction would encounter.

C. POSSIBLE OBJECTIONS

98. It may be convenient in this connection to deal with some
of the objections that have been mentioned against the proposal
outlined above.

99. One type of objection is that property transfers notified to
the Registrars are already transmitted to the relevant Income Tax
Officer on a routine basis; in the same way the companies notify
the Department of the interest and dividend payments made by
them. The answer to this objection is twofold. First, I am not, of
course, aware how regularly and efficiently the existing practice of
collecting data from the Registrars is working. Even if the existing
practice worked to the satisfaction of the authorities, it could still
be said that not only would considerable time and labour be
saved by having an automatic system of reporting whereby the
Registrars forward duly completed vouchers to the tax authorities
simultaneously with registration, but I.T.O.s by receiving information promptly of all important transactions of the assessees could
take prompt action concerning them. It is well known that prompt
action considerably facilitates investigations. In any case the
information extracted from the Registrars relates to transactions
in immovable property only. On the other hand, my system aims
at (a) the extension of this to transactions in stocks and shares,
and to transactions of a capital nature of all kinds, such as lending
and borrowing, etc.; and (b) the disclosure of the beneficial
owner on the supporting tax voucher in a manner that protects his
anonymity vis-à-vis third parties. Secondly, I am not aware either,
how efficiently and promptly the existing system of companies
sending copies of the list of interest and dividend payments to the

Central Collating Agency at Madras is working. It certainly cannot help in tracing the beneficial owner in case of properties registered in the name of the trustees or nominees or benami holders.

100. Nothing illustrates more the need for a comprehensive reporting system than the fact that with respect to the capital gains tax in operation in the years 1947–48 and 1948–49, only 199 assessments were raised in 1947–48, 469 in 1948–49, 440 in 1949–50, 245 in 1950–51, 329 in 1951–52 and 149 in 1952–53, or 1,814 altogether. There can be little doubt that even the six years' total only covered a fraction of the liable cases for those two years.

101. Another objection to the system proposed is that capital accounts are already submitted by assessees as a matter of routine; and these necessarily disclose capital transactions during the previous years. I understand, however, that full details of wealth and of capital transactions are only given with respect to business accounts. As the law stands today, a statement of net personal wealth can only be obtained with the prior approval of the Commissioner of Income Tax; and this is only made use of in rare cases, and even then not successively year by year.

102. It cannot, of course, be claimed that a system of the type suggested above would stop all evasion in all conceivable circumstances. When both the vendor and the vendee stand to gain from an under-statement of the value of the property the system will not prevent such under-statement (which could only be detected, in such cases, as a result of the detailed investigation of the individual cases). However, if the tax system included taxes on personal expenditure and capital gains (and not only taxes on income and capital), the interests of the vendor and the vendee would no longer be necessarily the same. Their interests may be opposed—the vendor might wish to over-state, and the vendee to under-state, the purchase price. It is not evident in these circumstances that a particular taxpayer gains from an under-statement of the value of transactions or from an over-statement of them. Given an expenditure tax as well as taxes on income and capital, the taxpayer still gains from an under-statement of receipts but he also gains from an over-statement of his tax-free

outlays, and it may thus pay him to pretend to have more assets than he possesses if he thereby saves more in expenditure tax and in future capital gains tax than he loses in the annual tax on property (or possibly in income tax). Hence the proportion of assets (including gold, jewellery and cash) which could be kept under cover and dealt with stealthily would undoubtedly be considerably reduced.

103. It should also be borne in mind that there is a very great difference between people's readiness to conceal transactions by furnishing an incomplete return (thus avoiding any declaration concerning some items altogether) and their willingness to make a false declaration in a public document. There is much to be said, therefore, for having a system which forces people into a position where they have to make a false statement "knowingly and wilfully" as against one where they need only commit the sin of omission and not of commission.[1]

104. As regards benami transactions my suggestion is that the benami holder should be asked to disclose the name of the beneficial owner at the time of the registration and in the event of his failing to do so (and declaring that he is not the beneficial owner himself) he should be treated as the beneficial owner in law. This provision is clearly intended to deter a person from entering into a benami transaction just for the purposes of tax evasion. While it may be true that a certain amount of personal trust is involved between the benami and the real owners in all such cases, I seriously doubt whether the system could continue to exist but for the recognition of benami in common law. Even retention of the title deed would not protect the true owner in case the benami holder formally declared that he was the beneficial owner of the property; and in case the true owner protected himself further through I.O.U.s, mortgage deeds etc., this would call for (as indicated in paragraph 93 (*g*) above) the same kind of disclosure.

105. It has been argued that the proposal would make it more difficult to defeat *male-fide* transfers of property undertaken to

---

[1] These latter remarks apply, of course, to the proposal for a comprehensive return required for the annual tax on capital and taxes on capital gains and personal expenditure and not only to the comprehensive reporting system discussed here.

prevent attachment of property in view of outstanding demands. I should be interested to know the number of cases in which the Revenue succeeded in breaking the benami through court action. My feeling is that the Revenue would gain far more from screening all benami transactions at the very outset than it would lose from any added difficulty in breaking the benami in the case of such fraudulent transactions.

106. With regard to jewellery, dealers should be compelled to complete and produce the requisite vouchers (together with the code numbers) for purchases and sales above Rs. 10,000. I would agree that such reporting system may not be completely foolproof, but it will certainly deter assessees from introducing "black money" into their business by pretending that they have obtained it through the sale of jewellery; and dealers will not be in a position to abet such transactions so freely since they will be forced to disclose the name and identity of the corresponding buyer.

107. The great indirect advantage of this system would be that the Revenue would be informed of all purchases of jewellery, and this would (in time) put them in a position to check the hoarding of jewellery etc., for purposes of an annual tax on capital or a capital gains tax. Here again the introduction of an expenditure tax (which would exempt purchase of works of arts, jewellery and ornaments from this tax—only taxing the "psychic income" derived from their possession—but only if the claim is properly supported by tax vouchers) would do a great deal in helping the disclosure of such transactions generally, since dealers in jewellery would take additional risks in unrecorded purchases if they knew that prospective buyers might demand from them the surrender of a voucher for the purpose of supporting their own claim for tax exemption. They would, no doubt, still be able to find buyers who would be willing to buy without request for a voucher, but such "black sales" of jewellery might well stand at a discount, and dealers may be reluctant to rely on them in making the purchases.

108. With regard to the hoarding of gold my own feeling is that the best way of dealing with this problem is to permit the sale and purchase of gold through officially registered dealers and making it

illegal to buy or sell gold through other dealers. Considering the widespread propensity to hoard gold in India, it is best to allow a "free market" for internally held gold (the price in this internal free market being permitted to vary so as to equalise supply and demand). The purchase of bar gold being purely a form of investment, it would not, of course, be subject to the personal expenditure tax (either as regards the initial purchase, or as regards any "psychic income" derived from its possession), though the value of hoarded gold would be subject to the annual wealth tax. Purchase and sale through registered dealers would, of course, have to be undertaken with duly completed tax vouchers which the dealers hand over to the seller in the case of sales, and to the buyer in the case of purchases. This would not prevent completely the existence of a "black market" for gold illegally bought and sold through non-authorised dealers. But it is probable that this black market would not be able to compete with the "white market" in the matter of prices and margins, so that the authorities would come to know about, and would be able to control, at any rate the greater part of the bar gold transactions.[1]

109. Apart from the hoarding of gold there may also be hoarding of bank notes as a means of concealing profits or (in connection with the initial introduction of an expenditure tax)[2] in order to be able to spend money without attracting expenditure tax. If the hoarding of bank notes is at all serious, the matter could be simply dealt with by calling in the existing note issue and replacing it with a new issue.

110. Finally, it has been suggested that in case of a large number of small property transfers in small towns and villages, where illiterate persons are involved, it would be impossible to enforce the proper completion of the tax vouchers and the use of code numbers. However, I have suggested an exemption limit of

[1] I think that people would not want to conceal gold, where such concealment is contrary to law, if all that they save as a result of such a concealment is the one-half to one per cent. per annum in property tax; though they would have a stronger incentive if the motive for hoarding gold is to prevent the discovery of "secret savings" made out of undeclared gains which escaped income tax. The question of the impact of taxation on gold hoarding is further discussed in Section IX.

[2] In connection with the expenditure tax, the hoarding of bank notes would only present a problem at the beginning—i.e. in connection with the initial introduction of the tax. In subsequent years there will only be a tendency to hoard in note form whatever was successfully concealed as a receipt in the income tax return—here the problem will be no different than exists at present.

Rs. 10,000, which I think would automatically exclude most transfers of small property in small towns and villages. My proposals involve the issue of code numbers to not more than two million persons. The probable number may be perhaps much smaller. There are, according to C.B.R. statistics, 60,500 holders of ordinary shares in the whole of India, 21,340 owners of interest-bearing securities, and around, say, 1,00,000 individuals owning property of Rs. 50,000 or more. The number of individuals involved in transactions of Rs. 10,000 or more cannot, therefore, be very large. Since a code number could be obtained on request from a local Income Tax Officer without any trouble (who would issue a duplicate code card in case the original one is lost) the use of code numbers should not raise any difficulty even if some people were only to make use of them once or twice in their lifetime. If people lose the code cards issued to them, they could always obtain duplicates. Since the purpose of presenting a code card issued by an Income Tax Officer is merely to ensure that the code number given in the documents agree with the name and address of the person who claims it as his own, there is no risk (as far as I can see) in the fraudulent use of lost code cards by other people (as in the case, for example, with lost ration cards) and, therefore, I do not think any restrictions are required for safe-guarding and circumscribing the issue of duplicate code cards.[1]

---

[1] There may be a risk of a person having more than one code number issued to him (by making a request for a card to different tax offices) but this is no different from the case of a taxpayer dealing with several I.T.O.s at the same time.

VII. THE TAX TREATMENT OF BUSINESS PROFITS

A. THE NATURE OF THE PROBLEM

111. According to both British and Indian laws, taxable income is arrived at by allowing certain expenses to be set off against a person's receipts during a period, but the expenses that are allowed as a deduction are defined differently for different kinds of income. Whereas in the case of (*a*) an office, employment or pension, the deductible expenses are defined as those which are "wholly, exclusively and necessarily incurred in the performance of the duties of" the office or employment, in the case of (*b*) a business, profession or vocation, the expenses deductible are defined as those which are "wholly or exclusively laid out or expended for the purpose of" the business, etc.[1]

112. This difference in wording denotes an important difference in treatment—a difference caused not solely, or even mainly, by the word "necessarily" which figures in the one case and not in the other, but by the fact that in the case of category (*a*) incomes the expenses must be incurred "in the performance of the duties of" and not simply "for the purpose of" the office or employment. The basic principle governing the deductibility of expenses is thus quite different. Indeed, it would be no exaggera-

---

[1] In the British Income Tax Act these words appear as a qualification to the enumeration of a list of items, the deduction of which is prohibited. The first item of the list mentions "any disbursement or expenses *not* being money wholly or exclusively laid out or expended for the purposes of the trade" etc. The Indian Income Tax Act proceeds exactly the other way round. It mentions the list of items which are allowed as deductions from the receipts, and ends up (in clause (xv) of subsection 2 of Section 10) with a general sweeping-up clause which asserts positively that "any expenditure . . . laid out or expended wholly or exclusively for the purposes of such business", etc., qualifies as a permissible deduction. The difference in the manner in which the definition is introduced in the British and Indian Acts is revealing. It shows that the definition was originally intended to strengthen the hands of Revenue in disallowing deductions. By the time the law was applied in India, it has come to serve the opposite purpose of ensuring that no type of expenditure which comes within the scope of this definition should fail to qualify.

tion to say that whereas in the case of profits the expenses allowed comprise everything which has been "laid out or expended" for the purpose of maintaining or improving the earnings prospect of a business, and, therefore, of the person or persons owning that business, in the case of an office or employment, the individual *qua* individual gets no expenses allowed at all for any form of expenditure incurred for maintaining or improving his own status or earning capacity as a person. Any allowance for expenses proceeds from the explicit or implied obligations assumed in a particular contract, not from the need or desire to maintain the earning capacity of the individual who enters into the contract. If the definition adopted for (*a*) were applied to (*b*), a business could only claim such expenses as could be shown to have been demonstrably and inevitably involved in the fulfilment of a particular contract, and not those which arise from the desire to maintain or improve upon the general profitability of the business as a continuing entity.

113. This sharp difference in conception is the cause of a serious injustice in tax treatment as between those who make their living as employees and those who work on their own account or live on property. The inequity of treatment takes the form of (i) the allowance for capital wastage which is recognised in the one case and entirely ignored in the other, and (ii) the allowance for a whole range of miscellaneous expenditure which, while not expenditure of a capital nature (i.e., which does not result in the acquisition of a physical asset), relates to the general improvement or maintenance of the earning capacity of a business, rather than to the fulfilment of a particular contract. Thus, in the case of persons who are taxed on the salary, etc., received, no allowance is made for the wastage of earning capacity due to the limited span of working life, or for the capital expenditure incurred in acquiring the skill, knowledge or the qualifications required for a particular employment. No allowance is made for expenses incurred wholly and exclusively for either the maintenance or the improvement of the status of a particular employee (as distinct from the expenses necessarily incurred in fulfilling his particular contract)—e.g., advertisement in a paper for a job, entertainments to present or to prospective employers or persons with

professional connections; expenditure on clothing in order to make oneself more acceptable to present or prospective employers, etc., etc.

114. In Britain (and I have little doubt that the situation is the same in India), the inequality of treatment only becomes fully apparent in those particular cases where a man pursuing some peculiar trade or vocation may be alternatively assessed as a salary recipient or treated as a person who makes a profit from a profession. Thus a Medical Officer of Health employed by a public authority is denied any allowance for his subscription to medical journals or his membership fee to the Medical Association, though an ordinary doctor would be allowed these things without question. An actor on a permanent contract and paid at a regular monthly rate would get no allowance for make-up, clothing, entertainment, etc., while an actor who contracts for individual shows separately would get all such expenses allowed quite irrespective of their amount, even if his services are habitually employed by the same firm. But perhaps the most important difference arises out of the fact that no depreciation allowance is given for the outlay incurred in acquiring personal qualifications, as distinct from the outlay on material assets, though both represent capital expenditure of an essentially identical character.

115. In some countries (particularly I believe, in some of the Scandinavian countries), an attempt has been made to widen the range of expenses allowed for an employee so as to embrace expenses incurred for the general maintenance of earning capacity.[1] The Majority of the British Royal Commission on the Taxation of Profits and Income, in an attempt to narrow the difference in treatment between the two types of income, recommended that the expenses rule of employees should be relaxed so as to cover "all expenses *reasonably* incurred for the *appropriate* performance of the duties", instead of "wholly, exclusively and *necessarily* incurred *in* the performance of the duties".[2] This relaxa-

---

[1] Recent Indian legislation also tended in this direction, i.e. in the provision to allow the cost of books up to a certain amount, and for the cost of maintenance of conveyances (cars etc.).

[2] Cf. para 140, page 47 of the Final Report (Cmd. 9474). The Indian Taxation Enquiry Commission ignored this problem altogether.

tion does not really meet the problem of the inequality caused by the basic difference in principle between expenses incurred "in the performance of the duties"—i.e., in the fulfilment of a particular contract, and expenses incurred "for the purpose of" i.e., for the general maintenance or improvement of earning capacity. The Minority strongly opposed this recommendation on the grounds that it would make it difficult to draw a clear line of distinction between business expenses and personal expenses; that the standard of "reasonably incurred" expenses would be steadily raised in the course of years; and finally, that all the difficulties and ambiguities which now beset the assessment of profits would be reproduced in the case of wages and salaries, with little, if any, compensating gain in equity as between one employee and another.

116. In the remainder of this chapter we shall consider this problem from three particular aspects—the general question of allowable expenses, the problem of capital allowances and, finally, the treatment of losses.

B. THE GENERAL RULE OF EXPENSES

The Proposed Rule

117. It seems to me beyond dispute that, whether we consider the problem from the point of view of administrative efficiency or of equity between the taxpayers,[1] the appropriate principle for arriving at chargeable "income" for tax purposes is the principle underlying the expenses rule for category (*a*) incomes rather than that for category (*b*). It is true, of course, that the actual wording of the former rule could only be applied to contractual employments, and not to profits derived from trading. However, it would not be impossible or even very difficult to invent a form of words which applied substantially the same basic conception to profits as is actually applied to contractual incomes. A simple definition that immediately suggests itself is that of *"expenses that are wholly exclusively and unavoidably incurred in earning the profits of the year"*. The insertion of the term "unavoidably" would fulfil the same

[1] These two aspects are not of course independent of one another. Provisions which cannot be effectively administered are themselves the cause of inequities.

functions for (*b*) as the word "necessarily" fulfils in the case of (*a*), whilst the restriction of expenses to those incurred in "earning the profits of the year" would be a proper equivalent in the case of (*b*) of the restriction "in the performance of the duties" applied to (*a*).

118. There can be little doubt that the original notion of "income" for tax purposes—the conception which underlay the original income tax legislation in the time of the Napoleonic wars —was intended to confine deductible expenses to direct and unavoidable outlays of this character. The extent to which the present conception of "income" departs from it is a measure of the erosion caused by over 100 years of relentless pressure exerted by vested interests.

119. The introduction of a more strictly defined expenses rule for the purpose of calculating the amount of taxable profits would have important advantages not only from the point of view of equity as between taxpayers, but also because of its repercussions on the efficiency with which the resources of the community are allocated between different uses. The kind of definition suggested above minimises the extent to which the amount of the taxable gain is dependent on the free choice of the taxpayer. The generous and elastic provisions for deductible expenses currently given in the case of profits put a trader in a privileged position in comparison with other taxpayers not only because he is taxed on a narrower conception of "income" than the others, but also because he is put in a favourable position to benefit from opportunities to evade taxation by dressing up personal expenses as business expenses.

120. The second of the two considerations, the need to avoid distortions in normal economic behaviour, is equally important as the first, the need to secure impartial treatment to different sections of the community. If expenses are allowed which are not a necessary or an inevitable concomitant of producing the receipts against which they are set off, the Government, in effect, is subsidising such expenditures through the instrument of taxation. In the case of outlays on unavoidable items no such subsidy is involved precisely because the trading receipts are directly dependent on them. The outlay on wages, fuel, materials, etc., per

unit of production, is virtually unaffected by the tax provisions. But if general expenses of all kinds—the scale of which is variable within wide limits relative to the scale of activity of a business— are made deductible, the very exemption is the equivalent of a direct subsidity from the Treasury, the rate of subsidy being the same as the marginal rate of taxation. When the marginal rate is as high as 90 per cent., the deductibility of avoidable or unnecessary expenses implies that nine-tenths of such expenses is financed. by the Government and only one-tenth by the taxpayer himself.

121. There is, of course, no general reason why private outlay should not be subsidised by the Government; nor is income tax the only instrument through which such subsidies are habitually given. It is important to recognise, however, that the tax exemption to such categories is but a variant of granting subsidies, and it, therefore, requires to be justified not on the principles of equity, but by the criteria of social utility. The avoidable and voluntary expenses which are outside the narrow definition suggested above comprise such varied categories as the acquisition of capital assets of all kinds, expenditure on research whether of a recurring or non-recurring nature, payments made to research and other scientific institutions, advertising and sales promotional expenses of all kinds, entertainments, and travelling expenses. (This list is not intended to be exhaustive.) Clearly, not all such expenses are equally deserving of a subsidy by the test of social utility. The important point is to recognise that the tax-exemptions accorded to all such outlays find their ultimate justification not in equity, but in economic or social expediency.

122. The ideal solution, therefore, appears to me to adopt a strict definition of expenses on the lines suggested in paragraph 117 and to allow any other kind of expenses only to the extent to which this appears justified in the social interest. Expenditure on scientific research, whether of a recurring or a non-recurring character, clearly deserves to be subsidised. But it is open to the Government to examine whether all research expenses should automatically be treated as deductible, or whether certain kinds of expenditure should be disallowed or only partially allowed. Equally, it is a matter for individual examination whether expenditure on such items as advertising, entertaining, etc., should

E

be disallowed altogether, or whether it should qualify as a deductible expense only up to a certain proportion of the turnover or up to a certain fraction of the expenses actually incurred.[1] (The relevance of these considerations to the question of allowances for capital expenditure generally will be discussed below.)

123. I realise that this approach runs counter to the prevailing trend, which shows a constant widening in the range of deductible expenses in most countries. Thus the recent Committees of Inquiry both in Britain and India appear to have conceded the claim that profits for purposes of taxation should be assimilated to profits computed on "sound accountancy principles", however incongrous such an assimilation may be in the light of its consequences on equity. The Committee on the Taxation of Trading Profits in the U.K., acknowledged the claim of businessmen that "the income tax system should give relief in respect of the wastage of all assets that are used up or consumed in the course of carrying on a business", without any recognition of the fact that assets are built up and not only consumed, in the course of a business (in the form of goodwill, for example), and to allow capital wastage to be deducted without bringing capital accretion into charge is completely at variance with the basic principles of equality of treatment. The assimilation of the concept of profit for tax purposes with the accounting concept is neither justifiable on grounds of equity, nor is it supportable from the point of view of administrative efficiency or economic expediency. In fact, almost all authorities on public finance who examined this question during the past 50 years or so have come to the conclusion that the concept of "income" that is most appropriate for tax purposes need have no particular relationship to the concept of income appropriate for accounting, or to the economist's concept of "income" as the individual counterpart of the "national income".

124. The Minority of the British Royal Commission following the above reasoning concluded that a tax on trading receipts less unavoidable expenses only (which comes broadly to the same

---

[1] In the autumn Budget of 1947, Dr. Dalton as Chancellor of the Exchequer proposed that only 50 per cent. of the expenditure on advertising and entertainment should qualify as deductible expense for tax purposes. As Dr. Dalton resigned from the Chancellorship immediately afterwards, and his successor did not press the proposals, they never got on the Statute Book.

thing as a tax on the "valued added" as defined for the Census of Manufactures less outlay on wages, salaries, interest, and rent) would be fairer and less arbitrary in its incidence than the present type of tax on profits; and that it would be a far simpler tax to administer; also since the tax base would be so much broader, it would make it possible to effect a reduction in the rates of taxation. Nevertheless, they felt that it would be futile to advocate for immediate adoption such a radical departure from existing practice so long as the taxation of profits in other countries remained on the present basis. For the traders engaged in overseas trade might be put at a competitive disadvantage if they were not allowed to treat as deductible expenses, selling and promotional outlays of various kinds which qualify for tax deduction in the case of their overseas trade competitors. They accordingly recommended that the U.K. should press through the United Nations or other international bodies for the adoption of binding international conventions concerning the principles to be followed in the taxation of trading profits which would make it possible to proceed towards a more rational, effective, and equitable system of profits taxation than any one country would be able to adopt acting in isolation. In the meantime as a second best they recommended that the difference in the treatment between the two categories of income should be compensated for in a broad manner through a differentiation in the rates of taxation applicable to each. This, they thought, could be most conveniently done through a change in the rules governing earned income relief.

Role of Earned Relief

125. The original purpose of earned income relief was to introduce a differentiation in favour of incomes from work as against incomes from property. The Select Committee of the British Parliament appointed to examine this question in 1906 was troubled by the problem of how to treat the profits which were in the nature of a joint return of the work of the trader and of the capital which he employed in the business. They concluded that the only practicable solution was to treat profits below a certain amount as if they were predominantly the reward of work and profits above that amount as if they were predominantly

the return on capital. On this reasoning, they thought that rough justice would be done if the earned income relief were extended to all "earned" incomes (including the trading profits of individuals and partnerships) when incomes were below £2,000, but not if they were above that figure.[1] There was never any justification for imposing such a limitation on income derived entirely or predominantly from work, i.e. salaries and the earnings of a profession or vocation. In the circumstances of 1906 this inconsistency did not trouble the legislators, since neither salaries not professional earnings were met within the over £2,000 range, except in a few very exceptional cases.

126. The Minority of the recent British Royal Commission came to the conclusion that the earned income relief could be made to serve the purpose of compensating for the difference in the expenses rule for salary incomes and profits if (*a*) the relief were extended in the case of salaries to all incomes, without any upper limit; (*b*) in the case of professional or vocational earnings, it is equally so extended, but only given to those taxpayers who at their own option are willing to be assessed under the strict expenses rule applicable to incomes from offices and employment; and (*c*) in the case of business profits, the relief should be subject to an upper limit as it is at present, but only extended to those traders who at their own option are willing to be assessed under the strict expenses rule.

127. I have described the current position in the U.K. and its historical origin in some detail because the Indian rules concerning earned income relief have obviously been taken over from the U.K. rules, and it is important, therefore, that Indians should be aware on what justification (or lack of justification) the existing delineation of that relief to certain categories of income, and its limitation to a certain maximum of income, rests. The Indian provisions concerning earned income relief until recently corresponded exactly with the U.K. provisions; recently, however, on the recommendation of the Taxation Enquiry Commission, a further provision was introduced in India whereby the relief, limited to the first Rs. 20,000 of taxable income, is progressively with-

---

[1] This rule was later amended, on the recommendation of the Royal Commission on Income Tax of 1920, so that the relief was made available to *all* earned incomes, whatever their amount, but only on the first £2,000 of taxable income.

drawn when incomes exceeded Rs. 25,000, so that for incomes of Rs. 45,000 or above, no relief is given at all.[1] (I confess, I cannot understand how the Taxation Enquiry Commission arrived at this particular recommendation. If one considers the variety of ways in which incomes from work are discriminated against by the present tax system through the more generous expenses rule applicable to profits, through the tax-exemption to capital gains, through the fact that the taxable capacity inherent in the owner-ship of wealth as such is unrecognised and that spending out of capital is tax-free, not to speak of all the evasion possibilities inherent in the one and absent in the other, this additional whittl-ing-down of an already inadequate concession appears singularly inappropriate.[2] The Taxation Enquiry Commission concede that of all the arguments in favour of the earned income relief the one which suggested that "the taxable capacity of those who receive unearned income is greater since they have also a fund of capital in addition to the income which arises from it" appears to them to be the most important. In the light of this remark their recom-mendation introduced immediately afterwards, and not supported by any argument, that "there should be a limit in terms of income beyond which the allowance should not be available"[3] is rather difficult to reconcile.)

128. If India were to adopt an annual tax on wealth and would reintroduce the taxation of capital gains, the arguments in favour of earned income relief would come to rest entirely on the difference in the treatment of expenses as between salary incomes and profit incomes. This is not meant to suggest that the case for the relief would no longer be a strong one—for the discrimination caused by the two different rules for expenses is a very powerful one indeed. But it would clearly imply that the relief should be confined to those who suffer from this discrimination, i.e. to the

[1] This means, in effect, a return to the system originally in force in the U.K. prior to the recommendation of the 1920 Royal Commission.
[2] It also has the incidental consequence that in the income range of Rs. 25,000—45,000, the progressive withdrawal of the relief is tantamount to a further increase in the marginal rate of taxation, which in these ranges is thus appreciably higher than for unearned incomes.
[3] Cf. T.E.C. Report, Vol. II, Ch. IX, para. 23. As indicated earlier in this section the Commission makes no mention of the inequities caused by the difference in the expenses rule applicable to salaries and profits.

salary recipient; and it should be given to them without any upper limit—i.e. what comes to the same thing, a sur-charge be imposed on all incomes from a business, profession or vocation, excepting only those of the professional and vocational category who at their own option are willing to be assessed under the strict expenses rule outlined in paragraph 117 above. The extension of the relief to all salaries without an upper limit coupled with its withdrawal in the case of income from other sources would (on the basis of the assessments in 1954–55) yield a small net gain in revenue.

The Case for a Strict Rule

129. I should like to emphasise, however, that a solution along the above lines is definitely a second best and is neither so satisfactory from an equity point of view nor does it secure the other important advantages that would follow from the adoption of a more strict expenses rule for profits. While the Minority of the British Royal Commission shied away from recommending such a radical change in the face of the opposition that its introduction would have encountered, I feel that the situation in India is a rather different one from that of the U.K. The argument of export promotion through entertainment and advertising is relatively far less important; the need of Indian industry for identity of tax treatment with foreign industry is far smaller, since Indian industry can be, and is, protected by tariffs from foreign competition (quite apart from the fact that the whole argument is a spurious one, since differences in the breadth of the tax base can be compensated for by differences in the rates of taxation), whilst the advantages from the point of view of administrative effectiveness of an income definition which is less ambiguous and less capable of manipulation by the taxpayers are considerably greater. By simplifying the concept of profit which is subjected to taxation—by reducing the range of items which qualify for deduction —the task of checking the accuracy of the remaining items by the tax officers is greatly simplified. The standards of administration are bound to be all the lower the more complicated are the taxes which the tax officers are asked to administer.

130. For all these reason, I would strongly urge the re-definition of deductible expenses on the lines recommended in paragraph 117

above in preference to all other solutions. This would mean, in effect, that only the outlays on wages, material, fuel, as well as the outlays specifically mentioned in clauses (i), (iii), (iv), (v) and (x) of Section 10 of the Income Tax Act would be automatically covered. With regard to the other items (including capital expenditure discussed below), the case for deduction would depend on considerations of economic expediency, and would thus be capable of adjustment and variation from time to time and from case to case.

131. There are no statistics in India to show the effects on tax revenue of either the allowance for indirect expenses or of the allowances for capital expenditure. I made an attempt, however, to estimate the possible magnitude of the items on the assumption that the relationship of the cost of materials and fuel on the one hand, and of "other costs" on the other hand, is the same in India as in the U.K. On that assumption (in the sector of manufacturing industry covered in Table 2), "other costs" (column 9) amounted to 5 per cent. of the material and fuel costs, to three times the amount of depreciation, to about 11 per cent. of "value added" and to about 26 per cent. the net profit. If this relationship held for India, not only in manufacturing industry but in trade, etc., as well, the additional amount of profits assessable as a result of disallowing all other but "direct" expenses and personnel costs (apart from allowances for capital expenditure) would come to about Rs. 150 crores. Not all of this would become taxable under the definition offered in paragraph 117; some items (those mentioned in paragraph 130) would continue to be allowed. Hence, the excluded expenditure may be put at the order of one-half of this sum, or Rs. 80 crores. This is not offered as an "estimate" but merely as an indication of the possible order of magnitude involved.

132. The suggestion for widening the concept of taxable profits by disallowing all but direct and unavoidable expenses is bound to arouse fierce opposition. The antagonists of this suggestion will employ every specious argument they can think of, to show that the proposed reform would have fatal economic effects. This opposition would lose a great deal of its force, however, if the proposal were combined with a simultaneous reduction of the

Table 2

ESTIMATES OF INDIRECT COSTS IN INDIAN INDUSTRIES ON THE BASIS OF THE UNITED KINGDOM RELATIONSHIP BETWEEN THE MATERIAL COSTS AND INDIRECT COSTS AND OF NET PROFIT FOR THE YEAR 1948

	United Kingdom			India							
Industry	Cost of materials	Other costs	Ratio of other costs to cost of materials (%)	Gross value of output (Rs. crores)	Cost of materials (Rs. crores)	Estimated other costs (Rs. crores) (4×6)	Work done for factory (Rs. crores)	Depreciation allowances (Rs. crores)	Estimated net value added (Rs. crores) (5 minus 6 to 9)	Salaries & Wages (Rs. crores)	Net profit (Rs. crores) (10−11)
	(In percentages of turn-over)										
1	2	3	4	5	6	7	8	9	10	11	12
1. Iron and Steel	61·7	3·4	5·50	42·45	20·63	1·13	0·14	2·13	18·42	10·93	7·49
2. Non-Ferrous Metals	77·2	2·5	3·21	18·87	13·45	0·43	0·18	0·44	4·37	2·65	1·72
3. El. Eng. & El. Goods	62·2	4·8	7·75	48·31	24·17	1·87	0·54	1·65	20·08	14·46	5·62
4. Leather goods	68·7	3·2	4·65	6·25	5·00	0·23	0·01	0·06	0·95	0·68	0·27
5. Cotton	71·9	3·5	4·85	354·58	186·58	9·05	2·05	3·01	153·43	83·41	70·02
6. Wool	72·2	2·5	3·45	8·41	4·14	0·14	0·03	0·08	4·02	1·78	2·24
7. Other Textiles	67·2	3·3	4·90	160·40	117·57	5·76	0·04	1·38	35·71	25·98	9·73
8. Food	78·4	3·4	4·32	237·79	203·40	8·79	0·15	2·94	22·51	12·98	9·53
9. Chemicals	71·8	5·4	7·51	20·65	11·69	0·88	0·03	0·73	7·32	3·25	4·07
10. Wood & Cork Manufacture	65·1	3·7	5·68	1·66	0·96	0·05	0·00	0·05	0·60	0·24	0·36
11. Paper	54·7	5·2	9·52	9·92	5·78	0·55	0·02	0·43	3·14	2·00	1·14
12. Other Manufacturing Industries	63·4	5·4	9·27	42·17	24·36	2·82	0·09	0·97	13·93	6·99	6·94
Total (12 Industries)	90·8	4·01	4·41	951·00	617·67	31·70	3·28	13·87	284·48	165·35	119·13

Sources: (1) 94th Report of the U.K. Board of Inland Revenue (1952). (Figures are for the year 1948 in Tables 54 to 67.)
(2) Cf., 7th Report of the Census of Manufacturing Industries for India (1952). (Figures are for the year 1948 in Tables B4, B5, B6; item 6: "Distilleries & Breweries", is excluded.)

rates of taxation; the advantage of charging tax at a lower rate on a broader base, as against a high rate on a narrow and uncertain base, should be apparent to everybody.

C. ALLOWANCES FOR CAPITAL EXPENDITURE

133. On the original conception of the income tax, the money invested in a fixed asset was regarded as capital and the depreciation of fixed assets a form of wastage of capital. The exclusion of any allowances for capital wastage was the logical counterpart of the exclusion of capital gains or capital appreciation from the scope of taxable income. This explains why for more than a generation after the re-imposition of income tax in England in 1843, no relief of any kind was given for the depreciation or wear-and-tear of fixed assets of any kind; and even after they were introduced during the economic depression of the 1880's, their scope was severely restricted to particular types of assets until 1944. In accordance with the findings of the Royal Commission of 1920, no allowance was given for the depreciation of any asset (1) which "was not created by the expenditure of capital" (mineral depletion is an example of this); and (2) whose useful life was 35 years or longer (hence all buildings were excluded).[1]

134. Looking at the matter from the point of view of equity alone, it is clear that an allowance for capital wastage without a corresponding charge being imposed on capital appreciation is quite indefensible. Even with a system of taxation on realised capital gains, capital wastage ought only to be taken into account in the form of a corresponding allowance for capital losses, which means that the allowance should be given as and when the capital loss resulting from wear-and-tear and wastage is actually realised. To hold the balance evenly between the charge on capital gains and the allowances for capital losses, wear-and-tear, etc., should only be allowed for tax purposes at the *end* of the useful life of an asset, when it is sold for scrap or otherwise disposed of. The current methods of allowing the write-off of capital expenditure by

[1] These principles were abandoned piecemeal in the U.K. after 1944, when the original reasoning behind the restrictions was long forgotten. The Report of the 1920 Royal Commission made it clear that the claim for capital allowances rests on expediency rather than equity.

means of annual depreciation allowances are far more favourable than this, even if one ignored the various forms of accelerated depreciation allowances (or the straight-forward subsidy to capital expenditure given in the form of the development rebate) now in vogue.

135. It follows that the depreciation allowances given for capital expenditure cannot be justified on grounds of equity, irrespective of whether capital gains are taxed or whether they are exempt from taxation. If capital gains are exempt, no allowance for capital expenditure can be so justified; if capital gains were taxed, the corresponding allowances should be given as and when capital losses are realised, and not earlier.[1]

136. The real justification for capital allowances is, therefore, not one of equity but expediency. It is in the social interest that capital expenditure should be encouraged; a system of income taxation, through the double taxation of savings and through its discriminatory effect on risk bearing, does the opposite—it tends severely to discourage it. Hence, the allowances given to capital expenditure are necessary to neutralise some of the worst disincentive effects of income taxation on the economy.

137. Once this is recognised it should be immediately apparent that the present form of these allowances are both unnecessarily complicated and unnecessarily costly in terms of revenue to the State. If neatly calculated annual wear-and-tear allowances (based on the probable lifetime of assets) are not part and parcel of an equitable definition of "income" for tax purposes, it is open to the State to select a form of allowances which is simplest to administer, and which is most effective for attaining the objectives aimed at per unit of cost to the State.

138. At the present time allowances are given at varying annual rates for different assets, the system generally followed being that of the so-called "reducing-balance" method, which implies the writing-off of an equal percentage of the outstanding amount of capital expenditure in each successive year. Table 3 exhibits the

---

[1] The tax system contains several "asymmetrical" provisions of this kind which put the man who is taxed on the profits of business in an anomalous position *vis-à-vis* other taxpayers. One of these consists in the permission given to traders to bring anticipated losses into account through the writing down of stocks below cost if market value is less than cost—without a corresponding obligation to bring into account unrealised gains (i.e. to write up stocks when market value is above cost).

effects of this method in the case of various types of capital expenditure. Thus in the most common case of plant and machinery of various kinds, where the annual allowance is 10 per cent., the method implies that 90 per cent. of the original cost is only written off in 22 years. In the case of first class buildings, where $2\frac{1}{2}$ per cent. is allowed, 90 per cent. of the original cost is only written off in a period of 91 years, and so on. From the point of view of a taxpayer who can freely borrow at the ruling interest rate, these allowances are thus the equivalent of the immediate remission of tax on an amount equal to the discounted value of the annual allowances. Thus, assuming a rate of interest of 5 per cent., an annual allowance of 2 per cent. on the whole capital expenditure is equivalent (as shown in column 2 of Table 3) to an immediate remission of tax on 35 per cent. of the total cost. In the case of machinery and plant where the annual allowance is 10 per cent. the annual depreciation allowance granted on the whole cost is the equivalent of an immediate remission on 67 per cent. of the cost; and so on.

139. Most businesses do not, however, have an unlimited borrowing power or an unlimited command over liquid resources; and to them a system which allows the discounted value of the depreciation allowances immediately is far more valuable than one which allows them to write off 100 per cent. of the cost, spread over a large number of years. For a man who builds up a successful business, the possible rate of expansion of the business is normally limited by its accumulated savings and borrowing power; and in these circumstances the immediate remission of taxation on capital expenditure is far more attractive, since it is the equivalent of an enlargement of his borrowing power. The latter therefore, is necessarily a more powerful lever for increasing capital expenditure than the former.

140. It follows that the ideal method of making allowances for capital expenditure is to allow the expenditure at the time when it is incurred in the same way as in the case of current expenditure; but unlike the latter, to allow only a proportion of the cost, a proportion that should vary with the probable life of the capital asset, as well as other factors such as the need to encourage the use of particular kinds of equipment, or to subsidise investment in

Table 3

PRESENT VALUE OF CAPITAL ALLOWANCES IN INDIA

Type of asset	Basic annual rate %	Case I		Case IIa		Case IIb	
		Period in years	Present discounted value Rs. lakhs	Period in years	Present discounted value Rs. lakhs	Period in years	Present discounted value Rs. lakhs
1	2	3	4	5	6	7	8
First class building & hydro-electric installations ..	2·5	91	34·97	86	38·50	58	46·53
Second class buildings, overhead cables, steamers & vessels	5·0	45	51·87	40	55·69	26	62·12
Machinery and plant (general rate)	7·0	32	59·90	27	88·39	18	96·47
Furniture and mills etc.	9·0	25	65·31	19	93·91	13	102·77
Machinery and plant (normal rate)	10·0	22	67·22	17	95·31	11	105·78
Salt works, excavators etc.	15·0	15	74·64	9	101·31	5	106·01
Batteries, X-ray, photographic recording & projecting equipment	20·0	11	78·46	5	108·36	4	115·55
Aerial photographic apparatus, and portable underground machinery	25·0	9	81·52	4	115·55	3	120·63

Notes

1. It is assumed that the reducing balance method is followed for 90% of the original cost and that the residual 10% is allowed in the year following the year when the written down value is reduced to 10% or under. The "period" of depreciation is calculated under this assumption.

2. Present value is calculated by discounting the allowances given subsequent to the year of installation at a rate of 5% interest.

3. Case I: Normal depreciation alone at the basic annual rates shown in column 2 is allowed.

    Case IIa: Normal depreciation and an equal amount of additional depreciation for the first five years only are allowed; 25% of the original cost is given at the beginning of the first year as development rebate for all types of assets except the first two types of assets.

    Case IIb: Normal depreciation, an equal amount of additional depreciation for the first five years only, and half the normal allowances for double shift are given throughout; also 25% of the original cost is given as development rebate for all but the first two types of assets.

Source: Appendix (iii) to C.B.R.'s *Income Tax for the Layman*, 1955, for basic annual rates.

certain industries.[1] Thus, for instance, if instead of an annual allowance of 10 per cent. an immediate allowance of 66⅔ per cent. is given on expenditure on machinery and plant; instead of an annual allowance of 2½ per cent. an immediate allowance of 33⅓ per cent. on first-class buildings; and instead of an annual allowance of 5 per cent., an immediate allowance of 50 per cent. on the cost of second-class buildings, the value of the allowance to the trader is at least as great or greater, whilst the cost ot the State (in the long run, at any rate) is appreciably less.[2] At the same time, on account of the fact that the allowances are given simultaneously with the expenditure and not afterwards, there can be no complaints on account of the difference between historical and replacement costs of the assets in times of rising prices; the allowance is always given in terms of currency of the same purchasing power as the one in which the expenditure is incurred.

141. The only objection that can be brought against this proposal is that the benefit to the trader is dependent on his ability to absorb the allowances (i.e. to set them off against current profits) in the year in which the expenditure is incurred. To the extent that there are not sufficient profits to absorb the allowance in the same business,[3] the benefit of making the allowances immediately available is correspondingly reduced. However, this difficulty can be perfectly adequately dealt with by a further provision, according to which any *unabsorbed* capital allowance carried forward to a future year earns a corresponding rate of interest. Thus, assuming a 5 per cent. rate of interest, if a trader incurs an expenditure of one lakh in a particular year, two-thirds of which are allowed, and there are only Rs. 20,000 of taxable profits to set off against the expenditure, the amount carried forward to the following year would be the unabsorbed allowance of Rs. 46,668 plus 5 per cent. interest, i.e. Rs. 49,000 altogether, and so on.

---

[1] If the Government wished, in accordance with the general aims of its economic plan, to encourage investment in particular industries and not in others, the ideal instrument is to vary the rate of these allowances accordingly; though from an administrative point of view the differentiation should not be based on the industrial classification of the user, but on the type of equipment purchased (e.g., engineering equipment, machine tools, power looms, etc.).

[2] The State (unlike private business) does not suffer from limited borrowing power.

[3] The question of allowances for losses will be examined below.

142. In India at the present time in addition to the "normal" depreciation allowance, additional depreciation allowances are given which double or more than double the normal rate for the first five years after installation, and then a development rebate of 25 per cent. is given on the whole amount of the capital expenditure which is additional to the depreciation allowances.[1] As Table 3 shows, the effect of these various concessions is that in many cases the discounted value of the various allowances exceeds the total expenditure. This is the case for plant and machinery, etc., with double shift working, when the basic annual allowance is 9 per cent. or more and double shift allowance is given; with single shift working, when the basic allowance is 15 per cent. or more. The result of these extra concessions is that for businesses which do not suffer from a shortage of cash and/or a limitation of borrowing power, the incentives for tax evasion are reversed—instead of there being a temptation to dress up capital expenditure as current expenditure, there exists the opposite temptation of dressing up current expenditure as capital expenditure.

143. It is a matter for consideration whether the current extent of these allowances are not unduly generous (even within the present framework of the tax system), and whether some of the extra concessions ought not to be dispensed with. (The case for this would, of course, become much stronger if the marginal rate of taxation on profits were reduced in accordance with the suggestions made earlier.) It is unfortunately not possible to find out how much these concessions cost in terms of revenue, as the amount of capital allowances granted against chargeable income are not computed for statistical purposes.

144. I am quite certain, however, that these allowances are greatly excessive in relation to the alternative system proposed. If depreciation allowances were altogether scrapped, and the whole of the capital allowance were given in the form of an initial allowance or development rebate (whichever term is preferred), with an accelerator clause for unabsorbed allowances, the actual amount of the allowances ought to be considerably reduced.

---

[1] The development rebates are also ignored for the purpose of calculating the balancing charges or allowances.

Subject to an annual addition of 5 per cent. for unabsorbed allowances, the amount should not exceed, say, 90 per cent. of the cost for equipment carrying a basic annual rate of 20 per cent. or more; 66·66 per cent of the cost where the present basic annual rate is between 10 and 20 per cent.; 50 per cent. of the cost when it is between 5 and 10 per cent.; and 33·3 per cent. of the cost where the annual rate is 2 per cent. These figures are not intended to be precise and are put forward mainly for illustrative purposes. The change-over to the new system may cause a temporary loss of revenue which, however, will be more than made good in future years through the saving in depreciation allowances.[1] Since on account of the present development rebate and the doubling or more of the normal depreciation for the first five years, a large part of these allowance are in any case given immediately (amounting at present to 45 per cent. of the total expenditure for equipment carrying a 10 per cent. basic annual rate and operated at a single shift, and to 50 per cent. of such expenditure in the case of double-shift operation), this temporary revenue loss is not likely to be appreciable.

145. The question still to be dealt with is how balancing charges and allowances are to be reckoned under the new system. If the taxation of capital gains were re-introduced, the amount of the balancing charge would in any case not be limited to the original cost, but would extend to the whole of the difference between the price at which an asset is sold and its written down value. Under the system I am recommending here, the written down value would be equal to the original cost less the allowances granted (including any additional allowance representing interest on unabsorbed allowances), and the balancing charges and allowances would be calculated on the difference between the sales-proceeds of an asset and the written down value.

---

[1] It would, of course, be necessary to continue to allow depreciation in regard to capital expenditure incurred prior to the introduction of the new system, so that the depreciation allowances would taper off gradually.

D. THE TREATMENT OF LOSSES

General Considerations

146. The original conception of the income tax as a tax on the recurrent yield from particular sources was no more consistent with the idea of granting relief for business losses than with the granting of allowances for capital expenditure. As the Majority of the British Royal Commission stated,[1] "if the idea of a loss of income involves that more money has been spent than has been received on income account during the period, the balance has in some sense been found out of capital, and to set the loss against taxable income, current or future, is to allow the depletion of capital to be made good at the expense of taxable income." Indeed, the very notion that the net yield from a positive source of income can be a negative one is questionable. No one is forced to carry on a business, and so long as the net worth of the business is positive the owner is always free to cut his losses (either by selling the business as a going concern or by liquidating it and selling the tangible assets separately) when the sale-proceeds from the realisation would put him in a position to earn a positive income corresponding to the interest on the value realised. Hence no one can really be said to derive a negative income from the ownership of any asset or a group of assets with a positive value (as distinct from a negative income from a negative source, such as interest paid on a debt), and if a man elects to keep on owning assets or to maintain a trading activity even though it brings him continued losses, there is no reason why the tax system should treat that as charge on his general income.[2] At the same time, as the Majority of the Royal Commission pointed

---

[1] Para 486, page 147 of the Final Report.

[2] This is the reason why the United Kingdom law has never recognised the possibility of a negative loss being incurred in connection with the ownership of property. If the maintenance and repair expenditure on property exceeds the income, the difference is not recognised for tax purposes except that for the purpose of calculating the income from property the taxpayer is permitted to substitute the average of the maintenance and repair expenditure of the last five years against the actual expenditure of the previous year, and to deduct such expenditure from the receipts of the year up to the limit of such receipts. Income from property therefore can be zero but cannot be negative. Under the Indian law, on the other hand, a loss on property is recognised for tax purposes in much the same way as a loss incurred from business activity.

out, "the ascertainment of business profits at fixed intervals of 12 months is so arbitrary a process, considering the continuous nature of business operations, that [to allow] the carry-forward of losses is an obvious concession to common sense."[1]

147. However, the Majority of the British Royal Commission did not, in my view, draw the right conclusion from this reasoning, in that they supported the existing provisions which permit a loss from any one source to be set off against any other income in the same year or in the following year as well as to be carried forward indefinitely against future income from the same source. They even recommended that unabsorbed capital allowances should qualify for a set-off against future income of any kind (and not only against future income from the same source).[2]

148. The question of the proper tax treatment of losses ought to be examined, like other questions, from the aspects of equity, economic effects, and administrative efficiency. From the point of view of equity, if capital gains are not brought into charge there is no case for recognising losses for tax purposes in any manner except perhaps as a means of averaging income over time; the latter consideration would only justify a carry-forward of losses against future income from the same source, and not as a set-off against income from other businesses or against non-business income.[3] If capital gains were taxed the notion of allowing losses as a deduction from taxable income would no longer be anomalous. But the present definition of a trading loss by no means corresponds with the definition of a capital loss which should be adopted for the purposes of a capital gains tax; nor is it consistent with the notion of income as a person's "increment

[1] They added that "theoretically, a carry-back against the taxed profits of past years would be equally reasonable, but the practical arguments against refunds of tax paid are sufficient to lead us to reject any extension on these lines".
[2] A concession which is already in force in India as a result of the wording of clause (b) of sub-section (vi) of Section 10(2).
[3] Though of the two methods of allowing an off-set of losses—against other income in the same year or against income from the same source in any future year—only the latter can be made consistent with the English conception of taxable income, historically it was the former, not the latter, which was the first to be introduced. The right to off-set was introduced in England in 1890 whereas the right to carry-forward a loss (originally for 6 years, now indefinitely) against any subsequent profits of the same business was only introduced in 1926. This explains why the justification of the right to set-off is rarely questioned, and the carry-forward is commonly treated as a marginal provision to be made use of only when, and to the extent to which, there is insufficient "other income" to absorb the losses in the same year.

of economic power". A trading loss is a loss on current (not capital) account. But since expenditures of a capital nature have come to be treated as deductions from current receipts, a trading loss on current account may result when certain capital outlays in a period exceed net current receipts, or even when certain capital outlays of a past period exceed net current receipts.[1]

149. The correct procedure from the point of view of equity—assuming that capital gains are brought into charge on the lines recommended in Section III—would be to allow only current losses in the strict sense (i.e. the excess of current unavoidable outlays over current receipts) as an offset against other income and to permit "losses" which represent unabsorbed capital allowances, etc., only to be carried forward against future income from the same source. If there is insufficient future income to absorb the allowances, the difference would be automatically allowed for when the assets are disposed of, either individually or upon the liquidation of the business, when the resultant capital loss can be offset against any current or subsequent capital gain.[2]

150. From the point of view of economic effects, to allow a

---

[1] Whenever development expenditure—either capital expenditure or expenditure on research, advertising, etc.—enters into the calculation of a current trading "loss", the effect of allowing such a loss to be off-set against income from other sources is that a taxpayer is able to build up a business at the direct expense of the revenue. In other words, capital for the development of a man's business "B" is provided by the tax abatement on his income from source "A". Part of the current tax bill is transformed into capital. Such an arrangement goes beyond the notion of subsidising certain types of investment to the extent of allowing expenditure upon them to be deducted from the receipts of the business concerned. In the latter case, if the developmental expenditure exceeds net current receipts the business must find the whole of the capital out of which to make the excess expenditure. In the former case the excess expenditure may be largely paid for by the Revenue. The situation in which a man is risking not his own capital but part of his tax bill in respect of income from other sources, in investing in a business a sum greater than his current receipts from that business, provides an incentive to take uneconomic risks together with wide opportunities for deliberate tax avoidance.

[2] From a strict equity point of view, net realised capital losses should qualify as an offset against other income in so far as they cannot be offset against realised capital gains—though the case for this is much less strong when income and capital gains (above a certain limit) are charged at a proportionate rate than when they are charged at a progressive rate. However, for reasons analysed in the Minority Report of the British Royal Commission (paragraphs 65–7, pages 375–6) and duly recognised in the tax codes of all the countries which tax capital gains, it would be very unwise to allow this since it might lead to wide abuse. If capital losses qualify as an off-set only against future capital gains, it is possible that the taxpayer will not have sufficient capital gains during his life-time to absorb them; and I think that in such cases it would be equitable to allow the tax claim on an unabsorbed capital loss to be credited against the liability to estate duty (or gift tax) at death.

loss from one source to be set off against income from other sources has the effect of encouraging the continuance of moribund or unproductive businesses at the expense of the Revenue and ultimately of taxpayers in general. A business which is not moribund will be able to absorb its own losses incurred in a bad trading year against the profits of future years. Hence, even under the conditions described in paragraph 149, where strict equity considerations would justify an off-set against other income, considerations of expediency suggest that it is better to limit the allowance to future income from the same source.

151. From the point of view of administrative efficiency, the main consideration is to prevent the abuse of the provisions through the creation of manufactured losses of various kinds, which take the form either of fictitious transactions between different taxpayers who are differently situated with regard to their overall tax position; or of the acquisition of concerns with accumulated past losses or current losses (in the sense of an excess of tax-free allowances over net receipts) for the purpose of tax avoidance. A general provision whereby a loss from any source can only be carried forward against future income from the same source, while it does not eliminate completely the possibilities of such manipulation—it would still be possible for a man to purchase a business with an accumulated loss and transfer to it profitable business which he would otherwise have carried on through another business—reduces its scope considerably.[1]

152. For all the above reasons, therefore, it appears that the ideal method is to treat income from each source as part of a separate "running account" between the taxpayer and the Revenue, and in consequence to allow a loss from any particular business to be carried foreward against future income from the same business but not to allow it to be set off against income from other sources, either in the same year or in subsequent years. The one respect in which some relaxation of this general rule may be permitted is in allowing a strict trading loss (i.e. an

[1] This loophole could be completely closed if, as suggested below, the provision recently introduced in India on the recommendation of the T.E.C. that the recognition of past losses should be disallowed when a business changes hands, would be made perfectly general (i.e. made applicable to companies as well as individuals, and to unabsorbed capital allowances as well as to accumulated trading losses in the strict sense).

excess of unavoidable current outlays against current receipts) to be off-set against other business income in the same year.

The Current Position in India

153. Under the existing Indian provisions (*a*) a loss from any source may be off-set against any other income of the taxpayer in the same year; (*b*) in the case of a business (but not in the case of other kinds of income) a loss which is not absorbed in the first year can be carried forward indefinitely against future business income from any source, provided the business to which the loss originally related has not changed hands, or identity or has not ceased to exist in the interval; (*c*) the so-called "speculative losses" cannot be off-set against other income and can only be carried forward against future speculative gains.[1]

154. It seems to me that the most urgent requirement would be to make the recently introduced proviso[2] concerning the business remaining in the same hands quite general in its application. The Taxation Enquiry Commission recommended that an analogous provision should be introduced in the case of companies, as well as in the case of individuals by providing that a carry-forward should only be allowed if the shareholders in the year of off-set are substantially the same as those in which the loss had occurred.[3] In addition, the restriction should be applied to unabsorbed capital allowances as well as to trading losses in the narrower sense. At present the income tax law treats unabsorbed capital losses more liberally than unabsorbed trading losses. The off-set of unabsorbed capital allowances is permissible against any income in any future year, whereas unabsorbed trading losses can be set off only against business income. For reasons explained in paragraphs 148 and 149 above, unabsorbed capital

[1] A speculative transaction is defined by Statute as one in which "a contract for purchase and sale of any commodity including stocks and shares is periodically or ultimately settled otherwise than by the actual delivery or transfer of the commodity or scrips", provided that it is not a hedging transaction or one incurred by a dealer or jobber in the ordinary course of his business. The effect of the restriction on speculative losses must obviously be very limited.

[2] Clause (ii) of sub-section (2) of Section 24 of Income Tax Act.

[3] I presume that this recommendation can only be made effective in the case of private companies and not public companies—at least the interpretation of the meaning of "shareholders remaining substantially the same" would be very difficult in the case of any company which has a large number of shareholders none of whom exercises any direct control over the business.

allowances ought to be treated more strictly than trading losses and not more liberally. Even if capital gains are charged to income tax and realised capital losses can be carried forward indefinitely against future capital gains,[1] the allowances for capital expenditure—the normal wear-and-tear allowances or the additional allowance in the form of extra depreciation or development rebate—should only be allowed to be carried forward against future income from the business to which these allowances relate, with the further proviso that off-set will be admissible only if the business in question continued to remain in the same ownership. If a business changes hands unabsorbed capital allowances would automatically be taken into account either in the direct form of balancing charges or allowances on the individual assets or indirectly in the resulting capital loss or gain on the sale-proceeds of the business as a whole. There is a strong case for limiting the offset of losses from any one source against income from any other source (whether in the same year or in the following year) to a trading loss in the restricted sense representing an excess of unavoidable current outlays over current receipts, and to disallow the recognition of a loss for the purpose of any such offset in all those cases where a profit and not a loss would have been shown, if development expenditures of all kinds had been excluded in the calculation of the trading profit.

VIII. COMPANY TAXATION

A. THE PRESENT SITUATION IN INDIA

155. The company taxation provisions of India (perhaps even more than those of other countries) are apt to strike a detached observer as a perfect maze of unnecessary complications, the accretion of years of futile endeavour to reconcile fundamentally contradictory objectives. In support of this statement it is sufficient to draw attention to the following characteristics of this legislation:

[1] With a proviso also for unabsorbed capital losses mentioned in the footnote to paragraph 149 above.

(i) Companies are charged to two different taxes, a refundable tax (income tax) levied at a uniform rate of 4 annas in the rupee, and a non-refundable tax (named super tax or corporation tax)[1] levied at different rates according to varying criteria, such as the nature of the company; the source from which the income is drawn (whether it represents profits of the assessee company, or dividends paid by another; if the latter, according to the kind of activity pursued by it); and according to whether the profits are distributed or retained.[2]

(ii) Companies other than public companies (the so-called Section 23A companies) pay an extra non-refundable tax on undistributed profits (in addition to the basic rate of $2\frac{3}{4}$ annas on total profits) of 4 annas for trading companies and 8 annas in the rupee for investment companies (i) if they distribute less than 60 per cent. of their current disposable income; or (ii) if they distribute less than 100 per cent. of such income, and (a) they are investment companies, or (b) they are trading companies whose accumulated reserves exceed their subscribed capital[3] plus loans, or the total cost of fixed assets, whichever is the greater. By a further clause introduced in the 1955 Finance Act,[4] all these provisions can be waived at the discretion of the Commissioner of Income Tax, if he is satisfied that "having regard to the current requirements of the company's business or such other requirements as may be necessary or advisable for the maintenance and development of that business" the declaration of a smaller dividend is called for. This legislation applies to all companies less than 50 per cent. of whose share capital (or less than 40 per cent. in the case of industrial companies) had been continuously held by the public in the previous year.

(iii) By the provisions of the 1956 Finance Bill, all companies, public or private, pay an extra tax on distributed profits equal to 2 annas in the rupee on that part of the distributed profit

---

[1] The terms "refundable" or "non-refundable" refer to the question whether the individual shareholder is credited or not with the taxes deemed to have been paid out of his dividend.

[2] I am ignoring complicated penalty provisions which are presumably of minor significance, such as the extra tax payable by companies who do not comply with prescribed requirements concerning dividend declarations, etc.

[3] Subscribed capital means paid up capital less the amount of capitalised reserves.

[4] Sub-section (3) Section 23A of Income Tax Act.

which represents more than 6 and less than 10 per cent. of the paid up capital, and at 3 annas in the rupee on distributions in excess of 10 per cent. To prevent avoidance of these provision through the future capitalisation of reserves, a tax of 12·5 per cent. is imposed on bonus issues.

(iv) Dividends received by companies from other companies are exempt from corporation tax, if the paying company is engaged in the pursuit of specific activities laid down in the Industries (Development and Regulation) Act, 1951 (mostly mining, heavy industries, chemicals, and paper). Dividends received by public companies from Indian subsidiary companies are allowed a rebate of $1\frac{1}{2}$ annas from corporation tax.[1]

(v) The profits of newly established industrial undertakings, subject to certain safeguards and certain minimum requirements as to size, are exempt from all taxation up to 6 per cent. of the capital employed for the first five assessment years, if they commenced the manufacture of goods in India after April 1st, 1948 and before March 31st, 1961.

156. The most notable features of the legislation on company taxation are the complex provisions designed to ensure, first, that incorporation is not used as a means of super tax avoidance by the individual taxpayer and, second, that companies retain as much of their profits as possible. Public companies are exempt from the first kind of provisions (though public companies retaining a large proportion of their profits can be equally suitable as vehicles of super tax avoidance as private companies), but private companies will be subject to both kinds of provisions at the same time, so that, in particular cases they may attract penal rates of taxation simultaneously both on account of the distribution and the non-distribution of their profits.

Penalties on Non-Distribution

157. The penal provisions concerning non-distribution by private companies impose, on the face of it, the most undesirable handicaps on industrial growth. To put a virtual limit of 40 per

---

[1] Thus apart from the cases covered in the Industries (Development and Regulation) Act, 1951, inter-company dividends are double taxed for corporation tax in India except that in the case of subsidiaries, the second tax is levied at a reduced rate.

cent. on the amount of current profits that companies can plough back[1] is not only severely discriminatory as between private and public companies (with all the attendant evils of an enhanced concentration of industry in the hands of a few large concerns) but is an extremely severe limitation in itself on the growth of enterprise. It is well known from the history of all capitalist countries that industrialisation depends on the rapid growth and multiplication of undertakings which almost invariably start as private businesses and can only become public companies with quotation on the Stock Exchange, after they attained considerable size.[2] If British or American experience is any guide, successful companies plough back, during the critical period of their expansion not 40, but 90 to 95 per cent. of their disposable profits or even more.[3] It is not always appreciated that the ploughing back of profits is an essential requirement for steady expansion in the case of a private business. It cannot grow through an increase in the share capital through public subscriptions; and its borrowing power is strictly limited to a proportion of the share capital employed in the business.

158. Even the permission to plough back 40 per cent. of current profit without penalty is withdrawn once accumulated reserves exceed the subscribed capital, unless the total amount expended by the company on the purchase of fixed assets is greater than the amount of the accumulated reserves.[4] Thus the

---

[1] I think it is correct to speak of a "virtual limit" in this case, in that the profits in excess of this amount pay a tax of 11 annas in the rupee, or almost 70 per cent. as against the 7 annas (43 per cent.) payable on ploughed-back profits generally.

[2] The Ford Motor Company in the U.S.A. has only become a public company a few months ago and even today it would not satisfy the criterion of a "public company" according to the Indian legislation.

[3] In India, taking all companies (public and private) together, the ratio of ploughed-back profits to net disposable profits after tax was 68 per cent. (i.e. Rs. 66·5 out of Rs. 98 crores) which makes the 40 per cent. limit applicable to all private companies the more absurd.

[4] Proviso (b) of sub-section (1) of Section 23A of the Income Tax Act where these qualifications are introduced, is a peculiarly badly drafted piece of legislation. The intention of the law is clearly to exempt from harsh treatment the ploughed-back profits (though only up to the critical limit of 40 per cent of disposable profits) needed for internal expansion, even though the company has accumulated reserves beyond the amount of capital subscribed. But the actual test applied is the relationship between the accumulated reserves and the total amount invested on fixed assets, and whether this enables a company to accumulate more than twice its subscribed capital or not (and if so, how much more) becomes dependent on a purely irrelevant consideration—i.e. on the ratio of fixed capital to circulating capital (or fixed assets to current assets) used in the business. If the required proportion of current assets is

provisions of Section 23A discriminate against private companies in relation to public companies, both by limiting the maximum rate at which they can grow to a percentage indicated by the formula:

$$\frac{\text{rate of profit earned on capital employed}}{2 \cdot 5}$$

and also by limiting the ultimate size to some multiple of the capital originally subscribed.[1] It is no answer to this to say that, in practice, the effect will not be so serious, either because under another provision new industrial undertakings enjoy a five-year tax holiday on profits up to 6 per cent. on the capital employed (the critical period of growth may well extend to more than five years after the original commencement of the undertaking, and the rate of profit earned may well exceed 6 per cent.), or because under a recent amendment of the law, all these provisions can be waived at the discretion of the Income Tax Commissioner, if he is satisfied that the reasonable needs of expansion require a higher rate of retention of profits. The point is that Revenue officials should not, in fairness, be entrusted with such wide discretionary powers. There is presumption that a Commissioner of Income Tax will be better able to separate the sheep from the goats than the legislature itself. If the law is unable to circumscribe the cases which ought reasonably to come under penal provisions with sufficient precision, there is no reason to

---

twice that of fixed assets, the alternative condition cannot be satisfied irrespective of whether the ploughed-back profits are used for internal expansion or not. If current assets are only one-half of the original cost of fixed assets, the alternative condition will permit the accumulation of reserves up to twice the amount of the original subscribed capital and no more. If the proportion is only one-fifth, the critical limit is five times the capital originally subscribed, and so on. The above examples ignore the possibility of stock-in-trade etc., being partly financed out of borrowed capital, but unless the company can borrow more than the whole of its current assets (so that its net liquid assets are negative) an allowance for this would merely alter the numerical limits and will not affect the principal conclusion—that under the proviso of this sub-section literally interpreted, the ultimate growth of private companies is limited to some multiple of their subscribed capital, the actual multiple depending on the technical relationship between fixed and circulating capital.

[1] The whole idea that there must be some ultimate limit beyond which a private company ought not to be allowed to grow through the accumulation of reserves seems to be throughly misguided. If the provisions of Section 23A had been in force in America in the early part of this century—and if they had been really enforced, which is probably not the case in India—Henry Ford might have been effectively prevented from growing beyond the stage at which he manufactured a 100 cars a year or so.

suppose that a Commissioner would be in a position to do so.[1] And even if the provisions of the new section 23A(3) could be perfectly reasonably administered, the requirement that a company must apply to the Commissioner for the determination of the minimum distribution in each individual case must be productive of considerable uncertainty in the planning of business expansion as well as being unnecessarily vexatious to the taxpayers.

Penalties on Distribution

159. The new provisions imposing penalties on distributions in excess of 6 per cent. of the paid-up capital are wholly incongruous with the Section 23A provisions prescribing minimum distributions. I presume it will be possible to avoid gross inequities by an administrative order which would prescribe that companies liable to the penal rate on their dividend distribution should not at the same time be subjected to an order under Section 23A (or perhaps the other way round). This does not, however, make the incongruity between these two pieces of legislation any the less glaring. The philosophy which on general economic grounds, or in order to limit Stock Exchange gains, wishes to encourage companies to plough back as much of their profits as possible, is not compatible with the philosophy of anti-avoidance provisions which require them to distribute all, or at least the greater part of, their profits.[2]

---

[1] It would be wrong to suppose that an analysis of a company's balance-sheet enables a Commissioner to determine whether there has been an undue with-holding of distribution or not. Assuming that a company satisfied the formal criteria of Section 23A(1)(b) requiring 100 per cent. distribution, all that the Commissioner can do to determine whether the application of Section 23A(3) is justified or not, is to examine whether the balance-sheet discloses an improvement or a deterioration in liquidity (through the growth or reduction of net indebtedness, or an improvement or otherwise in the holdings of cash and other financial assets). It is well known, however, that the growth in fixed assets and in stock-in-trade is not a steadily continuing process, and large fluctuations in the net liquid position are inevitable. It is impossible to separate out an increase in liquidity which is incidental to the normal activities of a business from one which is the consequence of an undue withholding of distributions prompted by the motive of super tax avoidance. (Not to mention the fact that if the holdings of cash and other liquid assets are to be made the test for the application of penal provisions, such holdings—and the profits which gave rise to them—are the more likely to be concealed from the accounts.)

[2] In the U.K., the provisions of the Income Tax Act concerning "closed corporations" (which are similar in intent, though not nearly so rigid or extensive as the Indian provisions) have been in abeyance since the war (except for investment companies), and in 1947 the Chancellor of the Exchequer (Sir Stafford Cripps) gave an assurance to Parliament that the provisions will not be applied so long as the policy of dividend restraint is in force.

160. The provisions introduced in the new budget for a discriminatory tax on dividend distributions are an adaptation of the existing U.K. rules which levy an additional profits tax of 25 per cent. on distributed profits. The Majority of the British Royal Commission recommended that these discriminatory provisions should be abolished forthwith. The Minority pointed out that the important function of a discriminatory tax on dividend distributions is to keep down Stock Exchange values (on account of the consequential modesty in dividend distributions in relation to earnings) and thereby to reduce the rate at which capital gains are being made in the economy.[1] The Minority stated[2] that they "do not disagree with the Majority's view that the artificial encouragement of the retention of profits by companies is not necessarily an economic advantage. Beyond a certain point it does not in itself stimulate the rate of capital formation—as is shown by the fact that in the last few years the net amounts retained by companies have greatly exceeded their financial requirements, both on account of capital expenditure and of investment in working capital. It can be argued also that the system of financing capital expenditure so largely out of the undistributed profits of companies does not ensure the best use of the community's savings. It makes it more difficult for fast-expanding firms to raise funds in the capital market; it strengthens the monopolistic tendencies in the economy; and it encourages wasteful expenditure on behalf of those firms who have more money than they can use and who are yet prevented (by custom and tradition as well as by the instruments of public control) from channelling these funds to their most profitable potential use". But they were opposed to the Majority's recommendation to abolish the differential tax independently of whether capital gains are taxed or not; instead they favoured the abolition as part of the wider reform which included the taxation of capital gains.

161. If it is correct to suggest, as the Minority of the British Royal Commission suggested, that the main function of a dis-

[1] Since the Stock Exchange normally values shares according to the dividend paid and not according to earnings.
[2] Para. 103, page 837, of the Final Report (Cmd. 9474).

criminatory tax on dividends is to serve as a crude and indirect method of taxing capital gains, the question may well be raised whether it would not have been better to re-activate the capital gains provisions which are still on the Statute Book in India rather than to introduce a further highly complicated set of provisions in the field of company taxation.

162. But granting the fact that a discriminatory tax on divi-dend distributions was preferred, on general grounds, to a re-activation of the capital gains tax, it still requires an explanation why these provisions should be introduced in a form that makes them both complicated and difficult to administer, and highly arbitrary in their incidence. The discriminatory tax in the United Kingdom is payable at a flat rate on the dividends de-clared and is not dependent on the ratio of this dividend to the amount of capital. The new Indian provisions operate so as to penalise the company which earns a high rate of profit and in consequence distributes a relatively high rate of dividend. Such provisions are not called for by any principle of equity (if a man makes a lot of money because he is successful in business, this should be reflected in his higher liability on account of personal taxation; it does not call for some variant of an excess profits tax) and are very ill-advised from the point of view of their general economic effects.

163. There is finally, a further criticism to be made in connec-tion with these particular provisions. Assuming that the Govern-ment on general grounds preferred a discriminatory tax on dividends to a straight-forward tax on capital gains and that they preferred a graduated tax which varied with the percentage of the capital paid (and presumably earned) to one which depended solely on the amount of the dividend payment, there is still the question which is the most reasonable measure of capital that should serve as a standard for the exemption and graduation of the dividend tax. There are, in principle, three such measures to choose from:

    (i) subscribed capital;

    (ii) paid-up capital (subscribed capital plus capitalised re-serves), and

    (iii) capital employed (paid-up capital plus reserves).

Of these three, the real choice is between (i) and (iii). There are reasons for preferring (i), since this measures the amount of capital which the owners have originally put into the business. Equally there are reasons for preferring (iii), since this measures the amount of the shareholders' capital which is effectively employed in the business; and if the current shareholders are not by and large the same persons as the original shareholders, the capital employed is a less discriminatory measure as between different shareholders than subscribed capital. The choice of paid-up capital as the standard (together with the new tax imposed on future bonus issues) discriminates against companies which (for the sake of good personnel relations or on other grounds) refrained from making bonus issues in the past, and in favour of companies which have capitalised a considerable part of their accumulated reserves. The choice of this standard is all the more incongruous within the framework of the Indian tax system since the standard for some of the penalty provisions of Section 23A is not paid-up capital, but subscribed capital.

164. The 12·5 per cent. tax on bonus issues is another consequence of the choice of paid-up capital (rather than capital employed, or subscribed capital) as the standard; and it was introduced in the current budget more as a measure to prevent avoidance of the new dividend tax than as a new tax justified on its own grounds. A tax on bonus issues has been urged from time to time (generally from trade union quarters), on the ground that a bonus issue is the method by which shareholders obtain profits on their holdings without paying tax on it. On closer examination, however, this claim is shown to be unfounded. It is true that shareholders may, and to some extent normally do, enjoy an appreciation in the value of their holdings resulting from bonus issues. The extent of this appreciation depends, however, on the consequential increase in aggregate dividend payments, and not on the amount of the bonus issue itself. There is no necessary connection between bonus issues and the increase in total dividend disbursements; though it is often suggested that companies prefer to keep the nominal rate of the dividend low, so as to give the appearance that the dividends paid to the shareholders are not excessive, and for that reason

the bonus issue is a means of increasing dividend payments. This may or may not be true of the majority of cases; but whether it is true or not, it should be evident that (*a*) the taxable capacity created by a bonus issue depends on the consequential appreciation in the market valuation of the company, and is not measured by the bonus issue itself; (*b*) this consequential appreciation cannot, in practice, be separated off from other factors affecting the market valuation of shares; and (*c*) there is no reason for treating capital appreciation resulting from bonus issues any differently than capital appreciation which is not due to this cause. Hence, the only equitable solution of the problem is a general tax on capital gains which automatically sweeps up gains created by bonus issues, along with all other gains. There is no case in equity for a special tax on bonus issues.[1]

165. Taking into account the number of different provisions affecting the rate of company taxation and the numerous qualifications attaching to each, it is quite impossible to assess the effect of the whole body of provisions on the incentives to invest, and on the growth of efficiency and output in the private sector. There can be little doubt, however, that the very multiplicity and complexity of these provisions is bound to act as a serious drag on the general efficiency of tax administration. When a very heavy burden is laid on Income Tax Officers merely in the interpretation of Statutes, the time and energy which they can devote to the task of checking the accuracy of returns must be seriously curtailed. In addition, the manner in which a succession of new provisions concerning company taxation have been introduced in the budgets of recent years must be productive of considerable uncertainty among investors and businessmen as to the true future return they can expect from the launching of new ventures. I feel sure that the real disadvantages of the present system lie as much in the general uncertainty which they create as in the inequities and burdens imposed.

---

[1] The Taxation Enquiry Commission in India and the Majority and Minority of the British Royal Commission have all rejected the idea of a tax on bonus issues.

B. SUGGESTIONS FOR REFORM

166. If our suggestions concerning the reform of personal taxation were adopted, the whole system of company taxation could be drastically simplified.

(i) In the first place, the taxation of capital gains and the substitution of an expenditure tax for the higher ranges of super tax makes the whole body of legislation under Section 23A superfluous. The justification for this legislation is that individuals can use incorporation as a means of avoiding the tax which ought in justice be levied on them. However, if the maximum rate of income tax on personal incomes were limited to 7 annas, the maximum amount of tax that can be avoided through an undue accumulation of reserves will be the difference between 7 annas and the effective marginal rate of company taxation. If the rate of company taxation is also 7 annas in the rupee (as is broadly the case at present) no income tax can be avoided in this manner. Nor can undue with-holding of distribution be used as a means of expenditure tax avoidance, provided only that the owner of the company is debited with any expenditure which the company incurs on his behalf or for his benefit as was suggested in paragraph 70 (Section IV) above. But even if the tax levied on companies were to be at a lower rate than the marginal rate of income tax levied on individuals, the difference no longer gives scope for tax avoidance once capital gains are charged to tax. All it means is that when a taxpayer uses incorporation for the purpose of reducing his personal income, a part of his immediate tax liability is postponed at a cost of incurring an additional liability later—either on account of the capital gain realised on the sale of the shares of the company or on account of the additional income tax that becomes payable on any future distribution of reserves.

(ii) In the second place, owing to the taxation of capital gains and the introduction of an expenditure tax, the case for a discriminatory differential tax on dividend distributions also disappears. If the original justification of the tax was that it operated as a crude indirect tax on capital gains (by reducing the rate at which capital gains are being made), the direct taxation of capital gains on the shareholders obviates the need for an indirect method of taxing the same thing. If the justification of the tax is sought as a means of reducing personal spending through keeping down dividends, the progressive expenditure tax is an infinitely more effective tool for the purpose. It is true that this tax will only affect the upper spending classes, but much the greatest part of the ordinary share capital of public companies (and it is only the dividends paid by public companies which come into question here) is owned (apart from institutional investors, like insurance companies) by the top income and property groups. Finally, if the justification is to be sought in a stimulation of capital investment brought about through higher company savings, the higher dividend distribution will not reduce the funds available for company investment, if the individual owners of the shares are effectively discouraged by the spendings tax from increasing their personal spending as a result of higher dividend distributions. Indeed, it can be argued that to allow companies to distribute their surplus funds to their shareholders will lead to a more efficient use of these funds (through reinvestment in different companies) than if they were retained by the companies earning them.

167. Assuming that these arguments are correct, we must still consider the question which is the most appropriate form of company taxation and, indeed on what principles this question is to be decided. The three principal questions that we need to discuss in this connection are as follows:

(1) Should there be any inherent relation between personal taxation and company taxation, or is it better to regard the taxes levied on companies as something entirely distinct from the taxation of individuals?

(2) Assuming that the answer to the latter part of the question is in the affirmative, what is the appropriate level of company taxation corresponding to any given level of personal taxation, having regard to the fact that company savings—or rather the capital appreciation resulting from company savings—are taxed also in the hands of the individual shareholders through a tax on realised capital gains?

(3) Is there a case for differentiation or graduation in the rates of company taxation at all, or should all company profits be charged at the uniform rate; and if so, should that rate be levied on the whole profit or only on the undistributed part of the profits?

168. In order to be able to answer these questions we must first of all discuss the role of company taxation within the original framework of the income tax system as developed in England (and adopted in India), and how far this role has been modified through the introduction of progressive income taxation and the proposed taxation of capital gains.

169. The original conception of income tax (a) ignored capital gains and losses; and (b) charged all income at a uniform rate. Under these two conditions, it was natural to tax the company on the whole of the profits at the same rate as the tax on individual income and to credit the tax paid by the company against the shareholder's individual liability on his dividend. When income tax became a progressive tax after 1911, the simple conception (which regarded company profits as part of the individual shareholders' income and deemed it to be taxed at the same rate as if it had been the personal income of the owners) was no longer appropriate. Whereas the shareholders' dividend income was taxed at varying rates depending on their total income (including dividend received), the pool of the undistributed profits of companies could only be taxed at a uniform rate. Hence, a distinction was introduced between income tax and a personal super tax; companies as such were charged to income tax at the maximum rate and individuals became liable to super tax on that part of their company income only which was distributed as dividend.[1] The profits tax introduced in the U.K. and the corresponding corporation tax in India after the last war are often regarded as a collective substitute for the individual super tax which the company's undistributed income would have borne in the hands of the owners had it been distributed as dividend.

170. However, under a system of progressive taxation it is not

---

[1] In pre-1914 days, when the exemption limit to super tax was very high in real terms, the charging of company income at the maximum income tax rate (or "standard" rate) on the whole of the income was probably not so different from the rate at which the profits would have borne tax in the aggregate, had they been distributed as dividends.

F

really possible to maintain that charging the pool of undistributed profits at a uniform rate comes to the same thing as taxing
it individually in the hands of the particular shareholders, even
if the effective rate on the one were the same as the average
rate on the other. For this reason the idea is sometimes put
forward that instead of taxing company profits it would be
better to compel companies to issue bonus shares to the full
equivalent value of the amount of profits retained each year and
to treat these bonus shares as part of the current income of the
shareholders for tax purposes. This view, however, ignores the
fact that a bonus share does not yield the same benefit to the shareholder as a cash dividend. As was argued in paragraph 164 above,
the benefit of a bonus issue to the shareholders depends upon the
resulting capital gain and this will be a variable fraction (varying
between 0 and 100 per cent.) of the nominal amount of the bonus
issue. An individual shareholder in the case of a public company
has very little say in determining how much of the profits should
be distributed or retained. No doubt all undistributed profits
benefit the shareholder in the long run but the benefit accrues
in the form of an appreciation in the value of shares which
occurs as and when, in consequence of the enhanced earning
power, dividend distributions increase. If each shareholder were
solemnly wedded to his shares, the contention that the undistributed profit is just another part of the income of the shareholders might be justified. But shareholders in public companies
come and go and the capital gain or loss which they realise on
any particular holding need have no relation whatever to the
accumulation of company reserves during the period of any
particular share-ownership.

171. The benefit which shareholders derive from the accumulation of company reserves can only be equitably taxed by taxing
the capital gains of individual shareholders, and not by taxing
the company savings as such. It follows, therefore, that under a
system of progressive taxation and assuming that individuals
are taxed on their capital gains as well as on their dividend income, the old conception which regarded the tax levied on
companies as part of the same income tax which is levied on
individuals can no longer be applied. It is better to recognise

this openly and to abolish the existing remnants of the old system by virtue of which companies are now charged to a refundable income tax as well as to a non-refunable corporation tax.

172. There is, therefore, everything to be said for a formal separation of personal and company taxation, which would at once simplify considerably the whole tax structure and make it possible to vary personal taxes and company taxes entirely independently of each other. This is already the case in a large number of countries (such as the U.S.A., the Scandinavian countries, etc.) and is indeed partly the case also in the U.K., and in India, but the old conception still lingers on. I feel the time has come both in Britain and in India for abandoning the idea altogether that companies should be charged the same income tax as individuals. Companies as such ought not to be charged to income tax at all (though they may be asked to deduct income tax at the maximum rate on all dividends, interest, etc., paid out as part of the normal system of collection at source) but should be charged to a single company tax, drawn up on principles which are appropriate to company taxation and which need not be identical either in structure or in weight with the personal income tax levied on individuals.[1] This is undoubtedly the right procedure; though in considering what is the right amount of taxation which companies should be asked to carry, the fact that income tax is imposed on any particularised benefit derived by a shareholder from his company must of course be borne in mind.

173. Indeed, the first question that requires to be answered is whether, if all realised capital gains are charged to income tax in the hands of the individuals, there is any justification left for levying a tax on the undistributed income of companies, in view of the fact that the distributed income is liable to income tax in the hands of the shareholder. Does the taxation both of company savings and of the appreciation resulting from company savings not imply taxing the same thing twice?

174. There are two answers to this argument. One is that whereas a tax on income taxes the savings made out of that income

[1] In India the adoption of this reform may require some consequential adjustment in the share-out of joint taxes between the Centre and States to compensate for the loss of revenue to the States due to the abolition of income tax on undistributed company profits.

simultaneously with the emergence of the savings, a tax on capital appreciation is an indirect tax on company savings paid with considerable delay—a delay caused partly by the time-lag between an increase in company reserves and the consequential increase in earnings and the capital appreciation resulting from it, and partly by the fact that realised capital gains lag behind by a fair number of years the rate of accrual of capital gains.[1] Hence if company savings were only taxed in the form of a tax on realised capital gains, whereas other savings were taxed simultaneously with income, the effective rate on company savings would be considerably less than on non-company savings.[2]

175. Another argument for a tax on the undistributed income of companies, additional to the one just mentioned, resides in the fact that company savings which are actually invested in fixed assets do get a partial exemption in the form of the allowances for capital expenditure.[3] The extent of this exemption is measured by the difference in the discounted value of the depreciation allowances granted on the capital expenditures of the year and the discounted value of the total capital loss realised (relative to the initial cost) when the assets are sold for scrap at the end of their useful life.[4] If the taxes on company

---

[1] Cf. para. 66 (Section III) above.

[2] Assuming a rate of discount of 5 per cent. per annum, the present value of Rs. 100 paid in tax ten years hence will be Rs. 63 while the present value of Rs. 100 paid 20 years hence will be Rs. 38. Assuming that personal income and capital gains are charged at the marginal rate of 45 per cent. and assuming that realised capital gains show an average time lag of 20 years as compared with the company savings which give rise to them, it would require a tax of 28 per cent. on company savings to equalise the burden of taxation on company savings and non-company savings.

[3] It is true, of course, that capital allowances are given on all expenditure on certain kinds of assets, irrespective of whether that expenditure is undertaken by companies or individuals. However, the amount of such capital expenditure is very much greater in relation to company income than in relation to non-company income.

[4] Thus, as shown in Table 3 (Section VII) above, the discounted value of basic depreciation allowances for machinery and plant carrying an annual rate of 10 per cent., and at 5 per cent. interest, is 67 per cent. The discounted value of the capital loss—assuming its scrap value at the end of 22 years to be 10 per cent.—is 34 per cent. This implies that if the capital expenditure for the year equals the company savings for the year, 33 per cent. of these savings are in effect exempted from tax. With the present additional allowances, as shown in Table 3, the discounted value (assuming single shift operation) comes to 95 per cent.; and the extent of effective tax remission therefore to 61 per cent. of capital expenditure. Assuming that the annual capital expenditure of companies amounts to two-thirds of company savings, the effective tax remission for the year amounts at present to around 40 per cent. of company savings. This justifies a further addition to the rate of company taxation by 66⅔ per cent. (i.e. by $\frac{100}{100-40} - 1$).

savings were abolished the allowances for capital expenditure would of course have to be abolished too; and the relief to the individual shareholder would be confined to the capital losses (or the lower capital gains) realised when either the business as a whole is sold, or when individual shares are sold. From the general economic point of view it is preferable to tax company savings and relieve this tax by subsidies on capital expenditure than to abstain from doing either. For the tax-cum-subsidy effectively re-distributes the income from companies whose savings are large relatively to their investments to companies whose investments are large relatively to their savings, and must, on balance increase the propensity to invest in the economy.[1]

176. It follows, therefore, that while in the absence of capital allowances and judging the matter on equity considerations alone, the effective rate of taxation on the undistributed profits of companies ought to be distinctly lower than the (average) marginal rate of income taxation on individuals, this is no longer necessarily the case when, for reasons of economic expediency, it is thought desirable to grant capital allowances— whether they are confined to annual allowances corresponding to the normal working lives of the various assets, or whether they comprise also accelerated allowances and straightforward subsidies in the form of development rebates. The higher the discounted value of the capital allowances granted in any or all these forms, the greater is the effective rate of taxation on company savings that is justified. Thus if the maximum rate of tax on individual income were to be put at 7 annas in the rupee (or, with surcharge, around 45 per cent.) the appropriate effective rate of taxation on the undistributed profits of companies works out at $7\frac{1}{2}$ annas in the rupee (or 46·5 per cent.) on the assumption that the present level of capital allowances is maintained; and to 36 per cent. or $5\frac{1}{4}$ annas in the rupee if the capital allowances were reduced in accordance with the suggestions made in paragraph

---

[1] It is sometimes argued that equity considerations justify an additional tax on company profits on account of the benefits which the owners of the company derive from the limited liability conferred on them through incorporation. On this view there is a case for a separate company tax as a kind of "franchise tax" over and above the income tax to which the owners would have been liable had the same profits been earned as individual income.

144 (Section VII) above;[1] and at appropriately lower rates (mentioned below) if the tax is expressed as a percentage of the whole profit.

177. There can be little doubt that irrespective of whether the company tax is levied by reference to the whole profit of companies or only the undistributed part of the profit, it ought to be charged at a unifrom rate independently of the total amount of profit assessed of a company.[2] The considerations which require a rich individual to be taxed at a higher rate than an individual of more moderate means do not apply to comparisons between large and small corporations.

178. This still leaves the question open, however, whether the tax should be levied on the whole of profits or on the undistributed part of the profits. Looking at the matter again from an equity point of view alone, there can be no doubt that the ideal system is one which treats dividend distributions in the same manner as interest charges and other expenses for the purpose of assessing profits to company tax, i.e. one which levies the tax on company savings rather than on the whole company income. Since distributed profits are charged to income tax, it is only the savings of companies which justify a tax levied on corporations as such.[3]

179. From an administrative point of view it may not be more difficult to levy a tax on undistributed profits (on profits less dividend distributions) than a tax on the whole profit.[4] But here again, the problem is not one that ought to be considered on equity considerations alone and without regard to economic expediency. It is perfectly possible, of course, to collect the same total revenue from companies irrespective of whether the tax is

---

[1] These estimates are based on the assumptions made and the methods of calculation employed in the notes to paragraphs 174 and 175 above.

[2] This is in fact the case today except that public companies earning Rs. 25,000 or less are exempted from the corporation tax. In case the present system of tax on companies is replaced by a single uniform company tax, I do not feel that there is any justification for maintaining this element of graduation in the case of public companies.

[3] Unless the equity argument for company taxation is to be based on the benefits derived from limited liability, i.e. on the "franchise tax" view referred to in a note to paragraph 175 above.

[4] If in any particular year the dividends distributed exceed the amount earned in that year, the difference can be treated as a "loss" which can be carried forward against future liability to company tax. But all such loss claims lapse on liquidation of the company.

levied on the whole income or only on the undistributed part of the income. Thus at present (on the basis of assessments in the year 1954–55) the average effective rate of tax on company profits is 42·74 per cent., or almost 7 annas in the rupee.[1] Since 32 per cent. of the consolidated disposable profit after tax was paid out to individuals as dividends, the same revenue levied on undistributed profits only would mean an effective tax of 52·34 per cent. or 8⅓ annas in the rupee.

180. Since the proposed company tax is a non-refundable tax, the whole of the tax would, of course, have been paid out of company savings quite irrespective of whether it was levied on the whole profit or on the undistributed part of the profit.[2] But the marginal rate of taxation (as distinct from the average or effective rate) and the distribution of the burden of the tax as between companies would have been quite different in the two cases. Under a system which levies the tax on the whole profit, companies which distribute a small proportion of their earnings are deprived of a smaller part of their savings through taxation than companies which distribute a large proportion of their profits. Since the expanding companies are likely to plough back a larger part of their earnings than companies which are not expanding, the system which levies taxes on the whole profit treats expanding companies relatively more leniently and stagnant companies relatively more severely than a system which charges tax on the undistributed profit only. Since, as explained in paragraph 157 above, the rate of increase of reserves is a critical factor in the rate of expansion of growing companies, the alternative of imposing the charge on the whole profit is undoubtedly preferable from the point of view of the social interest, even though it may be regarded as inferior when judged on strict equity considerations alone.[3]

---

[1] Cf. Annex to this Chapter for an explanation of these and the following estimates.

[2] Thus the average effective rate of tax on company savings in 1954–55 appears to have been 52·34 per cent. whilst the marginal rate was only 42·76 per cent.—the difference between the marginal and the average rate being accounted for by the fact that the company pays corporation tax on that part of the profit which is distributed as dividend; and which thus increases the average or effective rate on the remainder of its income.

[3] I think there is no case, however, for the existing practice of the double-taxation of inter-company dividends to corporation tax (i.e. for including dividends received

181. As was explained above, the appropriate rate of tax on the present level of capital allowances is $7\frac{1}{2}$ annas in the rupee on the undistributed income of companies.[1] In terms of a tax levied on the whole profit of companies, the equivalent rate (as shown by the computations in the Annex) works out at 38 per cent. or 6 annas in the rupee. This seems to me the rate of company taxation that is ultimately appropriate in relation to the rates of income tax and capital gains tax proposed earlier in this Report. Its immediate adoption, however, would involve a loss of Rs. 8·5 crores of revenue as compared with the taxation in force in 1955–56 (and rather more in relation to the taxation proposed for 1956–57) and, since the revenue from the newly imposed capital gains tax will have a fairly long gestation period, I do not feel that it would be either inequitable or particularly inexpedient to maintain the level of company taxation at the rate of 7 annas in the rupee until such time as the revenue collected from the tax on capital gains becomes substantial.[2]

182. It seems to me, therefore, that in place of all the present taxes on company income a single uniform tax of 7 annas in the rupee should be levied on the whole income of companies, assuming the continuance of the current depreciation allowances and the development rebates; or 6 annas in the rupee, if capital allowances were rationalised on the lines recommended in Section VII. Capital gains made by companies should be subject to this tax. The whole of this tax should be non-refundable; but income tax at the rate of 7 annas in the rupee should be deducted from all dividends, etc., paid out and credited to the account of the recipient. Dividend, received by companies should not be treated as part of a company's income for purposes of company tax.

---

from resident companies in the assessable income of other resident companies). The income tax deducted on all dividends paid out is, of course, refundable to a company in the same way as to any other non-liable person.

[1] On the capital allowances recommended in para. 144 (Section VII) above, it is $5\frac{1}{4}$ annas in the rupee.

[2] As shown in the Annex to this Chapter, the effective taxation falling on companies as shown by the assessments of 1954–55, works out at 7 annas in the rupee on the whole income of companies. This is an appreciably higher rate than what could be expected on the basis of the nominal rates in force, and must (presumably) be due to the application of higher rates under various penalty clauses and the partial double-taxation of inter-company dividends for corporation tax. (Our method of calculation of the yield of the proposed rates assumes that dividends received by companies from other companies are not charged to company tax in the hands of the recipient company.)

ANNEX

ESTIMATE OF THE YIELD OF COMPANY TAXATION

1. In 1954–55 the total assessed income of companies in India amounted to Rs. 197.5 crores. Of this sum, Rs. 58 crores were paid out in dividends; and of the dividend payments Rs. 26·75 crores were paid to other companies and Rs. 31·26 crores to individuals.[1]

2. The consolidated income of all companies (total assessed income less dividends received from other companies) thus amounted to Rs. 170·8 crores. The tax rates in force in that year were 3 annas in the rupee of income tax on the undistributed income of companies and a super tax (calculated at a normal rate) of $2\frac{3}{4}$ annas in the rupee on the *whole* income of the company. Had these rates represented the average effective rates, the yield of company taxation would have amounted to Rs. 26·2 crores in income tax (i.e. 3 annas in the rupee on the total undistributed income of Rs. 139·5 crores), a surcharge of Rs. 1.3 crores and a super tax of Rs. 29·3 crores ($2\frac{3}{4}$ annas in the rupee on the total consolidated income of Rs. 170·8 crores). In addition, it may be assumed that inter-company dividends bore, on the average, $1\frac{1}{2}$ annas super tax charge which yields another Rs. $2\frac{1}{2}$ crores, giving a total computed revenue of Rs. 59·3 crores.

3. As against that the actual yield of company taxation, according to C.B.R. statistics was Rs. 73·0 crores, made up of Rs. 32·6 crores income tax,[2] Rs. 2·2 crores surcharge, and Rs. 37·8 crores super tax.

4. The discrepancy of Rs. 6·5 crores with regard to income tax implies that the effective charge was $3\frac{3}{4}$ annas in the rupee and not 3 annas. This might be explained by the fact that a great deal of the assessments of the year 1954–55 related to earlier years when the rate of income tax payable was 5 annas in the rupee

---

[1] The dividend figures are based on individual assessments and may not provide a true comparison as they relate to an earlier year.

[2] This figure was reached by deducting from the gross income tax assessment of Rs. 46·8 crores a sum of Rs. 14·2 crores with respect to the income tax deducted at source on dividends.

and not 3 annas. The discrepancy of Rs. 6 crores with regard to super tax is not so easily explained however; and it can only reflect the combined result of the various penalty provisions imposed by the legislation.

5. Thus the actual yield of the taxes payable by companies in the year 1954–55 being Rs. 73 crores, the effective rate of company taxation works out at 7 annas in the rupee (as against the nominal rate of $5\frac{3}{4}$ annas), and this has been taken as the basis of the calculations given in the text.

IX. THE PROBLEM OF TAX EVASION

A. THE SCOPE OF THE PROBLEM

183. Everyone is agreed that apart from manipulations of various kinds which are broadly classed under the term "tax avoidance" there is considerable amount of evasion in India due to fraudulent concealment of income secured through false entries in the account books and the accounts. It is fairly generally agreed also that such practices have become more widespread since the last war. The important question is how much income is concealed in this manner in relation to the income which is assessed to tax. Conversations with individual business men, accountants, and revenue officials reveal guesses which range from 10–20 per cent. of assessed income at the minimum to 200–300 per cent. at the maximum.

184. We have made an estimate of the possible order of magnitude of evasion through a comparison of national income estimates with income tax assessments. The method involved first, an estimate of the distribution of the national income between wages and salaries, income of the self-employed and income derived from property in the form of profits, interest and rent according to each sector,[1] and second, making certain assumptions concerning the total of incomes excluding salaries which accrues to persons above the exemption limit. The figures shown

[1] I am indebted for the estimates on the distribution of the national income to Shri Mani Mukerji of the National Income Unit of the Central Statistical Organisation.

in Table 4 are very tentative and must be interpreted with great caution. The percentages assessed in column 7 in particular are based on very slender foundations. Nevertheless, I think an analysis of the resulting differences in the various sectors between the computed figures of assessable incomes and the actual figures of assessed income provides some indication of the order of magnitude of evasion. A defect of the method is that the national income estimates are not always derived from sources that are independent of income tax assessments. Thus in the sector of banking and insurance, for example, the national income estimates are based entirely on the published balance-sheets of companies, and since these are also the basis of income tax assessments, the correspondence between two figures is without significance. In the case of mining and factory establishments, the national income estimates are based on Census of Manufacturers and National Sample Survey data which again are not wholly independent sources, since businesses which conceal profits in the accounts which they submit to the income tax officers (and in the books which are open to inspection by I.T.O.s) will make the same adjustments (through an under-statement of receipts or an over-statement of outlays) in the forms which they fill up for purposes of the Census or the National Sample Survey. I understand, however, that the national income estimates make a certain allowance for this, in that a correction has been made for the over-statement of input prices in the National Sample Survey data.[1] On this evidence the disclosed income of factory establishments and mining is of the order of 50 per cent. of the total assessable income.

185. In comparison with factory establishments and mining (the so-called "organised sector" of the economy), the degree of under-assessment in commerce and distribution appears to be relatively moderate: assessed incomes appear to be over 60 per cent. of assessable incomes. This may merely reflect, however, the inadequacy of the national income estimates which are based on very slender material and the consequential under-estimation

---

[1] The broad effect of these corrections in the case of factory establishments is to raise both the value of the output and the share of non-wage and salary incomes by about Rs. 100 crores.

Table 4

ESTIMATED DISTRIBUTION OF INCOMES & TAX ASSESSMENTS IN THE INDIAN UNION FOR 1953-54 (*Rs. in crores*)

Sectors	Contribution to net domestic product at factor cost	Wages and salaries	Income of self-employed persons	Profit, interest, rent, etc.	Total non-salary income (4 plus 5)	Assumed proportion of non-salary income above exemption limit %	Estimated non-salary income above the exemption limit (6×7)	Non-salary income assessed to tax
1	2	3	4	5	6	7	8	9
I.								
1. Mining	100	30	—	70	70	95	66	26
2. Factory establishments	690	335	—	355	355	100	355	190
3. Small enterprises	950	270	525	155	680	0	—	—
Sub-Total	1,740	635	525	580	1,105		421	216
II.								
4. Railways & Communications	240	195	—	45	45	—	—	—
5. Banks & Insurance	75	55	—	20	20	100	20	20
6. Retail trade	1,025	100	800	125	925	20	185	87
7. Other trade	345	45	125	175	300	80	240	179
8. Transport	155	100	45	10	55	60	33	19
Sub-Total	1,840	495	970	375	1,345		478	305
III.								
9. Professions	515	300	175	40	215	50	107	24
10. Government Service	490	490	—	—	—	—	—	—
11. Domestic Service	135	135	—	—	—	—	—	—
12. House Property:—								
(i) Money	180	—	—	180	180	50	90	27
(ii) Imputed	260	—	—	260	260	20	52	—
Sub-Total	1,580	925	175	480	655		249	51
Total	5,160	2,055	1,670	1,435	3,105		1,148	572
IV. Agriculture and allied pursuits	5,305	835	2,885	1,585	4,470	7·5	335	(50)*
Grand Total	10,465	2,890	4,555	3,020	7,575		1,376	(622)

*Estimated.

Source: As indicated in the text.

of the contributions of retail and other trade.[1] In professions and income from house property, on the other hand, the ratio of the assessable to assessed incomes appears as much as 4.1. This may not seem unreasonable in the case of professions; but the assumed proportion of assessable income is based on such broad guesses that not much significance attaches to this result.

186. The total of assessable incomes in all sectors outside agriculture comes out at almost exactly twice the assessed income. No significance attaches to this precise figure, but it receives some confirmation from the fact that in the only sector in which the figures of income distribution are based on relatively solid material—in mining and factory industry, and where almost the whole of the activity is carried on by companies and hence income is not subject to an exemption limit—the ratio is also 2:1. If these figures are anywhere near the truth, the amount of income tax lost through tax evasion is more of the order of Rs. 200-300 crores[2] than the Rs. 20-30 crores which is sometimes quoted in this connection.[3]

187. As regards agriculture, the First Report on Land Holdings of the National Sample Survey suggests that 13 per cent. of the cultivable land is owned by persons whose individual holding is over 30 acres in area; and on the average the ownership of 30 acres or more should yield an income to the owner, which is in excess of the agricultural-income-tax exemption limit of Rs. 3,000. However, only 12 of the States levy an agricultural income tax and as these States account for over one-half of the total output, it is reasonable to assume that assessable agricultural incomes come to around $7\frac{1}{2}$ per cent. of non-wage incomes in agriculture. The total of agricultural incomes actually assessed by the 12 States is not known. It can be estimated, however, from the aggregate tax yield of Rs. 3.3 crores. On the experience of Uttar Pradesh, the average rate of tax on assessed agricultural incomes amounted to 6.7 per cent. On this basis the total amount of income assessed to agricultural income tax may be put at Rs. 50 crores, whilst the amount of assessable incomes, on the

---

[1] As was mentioned earlier, this appears to be the case also in banking and insurance.
[2] Since the average rate of tax on the additional incomes is at least 40 per cent., and much higher than the average rate on non-evaded income.
[3] Cf. speeches of the Minister of Finance in the 1956–57 budget debate.

assumptions made, is around six times this sum. So little is known, however, of agricultural income and property distribution of India, that no quantitative "estimate" can be anything but the wildest guess. But it certainly is not reasonable that the total yield of agricultural income tax—with an exemption limit of only Rs. 3,000—should amount to somewhat over Rs. 3 crores in an area accounting for over one half of the agricultural output of the country, valued at Rs. 5,000 crores.[1]

B. POSSIBLE REMEDIES

188. Our proposals concerning personal taxation should by themselves tend to reduce the extent of the evasion of business profits for two separate reasons: (1) smaller incentives; (2) greater obstacles.

189. As regards (1), the replacement of a single personal tax, charged at steeply progressive rates and mounting to over 90 per cent. of marginal income, by a number of different taxes with lower top marginal rates is bound to reduce the incentive to evade considerably. The extent to which people are willing to go—on keeping double sets of books, engaging the services of straw men and dummies etc.—in order to evade tax is much less when 45 per cent. of the gains made from any particular transaction can be saved by evasion than when nine-tenths of the amount can be so saved. The maximum rate proposed for the annual tax on net wealth is $1\frac{1}{2}$ per cent. per annum on estates of over Rs. 15 lakhs; the temptation to conceal property in order to save $1\frac{1}{2}$ per cent. per annum of the amount concealed must be very small. It is often forgotten that all such concealments involve a cost. Given an effective system for registering property which ensures the disclosure of the beneficial owner, as outlined in Section VI, the only possible method of concealing property is by hoarding cash, or gold, or jewellery. (In fact, to a considerable extent this is the case already—a man cannot be sure of "not being found out" unless he conceals his gains in hoards of cash or precious metals.)

[1] The land revenue is not an income tax, nor is the payment of land revenue credited against agricultural income tax liability. The land revenue is an expense to be set off against agricultural income, but since it only accounts at present for just 1 per cent. (on the average) of net agricultural income per acre, it has no significant effect on the amount of agricultural incomes liable to income tax.

Hoarding and the Wealth Tax

190. The cost of such hoarding is the annual income sacrificed —i.e., the income that would have been obtained if the capital had been invested productively. This should include the expected capital appreciation as well as the money return on capital productively employed and can, therefore, hardly be put at less than 5–6 per cent.; or, say, 3 per cent., after taking into consideration the consequential income tax payable on the income. There can be no incentive to conceal property in order to save at the maximum $1\frac{1}{2}$ per cent. per annum (in the bulk of cases only at $\frac{1}{2}$ to 1 per cent. per annum) at the cost of sacrificing an annual return of 3 per cent.[1] The case is different when the motive of hoarding is to evade income tax, since in that case a very large part of the hoarded money (amounting to nine tenths of the total under the present system and to 45 per cent. under my proposed system) might be "saved" as a result of the hoarding which, of course, makes it profitable to sacrifice the annual income for the sake of concealing the property for a large number of years.[2]

---

[1] In addition, the concealment of property by hoarding cash, gold or ornaments is always associated with some risk which increases the cost beyond the amount of income sacrificed:—
  (i) In the case of cash, the risk is that the Government might call in the existing note issue and replace it with a new issue (as happened in 1946), in which case the cash hoarding will have to be disclosed; or failing disclosure, it will become valueless, or else can only be sold to other persons for purposes of encashment with difficulty or at a considerable discount.
  (ii) In the case of gold, assuming there is a free gold market, the risk is a fall in the price of gold which should check the temptation to hoard as soon as the price of gold rises sufficiently out of line with the purchasing power of currency. (This happened in France in the post-war years, when as the result of hoarding of gold, the price of gold sovereigns, etc., had risen to a level at which they were quite out of line with the value of the currency. Subsequently, there was a steady fall in the price of gold over a period of years so that those who hoarded gold as an inflation hedge or in order to conceal wealth, lost considerably in value as well as in income forgone.)
  (iii) In the case of jewellery or ornaments, there is an additional cost in the form of a margin between buying and selling prices, since these objects cannot normally be obtained at the same price at which they can be sold.
[2] When concealed gains are hoarded the expectation is, I presume, that after a certain number of years the money thus concealed can safely be invested in income-yielding property without attracting the suspicion of the Income Tax Officers. As mentioned in Section VI, paragraph 106, in the absence of an annual wealth statement, it must often be difficult for an I.T.O. to rebut the plea that the new money introduced into the business comes from legitimate sources (such as the jewellery or dowry of the wife, etc.,) and not out of hoardings of concealed gains made in an earlier year.

Hoarding and the Expenditure Tax

191. There is no reason to assume, therefore, that an annual tax on property would provide an added incentive to the accumulation of secret hoards of cash and precious metals, whilst the reduction in the marginal rate of income tax would undoubtedly diminish existing incentives. It is different with the expenditure tax where the yield to the taxpayer of concealing particular items of expenditure might be very substantial. An expenditure tax might thus provide an incentive for hoarding out of secret gains in order to enable the taxpayer to spend these gains on a later occasion without revealing the consequential depletion of assets in the accounts. But the fundamental difference between an income tax and an expenditure tax is that *expenditure as such cannot be concealed* and if a man spends far more than he reveals in his declaration, whether on ordinary living expenses, or on extraordinary expenses, such as a wedding, he is bound to attract suspicion. Indeed, this is one of the reasons why concealed gains tend to be so largely saved and hoarded in cash, gold, or jewellery and not spent. The man who wishes to defraud the Revenue by concealing his true income simply cannot afford the risk of spending his gains. No doubt, some expenditure can safely be incurred without attracting suspicion. A man can spend more on liquor or on expensive foods provided he does not entertain on a large scale. Such additions to his consumption are not likely to attract notice but the amounts that can be spent in such ways can hardly exceed a certain proportion of his total living expenses.

192. The difference between the concealment of income and the concealment of expenditure lies precisely in this limitation. Provided that the proceeds are hoarded in cash and gold, there is no limit to the extent to which a man can evade income tax—he may conceal nine-tenths of his income, if only he can cover up the traces of the transactions which produced them. But he cannot evade nine tenths of his liability to an expenditure tax (or anything like it), for the simple reason that whatever his pattern of consumption, his standard and mode of living cannot be kept a secret.

Hoarding and the Gift Tax

193. It may be that an added stimulus to the concealment of business profits will be provided through the gift tax—that tax-payers will wish to conceal profits, not in order to save in income tax or in expenditure tax, or in the annual wealth tax, but in order to be able to pass money to their children or grand-children without attracting gift tax. Here again, I doubt whether the incentives will be anywhere near as strong as the present in-centives due to the very high rates of super tax. In order to save substantial amounts in gift tax (at an uncertain date in the future) the amount of profits which must be so concealed and hoarded in cash and gold must be very substantial, since other-wise the tax saving involved is proportionately too small to make it attractive. A man will not conceal income, in order that his son should save 10 or 20 per cent. in gift tax—parti-cularly when it is not a question of an immediate gift, but some-thing that is expected to be given at some future date. The case is different when the property to be passed on to a single heir is very large—say Rs. 10–15 lakhs—when the tax saving is of the order of 50 per cent. or more. But in that case the income loss due to the hoarding of such large sums (by the heir, as well as the testator, since the heir will have to continue to conceal his undisclosed wealth obtained through gift or inheritance) is equally very substantial. I believe also that the very fact that the gift tax is a charge on the recipient, and will have to be paid out of the gifts received by the recipient, will lessen the incentive on the donor to conceal income and property in order to save liability to a tax which is not a charge on him, but a charge on someone else, even if he (or she) is a near relation.

Evasion and the Comprehensive Return

194. As regards the second aspect mentioned above (obstacles), the proposal of requiring the submission of a comprehensive return concerning the personal accounts of each taxpayer, and the introduction of a reporting system on all capital transactions by means of tax vouchers, will tend to reduce the scope for evasion through the falsification of business accounts. The concealed income whether of a company, an individual business, or a

partnership must invariably reflect itself in the personal wealth
or expenditure of the owners or the managers of the business.
If profits are concealed for income tax purposes the resulting
savings must also be concealed in the annual statement—more
than it is the case at present. It may be argued, therefore, that
while the obligation to make an annual return of wealth, and
of all the casual receipts and property transactions of the taxpayers will make the concealment of income more difficult,
it would for that very reason increase the need to conceal the
savings made out of concealed income by hoarding them. The
enhanced attraction arises, not on account of the tax on wealth as
such, but on account of the stricter control over the savings
made in the year out of the income concealed for income tax
purposes. But the very fact that the savings made out of concealed
income cannot later be re-introduced into the business, or
invested profitably elsewhere will, together with the reduction of
income tax to a maximum rate of 45 per cent., make the concealment of income itself far less attractive. There is also the additional
factor that the hoarding of gold and jewellery can only be concealed in so far as gold and jewellery can be bought without the
seller demanding the surrender of a voucher for the purpose
of his own claim.[1] No doubt a provision of this kind cannot be
made fully effective, and it will not be possible to prevent completely transactions in gold and jewellery without surrendering
a voucher. But transactions of this sort are bound to command a
premium from the buyer and a discount to the seller, and thus
create further uncertainty as to the opportunities and ease with
which such hoards can be realised in the future; and this must
act as a further discouragement to the concealment of profits
for tax purposes.[2]

195. Provided, therefore, that the maximum charge on income
is reduced to the 45 per cent. suggested in my proposals—and
this appears in the light of the above discussion an essential
requirement in connection with the whole set of proposals put

[1] It was suggested in Section VI (paragraphs 106 to 108) that it should be made
obligatory to all authorised dealers in gold and jewellery to obtain (or supply) duly
completed vouchers in connection with selling and buying transactions.
[2] The question of the hoarding of gold in relation to taxation will be discussed further
below.

forth for the reform of personal taxation—I feel fairly certain that the extent of income tax evasion will be substantially reduced in consequence of the reform. But it would be sanguine to believe that it would solve the problem of the evasion of business profits through false book entries, etc., by itself or even that it will reduce its probable extent to dimensions at which its continuance could be tolerated without causing major damage to public morality or the community's sense of justice.

Other Methods of Attack

196. While there is no single magic formula that would render the evasion of tax on business income impossible, I feel that the problem could be tackled on a number of fronts and that substantial results could be gained from reforms in a number of directions. These relate to (i) the question of the compulsory auditing of the accounts of taxpayers whose income exceeds a certain minimum; (ii) the status, and the obligations imposed on the auditors; (iii) extension of the use of prescribed vouchers (with taxation registration numbers) to business transactions; (iv) increased powers of inspection and seizure of business books, etc., and (v) increased penalties and public exposure in the case of detection of fraud. I should like to discuss each of these questions in turn.

Compulsory Audit

197. Malpractices which consist in the presentation of false and misleading accounts should, of course, be sharply distinguished from the falsification of books from which the accounts are compiled. The compulsory auditing of accounts can only check the former and not the latter. Nevertheless, I think a great deal might be gained if it were made compulsory on taxpayers to present audited accounts in all cases in which income or property exceeds certain minimum limits. Owing to the shortage of auditors, this limit will have to be put rather high in the beginning but could be gradually lowered later. To start with, it may be prescribed that anyone whose income exceeds Rs. 1 lakh and/or whose capital exceeds Rs. 10 lakhs must produce audited accounts both as regards his personal

affairs and his business affairs. In the case of business accounts, the limit may be put at an annual profit of Rs. 50,000.

Status of Auditors

198. Even more important is to change the statutory regulations concerning the professional auditors. At the moment the obligation of a Chartered Accountant auditing company accounts is to ensure that the accounts are drawn up in a way which is not misleading from the point of view of the shareholders. Their duties, therefore, are satisfactorily discharged if they make sure that the shareholder is not given an inflated picture of the profits or the assets of the company (accounting conventions approve of turning a blind eye to the opposite kind of "cheating"—i.e., of giving a shareholder a less favourable impression of the affairs of the company than corresponds to reality). It is one of the main tenets of the ethics of the accountancy profession that it is much better to err on the conservative side, and to under-state results rather than to over-state them. Provided, therefore, that the accounts are formally correct— i.e., that the totals shown under the various heads agree with the individual items recorded in the books and are properly supported by vouchers—the accountant as a watch-dog of the shareholders is not unduly worried if deductions from the receipts are treated as provisions made against definite liabilities which ought more properly to be regarded as in the nature of reserves created against unknown and general contingencies; or when outlays are shown as a charge against current profits when, in fact, they represent capital expenditure; or when assets are written down in an immoderate manner, which business ethics approves as sound conservative practice. From the point of view of the State, all these, however, reduce the apparent income chargeable to tax, and make the task of the tax officers of discovering what is the true income legally liable to tax (which items are true charges on the profits, and which items should be disallowed as non-business expenses or capital expenditure) far more difficult. There is a great deal to be said, therefore, for the suggestion that professional auditors (at any rate, the Chartered Accountants) should be charged with a statutory obligation to examine whether

the accounts presented by companies and other firms for income tax purposes are drawn up in an appropriate manner so as to show the true chargeable income for tax purposes; and that they should be obliged to supply a certificate to that effect.

199. In this way auditors would become the watch-dogs of the other "silent partner" of businesses, the State, as well as being the watch-dogs of the shareholders and of the non-active partners of a firm. There is no reason why professional auditors should not be asked to carry out such a double obligation, but so long as the auditors are remunerated entirely by the owners of the firms their loyalties must primarily be towards their employers, and it would be wrong to impose upon them obligations which would set up a conflict of loyalties. For this reason a necessary complement to this proposal is either (a) that the whole of the auditing profession should be nationalised and professional auditors becoming full-time Civil Servants; or (b) that there should be a corps of Government auditors, distinct from the private auditors, and it should be made compulsory on firms above a certain size to have the accounts audited by a Government auditor as well as by private auditors; or (c) that a general scale of fees for auditors should be laid down by public regulation—the scale depending on the amount of work involved as well as the size of the business etc., and that 50 per cent. of the total fee should be paid by the Government and only 50 per cent. by the owners of the business; the formal approval of a Controller of Public Accounts being required for the appointment of any particular firm of auditors in any particular case. Each of these three proposals has its merits and each might provide a solution to the problem. Alternative (a) was discussed by the Taxation Enquiry Commission and rejected on the ground that the insufficiency of auditors makes the nationalisation of the auditing profession impracticable at the present time. Much the same kind of objection would be raised against proposal (b), in that it would take a number of years before a provision of this kind could be properly implemented. It seems to me however that suggestion (c) does not suffer from these defects, and offers the most practicable short-run solution of the problem.

200. It is not suggested that a reform on these lines would make it unnecessary for tax officers to subject the accounts submitted to a detailed scrutiny in particular cases. But it would greatly ease the task of this scrutiny; and it would tend to prevent many irregularities in the accounts, and a misleading form of presentation which might otherwise escape the watchfulness of the tax authorities.

Scrutiny of Accounts

201. Another line of attack lies in a more thorough check-up of the entries in the account books of the individual taxpayers. If the computation of the tax base were simplified in accordance with the suggestions made in Section VII, there would be a smaller number of entries to check up and the Department's ability to cope with this task would be automatically enhanced. It is also a matter for consideration whether the suggestion for the introduction of taxation code numbers should not be extended to business transactions, as well as capital transactions and whether an obligation to include the code number of the vendor on every voucher should not be generally imposed. It would certainly make it easier to route information obtained from the examination of A's return to B's file; and even if this were not done regularly or in any routine fashion, the very fact of the taxation code numbers being supplied with the vouchers would act as a deterrent to fraudulent over-statement of outlays and understatement of receipts.

Prevention through Deterrents

202. There is finally the question whether a great deal might not be achieved through more powerful deterrents to fraudulent practices. In India, as in Britain, tax-evaders are treated very leniently. Very few cases of fraudulent evasion are prosecuted before the courts,[1] and the taxpayer is generally promised immunity both from prosecution and publicity, if he makes a full disclosure and is willing to pay the relatively modest penalty

---

[1] In Britain, only a dozen or so cases a year on account of fraudulent accounts are prosecuted; whilst penalties imposed by the Department were collected in 18,114 cases in 1954 in addition to 133,757 small cases dealt with by the District Inspectors (Cf. 97th Report of the Commissioners of Inland Revenue. Cmd. 9351).

imposed. I suppose that, just as in Britain, this policy is based on the supposition that the Revenue will fare better and collect more if it allows the careless and sinful to come forward and confess their sins than if it threatens dire punishment.[1] In fact, in India there was a Voluntary Disclosure Scheme in operation for some years which promised complete immunity from pecuniary penalties as well as from prosecution and publicity if the taxpayer came forward and owned up voluntarily his concealed gains.

203. I very much doubt whether the policy of "softness" is of much avail, or whether, on the contrary, it tends to increase the scope of evasion. For it leads to a "heads I win, tails I do not lose" attitude, which must have the most destructive effect on tax morality. Indeed, even if a taxpayer knows that he cannot avoid penalties in case of detection it may still pay him to evade so long as the chances of detection are considered by him to be less than the proportion which the tax evaded bears to the total liability (i.e. penalty plus original tax charge) he would incur in the event of being detected. Thus, if the penalty imposed is equal to 100 per cent. of the tax evaded, it pays to evade so long as the chances of detection are less than 50 per cent. The maximum penalty that can be levied under the Income Tax Act in India is 150 per cent. and this deterrent is quite ineffective so long as the evader rates the chances of his detection at less than 1:2·5, or 40 per cent. I do not suppose that the likelihood of detection in India is above 1 in 10 in the average, so that to be a real deterrent the penalty imposed should be more than 9 times the sum risked and not $1\frac{1}{2}$ times.[2]

204. Very different is the situation in the U.S.A. where the tax-payer is left to assess himself to tax but if he is discovered having concealed income, he can be charged to an enormous penalty (amounting to between 10 to 20 times the tax escaped)

[1] This is the declared policy of the Board of Inland Revenue in the U.K., as stated by the Chancellor of the Exchequer (Sir John Anderson) in the House of Commons in 1944.

[2] Even the maximum penalty of 150 per cent. is not enforced except in rare cases. In the U.K., in seven years 1948–54, £47 million were collected in additional assessments as a result of the un-covering of under-assessments, in some 45,000 cases (Cf. 97th Report of the Inland Revenue, Cmd. 9351, p. 20). The total penalty raised amounted to £18 million which is 38 per cent. of the additional tax imposed. I do not suppose that the Indian data, if available, would show any different picture.

and is frequently dragged before the courts in a trial attracting a great deal of publicity and ending in long terms of imprisonment. Before the last war, no lesser personalities than the Vice-President of one of the biggest New York banks (The National City Bank) and the Chairman of the New York Stock Exchange were prosecuted for income tax evasion in trials attracting newspaper headlines for weeks on end; and only a few months ago the Head Porter of the Waldorf Astoria Hotel in New York was dragged before the court for having declared tips amounting to $33,000 in his income tax returns over a five-year period, whereas his bank account disclosed that he made over $60,000 in tips. No case of this type has ever been brought before the criminal courts either in Britain or in India. I feel quite certain that very heavy penalties and prosecution with a great deal of publicity is an infinitely more effective method of dealing with tax evasion than the policy of deliberate leniency and avoidance of public disclosure followed in Britain and India.

C. STANDARDS OF ADMINISTRATION

205. Finally, the prevention of evasion is very greatly dependent on the standard of administration in the Revenue Department—on the zeal, ability, efficiency, and the adequacy of numbers of tax officers. An efficient administration requires the ability of the Department to attract the best talent and to attract them in adequate numbers. This in turn is very greatly a matter of the conditions of pay and prospects in the service. In this respect I feel that there is too much of false and misguided economy in India. So long as the situation continues in which the local Income Tax Officer starts with a monthly salary of Rs. 350 (including extra allowances), and even after a number of years of service an officer occupying a position of considerable responsibility earns Rs. 500–600 a month, it is idle to expect that the highest standards of efficiency can be attained. Apart from the question of the ability and adequacy of qualified officers, I have a feeling that it is fundamentally wrong to pay officers, on whose attitude and conduct very large sums of money may depend, at such extremely meagre rates. Without in any way wishing to

cast aspersions on the general standard of integrity in the Department—which I am sure is very high—it seems clear that an Income Tax Officer living on a very modest scale cannot have the self-confidence and sense of social equality necessary to stand up to "great men" earning many lakhs of rupees, with whom he may have to deal. I feel that if an extra crore of rupees were spent on raising the standard of salaries in the Revenue Department—the cost of raising the monthly salary of Income Tax Officers to, say, Rs. 1,000 after a preliminary trial period of 5 years and rising to Rs. 2,000 a month in the normal course, could hardly exceed that amount—the return to the State in terms of additional revenue collected is bound to be many times the additional cost.

D. GOLD HOARDING AND TAXATION

206. It has been suggested in connection with the whole set of proposals put forward in this Report that their adoption would very greatly increase the tendency to hoard gold and other valuables, and will thus have highly undesirable effects on the employment of capital for productive uses and on the development of the economy. I should like to analyse this argument in some detail and to examine in particular (a) whether there is any genuine basis for the complaint that the tax reforms outlined here would lead to greatly enhanced hoarding of gold and jewellery; (b) the precise reasons why this should occur; (c) the economic effects of enhanced hoarding if it did occur; and (d) how far the danger of additional hoarding presents a valid argument against the proposals.

207. As we have already argued in paragraph 190 above, it is a mistake to suppose that the introduction of an annual tax on wealth would as such tend to enhance the hoarding of gold and valuables. Indeed the contrary is likely to be the case. Wealth held in the form of cash, gold, ornaments, jewellery, etc., would all be subject to taxation even though it yields no money income. In so far as these hoards are disclosed and included in the statement of net wealth on which tax is levied, the tax affords a stimulus in the opposite direction—it encourages investment in property

in forms which yield a relatively high return, and discourages the holding of wealth in sterile forms which yield no return.

208. If the gold and valuables are concealed and the tax authorities are unable to discover their existence, no tax will, of course, be levied on such hoards. But it is a mistake to suppose that the very imposition of an annual tax on wealth will lead people to hoard wealth which they would otherwise have invested productively merely in order to escape the tax. That could only be the case if the net yield of evasion were positive, i.e., if the tax-saving resulting from the concealment of assets is greater than the cost of doing so. The cost of concealing wealth in the form of hoards is the loss of the income which the same capital would have yielded otherwise. As we have shown above, with an annual tax on wealth the net return from evasion through concealment in hoards is bound to be negative, not positive. The maximum annual rate of tax is $1\frac{1}{2}$ per cent., whereas the minimum loss due to hoarding (even after taking into account the consequential saving in income tax due to having a smaller income) cannot be put at less than 3 per cent., and this is without taking into account the risks assumed and the specific costs associated with holding wealth in this form, which we have described in the note to paragraph 190 above. The argument, therefore, that an annual tax on wealth will serve as a stimulus to gold hoarding rests on a confusion—it applies considerations that are pertinent to an income tax, or a once-and-for-all capital levy (which levies tax at a high percentage of the total) to an annual tax on a capital levied at a low rate. People are willing to go to a great deal of dishonesty for the sake of escaping taxation when the net profit from successful avoidance is 900 per cent.—as is the case with income tax where the marginal rate is 90 per cent. They may even go to considerable trouble to escape tax when the net profit from tax evasion is 100 per cent., or even when it is only 20 per cent. But we cannot assume that apart from a few eccentrics, who would do it for sport—for the sheer love of the thing—people are willing to conceal their property fraudulently if there is net loss, and not a net profit in doing so.

209. Any increased tendency to the hoarding of gold cannot

therefore result from the desire to escape the annual tax on wealth but only from the desire to escape other taxes, particularly the income tax. In order to dodge income tax liability successfully the tax dodger must conceal not only the income, but the accretion of wealth resulting from that income. This problem arises now, in that a man who fraudulently conceals income for tax purposes must take care to ensure that the Income Tax Officer does not discover about it through circumstantial evidence —either because he spends noticeably more than he could out of his declared income, or because his capital assets have increased more than they could have out of savings made from his disclosed income. Indeed, an examination of a man's capital position over a period is probably the most effective method employed for the discovery of concealed income by the Special Investigations Branch of the C.B.R. or the Taxation Investigation Commission.

210. It can be argued also that the obligation to make an annual return of wealth, and the measures taken to ensure that property is not concealed through registration in bogus names, etc., will make it far more difficult than at present for a man to conceal income for tax purposes; and for that reason, he will tend to hoard his concealed gains to a far greater extent than now, this being the only safe method left to him of evading income tax with a prospect of success. (It may be argued that even with the present degree of vigilance of the tax officers, a large proportion of the concealed gains tend to get hoarded already, since no other method of concealing the money is considered really safe.)

211. No doubt, there is some validity in the argument that if you make income tax evasion so much more difficult than before, you stimulate those particular forms of concealment which you cannot control completely. If most loop-holes are plugged, the pressure on any remaining loop-hole is bound to increase. But as a basic criticism against our proposals it is really a most disreputable argument, since carried to its logical conclusion it simply says that anything that makes tax evasion more difficult will increase the economic ill-consequences of evasion; and that it is preferable, therefore, to refrain from measures

which make it more difficult to circumvent the laws. It would be impossible for a modern democratic Government to accept any such thesis as a guiding principle of conduct.

212. At the same time, in the particular context of my proposals, all such fears, I am convinced, are greatly exaggerated. The incentive to evade income tax is directly proportional to the marginal rate of taxation; it becomes powerful only when the marginal rate of tax amounts to a considerable part of the total amount. At a marginal rate of 90 per cent., the return from tax evasion is 900 per cent. on any particular amount concealed. At a marginal rate of 45 per cent., the return from successful concealment is only 82 per cent. Thus, while the successful concealment of income is rendered more difficult, the incentive to conceal income is also very greatly reduced. Moreover, if the proceeds of evaded income have to be kept in sterile forms, and cannot be invested in forms which yield a return, the attraction of saving the tax by evasion is still further reduced. It would be rash to predict, therefore, that my recommendations of tax reform would on balance enhance the propensity to hoard gold in any substantial degree. This is certainly not the case so far as the recommendations relating to the annual tax on capital and the income tax are concerned; and for reasons analysed in paragraphs 191 to 193 above, I am equally sceptical of any substantial tendency to hoard emerging as a result of the imposition of the expenditure tax or the gift tax.

213. But even if this were not so, it certainly ought not to be regarded as an argument of any weight against the case for a comprehensive tax reform. For exactly the same objection can be raised not only against the particular proposals put forward here but against any proposals designed to make the avoidance and evasion of progressive taxation less easy or less virulent, and which, therefore, would make a genuine contribution to the attainment of a greater degree of economic and social equality. I am prepared to believe that the proposal for a general income-ceiling may be less open to an objection of this sort, but if this is the case, it can only be so in so far as the proposed ceiling is only effective in relation to incomes from *work* and not in relation to the true incomes from *property*. If the idea of an income-

ceiling were to be effectively applied to incomes derived from property as well as to incomes derived from work, it would have to take the form of a 100 per cent. capital levy imposed on the owners of wealth above a certain maximum—since this is the only way in which the income of the property-owners could be effectively limited. (A ceiling on "income" alone, leaving property untouched, would be perfectly meaningless.) But this implies a capital levy with a marginal rate of 100 per. cent above a certain ceiling, surely the most powerful incentive that could be invented for concealing wealth through secret gold hoards.

APPENDICES

SUGGESTED FORM OF A COMPREHENSIVE
RETURN FOR PERSONAL TAXATION

SUMMARY STATEMENT

I. CAPITAL POSITION

1.1 Net wealth at 1st April, 1956
     (as per Statement A)

1.2 Net balance of gratuitous transactions
     (item 4.5 of Statement C)

1.3 Net balance of capital transactions
     (item 5.7 of Statement D)

1.4 Net balance of lending and borrowing
     (item 6.9 of Statement E)

1.5 Net balance of other capital and casual transactions
     (item 7.3 of Statement F)

1.6 Net wealth on the 1st April 1957
     (1.1 plus sum of 1.2 to 1.5 = Return as per statement A)

II. ACCRUALS AND DISPOSALS—1956–57

Accruals	Rs.	Disposals	Rs.
2.1 Income (Statement B)		3.1 Personal expenditure (item 8.6 of Statement G)	
2.2 Receipts from gifts (item 4.1 of Statement C)		3.2 Outlay on gifts (item 8.2 of Statement C)	
2.3 Proceeds from the sale of assets (items 5.2 and 5.5 of Statement D)		3.3 Purchase of capital assets (items 5.1 and 5.4 of Statement D)	
2.4 Receipts from borrowings and repayment of past loans (item 6.8 of Statement E)		3.4 Lending and/or debt repayments (item 6.8 of Statement E)	
2.5 Other casual or capital receipts (item 7.1 of Statement F)		3.5 Other capital payments (item 7.2 of Statement F)	
2.6 Total		3.6 Total	

STATEMENT A: *Personal Balance Sheet*

Net Wealth Statement, 1st April, 1956.   Rs.
Net Wealth Statement, 1st April, 1957.   Rs.
(Statements as prescribed at present, vide Appendix 'E' to Income Tax Inspectors' Manual)

STATEMENT B: *Income Account*

Detailed as in present return on income (I.T. 11) with business accounts attached.

STATEMENT C: *Gratuitous Transfers*

Gifts received during the year

Detailed nature of gifts (Cash or assets)	Donor	Value in Rs.
4.1 Total		

Gifts made during the year

Detailed nature of gifts	Recipient	Value in Rs.	No of Tax Voucher[1]
4.2 Total			

Balance of gratuitous transfers:
4.3   Net receipts of cash (plus or minus)
4.4   Net accession of other assets (plus or minus)
4.5   Net balance of gratuitous transfers (4.2 minus 4.1)

[1] All these entries must be supported by vouchers.

STATEMENT D: *Purchase and Sale of Capital Assets during the Year*
I. Income Yielding Assets and Bar Gold

Purchases			Sales				
Nature of assets (stocks and shares, immovable property, gold, etc.)	Price paid	Tax Voucher No.[1]	Nature of assets (stocks and shares, immovable property, gold, etc.)	Price received	Date of aquisition	Cost	Gain or loss
5.1 Total purchases			5.2 Total sales				

5.3   Net balance of purchases and sales of assets.   (5.1 minus 5.2)

II. Capital Assets for Personal Use

Purchases			Sales				
Nature of assets	Price paid	Tax voucher No.[1]	Nature of assets	Price received	Date of acquisition	Cost	Gain or loss
Houses for personal use			Houses for personal use				
Works of art			Works of art				
Jewellery			Jewellery				
Ornaments			Ornaments				
5.4 Total purchases			5.5 Total sales				

5.6   Net balance of purchases and sales (5.4 minus 5.5)
5.7   Net balance of capital transactions (5.3 plus 5.6)
5.8   Net capital gains made in the year (sum of last column *less* costs of acquisition).

[1] All these entries must be supported by vouchers.

STATEMENT E: *Borrowing and Lending*

Outlays	Amount[3]	No. of tax voucher[1]	Receipts	Amount
6.1 Net deposits in bank accounts or increase in cash holdings			6.5 Net withdrawals from bank accounts or depletion of cash holdings.	
6.2 Net lending— Mortgages			6.6 Net borrowing— Mortgages	
I.O.U.'s			I.O.U.'s	
Accrued credits for services rendered[3]			Accrued debts for goods and services supplied[3]	
6.3 Repayment of past debts			6.7 Replayment of past loans	
6.4 Total			6.8 Total	

6.9 Net Balance of lending and borrowing (6.4 minus 6.8)

[1] All these entries to be supported by vouchers.
[2] Credit can only be taken for cash deposited with banks or other financial institutions, in so far as these are not included in business accounts attached to Statement B.
[3] In so far as these items are not included in the business accounts furnished in Statement B.

STATEMENT F: *Other Capital or Casual Transactions*

Nature of receipts	Value	Nature of payments	Value
Sale of rights		Purchase of rights or leases etc.	
Betting and winnings		Payment of compensation	
7.1 Total		7.2 Total	

7.3   Balance of other capital or casual transactions (7.2 minus 7.1)

STATEMENT G: *Personal Expenditure*

Rs.

8.1   Income:
        (Statement B)
        Deduct if positive, *add,* if negative
8.2   Net balance of gratuitous transfers (item 4.5)
8.3   Net receipts from capital transactions (item 5.7)
8.4   Net receipts from lending or borrowing (item 6.9)
8.5   Net receipts from other capital transactions (item 7.3)

8.6   Net balance of above items (sum of 8.1 to 8.5)

I solemnly declare that to the best of my knowledge and belief the above balance agrees with the gross personal expenditure of my household during the year.

(Signature of Taxpayer)

Deductions from, and Adjustments to, Gross Personal Expenditure (item 8.6)—

8.7   Exempted outlays—
        Direct taxes paid during the year
        Fines
        Funeral and birth expenses
        Medical expenses
        Other exempt expenses
8.8   Gross chargeable expenditure
8.9   *Deduct* allowances for spreading expenditure on durable goods etc.
8.10 *Add* notional income for the year with regard to capital purchases for personal use (5 per cent of item 5.6 plus amounts outstanding from earlier years)
8.11 *Add* proportion of expenditure on durable goods etc., incurred in previous years and chargeable in the current year
8.12 Net chargeable expenditure for the year
        Number of members of household
        Number of adults units
8.13 Net chargeable expenditure per adult unit

G

APPENDIX B

PART ONE

SUGGESTED FORMS OF VOUCHERS FOR PROPERTY TRANSFERS*

*See Chapter 6.

FORM 1

1. Applicable to all property transactions requiring registration and attracting Stamp Duty.
2. To be filled in triplicate, A, B and C; copies A and B to be surrendered to the Registration or Stamp Office, and copy C to be retained by the transferee or beneficial owner.

[To be filled out by Transferor]

1. Brief description of property..
   (land, buildings, stocks and shares etc.)
2. Nature of transaction ....
3. Current value and/or consideration Rs. ....
   (enter both current value and consideration, if latter differs from current value)
   Name of Transferor................................
   Address..
   Taxation Code No..................................

[To be filled out by Transferee]

Name of Transferee...
Address..
Taxation Code No...

    I declare that I am the sole beneficial owner of this property.[1]
[1]Strike out if not applicable.

_____

(Signature of Transferee)

    I declare that I am part beneficial owner of this property.[2] The other beneficial owners are:

[2]To be filled in the case of HUF and other joint ownership.

  (1) Name ....
       Address......................................
       Taxation Code No.............................
  (2) etc. etc.

_____

(Signature of Transferee)

    I declare that I am a trustee/nominee/benamidar of the above property The beneficial owner(s) is (are):—

  (1) Name ....
       Address......................................
       Taxation Code No.............................
  (2) etc. etc.

[To be filled out by the Registration Office]

The above transfer of property was today duly registered under the Transfer of Property Act. I certify that the Taxation Code Nos. given above agree with the numbers on the Taxation Code Cards presented to me.

Date.................

Official Stamp.   (*Signature of Registration Officer*)

Notes:

1. The system can be extended to stocks and shares as well as immovable property by making the requirement that all transfer deeds must be handed to a Register Office or Stamping Office for stamping (as is the case in the U.K.).

2. The name(s) of the beneficial owner(s) is disclosed on the voucher as well as the taxation code number. Since, however, this is filled in by the transferee, the name(s) of the true owners is only disclosed in effect to the tax authorities and not the public at large. In the transfer deed, however, the code numbers of the beneficial owner (or the principal beneficial owner if there are several) should be given (along with the name of the transferee) and it should be the duty of the Registration Officer or Stamping Officer to ensure that the code number which figures in the transfer deed corresponds with the code number of the principal beneficial owner (and not of the nominal holder). These code numbers must be included along with the names of the nominal holders, in the companies' share registers and in any dividend vouchers etc., issued by them.

FORM 2

1. Applicable in case of loans, deposits, gifts, purchases of goods in the exempt categories, etc.

2. To be filled in triplicate, A, B and C; Copies A and B to be surrendered to the Registration or Stamping Office, copy C to be retained by the payor.

[To be filled out by Payee]

1. Brief description of transaction...
   (loan, repayment of debt, gift, bequest, purchase of........etc.)

2. Current value and/or consideration Rs...................................
   (enter both current value and consideration, if latter differs from current value)

3. Name of Payee......................................
   Address...
   Taxation Code No..................................

[To be filled out by Payor]

Name of Payor......................................
Address...
Taxation Code No..................................

[To be filled out by the Registration Office]

I certify that the Taxation Code Numbers given above agree with the numbers in the Taxation Code Cards presented to me.

Dates.................

Official Stamp.   (*Signature of Registration Officer*)

Notes:

1. This form is simpler as no question of benami or nominal ownership arises. Under "Brief description of transaction" an indication of its character should be given (debt, repayment, gift, legacy, purchase of jewellery etc.)

2. It should be obligatory on all payees to hand over such vouchers, with relevant portions duly filled in to the payor, who, if he wishes to utilise it as a voucher in connection with a tax-claim, must have it stamped first by a Registration Officer who detaches copies A and B and returns copy C duly completed.

PART TWO

A SAMPLE OF SWEDISH INCOME TAX VOUCHERS

Form 18a

Dividends on Swedish shares not Exempt from Dividend Tax
(Section 42 § 3 of Income Tax Act)

This statement should be completed by the recipient of the dividend and handed to the payor. It is the payor's responsibility to ensure that this is done. If the dividend payment relates to a series of years a special form should be filled in with respect to each year. It is forbidden to use any other but this printed form for the purpose. You may specify particulars of different dividends on the back of this form. This form should be used only if both the questions stated below are answered in the affirmative. In all other cases Form 18b should be completed. Form 18b is invariably required for receipts by residents abroad.

Questions should be answered by X

1. Is the person entitled to receive the dividend, *the beneficial owner* of the share (or shares) on the date when the dividend is first payable?

   If the person completing this form does not know who is the beneficial owner of the share or shares, or else does not know how to answer this question, Form 18b should be used.

   Answer ☐ Yes

2. Was the person entitled to receive the dividend a permanent resident of Sweden at the time of payment and continuously thereafter?

   A juridical person (company, corporation, association, etc.) is always treated as a permanent resident in Sweden. A foreign juridical person is never so regarded.

   Answer ☐ Yes

Full Name of the Recipient   Title or Profession

Address on Nov. 1st preceding the income year

Street and Number   District   Area   Village or town   Parish   County

In case of foreign address, name of country should also be included.

Dividends receivable in accounting year	Coupon No. for the year	Types of shares Ordinary/Preference	Total Receipts

Name of company

I solemnly declare that the above particulars are true and correct.	Declaration by payor
Date	Nothing known at the time of payment to dispute the accuracy of the above.
Signature of the payee.	*Signature of the payor.*
This should be signed by the receipent of the payment or his representative. Address of Representative.	Payor's name and address Stamp of paying agent if payment made by bank

FORM 17
INTEREST ON DEBENTURES & BONDS
(Section 42 § 3 of Income Tax Act)

This statement should be completed by the recipient of the interest payment and handed over to the payor. It is the payor's responsibility to ensure compliance with above. If the owner acquired security after the last interest payment was due and the new owner is obliged to compensate the previous owner for part of the payment covered by this statement the new owner should state this in the I.T. return furnished by him, but on this form the full amount should be stated. The statement for the tax-obligations on the interest should be given even if the recipient is not the true beneficiary of the interest paid.

Full Name of Recipient of Payment   Title or profession

Address on November 1st of the income year preceding

Street and Number	District	Area	Village or town	Parish	County

If payment is made against a coupon without the security from which it was detached, recipient of coupon should state name(s) of person(s) from whom coupons were acquired.   Title or profession

Name....................   Address etc.

Nominal amount of security   By whom issued

Debentures	%	Year of issue	Date of payment falling due (as per coupon)	Amount of interest payment in Sw. Crowns

Bonds

I hereby solemnly declare that to the best of my knowledge and belief the statements given above are correct and I hereby undertake to encash any coupons through SVENSKA HANDELSBANKEN that have not been paid on the instructions of the debtor

Name and address of payor
Stamp

Signature

Date

This statement should be signed by the recipient of the payment or his representative.

Address of representative.

Perforated slip attached listing details of security and interest payment.

THE YIELD ON AN ANNUAL TAX ON WEALTH—AN ESTIMATE
BASED ON SWEDISH EXPERIENCE

1. I received in response to enquiries, figures relating to the operation of the annual wealth tax (officially styled, the State Capital Tax) in Sweden which may serve to supplement the estimates concerning the yield of an annual wealth tax in India.

2. The Swedish income tax statistics record the number of assessees, the total property value, and the median income per assessee for each property class which (together with the number of assessees) makes it possible to calculate the total income, as well as the total property value, for each property group. These figures are shown in Table 5. The relationship between the total income and total property value for each property group gives the income/property ratio for that group shown in column 6 of Table 5. The interesting result which emerges from this is that there is a clear negative correlation between the income/property ratio and the size of property; the larger the property, the higher the income, but the lower the relationship of income to property value. Thus while for the lowest property group of Rs. 50–60,000[1] the ratio is 15·8 per cent., for the highest group of Rs. 10 lakhs and over the ratio is as low as 3·8 per cent. The average ratio for all estates of Rs. 50,000 and over is 10·55 per cent.

3. The explanation for the steady decline of the income/property ratio with property-size is, I believe, two-fold. First, in the case of the smaller property owners, the total income is the joint outcome of labour and capital, and the percentage which can be attributed to labour would steadily decline with the size of property. Amongst the large property owners the proportion of income attributable to managerial activities or to salaries

---

[1] One Swedish Crown has been taken as the equivalent of one Indian rupee for the purposes of our calculations. (The official rate of exchange is 100 rupees = 107·5 Swedish Crowns.)

earned must be comparatively small in relation to property income. Second, in the higher income and property brackets the income/property ratio is unduly depressed as a result of income tax avoidance, the main form of which is the conversion of income into capital gains. Although short-term capital gains are taxed in Sweden at the same rate as income, it is still, of course, greatly to the advantage of a rich man to convert income into capital appreciation. According to Swedish law, capital gains are treated fully as income when the gains arise on the realisation of assets held for less than two years; 25 per cent. is remitted from the taxable net gain if the asset was held for more than 2 but less than 3 years; 50 per cent. if more than 3 but less than 4 years, etc., and there is complete exemption for realised gains on assets held for more than 5 years.[1]

Table 5

INCOME/PROPERTY RELATIONSHIP IN SWEDEN FOR PERSONS WITH PROPERTIES OVER SW. CROWNS 50,000

Property class value in Crs. thousands	No. of assessees	Property value Swedish Crs. crores	Median income by property group	Total income Swedish Crs. crores	Income-property ratio (per cent)
1	2	3	4	5	6
50– 60	39,967	218·79	8,690	34·73	15·87
60– 70	28,466	184·20	9,409	26·78	14·53
70– 80	20,312	151·77	10,213	20·74	13·66
80– 90	14,820	125·58	10,960	16·24	12·93
90– 100	11,722	111·10	11,747	13·77	12·39
100– 125	19,200	213·83	13,117	15·18	11·77
125– 150	11,474	156·61	15,201	17·44	11·13
150– 175	7,410	119·75	17,043	12·63	10·54
175– 200	5,202	97·26	18,680	9·72	9·99
200– 300	10,288	248·23	22,956	23·62	9·51
300– 500	6,279	236·95	31,637	19·86	8·38
500–1000	2,887	194·50	47,059	13·59	6·99
1000–	1,076	253·14	90,049	9·69	3·83
Total	179,103	2311·70	11,730	243·99	10·55

Note: Entries in columns 1 to 5 are taken from the Swedish tables while entries in column 6 were obtained by dividing the figures in column 5 by those in column 3.

Source: Official Statistics of Sweden: Income and Property for the Assessment year 1954; Central Bureau of Statistics, Stockholm, 1955.

[1] The above applies to stocks and shares; in the case of immovable property the same principle is applied but the period of ownership required for partial or full remission of taxation is approximately doubled.

4. There is of course no *a priori* reason for assuming that income/property ratios are the same for different countries. There are reasons for assuming, however, that the figures applicable to India are lower than those applicable to Sweden. These reasons are: (i) the market rates of interest (i.e., the yield of bonds and debentures) and the market valuation of ordinary shares (i.e., the dividend yield of shares quoted on the Stock Exchanges) are no higher in India than in Sweden; (ii) the value of labour—i.e., the market price of services rendered—is very much lower in India than in Sweden, so that in the case of joint incomes, the percentage attributable to labour in any particular property-group is likely to be much smaller, and that attributable to capital much greater. Hence, while the income/property ratios in the high property brackets are not likely to differ much on account of differences in the level of interest rates, the rise in this ratio with decreasing property size is likely to be much less in India than in Sweden; (iii) since the top marginal rates of income tax at 90 per cent., are greatly in excess of the Swedish top rate of 66 per cent.; whilst capital gains, fully exempt in India, are only exempt on longer-term holdings in Sweden, both the incentive for, and the possibilities of, converting income into capital gains must be much greater in the one country than in the other. For all these reasons the Swedish figures can only be applied to India as an indication of the *upper limits* of these ratios (i.e., of affording a *lower limit* to an estimate of property values).

5. While the Swedish statistics show the median income by property group, they do not show the median amount of property owned by each income group and the two relationships need not, of course, to be identical. It is possible, however, to build up an estimate of property value by income groups by applying the income/property ratios derived from the property-class classification to incomes classified by income-classes, and to correct for the error in the resulting estimate through a comparison of the estimated with the actual figures. This is shown in Tables 6 and 7. In Table 6 the incomes of the self-employed and of persons with no occupation (i.e., all income recipients other than salary earners) with incomes of Rs. 10,000 and over are classified. They show that there were 139,000 assessees in this

category in Sweden and their total aggregate income amounted to Rs. 267 crores. This should be compared with 179,000 assessees owning property of Rs. 50,000 and over shown in Table 5, whose total income amounted to Rs. 243 crores. The differences (an appreciably smaller number of assessees and a somewhat larger total income) are to be explained by the fact that the number of self-employed with incomes of more than Rs. 10,000 whose property was less than Rs. 50,000, was smaller relatively to the number of assessees with property of more than 50,000 whose income was *less* than Rs. 10,000; at the same time the total income of the persons in the former category (consisting, I presume, of the professions and vocations) was appreciably *greater* than that of the latter (consisting of small rentiers).

6. Table 6 includes a comparable estimate for India based on C.B.R. figures. It is interesting to note that the comparable total of assessed incomes is almost exactly the same (263 as against 267 crores) in the two countries. In India, however, there were only 115,000 such assessees (as against 139,000 in Sweden), the average income per assessee thus being almost 15 per cent. larger. Moreover, the distribution of the two populations is very different, since the proportion of income attributable to the highest class, as well as the proportion of income-earners in the highest class, is much greater, while the percentage of cases in the lowest categories is much less, in India than in Sweden. Thus, in India 2,650 persons had incomes of more than Rs. 1 lakh, and their total income was Rs. 58 crores. In Sweden there were only 632 such persons and their total income was Rs. 13 crores. On the other hand, in the bottom category of incomes between Rs. 10–15,000, the number of assessees was 50 per cent. higher, and the total income of assessees 80 per cent. greater, in Sweden than in India.

7. These differences reflect partly the differences in the degree of concentration in the ownership of wealth, and partly also differences in the extent of income tax evasion. The population of India is almost fifty times the population of Sweden, whilst the national income of India is about three times as high. While the proportion of the total national income accruing to property owners of all kinds must be lower in India than in Sweden

Table 6

STATISTICS OF ASSESSEES (EXCLUDING SALARY-EARNERS)
WITH INCOME OVER Rs. 10,000 IN SWEDEN AND INDIA

Range of income Rs. thousands	Sweden		India	
	Number of assessees	Total income Rs. Crores	Number of assessees	Total income Rs. crores
1	2	3	4	5
10– 15	75,420	93·76	50,364	54·14
16– 25	42,240	81·65	35,640	57·73
26– 40	14,287	41·68	16,220	43·18
41– 55	4,252	17·92	5,468	21·68
56– 70			2,381	12·84
71– 85	2,476	18·57	1,339	9·06
86–100			834	6·91
101–	632	12·97	2,652	57·79
Total	139,307	266·60	114,908	263·33

Notes:
(1) One Swedish Crown is taken as equivalent to one rupee.
(2) Since the income ranges given in the income tax statistics of the two countries are not identical, some of the Swedish figures had been estimated by interpolation.
(3) The Indian figures relate to the categories "Individuals with salaries and other sources", "All other sources", "H.U.F.'s and unregistered firms", etc. In the category of "Individuals with salaries and other sources", only income under "other sources" has been included.
Source: Swedish figures as in Table 5 and Indian figures according to C.B.R.s All-India Income-Tax Revenue Statistics, 1954–55.

(since property income can only emerge out of a surplus of production over the bare minimum consumption) wages per head are also 10–12 times as great in Sweden as in India, so that the difference in the proportion of the national income accruing to property owners is hardly sufficient to explain the fact that the number of persons (other than salary earners) with incomes of more than Rs. 10,000 a year should actually be less in the one country than in another and their total income no higher.

8. In Table 7, the data shown in Tables 5 and 6 are combined to obtain an estimate of total property and its distribution, and to estimate the yield of an annual tax on capital in the two countries. For this purpose the incomes shown in Table 5 were divided by the income/property ratios applicable to the mean values of the different income groups, estimated by interpolation from column 4, Table 5. The resulting estimate for Sweden gives total property values of Rs. 3,049 crores which is somewhat

Table 7

ESTIMATES OF THE DISTRIBUTION OF PROPERTY (DERIVED FROM INCOME STATISTICS) AND OF THE YIELD OF AN ANNUAL TAX ON WEALTH IN SWEDEN AND INDIA

| | SWEDEN | | | | | | INDIA | | | | | |
Range of income	Number of assessees	Total income Swedish Crowns Crores	Income-property ratio %	Total property Swedish Crowns Crores	Estimated tax yield schedule A Swedish Cr. Lakhs	schedule B Swedish Cr. Lakhs	Number of assessees	Total income Rs. crores	Income-property ratio %	Total property Rs. crores	Estimated tax yield schedule A Rs. Lakhs	schedule B Rs. Lakhs
1	2	3	4	5	6	7	8	9	10	11	12	13
10– 15,000	75,420	93·76	12·8	732·4	—	177·6	50,364	54·14	12·8	422·9	—	83·5
15– 25,000	42,240	81·65	10·2	800·5	126·0	344·6	35,640	57·73	10·2	566·0	58·0	203·1
25– 40,000	14,287	41·68	8·0	521·0	126·0	335·3	16,220	43·18	8·0	539·7	125·8	328·8
40– 55,000	4,252	17·97	7·0	256·3	78·5	214·1	5,468	21·68	7·0	309·7	91·0	249·1
55– 70,000	} 2,476	} 18·57	5·0	} 368·9	} 174·5	} 454·0	2,391	12·84	6·5	197·5	70·8	189·8
70– 85,000							1,339	9·06	5·2	174·4	75·0	205·3
85–100,000							834	6·91	4·0	172·8	94·8	236·3
100,000—	632	12·97	3·5	370·6	377·9	608·3	2,652	57·79	3·5	1651·1	1729·7	2725·3
Total	139,307	266·60	8·7	3049·7	882·9	2133·9	114,908	263·33	6·5	4034·1	2245·1	4221·2

Notes: (1) The values of properties in columns 5 and 11 have been estimated from the income figures in columns 3 and 9 and the property ratios in columns 4 and 10.

(2) Since income-ranges given in the statistics of the two countries are not identical, some of the figures have been estimated graphically for the income-ranges shown here.

(3) Tax yields have been calculated on a slab system on the following basis:

Schedule A
(Suggested rates for India)

	%
up to 100,000	nil
100,000–400,000	0·33
400,000–700,000	0·50
700,000–1,000,000	0·75
1,000,000–1,500,000	1·00
1,500,000 and over	1·50

Schedule B
(Actual rates in Sweden)

	%		%
up to 50,000	nil	200,000– 400,000	1·3
50,000–100,000	0·5	400,000–1,000,000	1·6
100,000–150,000	0·8	1,000,000 and over	1·8
150,000–200,000	1·0		

Sources: As in Tables 5 and 6.

over 24 per cent. in excess of the actual property values of Rs. 2,311 crores shown in column 3 of Table 5. A comparison of column 5 of Table 7 with column 3 of Table 5 shows that the discrepancy between the estimated and the actual figures is greatest in the medium income and property classes. This confirms the inference made in paragraph 5 above, that the relatively high average level of professional and vocational earnings (in relation to the income of "small rentiers" excluded from the figures) is the chief source of error in our method of computation. This in turn indicates that the error involved in the use of the method is likely to be appreciably less for India than for Sweden and if for Sweden the inference from income to property figures on the basis of property/income relationships yields an over-estimate of 20 per cent., for India the over-estimate cannot exceed 10 per cent.[1] and may indeed be far smaller, quite apart from the underestimate due to the factors referred to in paragraph 4 above. Hence the inference to be drawn from the estimate in column 11 of Table 7 is that in India the total property values from which the disclosed income of taxpayers in the relevant categories are derived cannot be put at less than Rs. 3,600 crores. This is remarkably close to the lower of the two estimates of property values viz. Rs. 3,700 crores, given in Table 1 (Section II).

9. For the reasons given in paragraph 4 above this can be only taken as the *lower limit* of estimate since it assumes that the income/property relationships in each particular property-category are the same in both countries whereas in India, owing to the lesser value of labour, the additional return, as percentage of property value, in the case of "joint incomes" (i.e. due to managerial etc. activities) is likely to be much smaller. As an *upper limit* of estimate the average income/property relationship may be put at 5 per cent. (rather than 7·1 per cent. implied in our estimate) which would make the total property value Rs. 5,200 crores.

10. Columns 6–7 and 12–13 of Table 7 indicate the wealth

---

[1] The *total* amount of professional and vocational earnings assessed to income tax is only Rs. 24·3 crores (see C.B.R. All-India Statement No. 4, Group 9) or less than 10 per cent. of the total of profits etc. capitalised for purposes of our estimate, and some of this must be in income categories below Rs. 10,000 which are excluded from our figures.

tax yield derived from the estimated property figures in the two countries. For this purpose the tax yield was calculated for both countries by reference to (*a*) the actual rates of capital tax in Sweden (shown as Schedule B) and (*b*) the tax rates suggested for India (shown as Schedule A). It is evident that whether we take the Swedish or the Indian property distribution, the suggested tax rates for India would only yield about one-half as much as the actual tax rates in force in Sweden.[1]

11. The actual return from the wealth tax in Sweden was Rs. 13·1 crores as against the Rs. 8·8 crores estimated on Schedule A and Rs. 21·3 crores estimated on Schedule B. For reasons indicated, the actual yield of the tax in India is not likely to fall short of the estimates given in Table 7 by more than 10 per cent. so that on the lower rate schedule, the *minimum* estimate of the yield comes to Rs. 20 crores. If the Swedish rate schedule were adopted, the minimum yield of the tax would be of the order of Rs. 38 crores a year.[2]

12. None of these figures takes into account the additional yield of either the income tax or of the proposed wealth tax that could be expected to follow from the reduction of the tax-evasion due to the introduction of the new tax and the consequent need to produce consistent and comprehensive returns relating to both income and property.[3]

---

[1] The difference between the suggested Indian tax rates and the actual Swedish rates is due more to the width of successive rate slabs than to a higher maximum rate. This explains why the differing structure of income and property distribution causes the Schedule A estimate to amount to only about 40 per cent. of Schedule B estimate in the case of Sweden and well over 50 per cent. in case of India.

[2] On the basis of the *maximum* estimate of property values given in para. 9 above the yield might be put at Rs. 25 crores with Schedule A and Rs. 50 crores with Schedule B.

[3] An estimate of the probable extent of tax evasion is given in Chapter IX.

3

SUGGESTIONS FOR A COMPREHENSIVE
REFORM OF DIRECT TAXATION
IN CEYLON[1]

THIS memorandum puts forward a set of inter-related proposals designed to create a system of progressive direct taxation suited to the needs of a democratic socialist community. Their object is to provide incentives to progress at the same time as to bring about greater social and economic equality.

The proposals aim to eliminate both tax avoidance and tax evasion and to bring the taxes levied on individuals into a far closer relationship with capacity to pay. They also aim at achieving the maximum simplicity of administration (consistent with an efficient tax system) by eliminating numerous features in the existing structure which cause needless difficulties in administration and delays in assessment.

It is suggested that the taxpayer should be asked to make a single return with respect to all the five taxes—Income Tax (including Profits Tax), Capital Gains Tax, Wealth Tax, Expenditure Tax and Gift Tax—and the liability to all these taxes should be assessed simultaneously. It is also suggested that a comprehensive reporting system be introduced on all property transfers and other transactions of a capital nature.

In the field of administration, it is suggested that the status of the present Income Tax Department be raised to the equivalent of the Board of Inland Revenue of the United Kingdom and the Central Board of Revenue of India, and the strength of the Department be increased at all levels.

Some of the above reforms (those relating to personal income

---

[1] Prepared in Colombo, Ceylon, at the invitation of the Government of Ceylon in April 1958 and published as a White Paper by the Government of Ceylon in April, 1960.

tax and company taxation) could take effect in the coming financial year and the others in the financial year 1959–60.

The present memorandum is restricted to a bare outline of the suggested reforms. For a more detailed exposition of the case for these reforms, reference may be made to the author's Report on Indian Tax Reform and to the Second and Final Reports of the British Royal Commission on the Taxation of Profits and Income (Memorandum of Dissent).

I. INCOME TAX

(1) *The Taxation of Capital Gains*

It is proposed that all profits which now rank as a capital profit and, therefore, not liable to tax should henceforth be charged to income tax in the same way as a trading profit. This means taxing the profits made on the realisation of capital assets of all kinds (immovable property; movable property, such as stocks and shares, business plant and equipment; also furniture and jewellery above a certain value). "Realisation" is to be defined as the change in the ownership of property as the result of sale, the liquidation of a business, or transfer under a deed of gift, or will, or to an irrevocable trust. Realised capital losses should be set off against realised capital gains, and unabsorbed capital losses of any year should be carried forward as a set-off against future capital gains for an indefinite period. If a person's estate shows net unabsorbed losses at death, the tax which would have been reclaimable on these losses should be credited against Estate Duty liabilities. This method ensures that the accumulated total of realised capital gains, over a taxpayer's whole life comes to the same as the accumulated total of accrued capital gains, i.e., that each individual pays tax over his lifetime on the net accrual of capital gains during his lifetime.

Apart from gains resulting from the sale or transfer of assets, capital receipts that arise from the sale of certain rights over assets should also be taxed (such as premiums received on leases, money received for the surrender of leases, receipts on account of the sale of terminal rights of enjoyment of possession, such as the sale of mineral rights, &c.).

To ensure the full and accurate reporting of capital gains, each taxpayer should be asked to return all capital transactions within the year, i.e., his purchases as well as sales (the return on purchases to be supported by means of vouchers in accordance with the reporting system described below). The return of assets purchased provides a record for the Tax Department, that serves as a check on future gains arising out of the sale of these assets. For the purpose of the initial introduction of the tax, the following procedure is suggested:

(a) In the case of movable property of all kinds, for assets purchased prior to the "appointed date" and sold subsequently, the current value on "the appointed date" should be deemed to be the cost for the purpose of calculating the net gain. (The taxpayer's declared value of stocks and shares, &c., for the purpose of the Wealth Tax, should also serve as the "value on the appointed date" for the purpose of the capital gains tax).

(b) In the case of immovable property, if the property was purchased within a 10-year period prior to the appointed date, the actual purchase cost (or probate value in case the property was acquired through inheritance, or the value stated in the deed of gift, in the case of a gift) shall be the cost for the purpose of tax; provided that—

　(i) only that proportion of the gain should be taxable which the period elapsing between the "appointed date" and the date of realisation bears to the total period of ownership;

　(ii) the written-down value of any development expenditure in respect of which capital allowance or depreciation allowance has been granted should be added to the original cost of acquisition.

Unrealised capital gains in an estate on decease should be added to the income of the deceased of the last year prior to death. The tax credit for unabsorbed capital losses should be based on the average of the marginal rates of income tax paid in the last five years prior to death.

It is suggested that in the case of taxpayers who had no taxable income for the previous three years, capital gains up to Rs. 5,000 should be exempt. Capital gains on movable property other than stocks and shares should be only charged if the gains exceed Rs. 2,000 in any one year.

(2) *Allowable Deductions for Expenses*

Although the Ceylon Income Tax Ordinance gives a stricter definition of allowable deductions for expenses than the U.K. law (since only such deductions are allowed as are "incurred in the production of" the profit or income), in practice this makes little difference, and certain classes of expenses have come to be treated as legitimate deductions.

To secure equality of treatment between various classes of tax-payers, it is suggested that the deduction of certain classes of expenses should be prohibited. These should comprise:

(i) entertainment expenses (of all kinds);
(ii) expense allowances given by a business to its executive staff (the so called "Expense Accounts");
(iii) travelling expenses of all kinds for the benefit of the owner, partner, director or a higher-grade executive of a business;
(iv) one-half of the expenditure incurred for advertising.[1]

As regards (i), (ii), (iii), this would mean that all such allowances and expenses would have to be met out of the taxed profits of the business; they should not, therefore, be charged in the hands of the director or employee who receives them; though in so far as they include an element of personal benefit they would be liable to expenditure tax in the hands of the beneficiary. As a complementary measure it should be laid down that no deduction for expenses (on account of entertaining, travelling, &c.), should be allowed from employment income.

As regards (ii), the disallowance of travelling expenses to the owners, directors or higher grade executives of businesses should imply *inter alia* that all expenses connected with the use of motor cars (depreciation, running expenses and other connected ex-

[1] In addition it may be considered to amend Section 9 (1) of the Income Tax Ordinance by substituting for the words "in the production thereof" the words "in the production of the profits or income of the year" in order to make it clear that only such expenses qualify for deduction as are unavoidably incurred in earning the profits that are assessed to tax.

penses such as the driver's wages) should [be disallowed, unless such cars are for the exclusive use of the subordinate staff in the performance of their duties. Certain classes of professional persons, such as doctors, and possibly lawyers and accountants, should be explicitly exempted from this provision.

In order to ensure compliance with these provisions, it should be made a statutory requirement to separate clearly all entertainment, travelling and advertising expenses incurred by a business in the accounts submitted.

(3) *Rules Concerning Aggregation and Allowances to the Family*

In view of the prevailing practice of making gifts of properties to minors, setting up trusts with minors as beneficiaries, allotting shares to minors in private limited liability companies, or providing annuities to minors in order to reduce liability to income tax, it is suggested that the income of children should be aggregated with that of their parents (in the same manner as that of husband and wife) up to the age of 25, or marriage, whichever is earlier. (The age of 25 is suggested since this is the present limit for children's allowances.) In the case of a child who sets up a separate household, aggregation should cease when that child is over 21 years old.

At the same time, it is suggested that the present method of granting personal, wife and children allowances should be replaced by the quotient method which is a far more equitable one where the incomes of all the members of the family are aggregated. Under this method, the aggregate income of the taxpaying unit is divided into a number of parts, depending on the number of persons in the family, and tax charged separately on each part. For this purpose, the husband and wife should each be considered as one unit, and each child as half a unit. By this method a married man and wife with two children would constitute three adult units and a man and wife with 4 children, 4 adult units. It is suggested that an upper limit should be placed to the number of units in a family, and that this limit should be fixed at four—which means in effect that no further tax concessions are given after the fourth child. Dependent relatives living in the household (such as parents, or uncles and aunts, &c.) should be considered in the same way as children, provided only that their income is aggregated with the family, in the same way as the children's income and always subject to the over-riding maximum of 4 adult units per family. (However the aggregation of dependent relatives' income should be made optional—depending on whether the taxpayer wishes to have the quotient method applied to them— whereas the aggregation of minors' income should be made compulsory.)

(4) *Suggested Schedule of Income Tax Rates*

It is suggested that each adult is given a tax-free allowance of Rs. 2,000 a year, the balance of income of each unit being charged on the slab system. Since a single person living separately normally incurs a higher expenditure than half the expenditure of a married couple, it is suggested that a single person be given an extra tax-free allowance of Rs. 1,000. The exemption limit for income tax could, at the same time, be brought down to Rs. 3,000 for a single person and Rs. 4,000 for a married couple in place of the Rs. 4,800 prevailing today.

In view of the introduction of the net wealth tax as a method of differentiating income from work and income from property, it is suggested that the existing earned income relief be abolished and that there should be only a single schedule of income tax rates. The following schedule of allowances and tax rates was worked

(a) *Tax free allowances*		Rs.
A single person		3,000
Married man with wife living but no children	(2 units)	4,000
Married man with wife and one child ..	(2½ units)	5,000
Married man with wife and two children ..	(3 units)	6,000
Married man with wife and three children	(3½ units)	7,000
Married man with wife and four children .	(4 units)	8,000
		(maximum allowance possible)

(b) *Slabs and rates applicable to each unit*		
First Rs. 1,500 after tax-free allowance	@	5%
Next Rs. 1,500 ,,	@	10%
Next Rs. 1,500 ,,	@	15%
Next Rs. 1,500 ,,	@	20%
Next Rs. 1,500 ,,	@	25%
Next Rs. 1,500 ,,	@	30%
Next Rs. 1,500 ,,	@	35%
Next Rs. 1,500 ,,	@	40%
Balance ,,	@	45%

out on the assumption that the *average* burden at each income level should remain unchanged until the suggested maximum rate is reached. This means a higher burden than at present on a single person, and on married couples without children, and a lower burden than at present on families with more than two children.

On these schedules, the marginal rate of 45 per cent. would be reached at an income of Rs. 15,000 for a single person, Rs. 26,000 for a married couple and Rs. 42,000 for the married couple with two children. It is suggested that 45 per cent. should be the maximum rate of income tax, any higher tax charge being secured by means of the Expenditure Tax. In view of the taxation of capital gains, it would not be practicable to charge capital gains at the same rates as ordinary income if the maximum rate of income tax were higher than 45 per cent.[1] There are enormous advantages, however (from the point of view of simplicity and the elimination of tax avoidance), in avoiding any differentiation between capital profits and other types of profit for tax purposes. Also if the 45 per cent. rate were chosen for both personal income tax and company tax (as is suggested below), the possibility of avoiding personal income tax through the undue retention of profits in closed corporations would also be eliminated, and this again would greatly simplify tax administration.

In the case of *non-resident individuals* who cannot be made subject to an Expenditure Tax, it is suggested that the present schedule of income tax rates (mounting up to 85 per cent.) be generally retained, but relief be given for tax charged at a rate in excess of 45 per cent. in so far as the amount of tax thus forgone is retained in this country and not remitted abroad. The justification for this proposal is to secure equality of treatment between resident and non-resident individuals.

Income remitted from Ceylon may be considered as income expended rather than saved by the recipient, so that the retention of the present rate schedule together with non-remittance relief

---

[1] In all countries where capital gains are taxed but high marginal rates of income tax prevail, capital gains are treated more favourably for income tax purposes than ordinary income. Thus in India only one-third of realised capital gains is taxable as income, while in the U.S. long-term capital gains are taxed at the maximum rate of 25 per cent. irrespective of the marginal rate of tax of the individual taxpayer's ordinary income.

for tax in excess of 45 per cent. secures analogous treatment to non-residents as is imposed through the combination of income tax and expenditure tax on residents.

II. THE TAXATION OF BUSINESS INCOME

(1) *Profits Tax on Income from Professions and Unincorporated Businesses*

The existing system which levies two separate taxes on business income, a profits tax and an income tax, is a source of unnecessary complications in administration, apart from the fact that it differentiates between the taxation of business income and non-business income in a manner that is only justified in so far as the effective burden of income tax is smaller on business income than on incomes from employment. Such is undoubtedly the case at present owing to the non-taxable perquisites (capital profits and allowances for expenses) associated with business income and not with employment income. Once, however, capital gains are brought into charge and the range of allowable expenses is tightened up in the manner suggested above, the justification for a differential charge on business income disappears.

There may, however, be a case for retaining the profits tax on unincorporated businesses (in the case of companies a new uniform tax is suggested below) for a strictly temporary period on account of the fact that its sudden abolition would create inequities between different taxpayers (due to the fact that the profits tax is now assessed to a different period from the income tax); that the new taxes on wealth and expenditure are not to take effect immediately, and that the tax on capital gains will not produce its full effect for a certain number of years after its initial introduction (owing to the time lag between the accrual of gains and their realisation). However, to save the administrative complications due to this tax, the following reforms are suggested for immediate adoption:

  (i) Income tax should be charged on the full income without any deduction for profits tax;
  (ii) The exemption for profits tax should be Rs. 50,000 as at present, but the alternative standard of exemption based on 6 per cent. of the capital employed should be abolished;

(iii) Profits tax above the exemption limit should be charged at a uniform rate of 15 per cent., instead of the 30 per cent. This is a purely nominal change which is balanced by the provision suggested in (i) above that profits tax is no longer a deductible charge for the purposes of calculating income tax.

> (A 45 per cent. income tax plus 15 per cent. profits tax implies a combined marginal rate of 60 per cent., whereas the existing 30 per cent. rate of profits tax rate plus a 45 per cent. income tax rate on the remainder gives a combined charge of $61\frac{1}{2}$ per cent. The small reduction of $1\frac{1}{2}$ per cent is off-set by the abolition of the alternative exemption limit based on the capital employed.)

(iv) The profits tax assessment for the *next* assessment year should not be for a twelve-month period, but for whatever period is necessary to bring the profits tax assessment into line with the income tax assessment, and thereafter profits tax and income tax should always be assessed simultaneously on the basis of a single return.

My own preference would be, however, to abolish the profits tax altogether from the date of commencement of the wealth tax and the expenditure tax—for otherwise the taxation of business income might appear to be unnecessarily severe. (The revenue loss due to its complete abolition, bearing in mind the additional revenue from income tax, amounts to only Rs. 5 million a year.) In that case I would suggest adopting the proposals (i)–(iv) above for the next financial year only.

(2) *The Taxation of Companies*

It is proposed to replace the existing system, according to which companies are liable to a profits tax plus an income tax which is refundable on the dividends paid to the individual shareholder, by a new system (analogous to the American system) according to which a single non-refundable tax is charged on the *whole* income of companies; and in addition a tax on the dividends declared which is credited to the account of the resident shareholder. It is proposed that both the company profits tax and the dividend tax should be levied on non-resident as well as resident companies, but in order to comply with existing provisions, the two taxes would appear in the legislation as part of a single tax on company income. It is estimated that in order to obtain the same revenue as the present profit and income taxes on companies, the rate of tax would have to be 45 per cent. on the whole profit of the year plus 33⅓ per cent. on the *gross* dividends declared in the year. (This is based on an estimate of one-third of profits earned being distributed as dividend.) The 33⅓ per cent. on the gross dividends is the equivalent of 50 per cent. of the actual dividend payments and for the purposes of the initial change-over to the new system, it is preferable to define the charge as 45 per cent. of the profit earned in the accounting period ending in the year previous to the year of assessment, plus 50 per cent. of the *net* dividend payments made to shareholders during the same accounting period. But whether the tax on the dividends is defined on a net or on a gross basis, it is in effect a withholding tax which is credited against the income tax liabilities of the resident shareholder, whose dividends are grossed up for the purpose in the same manner as under the present system. (Non-resident shareholders are not entitled to a refund, but they obtain double tax relief from their own revenue authorities.)

The advantages of this reform, apart from greater simplicity of administration, are that it improves incentives by lowering the effective marginal rate of taxation (at present this marginal rate amounts to 57 per cent. in the case of resident companies and 61½ in the case of non-resident companies) and at the same time offers a strong inducement to the companies to plough back profits, since the tax actually levied on them will be the heavier the higher the proportion of profits distributed.

In the case of non-resident companies whose main centre of operation lies abroad, and who maintain branch establishments or subsidiaries in Ceylon, one-third of the profit earned should be deemed to have been distributed as dividend for the purposes of this tax unless the amounts actually remitted abroad are below this amount, in which case the dividend charge should be based on the amounts so remitted.

The existing differential charge of 6 per cent. on non-resident companies, in lieu of Estate Duties, should be retained, so that the profit tax on non-resident companies becomes 51 per cent. (This is in fact a higher differentiation than the present one, which amounts to an effective rate of only 4·5 per cent. but can be justified by reference to the wealth tax and the gift tax from which non-residents are exempt.)

(3) *Commencement and Cessation Provisions*

It is suggested that, in connection with the above reform of the taxation of individuals and companies, the existing commencement and cessation provisions for income-tax be abolished, as these frequently provide a means of tax evasion, since it is open to both companies and partnerships to avoid tax by liquidating the existing business in years of exceptionally high profit, and recommencing in years of low profit. Henceforth taxes for the current year should be uniformly based on the profits of the previous year, without exemptions from tax for the last year of operation and without new firms being assessed twice on the profits of the second year of their operation. As a special concession, it is suggested that businesses which cease operating within 10 years of the introduction of the new system should be entitled to a refund with regard to that part of the tax on the profits of the last year of their operation which corresponds to the profits earned in the second year after commencement.

(4) *Capital Allowances*

In order to provide a more powerful incentive for the re-investment of profits for the purpose of expansion, it is suggested that the existing system of initial allowances and depreciation allowances be replaced by a once-and-for-all capital allowance which is credited to the taxpayer in the same year in which the expenditure is incurred. This single capital allowance should broadly correspond to the discounted value of the depreciation allowances now granted over the lifetime of the capital assets. Assuming that the depreciation is calculated on the "reducing balance method" (i.e., as some constant percentage of the written-down value of the assets at the beginning of each year) and assuming a rate of interest of 5 per cent., the value of this capital allowance (being the equivalent of the discounted value of the depreciation allowances under the old system) for different kinds of assets would be as follows:

For assets with a rate of depreciation of 2½ per cent. (buildings and installations)	35% of expenditure
For assets with a rate of depreciation of 5 per cent. (installations, steamers and vessels)	50% ,
For assets with a rate of depreciation of 7½ per cent. ..	60% ,,
For assets with a rate of depreciation of 10 per cent. (the usual rate for machinery and plant)	66⅔% ,,
For assets with a rate of depreciation of 20 per cent. ..	80% ,,
For assets with a rate of depreciation of 25 per cent. ..	82% ,,

It is suggested that for simplicity the existing categories should be reduced to four types, carrying the following capital allowances:

Buildings &c.	33⅓%
Durable plant and machinery	50%
Normal machinery &c.	66⅔%
Short-lived equipment	80%

If the capital allowances for any year cannot be fully absorbed by the profits of that year, the unabsorbed capital allowances should be carried forward to future years augmented by an annual interest allowance of 5 per cent. to compensate for the shrinkage of the discount factor. Thus, assuming that a trader incurs a capital expenditure of one lakh in a particular year on which the capital allowance due is Rs. 66,668, but there is only Rs. 20,000 taxable profit to set off against this expenditure, the amount carried forward to the following year will be the unabsorbed allowance of Rs. 44,668 plus 5 per cent. interest, i.e., Rs. 49,000 altogether, and so on.

No annual depreciation allowances are to be granted on capital expenditure in respect of which a capital allowance is given, but depreciation allowances would continue to be given with respect to capital expenditure incurred previous to the introduction of the new system. It should be open to the Income Tax Commissioner, however, at any time to compound outstanding depreciation allowances by a single allowance whenever this can be done without undue loss of revenue, so as to simplify the work of future assessment.

In addition to the normal capital allowance, representing the discounted value of depreciation, I suggest that a special *develop-ment subsidy* be introduced which should be added to the normal capital allowance. This development subsidy should be a flat addition to the normal capital allowance of 20 per cent. of the capital expenditure for assets of all types, but it is only to be given in the case of the acquisition of a *new* asset and not in the case of the purchase of an existing asset. This development subsidy may be extended to certain types of commercial buildings, such as hotels, which do not at present qualify for either initial allowance or depreciation allowance.

For the purpose of ascertaining the profits on the sale of assets, the sales proceeds should be related to the written-down value, (i.e. the original cost less the normal capital allowance) but ex-cluding the development subsidy. The capital allowance should be granted in all cases in which a depreciation allowance is given at present. Thus, in the event of a person purchasing a plantation estate, a capital allowance may be given on the machinery &c. based on the cost to the vendor, whilst a corresponding charge on the excess of the sales price of the machinery over its written-down value is imposed on the seller.

Unabsorbed capital allowances should not qualify as set-off against other income, but should be carried forward indefinitely as set-off against future income from the same source. All loss claims should lapse on the sale or liquidation of a business (since any genuine loss will be allowed as a set-off against capital gains to the owner).

III. A TAX ON NET WEALTH

It is proposed that a new annual levy be imposed on resident individuals based on net wealth (i.e. the excess of the value of the taxpayer's assets over his total liabilities). The tax should be based on the current market value of the immovable and movable property enumerated by individual items, and the responsibility for the initial valuation of all property would rest on the tax-payer. In the case of movable property (particularly stocks and shares) value declared for wealth tax purposes should be the basis for any future charge of capital gains in connection with the transfer of the property by way of sale, deed of gift or will. As a penalty for under-valuation, a provision should be made for imposing an automatic penalty of three times the tax if the declaration is found to be more than 25 per cent. below the correct figure.

In order to save bother to both the taxpayer and the tax authorities, it is suggested that the initially declared values of property should stand for at least 5 years, subsequent revision being undertaken at five-year intervals. For assets purchased subsequent to the introduction of the tax (but before a revaluation takes place) the valuation should be based on actual cost.

It is suggested that the property owned by husband, wife and children should be aggregated for wealth tax purposes in the same way as for individual tax. Similarly, if the application of the quotient system is claimed with respect to dependent relatives for purposes of either income tax or the expenditure tax, the wealth of such dependent relatives should also be aggregated, but the levy should be imposed on total wealth, without the application of the quotient method. The net wealth of a person for the purpose of this tax should include property held in trust with respect to which the taxpayer or member of his family are life beneficiaries. The wealth tax levied on trusts should primarily be collected from the beneficiaries, but if necessary recourse should be had to the trustees.

The suggested rates for wealth tax are:

On the first Rs. 100,000 of net wealth	..	..	..	Exempt	
,,	next Rs. 400,000	,,	..	..	..	$\frac{1}{2}$% per annum
,,	next Rs. 500,000	,,	..	..	..	1% ,,
,,	remainder		..	..	..	2% ,,

The high exemption limit is recommended more for administrative convenience than as a matter of principle. In fact, once the wealth tax is in operation, it may be found to be a much more convenient method for levying tax on small traders and on small farmers than the income tax. By lowering the exemption limit of the wealth tax it may be possible to make it perform much the same functions—of encouraging the productive use of land and increasing the agricultural surplus—as the land tax performs in other countries.

It is not suggested that companies should be made liable to the wealth tax. The arguments in equity which favour the imposition of a wealth tax on individuals alongside taxes on income—i.e., that the possession of disposable wealth provides an additional source of spending power—do not apply to companies; nor is it likely, in the case of Ceylon, that individual wealth can be hidden on any considerable scale through transferring assets to companies. (If this were the case, the problem could be met by valuing the shares of private companies—in the same way as for Estate Duty at present—on the basis of the current break-up value of the assets of the companies.)

IV. AN EXPENDITURE TAX

It is suggested that in place of the higher brackets of income tax (i.e., the rates in excess of 45 per cent.) and in order to bring into charge expenditure which is not financed out of the taxed income of the taxpayer, whilst giving exemption from tax in excess of 45 per cent. to that part of income which is saved, a progressive tax should be levied on personal expenditure. This tax, unlike the income tax, should be levied on a *net* basis, i.e., after the deduction of the various taxes (income tax, wealth tax, expenditure tax, and gifts tax) paid by the taxpayer.

Personal expenditure is to be defined for the purpose of this tax as including not only items financed by the taxpayer's own outlays but also the money's worth of benefits and gifts received in kind, expenses met by the employer, friend or relative, subject to an annual exemption for such benefits in kind up to a limit of Rs. 2,000 a year.

"Personal expenditure" excludes outlays on the following items:

(a) Business expenses.

(b) All investment outlays, i.e., sums devoted to the purchase of income yielding property (like land, stocks and shares, securities of all kinds, payments made under insurance policies, bank deposits, &c.) or non-income-yielding sources of wealth (like bar gold, current deposits, loans of all kinds and sums devoted to the repayment of past indebtedness).

(c) Capital investment for personal use, such as purchase of a dwelling house for owner occupation and the purchase of works of art, jewellery, and ornaments. The annual value of a dwelling house should, however, be added to expenditure in the same way, as it is added to income.

(d) Gifts made to other persons in excess of an aggregate of Rs. 2,000 a year. (These, however, will attract gifts tax.)

Outlays not falling in categories (a) to (d) above may be defined as the gross personal expenditure, but not all such expenditure would be charged to tax. I suggest exemption of the following categories of necessitous expenditure:

(e) All direct taxes paid by the taxpayer during the assessment year (income tax, profits tax, wealth tax, expenditure tax, gifts tax).

(f) Fines imposed in criminal proceedings, and expenditure incurred on both criminal and civil legal proceedings.

(g) Funeral and birth expenses up to a maximum of Rs. 2,000 in each instance.

(h) Marriage expenses up to Rs. 3,000 in each instance.

(i) The expenditure incurred as a result of fire, burglary, theft, flood-damage, &c., in so far as they qualify for insurance. (Payments received under insurance policies rather than the outlays themselves should be exempt.)

(j) Medical expenses up to a maximum of Rs. 3,000 a year.

(k) Education of children abroad up to a maximum of Rs. 8,000 a year.

In addition, the taxpayer should have the option of spreading non-recurrent expenditure of any kind (such as expenditure on a journey abroad, the purchase of furniture, motor cars, &c.) which are not in themselves exempt, over a period of five years. The amount of expenditure with respect to which spreading is claimed can be left to the taxpayer's discretion, since he would incur higher charges if he claimed more than what is necessary to even out his flow of expenditure over time.

The expenditure tax is to be assessed on the quotient method, in the same manner as the income tax. The following tax-free allowances and rates-schedules have been worked out on the assumption that the expenditure tax should only begin to operate where the progression of the income tax leaves off—i.e., for expenditure in excess of the net income corresponding to the maximum rate of income tax:

Tax-free Allowance	Rs.	
Single person	10,000	
Married man with wife living but no children (2 units)	16,000	
Married man with wife and 1 child (2½ units) ..	20,000	
Married man with wife and 2 children (3 units) ..	24,000	
Married man with wife and 3 children (3½ units) ..	28,000	
Married man with wife and 4 children (4 units) ..	32,000	(maximum possible allowance)

Rate Schedule for each unit		
On the first Rs. 5,000 expenditure after tax-free allowance ..	25%
„ next Rs. 5,000 „ ..	50%
„ next Rs. 5,000 „ ..	100%
„ next Rs. 5,000 „ ..	200%
„ balance „ ..	300%

For administrative reasons the expenditure tax, along with the wealth tax and the gift tax, should take effect in the financial year 1959–60 and be assessed on the basis of expenditure incurred in the financial year 1958–59. It is important, however, to make it clear in the first official announcement concerning this tax that the tax will be assessed with respect to the expenditure of the period commencing with the date of this announcement—since otherwise there might be a tendency to anticipate expenditure on postponable items with a view of tax avoidance.

The actual method of administration of the tax would follow the lines set out in my Indian Tax Reform and recently adopted in India.

V. A GIFT TAX

The gift tax is a necessary complement to the Estate Duty in that it levies a charge on gifts *inter vivos* which can now escape duty. The ideal method of levying the gift tax would be to make a charge on the recipient, at rates depending on the total wealth of the recipient including the gift, and this would serve to replace the existing Estate Duty altogether, since gratuitous transfers by way of inheritance would be charged under the same tax as gratuitous transfers *inter vivos*. I am persuaded, however, that until the new system of taxation has been in operation for a number of years, the adoption of such a tax might raise serious administrative difficulties. It is proposed, therefore, that the existing Estate Duty should be retained and supplemented by a cumulative gift tax levied on the *donor*; but the ultimate replacement of this system by a single gift tax levied on the *recipient* should be borne in mind.

A gift tax on the donor requires the aggregation of successive gifts for tax purposes—for if the rates were made dependent on the size of each individual gift, the tax would be avoided merely by the spreading of gifts over time. Hence, for the purposes of this tax, successive gifts by a taxpayer are to be aggregated, and the rate of tax on any particular gift should depend on the cumulative total of all previous gifts, the cumulation starting from the date of the initial introduction of the tax and extending over the tax-payer's lifetime.

The rates-schedule for the gift tax should be identical with the rates-schedule for Estate Duty, bearing in mind that whereas the Estate Duty rates are expressed on a *gross* basis (since the duty is deducted from the total estates) the rates of the gift tax are expressed on a *net* basis (since the duty is levied on the amounts actually transferred by a deed of gift). To ensure this identity, it is necessary to re-cast the schedule of Estate Duty rates on the slab system (in place of the existing schedule in terms of effective rates). A suggested schedule for the Estate Duty and the gift tax is given below. The Estate Duty rates, apart from minor differences due to rounding, are the same as the gift tax rates "grossed up".

The operation of a cumulative gift tax may best be explained in terms of an example. Supposing an individual makes a gift of Rs. 50,000 in the first year after the commencement of the tax on which the charge is 5 per cent. Supposing in the next year he makes another gift of Rs. 50,000 the charge on this will be the charge as for a total gift of Rs. 100,000 less the charge on a gift of Rs. 50,000. If he makes a third gift of Rs. 50,000 in the third year, the charge on that will be the tax on a gift of Rs. 150,000 less the tax on a gift of Rs. 100,000 and so on. (In terms of the rates-schedule suggested below, the charge would be 5 per cent. for the first year, 9 per cent. for the second year, 12·25 per cent. for the third year and so on). If a taxpayer is found to have made Rs. 500,000 gifts at the time of his death on which (on the rates-schedule suggested below) he would have paid Rs. 91,400 in gift tax, and he left an estate of Rs. 1,000,000, the charge for

Estate Duty will be the duty on estate Rs. 1,591,400 (i.e., the probate value of his estate *plus* the cumulative total of gifts made in his lifetime, *plus* the gift tax paid on those gifts) *less* the Estate Duty on Rs. 591,400 which should normally (i.e., but for small differences due to rounding, &c.) equal the gift tax paid during his lifetime. By this method it is ensured that each person who parts with property either through *inter vivos* gifts or through death pays the same total duty on the value of property transferred gratuitously irrespective of whether he parted with it wholly or in part during his lifetime or whether it fell in for estate duty at his death.

RATES SCHEDULES FOR GIFTS TAX AND ESTATE DUTY

Rates Schedule for Gifts Tax				*Rates Schedule for Estate Duty*				
Gifts aggregating to Rs. 2,000 in a year			Exempt	First	Rs.	20,000	..	Exempt
First Rs.	50,000 of taxable gifts @		5%	Next	Rs.	30,000	.. @	5%
Next Rs.	25,000	.. @	8%	Next	Rs.	30,000	.. @	7½%
Next Rs.	25,000	.. @	10%	Next	Rs.	30,000	.. @	10%
Next Rs.	40,000	.. @	12%	Next	Rs.	40,000	.. @	11%
Next Rs.	40,000	.. @	13%	Next	Rs.	50,000	.. @	12%
Next Rs.	80,000	.. @	18%	Next	Rs.	100,000	.. @	13%
Next Rs.	80,000	.. @	20%	Next	Rs.	100,000	.. @	15%
Next Rs.	80,000	.. @	25%	Next	Rs.	100,000	.. @	20%
Next Rs.	80,000	.. @	30%	Next	Rs.	100,000	.. @	25%
Next Rs.	80,000	.. @	35%	Next	Rs.	100,000	.. @	27%
Next Rs.	80,000	.. @	45%	Next	Rs.	100,000	.. @	30%
Next Rs.	80,000	.. @	50%	Next	Rs.	100,000	.. @	35%
Next Rs.	250,000	.. @	60%	Next	Rs.	350,000	.. @	40%
Next Rs.	450,000	.. @	80%	Next	Rs.	750,000	.. @	45%
Balance		.. @	100%	Balance			.. @	50%

Non-residents' Estates

The change-over to the slab system in the schedule of rates for Estate Duty involves certain adjustments in the method of charging duty in the case of non-residents' estates. At present the value of the Ceylon Estates of a non-resident is added to the value of his Estate outside Ceylon in order to ascertain the rate at which the Ceylon Estate should be taxed. Under the new system it will be necessary to aggregate the value of the estates as above, and charge duty on the Ceylon Estate at the *effective* rate of duty that would be applicable to the non-resident's world Estate if it were considered chargeable to Estate Duty at Ceylon rates.

Example	*Rs.*
Value of Estate in Ceylon	50,000
Value of Estate outside Ceylon ..	150,000

Duty chargeable on basis that total Estate is chargeable to duty at Ceylon rates:

First	Rs. 20,000..	..	..	..	..	exempt
Next	Rs. 30,000 @ 5%	..	..	..	Rs.	1,500
Next	Rs. 30,000 @ 7½%	..	..	..	Rs.	2,250
Next	Rs. 30,000 @ 10%	..	..	..	Rs.	3,000
Next	Rs. 40,000 @ 11%	..	..	..	Rs.	4,400
Next	Rs. 50,000 @ 12%	..	..	..	Rs.	6,000
					Rs.	17,150

Effective rate $= \dfrac{17,150}{200,000} \times 100 = 8.6\%$ approx.

Therefore duty payable on Ceylon Estate is 8·6% of
    Rs. 50,000 = Rs. 4,300 approx.

(It would obviously be inequitable to charge the Ceylon Estate at 12 per cent. at the highest marginal rate applicable to the total Estate if liable to Ceylon Estate Duty.)

Stamp Duty Payable on Gifts

The present practice as far as Estate Duty is concerned is to give credit for the stamp duty paid on a gift *inter vivos* within five years which now gets caught up in liability to Estate Duty. Under Section 16 of the Estate Duty Ordinance, if in any particular case the credit for stamp duty exceeds the Estate Duty, no refund is made to the donee. It is suggested that analogous principles be applied to the gift tax—i.e., to credit stamp duty against the gift tax liability, but without making a refund in cases in which the stamp duty exceeds the gift tax. Similarly, no refund of gift tax is to be made if the above method of calculating the estate duty results in a negative liability. (This could only arise in cases where the net probate value of the estate is negative, i.e. the liabilities exceed the assets.)

Gifts up to Rs. 2,000 a year made by any one donor should be exempt from gift tax though they will be charged for expenditure tax. Apart from this limitation, all gifts should be included for purposes of the gift tax, including gifts made to charities or charitable trusts and voluntary annuities, but not the payment of alimony imposed by Court order.

H

VI. SYSTEM OF ADMINISTRATION

The combination of the various taxes suggested here should serve to improve greatly the efficiency of tax administration. At present there is undoubtedly a great deal of evasion of both profits and income tax. The new taxes, provided that they are administered as part of a single system, should make evasion far more difficult—partly because the taxpayer must provide far more comprehensive information concerning his affairs than at present, i.e. his wealth position at the beginning and at the end of the income tax year, his purchases and sales of capital assets, and receipts by way of gifts, bequests &c.; partly because concealment or under-statement of items in order to minimise liability to some of the taxes may increase the liability with regard to others, and partly also because the information furnished by the taxpayer in the interest of preventing over-assessment with regard to his own liability automatically brings to light the receipts and gains of other taxpayers.

In order to operate the system at full efficiency, it is necessary however:

(i)   that all these taxes should be administered, jointly, i.e. that there should be a single file relating to each taxpayer with regard to all these taxes and that they should all be assessed at the same time, preferably on the basis of a single comprehensive return submitted by the taxpayer; and

(ii) that there should be an automatic reporting system extending to property transactions and to cash payments over a certain sum on account of gifts and loan transactions.

(1) *The Form of the Return*

I am persuaded that the full "comprehensive account" recommended in my Indian Tax Reform (Appendix A) could only be brought into operation after both taxpayers and tax assessors had a certain amount of experience with the new taxes. However, I think it would be far more convenient if from the start the taxpayer were asked to make one return only instead of a series of returns (as is the case in India at present) even if the return fell short of the requirements of a comprehensive account (i.e., without the need of a full reconciliation of the various statements).

It would not be necessary, however, for each taxpayer to fill up the whole return. Part A, relating to income and capital gains (including an enumeration of purchases and sales of assets during the year) would have to be filled up by every income-tax payer. Part B, containing the Return of Net Wealth, would not have to be completed by persons who make a statutory declaration (which is part of the form) that their net wealth is below, say, Rs. 50,000. Part C, relating to expenditure tax, would not have to be completed by those (i) whose declared wealth is under Rs. 50,000 and (ii) whose income is below Rs. 12,000 in the case of a single person Rs. 20,000 in the case of a married couple, &c. Part D, relating to the Gift Tax, would not have to be filled in by persons who declare they have not made gifts or received gifts of over Rs. 2,000 in the year.

The advantage of having one return only is, first, that it saves a great deal of bother and harrassment to the taxpayer; second, that it makes it easier for the Revenue department to ensure that taxpayers comply with their obligations, and saves a great deal of time and bother involved in chasing after separate returns; third, that it accustoms both taxpayers and assessors to look upon these taxes as part of a single system. Similarly, I suggest that all these taxes should be assessed simultaneously, in a single notice of assessment.

(2) *An Automatic Reporting System*

The evasion of income tax, as well as certain administrative difficulties that may be experienced in connection with the taxation of capital gains, the wealth tax, the gift tax and the personal expenditure, could be effectively overcome by an automatic reporting system on capital transactions. This system can be briefly described as follows:

(i) Every income-tax payer is given and supplied with a code number by the Income Tax Department on a code number card. Any person who is not on the register of income-tax payers should also be given a code number at his request and supplied with a code number card. (The system of code numbering should be on a district basis; and the Revenue Districts into which the Island is at present divided might form the basis for the system of code numbering.) Any person should be supplied with a duplicate code number card on request, if he requires one.

(ii) It would be made obligatory in the case of all property transfers for the transferor and transferee to disclose their code numbers. A form will be so designed and it will be laid down that one part should be completed by the transferor and the rest of the form by the transferee. The transferor should have the obligation to fill in triplicate that part of the form relevant to him first, and hand all three copies over to the transferee. The transferee having completed the rest of the form should hand over two copies to the Registrar-General with the deed. The Registrar-General's Office will forward it to the Income Tax Department where it can be routed to the files of the transferor and transferee. The copy that the transferee retains will be his evidence for claims of exemption for expenditure tax purposes.

(iii) If the purchaser of property is not the beneficial owner, but a trustee or a nominee, it should be obligatory on him to disclose the name and code number of the beneficial owner(s).

(iv) In addition to transactions in immovable property and stock and shares, this system can be extended for various other classes of transactions, such as loan transactions, gifts, purchase of jewellery, ornaments, &c., which are exempt from expenditure tax and where, therefore, the taxpayer may be required to support his claims for exemption with duly completed vouchers. In all such cases the recipient of cash may be required to complete a form and hand it over to the payer, i.e., the lender in the case of a loan, the debtor in the case of a repayment of debt, the depositor in the case of a bank deposit, the donor in the case of a gift, bequest and legacy, the purchaser of jewellery gold ornaments, &c.,—we have an incentive to insist on the completion of such vouchers, which they may be required to produce in connection with their tax returns. This should be made obligatory whenever the payment involved exceeds, say, Rs. 5,000 and optional in other cases.

(v) The code numbers of nominal holders and beneficial owners may be included also in the share registers of companies, and copies of dividend vouchers (containing the code number) issued to shareholders required to be sent to the Revenue Department.

I am satisfied, after discussing the matter with the Income Tax Department, that this scheme is workable and its introduction would be a great deal easier (arousing less virulent opposition) if it is made in connection with a major reform of the tax system than if it is left to a later stage. The need for it, it should be emphasised, arises not only in connection with the new taxes but for the sake of eliminating (or at least circumscribing) the serious evasion of the present income tax and profits tax.

If it is felt that the full scheme would encounter too much opposition, the scheme may initially be confined to the proposals outlined in (i), (ii), (iii), leaving (iv) and (v) to a later stage.

4

REPORT ON MEXICAN TAX REFORM[1]

---

[1] This is a somewhat abbreviated version of a report prepared at the invitation of the Mexican Ministry of Finance and written in Mexico in September 1960. Letter of transmittal omitted.

1. There is urgent need for a radical and comprehensive reform of the tax system of Mexico for two major reasons.

2. The first is that the current revenue from taxation is inadequate for the needs of a dynamic community with a rapid growth of population and its requirements for accelerated developments, both in its economic and its cultural aspects. The current revenue from taxation (Federal, State and Municipal) in Mexico is around 9 per cent. of the gross national product and is among the lowest in the world. It has been kept steady at this figure only by continued modification of the rules and by increasing the rates of taxation; and expert opinion appears agreed that within the present framework it would be very difficult to enlarge it. While the taxable capacity of a country (as measured by the percentage of the national product that can be taken in taxation) is obviously greatly dependent on its income per head, there is little doubt that the public revenue of Mexico is too small not only absolutely, but relatively to its stage of underdevelopment. In Ceylon, for example, where income per head is only about one half as high as it is in Mexico, the level of taxation amounts to 20 per cent. of the gross national product. Even in India, whose income per head at 60–70 dollars a year is only about one-fourth of that of Mexico, the ratio of public revenue to the G.N.P. exceeds 10 per cent. The proportion is appreciably higher also in most other Latin American countries in a similar stage of development.

3. The inadequacy of public revenue has two important consequences. It forces undue economies precisely in those fields of public expenditure (like health and education) which may be

dispensable in the short-run, but which are the most important from the point of view of long-run progress. It also yields persistent budgetary deficits which force the Central Bank to follow a highly restrictive credit policy (in the interest of protecting the balance of payments and of the internal purchasing power of the currency) which in turn has highly undesirable effects on the pace of economic growth, without fully compensating for the effects of the weakness in the state of public finances on the stability of the peso.

4. A higher level of public revenue would make it possible not only to increase the social and developmental expenditures of the State but also to pursue a more expansionary credit policy, and thereby accelerate the pace of industrial development. The rate of population increase of Mexico, around 3 per cent., is among the highest in the world. This means that even to maintain the current living standards there must be a sizable proportion (amounting perhaps to 6–8 per cent.) of the national income devoted to *net* investment. In order to ensure that there is a sufficient growth of income per head to double the standards of living of the population in 25 years (which cannot be regarded as an immoderate aspiration) the rate of growth of the national product must average 6 per cent. per year, which means that the share of net investment in the national income must reach 12 to 16 per cent. There is no possible way of securing these objectives except by a much higher public revenue both absolutely and in relation to public expenditure.

5. The second major reason for a comprehensive reform of the tax system is partly a political one. It resides in the fact that the growing economic inequality between the different classes, together with the regressive character of the existing system of taxation, threatens to undermine the social fabric and thus endangers the prospects of a peaceful, constitutional evolution of society.

6. The need for a fiscal reform that would strengthen social stability and democratic institutions is increasingly felt over wider areas of Latin America and has recently been stressed at the Meeting of the O.S.A. in Bogota.

7. The economic development of Mexico over the last twenty

years (greatly helped by the delayed consequences of the agricultural reform releasing the productive forces on the land and also by governmental policies in assisting agriculture) has certainly been impressive: its percentage rate of growth was amongst the highest among the countries of the Western Hemisphere. But it was attended (just like the industrial revolutions of Europe in the nineteenth century) by a rapid build-up of large fortunes, with a consequent sharp increase in the inequality in the distribution of wealth. Though firm or detailed statistics are not available, it does not appear that the masses of the population (the urban workers and the peasants) have yet participated anywhere near proportionately in the growth of productivity and of incomes per head. As a result the inequality in the distribution of incomes (the skewness of income distribution) has attained dimensions which make it among the highest in the world. According to calculations of Mrs. Navarrete (based on a sample study of the Office of Statistics) 300,000 families amounting to some 5 per cent. of the total number, appropriated to themselves in 1957 more than 40 per cent. of the total national income. Of these, 135,000 families accounting for 2·3 per cent. of the total, alone received over 26 per cent. of the national income. As against this in Britain and the United States the share of the highest 5 per cent. of the families was only around 30 per cent. These figures moreover are before adjustment for the share of income taken in taxation. In Britain and the United States an appreciable share of the high incomes is effectively taxed. In Mexico, on the other hand— owing to both legislative provisions and administrative defects— the effective rate of taxation on large incomes from property appears to be very low. Taking both direct and indirect taxes together there can be little doubt that the proportion of income effectively paid in taxation is lower in the high income ranges (with the exception of high salary incomes taxed under Schedule IV) than in the case of average incomes.

In fact, the only form in which property seems to be genuinely taxed at present is through the taxation of business profits (much of which is paid by large corporations); and it is questionable how far the incidence of this tax falls on the shareholder, and how far it falls on the community at large.

8. The existing tax system of Mexico is both inefficient and unjust in its incidence. It is inefficient because with the instruments at its disposal it is incapable of preventing large-scale tax evasion or of bringing important classes of gains, which are legally liable, within the scope of taxation. (Nor is it possible to change this situation by mere administrative improvements.) The system is unjust because it favours income from the ownership of capital as against income from work (owing to a whole host of omissions and exemptions as well as an unconcealed bias in the law) to a degree that must be unparalleled among the countries that set themselves economic and social objectives such as Mexico has.

9. The present tax immunity of the wealthy classes is a serious drag on the growth of the economy, mainly because it causes a considerable proportion of the national resources to be devoted to unnecessary luxury consumption; and also because, given the low levels of consumption of the masses of the population, these resources provide the only potential source from which the resources devoted to development could be enlarged. Furthermore, luxury consumption is that component of the national expenditure which has the highest import content, so that the failure to tax the wealthy classes also aggravates considerably the problem of the balance of payments.

10. The adoption of the proposals in this report would result in the introduction of an effective and impartial system of progressive taxation which would ensure—as far as it is possible to do so—that the burden of taxation is equitably shared between rich and poor, between those who derive their income from property and those who derive income from work. Their adoption would necessitate far-reaching institutional as well as legal changes. The most important stumbling block to the institution of an effective system of taxation on property incomes is the anonymity of mobile property (owing to the prevailing system of bearer shares); and I am convinced that until effective steps are taken to prevent wealthy individuals from hiding behind the cloak of anonymity, the creation of a just system of taxation will prove impossible. In the long-run a situation under which a privileged group of citizens can secure immunity from the com-

mon social burdens and obligations under the protection of a secrecy which is denied to all other citizens will be found intolerable. But it is greatly to be hoped that this highly anomalous situation will be brought to an end sooner rather than later, and by means of orderly and constitutional, rather than violent, change.

11. I am under no illusion that in the political and social context of Mexico the implementation of these proposals will cause a change that is little short of a social revolution, comparable in nature to that caused by the land reform which followed the Revolution in 1910. It is hopeless to expect that it would not be strongly resisted by the classes whose privileges would be impaired any more than was the case with the land reform itself. But whatever justification there may have been for the protection and preservation of these immunities and privileges for the sake of encouraging economic development in the early stages of Mexico's industrialisation, I feel certain that the time has now come when the adoption of fundamental reforms is essential if further social and economic progress is to be guaranteed within the framework of a free and democratic society which gives reality to the basic objectives of the Revolution of 1910.

12. It has not been possible, within the time available to me, to work out the scheme of tax reform in more than general outline, and the administrative and legal implications of the proposals need to be considered in far more detail before they can be implemented. Nor has it been possible to review the existing system of taxation outside the field of income and property taxes, though I feel sure that in this field also rationalisation of existing techniques would lead to a considerable increase in revenue as well as to improvements in their effects on the economy. Nor was either time or sufficient data available to make any detailed estimate of the revenue effects of the present proposals. Estimates, given at the end of this Report[1], based on such statistical data as were available (derived from sample studies) indicate that the adoption of the proposals in regard to *personal taxation* might ultimately increase the existing revenue (not counting any increase in revenue due to the growth of the national income since 1957) six or seven times. As regards company taxation,

[1] The detailed estimates are omitted from this version.

it appears that on the basis of the present declaration of gross receipts under Schedules I and II the restrictions recommended on the range of deductible expenses, together with the closer scrutiny of company accounts which is now undertaken by public auditors, would increase the current revenue by three to four times. The ultimate yield of income tax and profits tax (not counting the yield from the taxation of capital gains, the annual tax on net wealth, or the gift tax) assuming a 100 per cent. enforcement of liability, and on the schedule of tax rates recommended, would thus amount to some 14–15 thousand millions of pesos on the basis of the national income of 1957, as against the actual yield of 2·7 thousand million in that year. While a 100 per cent. coverage is only a theoretical limit, it is not too sanguine to expect that within 2–3 years of the adoption of the new system the revenue from personal taxation should increase by 2·5 thousand million, and the revenue from company taxation by 2 thousand millions, raising the total revenue from taxes on income to two and a half times the present level.

13. It should be emphasised that this additional taxation, so far from being a "burden" on development, would imply a transfer in resources from luxury consumption to investment and thus secure a far better balance in the use of the national resources.

14. As the political history of many Western countries shows, the long-term effects of the introduction of effective progressive taxation are not to be measured, however, by their financial consequences alone. Their effect on the degree of social cohesion and on the attitudes and co-operation of the various social classes are further benefits which cannot be expressed in quantitative terms.

II. INCOME TAX AND CORPORATION TAX

15. The first part of the proposals aims at the introduction of a global income tax on individuals and a corporation profits tax on limited companies, in replacement of the current cedular taxes on income and of the distributable profits tax and the excess profits tax on businesses. It is proposed that the existing cedular

income taxes should be transformed into a single income tax which differs from the existing system in the following main respects:

(*a*) It is levied on the *total* income of an individual from all sources, instead of separately on each particular source;

(*b*) It operates with a single rate schedule, applicable to all kinds of income and not by separate schedules for different kinds of income;

(*c*) It is based on a comprehensive notion of income which embraces all such gains or benefits as increase an individual's net worth over a period, whilst the present system leaves important kinds of such benefits untaxed;

(*d*) It regards the family rather than the individual as the basic economic unit for progressive personal taxation.

16. The adoption of such a system would not involve the introduction of entirely new methods of tax assessment and collection. Many features of the existing cedular system would be retained though it would be possible (and advisable) to reduce the number of separate schedules. It would be more correct to say that the adoption of these proposals would involve the absorption of the existing system into a single comprehensive tax on income.

17. It is suggested that unlike the present cedular tax, the new income tax should be levied on individuals only and not on legal entities as such. The tax would continue to be charged to businesses run by individuals or to partnerships with unlimited liability, but the assessment of such businesses to income tax would merely be a convenient method of getting at the income of the individuals who own them. The final tax liability on the profits of such businesses would depend on the total income and the family circumstances of their individual owners.

18. Legal entities would also be taxed as legal entities in so far as they are limited liability companies (i.e. Sociedad Anonima or Sociedad de Responsabilidad Limitada). But they should be assessed to a separate tax, which may simply be called the *Profits Tax*, and which would differ from the income tax in being a flat-rate tax charged at a single rate (i.e. subject to the exception considered below, this tax would be a *proportionate* tax, and not, as the income tax, one which is progressive, at any rate within a

certain range). The considerations which argue in favour of a progressive tax on the total income of *individuals* have no counterpart in the case of *companies*. There is no reason, in equity, why the profits of a large company should be taxed more heavily than the profits of a small company, considering that both companies may be owned by shareholders with varying degrees of individual wealth (who would be taxed at a progressive rate on their personal income and capital gains). Considerations of economic efficiency argue strongly in favour of a flat-rate on company profits, irrespective of the size of these profits or their relation to the amount of capital employed by the business. If business profits are taxed at a progressive rate the marginal rate of taxation is bound to be much higher than the average or effective rate, and the effective rate itself will be rising with every increase in profits. These penalties on size and expansion militate against rational allocation of resources without any corresponding gain in the equity of the allocation of the burden between persons. For this reason the existing *excess profit tax* which taxes profits the more heavily the higher the amount of profits earned in relation to the amount of capital employed by the business (subject to a limit of 10 per cent. on total profits), quite apart from its extreme cumbrousness, seems to be conceived on the wrong lines. There is no reason in equity nor in economic expediency why a higher ratio of profit to capital employed should attract heavier taxation. On the contrary the general presumption is that a business which earns a higher ratio of profit on its capital uses the resources at its command more efficiently, and would therefore deserve special encouragement in relation to some other businesses which make a lesser profit on the resources which they employ.

19. Whenever separate taxes are imposed on businesses *qua* businesses, special problems arise on the tax treatment of that part of the profits which is distributed to the owners in the form of dividends and therefore enters into the shareholder's personal income. In some countries that part of the tax on the corporation which is attributable to the dividend is credited to the personal tax account of the shareholder. (This was the original British conception modified since the Second World War.) In other countries

(such as the U.S., France, etc.), the tax on the corporation is regarded as something quite independent of the individual income tax, and the company dividend, which is *paid* net of corporation tax, is further subjected to income tax in the hands of the shareholders.

20. As is readily seen, the former system is equivalent to a company tax confined to the undistributed profits of companies whereas the latter system is a tax on the whole profit, irrespective of how much or how little of that profit is distributed. With the latter tax, therefore, the burden on the company is the lighter the higher the ratio of total earnings to dividends, and vice versa. It is also evident that the latter system is capable of yielding the same total revenue with a lower rate of tax than the former system. Since the companies which retain a higher proportion of their current earnings are, by and large, the fast expanding companies which contribute most to industrial growth, the economic implications of a tax of the latter kind (i.e. of the "American" rather than the "British" kind) are definitely more favourable. I therefore recommend that the Profits Tax on companies should be treated as something distinct from the income tax on individuals and that the dividends paid out of profits which have already borne the Profit Tax should be further liable to income tax in the hands of the shareholders who receive them.

21. The implications of these proposals, together with more detailed suggestions for improving the existing rules concerning income tax will be discussed below under the following headings:

(1) Consolidation of the current cedular system.
(2) The proposed rate schedule and allowances.
(3) Aggregation.
(4) Suggested changes in the definition of income.
(5) Required changes in commercial and company law, and institutions.

1. *Consolidation of the Current Cedular System*

22. Since the income tax will be a single tax on the individual and not a series of separate taxes on the revenue yielded by particular sources of income, the classification of incomes according to various "schedules" need be retained only for the purpose

of facilitating the process of administration (i.e. the machinery of assessment and collection). The different kinds of incomes involve different problems of legal definition and administrative treatment and for this reason, the division of income into separate schedules should be retained. (In this the proposed system closely resembles the existing British system, which is also administered under separate schedules, though as part of a single uniform tax on all income.) With a uniform rate schedule it should be possible, however, to consolidate the existing seven schedules into four, corresponding to the four different kinds of income involving peculiar problems both of law and of administration. To avoid confusion I shall use the letters A to D to denote the schedules of the new classification as against Schedules I to VII of the existing system.

The system I propose is as follows:

Type of Income	New System	Incorporating Schedules of existing system
Profits of business activity	A	I, II, III
Earnings of professional activity	B	V
Salaries and wages	C	IV
Income from capital (rent, interest, dividends, capital gains)	D	VI, VII

23. The profits of business activity of individuals and partnerships should be assessed to tax in the same manner as the profits tax on companies (described in paragraphs 33–35 below) but the ultimate tax liability would be determined by reference to the total income of the owner (or owners) of the business and of his personal allowances. Since the tax assessed and collected from the business would be credited to the personal account of the owner (the tax credit being divided among the owners, in the case of a partnership, according to their aliquot share of the profits) when the individual owner made a full return of his income from all sources, appropriate refund should be made for any excess in the amount of tax paid by the business over his personal tax liability.

24. In the case of income from professional activity in similar

manner a return should be asked for, disclosing the total income of the taxpayer from all sources (as well as his personal circumstances) and the assessment made accordingly.

25. With regard to salaries and wages there is no need to ask each taxpayer for a full return; since in the case of the great majority who do not engage in regular professional or business activity, or have any property from which they derive any income, a simple declaration made in an initial year that they do *not* possess capital above a certain amount and do *not* run a business should be sufficient. This initial return, however, should disclose their family circumstances, and some simple coding system would have to be adopted (as e.g. a single person having Code No. 1, married couple Code No. 2, married couple with one child No. 3, etc.), to instruct the employer in connection with tax tables how much tax to deduct from any particular income of each employee. Thus the income tax on salaries and wages will be deducted at source as at present, but there will be a more complicated procedure of withholding, and a final adjustment of liability, which will be further discussed below.

26. In the case of taxpayers who derive any substantial income from capital, a full return will have to be asked for, to disclose both their total income from all sources and also the annual capital transactions (purchase and sale of capital assets during the year).

27. Since the tax under Schedules C and D will be deducted at source, in many cases by a higher amount than the ultimate liability, there may be frequent cases of claims for refund tax. It is suggested that in all cases where an excessive amount of tax was deducted and a refund is due to the taxpayer, the amount so involved should carry an interest of 10 per cent. per annum as between the date when the income payment was due (and the tax was withheld) and the date when the refund was made.

2. *The Proposed Rate Schedule and Allowances*

28. There is no justification for the existing differences in the rates of tax charged under the different schedules either from the point of view of equity or its economic effects. If the State wishes to subsidise certain lines of activity or to penalise others, it has

many instruments at its disposal other than the income tax. From
the point of view of a fair and equitable system of taxation, it is
essential that the tax levied on different individuals (or rather
families) should be based on criteria that are manifestly impartial, comprehensive and uniform in their incidence.

29. There is a strong case, however, for introducing two further
alterations into the existing rate structure of Mexico. The first
is the raising of exemption limits which would reduce considerably the number of individuals liable to income tax without a
great loss of revenue. The second is a much higher "starting
rate" of taxation, and a more rapid progression so that the
highest or "ceiling rate" of income tax would be reached at a
lower level of income than under the present system. There
are also considerable advantages in retaining a comparatively
low *ceiling* rate of taxation.

30. With these considerations in view I would like to suggest
that the lowest marginal rate of income tax should be not less
than 10 per cent., and that this rate should be raised in steps
of not less than 5 per cent. to an ultimate "ceiling" rate of not
more than 40 per cent. I would also like to suggest that a single
individual should be exempt on the first 12,000 pesos of his
annual income, and the amount of exempted income should be
raised by a further 12,000 pesos for a married couple (without
children or other dependants) and by a further annual 6,000
pesos for each child or other dependant. It is suggested that the
rate of tax starting at 10 per cent. should be raised by 5 per cent.
on each successive slab of 12,000 pesos of annual income. This
would yield the following rate schedule for the single *person*:

On income not exceeding 12,000	*Exempt*
On the bracket 12,000–24,000	10 per cent.
24,001–36,000	15 per cent.
36,001–48,000	20 per cent.
48,001–60,000	25 per cent.
66,001–72,000	30 per cent.
72,001–84,000	35 per cent.
On the excess of income over 84,000	40 per cent.

31. Thus, the maximum marginal rate will be reached at the

income of 84,000 pesos for a single person, 96,000 pesos for a
married couple without children, 108,000 pesos for married
couple with one child or other dependant, etc. It will be seen
that in comparison with the existing schedule of rates, the exemption limits are much higher and the maximum tax rates are
reached very much earlier. Both these changes will contribute
greatly to the efficiency and simplicity of tax administration. Thus,
with the existing system in Mexico in most cases tax begins to
be paid (at the very low rates of 1–3 per cent., rising very gradually) on incomes in excess of 2,000 to 6,000 pesos a year, but the
ceiling rate (which varies between 33 per cent. and 46 per cent.
on the various Schedules) is not reached until an income of
1,000,000 to 2,000,000 pesos is attained (except in the case of
salaries where a ceiling rate of 46 per cent. is reached at 600,000
pesos a year and of Schedule VII with a ceiling rate of 41·2 per
cent. at 500,000 pesos a year).

32. From the point of view of a fair distribution of the tax
burden, it is a matter for consideration whether the allowances
given to the wife and other family dependants should not themselves increase with the size of income, at any rate up to a certain
maximum. If this were adopted I would recommend that the
wife's allowance should be either 12,000 pesos a year or 10 per
cent. of total income, which ever is greater, subject to a maximum
allowance of 24,000 pesos a year; whereas the allowance for a
child or other dependent should be defined as "6,000 pesos or
5 per cent. of total income, whichever is the greater, subject
to a maximum allowance of 12,000 pesos a year." These variable
family allowances would, however, considerably complicate the
problem of deducting income tax at source on wage and salary
earners and for that reason I recommend this system with hesi-
tation.

33. With regard to the profits tax on companies, I suggest
that the single uniform rate of company tax should also be 40
per cent., as there are very considerable administrative advantages
in having the *same* rate of tax both on companies and (as the
marginal or ceiling rate) on individuals. Since, however, this
rate may operate too harshly on small businesses which adopt or
have adopted the legal form of limited liability for reasons

unconnected with taxation, I would recommend that there should be a *special relief for small companies* which could be defined as "one-half of the tax on the first 500,000 pesos of taxable profit or one-third of the tax on the amount by which 1,500,000 pesos exceeds the taxable profit of the year, whichever is less". The effect of such a provision would be to reduce the Profit Tax to 20 per cent. for companies whose profits are 500,000 pesos a year or less, but to withdraw this concession gradually, so that the *effective* rate of taxation approaches 40 per cent. as the profit approaches 1,500,000 pesos. The operation of this concession can be shown in the following table:

Annual profit Pesos	*Tax at full rate* (40%)	*Small company relief*	*Effective tax* (1)–(2)	*Effective tax* %
500,000	200,000	100,000	100,000	20
800,000	320,000	93,000	227,000	28
1,000,000	400,000	66,600	333,300	33⅓
1,250,000	500,000	33,300	466,600	37½
1,500,000	600,000	—	600,000	40

34. I recommend that companies should also be asked to act as agents of the Treasury and deduct income tax at the *full* rate (40 per cent.) on all interest and dividends paid by them to creditors and shareholders, this payment being credited to the tax account of the recipients. If the recipient is a resident individual liable to the personal income tax he would receive a voucher showing the amount of tax deducted, entitling him to a tax refund on all such income on which he is either fully exempt from tax or liable to pay tax at less than the full rate (i.e. in the case of a single person, he would be entitled to a partial refund on the first 84,000 pesos of gross annual interest and dividends received, or in terms of actual receipts, on the first 50,400 pesos *net* interest and dividends received in the year, assuming that he has no income on other schedules on which tax may be due from him). In the case when the recipient is a domestic company liable to the profits tax, the interest and dividend paid should be credited against the profit tax liability of the recipient company, which means simply that for all companies which pay

profits tax at the full rate of 40 per cent., interest and dividends received from other companies can simply be ignored in calculating their taxable profit. If the recipient is a non-resident company or individual, the effect of 40 per cent. deduction at source will generally be offset by a corresponding tax credit from their domestic tax authorities.[1] Thus in the case of U.S. companies or individuals receiving dividends or interest payments from Mexico, on which a 40 per cent. income tax deduction is made, the effect will merely be that (in the case of a company) the effective domestic corporation tax will be 12 instead of 52 per cent. Similarly, a U.S. individual receiving income from Mexico will not be adversely affected by the 40 per cent. income tax deduction at source so long as his marginal rate of income tax in the U.S. is 40 per cent. or more.

3. *Aggregation*

35. Since under the proposed system the family is considered as the basic tax paying unit, rather than the single individual, it is necessary that the income of the various members of the family should be aggregated and that the head of the family (normally the father) should be made responsible for making the tax return for the whole family, and also for being primarily liable for the payment of tax. This matter of aggregation is only of practical importance in the case of wealthy families where, from a tax point of view, it may make a considerable difference whether the wealth and income of the different members of the family are treated separately or together, and where in the absence of aggregation, wealth and income may be diffused among the family members for the purposes of tax avoidance. The aggregation should be compulsory as between husband and wife and minor children (that is to say children up to 21 or up to marriage, whichever occurs sooner) and also with regard to all such dependent relatives (other than minor children or con-

---

[1] In case foreign companies maintain a permanent establishment in Mexico which is not a subsidiary but merely a branch of the foreign undertaking, it is suggested that in addition to the profit tax assessed on the branch, there should be deducted a tax of 40 per cent. on one-third of the profits remaining after deducting the profits tax, in lieu of the deduction that would have been made on dividends if the branch had been organized as a resident subsidiary company.

cubines) with regard to whom a dependants' allowance is claimed.[1] It is not necessary, however, that the *earned* income of wives, concubines or minors should be aggregated with those of the parents which may give rise to considerable administrative complications, without any strong claim in equity. It is therefore suggested that incomes of wives, concubines or minors under Schedules B and C (the present Schedules IV and V) should not be aggregated with the husband or father. (The number of minors in Mexico liable to be taxed on the Schedules IV or V at present must in any case be small, and would become considerably smaller if the tax exemption limits are increased in the manner recommended above.)

4. *Suggested Changes in the Definition of Income*

36. The Mexican system of income tax operates in a discriminatory fashion as between different *kinds* of income-receivers to an extent that is hardly suspected. This partly results from the fact that certain important kinds of gains escape the tax net altogether (whether as a result of explicit provisions of the law or the failure to administer the law effectively), and partly from the fact that the provisions of the law permit deductions from the gross receipts in arriving at "taxable income" for certain kinds of income and not for others, so that the notion of what constitutes "income" for tax purposes is very far from being uniform for different taxpayers. Since the important gains which are outside the scope of the tax net are mostly those which directly arise from, or are closely connected with, the ownership of capital, and the preferential treatment of certain kinds of income, as regards deductible expenses, benefits those who derive income from business activity, and is therefore also closely associated with the ownership of capital, the cumulative effect of these deficiencies in the law or in administration is to give the owners of capital a far more favourable treatment than those who derive their income from work. The proposals detailed below are intended to reduce this bias in favour of capitalists, and thereby

---

[1] Concubines sharing a household with a taxpayer should be entitled to a married woman's allowance if they so desire. Dependents would only qualify for an allowance if (a) they are relatives of the 1st or 2nd degree; (b) they have no independent source of income or wealth other than pensions not exceeding 300 pesos a month.

make a contribution to the democratic ideal of equality of treatment for all citizens. It is not claimed that it would be possible to eliminate this bias altogether. But the proposals listed below, if adopted, would undoubtedly make the allocation of the burden of taxation considerably more equitable than it is at present.[1]

37. For convenience the various proposals are listed according to the types of income classified under the proposed schedules.

A. *Income from Business Activity*
   (i) *The distinction between "greater" and "lesser" income from business*

38. Under the present system taxpayers with "lesser" income (i.e. those under 300,000 pesos a year) are taxed on the basis of their "gross income" (i.e. their business turnover). They are not required to keep the books prescribed by the commercial code or the income tax regulations, and they are only required to report their business turnover in the previous year. Their tax is derived directly from their turnover according, as I understand, to a published table which shows a fixed amount of tax applicable to each gross income bracket for each of seven categories of business activity. These provisions make the income tax on "lesser" taxpayers nothing but a species of a turnover tax. The essence of an income tax is that it is a tax on the profit realised on business transactions and not on the business transactions themselves. The effect of these provisions is therefore that a special turnover tax is imposed on smaller businesses and the exemption limits for income tax proper are raised by an unascertainable (and of course variable) amount.

39. I would suggest that the present provisions should be abolished altogether in the case of *companies*. There is no reason why small companies should not be obliged to follow the requirements of the commercial code and income tax regulations with regard to the keeping of books and the presentation of accounts,

[1] It should be remembered that the taxation of income and profits, and other personal or direct taxes, take up only a proportion of the total taxation imposed by the State; the great bulk of indirect taxes on commodities or transactions (which make up the remainder) very largely falls on the great mass of consumers who derive their income from work and not from property. Taking both direct and indirect taxes into account there can be little doubt that owners of capital bear only a small fraction of the burden which an impartial allocation would require.

in the same way as large companies. With regard to individuals on the other hand I think it would be impracticable to impose the same rigid requirements concerning bookkeeping and accounts on small businesses, as it is unlikely that such provisions could be enforced. I would recommend, however, that the present exemption limit of 300,000 pesos be gradually reduced, and in the meantime the provisions under which the tax payable by such small taxpayers is automatically derived from their turnover on the basis of published tax tables should be abandoned, and instead the tax should be assessed not solely in relation to the size of the turnover but on the basis of a number of criteria, such as the scale of living (the living expenses of a taxpayer can be determined within limits fairly easily) and also a declaration as to the profit made. The taxation of the profits of small businesses constitutes a difficult problem not only in Mexico but in most countries; and I think one has to reckon that there will always be a considerable amount of tax evasion in this category. I do not feel, however, that the particular provisions now in force in Mexico for dealing with this problem are suitable or even consistent with the basic principles of an income tax. If our suggestions concerning exemption limits and family allowances were adopted, the number of taxpayers with a "lesser" gross income who would be liable to income tax would be considerably reduced.

(ii) *Casual profits*

40 Under the present rules profits arising from casual transactions, as against the profits of regular business activity, are taxed at a reduced rate of 20 per cent. There is no justification for this in equity and its retention would be wholly anomalous if the capital gains which now generally escape tax altogether (because they are deemed to arise from civil transactions[1]) are treated as taxable income and taxed in the same way as other income. I suggest, therefore, that the distinction between casual and regular profits be abolished, and casual profit be taxed in the same way as other profits.

---

[1] See para. 65 below.

(iii) *Exemptions to new industries, etc.*

41. If the existing income and profit taxes are revised in the manner suggested it will be necessary to review the existing provisions concerning the tax exemption of new or essential industries. It would of course be possible to apply the existing 40 per cent. exemption to the new company profits tax as well as to the income tax. My own feeling is that a partial or full exemption from profits taxation is an inappropriate instrument for promoting industrial growth and is of doubtful efficiency. I should recommend that the existing provisions for tax exemptions for new or essential industries should be terminated as soon as possible (at least in regard to income tax and profits tax; the question requires more detailed consideration in the case of import and export duties) but that instead, direct subsidies be given for expenditure on fixed capital (industrial buildings, plant and machinery) the magnitude of which could be varied from time to time (and also as between industries) in accordance with the changing needs of the general economic situation. This suggestion is further considered below.

42. I also recommend that the existing exemption of profits arising from the operation of private schools or publishing houses and the preferential treatment of motion picture producers and distributors be abolished.

(iv) *Deductible expenses*

43. Since the Mexican law does not recognise any legitimate expenses whatever in the production of contractual income (under Schedule IV tax is chargeable on the gross compensation received by an employee from his employer, without any deduction whatever, not even exempting reimbursement for travelling expenses, etc.) the range of expenses which should be allowed for deduction in the case of business income ought to be narrowly circumscribed, and confined to those which are directly and inevitably incurred in producing the income that is subject to taxation, such as the direct cost of the raw materials, fuel, etc., consumed and the wages of direct labour. It is doubtful whether even the deduction of general or indirect business

expenses such as the rent of business promises or the salary of managerial or supervisory personnel is consistent with the very broad concept of income which underlies the notion of income under Schedule IV. I would not recommend that the rigid provisions concerning deductions in the case of Schedule IV income should be relaxed, since any relaxation is bound to lead to considerable abuse. But the very fact that no deductions are allowed under Schedule IV for such things as subscriptions to charities, subscriptions to scientific journals or societies, or to professional associations, constitutes a very good reason for disallowing such expenses also for (the present) Schedule I and II tax-payers where, I am sure, such provisions are equally liable to abuse.

44. There is an even stronger case for disallowing the so-called sales promotion outlays such as entertaining, travelling and advertising expenses. When items like entertaining and travelling are allowed as business expenses it is inevitable that personal expenses should masquerade as business expenses, and outlays which are applications of income should come to be treated as deductions in arriving at income. Advertising expenses are more in the nature of expenses for maintaining or improving general earning capacity than of expenditures which are directly and inevitably involved in producing the income. I would suggest that entertainment expenses should be disallowed altogether as a business expense (unless they are given in the form of "entertainment allowances" or "expense accounts" in which case they should be taxable in the hands of the directors, etc., who receive them). In the same way, travelling expenses for the benefit of the owner, partner, director, or higher grade executive of a company should only be allowed as a business expense to the company when it is entered as part of the taxable compensation of the recipient. Finally, I would recommend that classification of outlay on commercial advertising as a business expense should be partially disallowed: the amount deductible should be only a proportion, say one-half of the actual outlay.

45. The allowances for capital wastage under the present system (i.e. depreciation, amortisation and depletion) are equally anomalous within the framework of a system which does not

effectively recognise capital gains for tax purposes. If, as is suggested below, realised capital gains of all kinds are brought within the scope of income taxation, a corresponding allowance should be made for realised capital losses (in the case of business assets these should be allowed as an offset against profits of all kinds; in the case of non-business assets, as an offset against capital gains, present or future). This will make the current allowances in the form of depreciation, amortisation, and depletion unnecessary, since a proper allowance will in any case be made for all capital wastage as and when the losses due to that wastage are actually realised.

46. There is no case, therefore, for any of these allowances on grounds of equity. There is, however, a strong case on grounds of economic expediency for giving special encouragement to expenditure on capital assets, since the rate of expenditure on such assets is one of the most important factors determining the rate of economic progress of society. Depreciation allowances on physical assets (though *not* the amortisation or depletion, which do not relate to physical assets *created* by investment expenditure) can be looked upon as a means of promoting capital expenditure through giving more favourable tax treatment to such expenditure than equity considerations alone would justify. The favourable treatment consists in allowing these expenses to be brought in as a charge at a much earlier date than the date of the actual realisation of the loss. But if depreciation allowances thus contain an element of concealed subsidy which is justified and can only be justified, on account of their effect in promoting economic growth, there is a strong case for selecting a system of allowances which is the most efficacious for that purpose. From this point of view, it is clearly much better if whatever allowances are given are granted simultaneously with the expenditures, than if they are spread over the lifetime of the capital assets in respect of which they are given. I recommend, therefore, that both on economic grounds and also on grounds of administrative simplicity, the existing system of depreciation allowances be replaced by a system of once-and-for-all capital allowances given simultaneously with capital expenditure, which should be at least equal in amount to the *discounted value* of the present depreci-

ation allowances. According to the present law, there are three standard rates of depreciation:

1. Buildings, constructions, and permanent improvements made thereto.   5 %
2. Machinery (including the expense of its installation), scientific apparatus and instruments, etc.   10 %
3. Vehicles, ships, airplanes, rolling stock, machinery used in the construction of industry, etc.   20 %

The depreciation rates are given on a straight line basis (i.e. an equal percentage of the original cost being allowed on each successive year) and taking 10 per cent. as the normal rate of interest these depreciation allowances are equivalent, in terms of present discounted value to (roughly) 33⅓ per cent. of expenditure under Category 1, 50 per cent. of expenditure under Category 2, and 75 per cent. of expenditure under Category 3.

47. From the point of view of the enterprises this alternative system of current capital allowances has the advantage that it eases their financial strain precisely at the time when they most need it; i.e. when the capital expenditure is actually incurred, and not when the profits made as a result of that expenditure are subsequently brought into charge. The scheme is analogous, therefore, to an automatic matching credit on all capital expenditure given by the State in a proportion varying inversely with the durability of the capital assets.[1]

48. I suggest, therefore, that with the adoption of the new system of taxation there should be introduced a new scheme of *capital allowances* charged against current profits and amounting to 33⅓ per cent., 50 per cent. and 75 per cent. respectively on the three categories of capital expenditure described above. If the allowances cannot be fully absorbed out of the year's profit, any unabsorbed portion should be carried forward against the profits of the following year, the unabsorbed amount being

---

[1] The scheme has the further advantage from the point of view of the businessman that the capital allowances are given in money of the same purchasing power as the one in which the capital expenditure was incurred. With a continued inflationary trend of prices there is a frequent complaint that depreciation allowances are given in terms of depreciated currency and are insufficient to cover replacement costs. With the suggested scheme the allowance on each piece of equipment is given in money of the same purchasing power as that in which the expenditure was laid out.

augmented by an annual interest allowance of 10 per cent.

49. I would also recommend that in addition to this basic capital allowance, which should be established on a permanent basis, there should be granted a special development allowance on *newly created* capital assets, the amount of which could be varied from time to time in accordance with the state of the economy and also as between industries in accordance with their importance to economic development. I would suggest that the *special development rebate* should amount to 20 per cent. for all categories of assets and to 40 per cent. for assets used by industries designated as essential industries by the Government. (As already mentioned, I would recommend that with the introduction of the system of capital allowances and development rebates, the existing income and profits tax concessions to new or essential industries be withdrawn.)

50. There is no case, however, for the retention, in whatever form, of the present amortisation and depletion allowances. Amortisation allowances represent the write-off of capitalised goodwill and there is no justification for the tax system giving any allowance on such expenditure. Unlike physical assets, the creation of goodwill cannot be promoted by tax allowances: the only result of such allowances is that businesses as going concerns change hands at a higher price than they would otherwise, and the seller of a business makes a larger (and, so far, normally completely untaxed) gain. If capital gains and losses are effectively brought within the tax net, losses on capitalised goodwill will be automatically allowed for as and when such losses are realised, and the gains from the sale of goodwill will be correspondingly taxed. Exactly analogous arguments hold for mineral depletion. Minerals cannot be created, nor is their exploitation in any way promoted by the depletion allowance: the only effect of such an allowance is to enable the owner of land or the holder of the concession to charge a higher price for the sale of the concession than he would have been able to charge otherwise.

5. *Allowances for Losses*

51. Present Mexican law does not recognise an operating loss for tax purposes, except in so far as the profits and losses resulting

from different business operations are consolidated if they arise within the same schedule. But there is no carry-forward of un-absorbed losses against the profit of future years. This asymmetrical treatment of gains and losses is bound to have undesirable effects on willingness to bear risks: as most economists working in this field recognise, the deleterious effects on risk-bearing and on investment arise, not from taxation as such, but only from the fact that while gains are taxed, losses are not correspondingly allowed. It is generally recognised, of course, that *full* allowance for losses (which would mean the recognition of a negative tax or subsidy payment whenever the accounts show a negative profit) is capable of such wide abuse as to make it thoroughly impracticable. There is no such valid objection, however, to allowing an operating loss to be carried forward against future income from the same source, provided only that all such loss claims automatically lapse whenever the ownership of a business changes hands (in the case of a company, whenever there is a change in the ownership of the majority of the shares). I recommend, therefore, that the indefinite carry-forward of the net operating losses of businesses be allowed.

52. I also recommend that net realised losses on the sale of capital assets should be carried forward against future capital gains of the taxpayer, but should not be offset against income from other sources. If a taxpayer's estate shows net unabsorbed capital losses at death, this should be allowed to be carried back against tax paid in the previous five years either on account of capital gains or other income. Capital losses realised on business assets (defined as assets on which a capital or depreciation allowance has been given) in excess of the depreciation or capital allowance granted, should be deductible against operating gains; but the capital losses of businesses on assets on which no capital allowance is given (losses on the sale of real property or stocks and shares) should not be offset against operating gains, but should be allowed to be carried forward to be offset only against future capital gains of the same kind.

B. *Income from Professional Activity*

53. The comments made above on the liberal treatment of

expenses concerning the profits of business activity are equally applicable concerning the income of professional services now taxed under Schedule V. There is no justification for the discriminatory treatment as between Schedule IV and V taxpayers in matters such as charitable contributions, subscriptions to professional publications, automobile expenses, depreciation, amortisation, etc. This discrimination is the more glaring since Schedule IV taxpayers cannot escape tax by concealing their income, whereas Schedule V taxpayers benefit from tax evasion through under-reporting. (In addition they also benefit at present from a more favourable schedule of tax rates.[1])

54. I cannot see the rationale of the present elaborate scheme by which the payor of income of professional, etc., services withholds 2 per cent. of the payment on account of income tax which is then credited to the account of the taxpayer. If a withholding scheme of this sort is put into operation at all the provision for tax withholding ought surely to be more like 20 per cent. than 2 per cent.

55. I suggest that the tax should be withheld at the rate of 20 per cent. but that, in a manner similar to interest and dividend payments, any subsequent refund of tax should be augmented by an annual interest allowance of 10 per cent., the interest being reckoned from the date when the tax was withheld to the date when the re-payment is actually made.

C. *Income from Services as an Employee (Salaries and Wages)*

56. I feel that unless the allowances for expenses under present Schedules I, II, III and V are considerably tightened up there is a strong case for allowing certain kinds of expenses (such as charitable expenses, expenses on scientific or professional journals, etc.) to employees in the same manner as they are allowed to independent professional workers. On the other hand, I cannot see the justification for excluding from taxable income bonuses received by company directors which are now considered as "additional voluntary payments in the nature of profit parti-

---

[1] In some other countries the income of self-employers and of small businesses is taxed, on the contrary, at a *heavier* rate so as to compensate for the greater likelihood of under-reporting.

cipations". Similarly there is no case for exempting the year-end bonuses granted to public employees without any limitation as to their amount or of the salary of the recipient. The provisions relating to public employees in this context should be assimilated to those of private enterprises.

57. But the main respect in which the present law concerning Schedule IV requires amendment is that taxable income under Schedule IV is a *monthly concept* and not an *annual concept* (i.e. the object of taxation under Schedule IV is the monthly income, and not the annual income). This is clearly discriminatory and its retention would militate against the introduction of a single comprehensive income tax on the lines recommended.[1]

58. In most other countries in which the income tax on the wages and salaries of the employees is withheld at its source, the tax liability is nevertheless computed on annual, and not on monthly income, and a final adjustment is made when at the end of the year the total income is known and the final liability is computed. Under the British system where the deductions proceed by a rather ingenious method of cumulative averaging, the taxpayer automatically gets the benefit of tax repayment due to excessive weekly or monthly deductions as his weekly or monthly income fluctuates. Under the American system the provisional deductions made in the course of the year are adjusted in the following year on the basis of the taxpayer's return of his annual income. I suggest that the existing system of tax deductions for employees be revised either on the British or on the American pattern and that a special study be made as to which of these two systems is more appropriate in the circumstances of Mexico.

D. *Income from Capital*

59. Of all the schedules of the present Mexican income tax

---

[1] For wage and salary earners whose monthly income is the same for each successive month of a fiscal year it clearly makes no difference whether the tax is computed on a monthly basis or an annual basis. But whenever the monthly income fluctuates in the course of the year—and it can do so either on account of illness or unemployment or simply on account of overtime or promotion to a higher grade in the course of the year—the sum of the taxes computed on a monthly basis will invariably exceed the tax on the *same annual income* computed on an annual basis. Since all other taxpayers have their income computed on an annual basis this constitutes a further serious discrimination against the wage and salary earners.

system the provisions and manner of operation of the present Schedule VI are undoubtedly the least satisfactory. Indeed, one is tempted to say that the exceptional favours which they accord to various forms of income from property are almost without parallel in the income tax legislation of other countries. To substantiate this statement it is sufficient to draw attention to the following features of the present rules under Schedule VI:

(1) Income from immobile property (land and houses) is left almost entirely untaxed, presumably on the ground that this "source" is already taxed in the form of an annual property tax by the individual states.

(2) Dividends (which form the great bulk of the income from the capital of industrial and commercial enterprises) are not taxed at all in the hands of the recipient, apart from the flat rate 15 per cent. tax on distributable profits which is more in the nature of a corporation's profits tax, with varying reliefs for reinvestment which can attain 100 per cent. in which case the tax is not payable at all (not even on that part of the profit which is distributed as dividend).[1]

(3) Many forms of interest payment are not taxed at the full progressive rate but only at a proportionate rate of 10 per cent., while other kind of interest payment (interest paid by banks and savings institutions; interest on government and public utility bonds, and also on bonds of private corporations if so directed by the Minister of Finance; bonds of international credit institutions; finally all mortgage bonds and mortgage certificates issued by credit institutions or issued with their participation) are exempt altogether from income tax.

(4) Capital gains made either on mobile or immobile property are not brought into charge except those gains arising out of real property transactions of companies which are taxed under Schedule I and II.

60. There can be little doubt that any genuine reform of the Mexican tax system must involve a radical change in the present state of affairs concerning the taxation of income and of gains

---

[1] The wide discretionary powers given to the Ministry of Finance to exempt individual companies in whole or in part from the distributable profits tax is one of the least desirable features of the present legislation. Under the scheme proposed in this report, the distributable profits tax is abolished altogether.

I

from capital. Some of the present provisions (such as the flat-rate deduction in the case of dividend and certain kinds of interest income) are probably just a consequence of the impossibility of assessing individual recipients at their proper rate, when their total income from dividends and interest is unknown and when no effective machinery exists for discovering it. Other provisions (such as the tax exempion on bonds and mortgages) are the consequence of the desire of the authorities to promote the more widespread holding of financial assets, which, incidentally, was more effectively promoted by the re-purchase practices of the Bank of Mexico and the "Nacional Financiera" than by the tax exemptions. Yet others are the result of the anonymous character of all mobile capital (i.e. stock and share capital) which, under the prevailing legal system of bearer bonds and bearer shares, makes it impossible for the Government to discover either the wealth or the income of a particular individual. So long as this anonymity obtains it will prove impossible to evolve a satisfactory system of taxation; and in a following section proposals will be put forward which aim at overcoming the effects of anonymity without basically altering the present civil or commercial law. Apart from this, the system of taxation under Schedule VI could be considerably improved if the system of deducting tax at source were made quite general and if the tax so deducted were at the maximum rate (i.e. at the suggested 40 per cent. rate) with the income recipient being obliged to claim a refund of tax on all such income on which less than the maximum rate is payable. There is no justification either in equity or in expediency why tax withholding should be at such low rates as 10 per cent. or 15 per cent. (a rate that must be much below the true rate applicable to the great majority of the recipients) particularly if, as was suggested above, interest were paid by the Government for the period for which the taxpayer is out of pocket owing to any excessive deduction.

61. Our recommendations for a fundamental reform of the taxation of income from capital are set out below under the following headings:

(i) Universal deduction at source at maximum rates;
(ii) Abolition of tax exemptions;

(iii) General inclusion of rental income from real property;

(iv) New and detailed provisions for the taxation of capital gains.

The effective implementation of these recommendations will also involve legal and administrative changes, and the introduction of complementary tax on net wealth which will be described later.

(i) *Universal deduction at source at maximum rates*

62. It is suggested that there should be a general obligation on the payor of income for the use of capital (in its broadest sense, i.e. on anyone who pays a rental for the use of either mobile or immobile property or pays interest on funds borrowed in whatever form, and on any company or business which pays out shares of profit whether under the name of dividends, bonuses or premiums, or under any other name) to deduct tax from the money so paid out at the rate of 40 per cent. and to issue a certificate to the recipient to this effect. Copies of these certificates (one to be issued with respect to each transaction, that is, each payment to each recipient) should be forwarded to the income tax department at the time when the monies so deducted are remitted. The certificates should detail the name and address of the payor and of the payee, and if the system of code numbers (explained below) were adopted, the code number of the payor and the payee. In the case of payment of interest and dividend on bearer securities, such payment should be rendered through one of the nominated banks (who would also be responsible for issuing tax deduction certificates) and not by the firms or individuals who are making the payments.

63. The individual recipients in possession of duly made out certificates of tax deduction should claim a refund of tax on all that part of their income which is not subject to tax at the maximum rate. The submission of a full income and wealth tax return, including a full report of the purchases and sales of capital assets during the year (described more fully in Section VI below), should be made a pre-condition for the refund of tax: but it should not be required that a taxpayer should submit more certificates than are necessary to establish his claim, (i.e. which

relate to that part of his income on which a refund is claimed). Interest at 10 per cent. should be allowed for the whole period between the effective date of tax withholding and the effective date of tax repayment, except for such period of delay as is caused by the failure of the taxpayer to submit his income and wealth tax return by the date due. The "due date" should be the end of the period of three months following the fiscal or calendar year to which the return relates.

(ii) *Abolitions of tax exemptions*

64. It is suggested that *all* existing exemptions from income tax on interest paid on federal, state or private bonds or obligations should be abolished. There is no reason for supposing that these exemptions effectively promote the processes of savings and investment; in so far as they do have an effect in enabling the borrower to borrow at a lower rate of interest (which itself is questionable) it would be greatly preferable if the Government promoted investment in some other manner (for example through subsidies or subventions on actual capital outlay, or through providing a matching loan at relatively low rates of interest, which are in any case more effective) rather than through provisions which ride roughshod over the whole system of equitable personal taxation. In all countries in which such tax exemptions exist (as for example in the U.S.A. in regard to state bonds) their presence is universally condemned by experts on public finance. In Mexico these tax exemptions cover such a wide range of financial transactions that their *differential* effect in making borrowing easier for particular classes must be almost nil. This should make their abolition easier, since it will make less difference to the facility of borrowing than would be the case if exemptions had been confined to a narrower category of borrowers.

(iii) *General inclusion of rental income from real property*

65. Except in a few special cases where rentals are taxed as business income or when they come under the notion of a lease of an entire business, or else a lease destined for a commercial purpose (such as a factory, hotel, etc.), the rentals, as well as the

sales of real property are classified as "civil transactions", and as such are outside the scope of the income tax law. It seems to me essential that they should be brought within the scope of income taxation since an individual's capacity to pay is measured by his income as such, and not by income from certain sources to the exclusion of others. Nor does the fact that real property is subjected to a state tax provide any real justification for its exemption from federal income tax. Territorial entities within sovereign nations, like states or municipalities, find it convenient to levy taxes on the real property situated within their territory, for the simple reason that the taxation of real property does not raise difficult problems of residence which arise, e.g., in the case of a local income tax. But the fact that real property is a convenient object of local taxation does not constitute a ground for its exemption from federal taxation: there is no reason why the same individual or the same property-owner should not be subjected to separate taxes in the hands of two or more taxing jurisdictions. The dual taxation arises simply and solely from the fact that a state administration exists, over and above the federal administration. In the case of the commercial receipts tax, the existence of a state tax is not regarded as ground for exemption from the federal tax, or vice versa; and there is no more justification for such grounds of exemption in the case of income from real property. (In Britain and many other countries there is both local and state taxation on real property.) Excluding rental income from income tax again favours the higher income groups which possess such income in much greater proportion than the rest of the community.

66. If the tax system is to be equitable it is important that income from land should be taxable, irrespective of whether the property is lent for a money rental, or whether it is for the direct use of the owner. This is the principle of the British system of income tax (as well as of the state property tax in Mexico) though not of the U.S. tax. Without the inclusion of the imputed rent of the owner-occupier it is impossible to do justice as between those who live in their own houses and those (the great majority of wage and salary earners) who occupy rented houses. If the imputed rents of the owner-occupier are not charged,

justice requires that the rents paid by other taxpayers (under Schedule IV and V) should be deducted from taxable income.

67. I suggest therefore that the *net income* of real property of all kinds should be explicitly included under taxable incomes under Schedule D (the present Schedule VI); that *net income* should be defined as gross income less permitted deductions categorised by law; and that *gross income* should be defined as *either* 10 per cent. per annum of the value of the property, *or* the gross rent actually received from the lease of the property, whichever is the *greater*. The value of the property should be the value declared for wealth tax purposes (see below paragraph 80) and if the property is owned by persons exempt from the wealth tax, it should be the current market value, as would be ascertained for purpose of the gift or inheritance tax.

68. The *permitted deductions* from gross income or gross rental in arriving at the net income taxable under this schedule should be as follows:

1. Real property taxes payable to the states or municipalities;
2. Interest on loans which are a charge on the property (secured by mortgage bonds or certificates); also, to encourage the construction of houses designed for owner occupancy, the amortisation of mortgages—of owner-occupied houses.
3. Insurance premia on fire and casualty insurance on buildings and permanent installations, excluding insurance on movable contents of premises;
4. Maintenance expenses on the property, including wages or salaries of personnel wholly or mainly engaged in looking after the property;
5. All repair expenditures provided that they do not constitute an improvement to the property (such as an addition of a new wing to a house, the modernisation of buildings like the installation of additional bathrooms, etc.). Since all repair expenditure is allowed there is no case for granting a depreciation allowance, with the exception of the capital allowance recommended above and restricted to *business* capital expenditures.

69. The total amount of deductions under (1) to (5) above

must not exceed the gross income as defined, but it should be permitted to enter the *average* expenditure of the last five years as a charge against the current year's gross income.

70. I would further suggest that the taxpayer should have the option of claiming an overall allowance of 20 per cent. of the gross income for deductible expenses under (1) to (5), without proof of actual expenditure, i.e., that a 20 per cent. deduction should in any case be allowed as a minimum, and a detailed statement of actual expenditure supported by evidence should only be necessary when a deduction of more than 20 per cent. is claimed.

(iv) *New and detailed provisions for the taxation of capital gains*

71. I regard the effective taxation of capital gains as an essential feature of an equitable system of personal taxation. This is so, not only because capital gains are a very important source of income of the *large* owners of property (in the case of really wealthy families, the increments of economic power that take the form of capital gains probably exceed by several times the rent, interest and dividend income derived from the properties) but also because, while capital gains remain untaxed, there are innumerable kinds of manipulations by which a particular taxpayer can minimise his tax liability through the conversion of taxable income into capital gains, thereby reducing his taxable income to an arbitrary extent. The exemption of capital gains from taxation is the single most glaring feature of "one law for the rich and another law for the poor", an inequity which is not less objectionable for its being so widespread among the Western democratic nations, almost none of which taxes capital gains as fully or as effectively as fairness and impartiality demand.

72. Most of the objections commonly made against the taxation of capital gains are without validity. One argument which has *partial* validity is that in times of inflation the increase in the value of capital assets in terms of money is not, or not wholly, a true gain, since to the extent that appreciation reflects the general rise in prices there has been no *real* accumulation – no real increase of economic power. However, the main purpose of income taxation is to do justice between persons; if the gains of the gainers

are excluded from charge on the ground that the gains were fictitious, it would be necessary to make an explicit deduction from taxable income for all those whose position deteriorated on account of the rise in prices (the holders of bonds, savings deposits, etc.). In times of inflation those who manage to preserve their real capital intact through capital appreciation still gain *relatively* to those whose real wealth is reduced in consequence, and who do not get any relief on that account from the tax system. There is no case, therefore, for any special provisions exempting capital gains on account of inflation from the point of view of *equity*. Nevertheless in order to minimise the political agitation in opposition to this tax, I would recommend inserting a provision in the law according to which, whenever a major rise in prices has occurred, i.e. whenever the retail price level had risen by 50 per cent. or more in the ten years prior to realisation, such part of the appreciation of the value of property during the relevant period (i.e. the period of "ownership" for tax purposes as defined below) as corresponds to the increase in the official wholesale price index, should be deducted from the taxable gain or added to the allowable loss.

73. The opposition to the introduction of the taxation of capital gains would be considerably lessened also if the tax were not intended to be (and were not considered by the public to be) retrospective in character. The introduction of retroactive taxes is in any case forbidden under Article 14 of the Constitution, which says that taxes can only relate to events which occur subsequent to the publication of a tax law, irrespective of whether the law introduces a new tax or modifies an existing tax. The interpretation of this clause in the particular case under discussion is by no means clear, however, first because the term "taxable event" could be taken to refer either to the sale of an asset on which the gain is charged, in which case the constitutional requirement would be satisfied, or else to the purchase, or the mere possession of an asset giving rise to the taxable gain, in which case only gains accruing after the publication of the new law would be taxable; and secondly, because it is a matter of some uncertainty how far the gains in question are already taxable under the present law, in which case the new

provisions would merely serve the purpose of making the law effective, rather than of changing the law. However that may be, it is evident that if an attempt were made now to bring into charge gains which have accrued over a number of years in the past and which were not regarded as or were not known to be, taxable at the time of their accrual[1], the measures would be regarded as retroactive in character and seen as violating the spirit of the Constitution.

74. I would recommend therefore that, in the case of individuals as distinct from companies, only such gains should be brought into charge as *accrue* following the publication of the new tax system. For this purpose I would suggest that all owners of wealth (all individuals owning property above a certain value) should be asked to make a return of the various kinds of mobile and immobile property in their possession at a particular date and to declare their current market values. This valuation, which would be the taxpayer's responsibility, would serve both for the purpose of an annual wealth tax (described below, paragraphs 78–86) and also for the purpose of the capital gains tax since for all assets acquired *prior* to the introduction of the new law (prior to a certain "appointed day"), the taxpayer's own declared values will be construed as the "cost of acquisition" of the assets, i.e. they will form the base from which the taxable gain is measured when the ownership of the assets changes hands subsequently and the gains are brought into charge. This means that the revenue from this tax will not be large in the initial years. However, the taxpayers will know that a part of the currently accruing capital gains will be taken in taxation as and when these gains are realised, and so the tax will have much the same effect in

---

[1] The Mexican law makes no distinction between capital gains and revenue or operating gains, which means that in theory capital gains are taxable in the same way as revenue gains. However, the tax law only applies to "commercial" as distinct from "civil" transactions; the purchase or sale of real property has until recently been presumed to have been a civil transaction unless undertaken by a business; the purchase and sale of securities is, on the other hand, declared to be an act of commerce according to Article 1 of the Law on Securities and Securities Transactions. This means that the gains on the holdings of ordinary shares are generally taxable, whilst the gains on the holdings of real property are only taxable in special cases, or in the hands of special classes of persons. However, no attempt has so far been made to enforce the law with regard to capital gains realised on securities, and if an attempt were made to enforce the taxation of such gains systematically, it would be generally regarded as a substantive modification of the law, and not only a change in administrative procedures relating to its enforcement.

restraining personal expenditure as it would had it been levied and collected concurrently with the accrual of the gains.

75. Subject to the above I would recommend that the taxation of capital gains in Mexico should follow the general lines of recent Ceylon Income Tax (Amendment) Act of 1959. The main features of such a scheme (which in my view ought to be spelled out in considerable detail in the income tax law itself) are as follows:

(a) "Capital gains" form a species of taxable income, which arises in the following circumstances:

  (i) In connection with the *change of ownership* of property by way of sale, exchange, disposal by deed of gift or will;

 (ii) From the surrender or relinquishment of any right to property, such as the right to the use or the exploitation of a property (the lease of a house or apartment, etc.)

(iii) From the redemption of shares, debentures or other obligations;

 (iv) From the dissolution of a business and the formation, amalgamation or dissolution of companies.

(b) The capital gain, arising in connection with a change of ownership, to the person who was the owner immediately before such a change, is defined as the excess of the value of the property at the time of the change of ownership over the value of the property when it was acquired. If both the original acquisition and the current change of ownership was the result of a sale for full consideration, the selling price in each case (i.e. the consideration given or received) is deemed to be the value of the property at the relevant date for the purpose of calculating the taxable gain. If the property was acquired by gift or inheritance subsequent to the introduction of the new tax system, the value of the property as ascertained for gift and inheritance tax purposes shall be deemed to be the value at the time of acquisition; in the same way, when the ownership is relinquished by deed of gift or will, the value at the time of the disposal of property shall be the value as ascertained by the public valuer for gift or inheritance tax purposes. Similarly capital gains arising from redemption of shares are the excess of the money or other property received over the cost of acquisition of the shares, etc., and the capital gain arising from the dissolution of a business or the liquidation of a company is the excess of the value of all the property received on such dissolution or liquidation over the cost of the share capital owned. Expenses incurred in improving the property (but not on repair or maintenance) subsequent to its acquisition, shall be added to the cost of acquisition.

(c) In the case of capital gains arising from the surrender, relinquishment or transfer of any right, from the amalgamation or merger of two businesses or companies, the gain is simply the amount of money or other property received in connection with these events.

(d) The law should also recognise a *capital loss* arising from a change of ownership, redemption of any shares, etc., or on the dissolution of a business or liquidation of a company. Such capital losses should in the first place be offset against capital gains on other transactions in the same year, the amount to be brought into charge being the net capital gain of the year, which is the excess of capital gains over capital losses. If capital losses exceed capital gains for any particular year, the un-absorbed loss should be carried forward for an indefinitive period as an offset against future capital gains; it should not be allowed as an offset against operating gains on the same schedule, or of income under a different schedule. If a tax-payer's estate shows net unabsorbed losses at death, such losses should be carried backwards and offset against past capital gains or other income on which income tax was levied, in the five years prior to the death.

(e) The kind of property on which capital gains and losses are recognised should be limited to real property and to stocks and securities, and titles to valuable rights, such as patents, copyrights, or other "intangible" property. Furniture, jewellery, works of art, etc., should be explicitly excluded, owing to the difficulty of enforcement; for the same reason, also gambling winnings.

(f) Capital gains arising from the sale of a house which has been effectively occupied by the owner should be exempt from tax, provided the proceeds are wholly or at least in greater part reinvested within twelve months in the purchase of another house intended for occupation by the owner. This concession should be limited to the sale of the *principal residence* of the tax-payer, and should not extend to the sale of summer residences, week-end houses, etc.

(*g*) Net capital gains arising from any of the transactions specified should be treated as taxable income under Schedule D (in so far as they are not taxed as business income under Schedule A) and consolidated with the rest of the income for tax purposes, except that in the case of a net capital loss, the loss should not be consolidated as other income, but carried forward and offset against future capital gains.

To ensure full and accurate reporting of capital gains each tax-payer should be asked to make a full return of all his purchases and of his sales of all assets on which chargeable gains could arise (i.e. real property, stocks and shares, intangible property rights of all kinds) in the course of the year. There should also be a reporting system, described in more detail in the next section (paragraph 77), by which the income tax authorities receive current information independently on all real property and securities transactions on a form that can conveniently be routed and attached to the files of the individual taxpayer and items checked against his return.

(5) *Required changes in commercial and company law and institutions*

76. The introduction of a system of comprehensive income taxation and its effective enforcement necessitate certain basic legal and institutional changes of which the most important are: 1. the abolition of the distinction between "commercial" and "civil" transactions; 2. the effective abolition of anonymity in the holding of mobile property, i.e. bonds, obligations and ordinary shares.

1. On the first point relatively little needs to be said. Once it is recognised that taxable capacity is measured by a man's personal spending power, or increment of economic power (i.e. the increase in his net worth over a period) it is evident that the question whether a gain results from a commercial or a civil transaction is wholly irrelevant. I understand that an amendment to the income tax law introduced last year already goes a

certain way towards removing this distinction for tax purposes. However, when the new income tax law is introduced, I think it should be stated in the preamble that all gains are taxable, irrespective of whether they arise from a commercial or a civil transaction, but that gains and losses are only recognised for tax purposes when they are actually *realised* through a transaction of some kind. Anticipated losses are not taken into account, nor is a charge made on anticipated or unrealised gains.

2. Far more important and difficult is the question of the anonymity of ownership of mobile capital. It goes without saying that so long as this anonymity is left intact the creation of a fair and effective system of taxation will prove impossible. Progressive personal taxation of property or of the income from property is quite incompatible with the anonymity of property. The countries in which a progressive income tax is effectively enforced are either those where the system of anonymous shares and property titles has never existed (as in England, the British Dominions, the United States and in the Scandinavian countries) or where it has been abolished (as in Italy and France). So long as wealth can retreat into anonymity by the simple act of the ownership of physical assets being transferred to legal entities the titles to which are held in the form of bearer shares, it will be impossible to do justice not only as between property owners and non-property owners, but also as between different kinds of property owners. Some people are bound to be undertaxed and others (relatively) overtaxed, depending on the wholly irrelevant criterion of how much of their total wealth is held in anonymous forms.

77. The complete abolition of the system of bearer securities would necessitate such far-reaching changes in basic commercial and company law that a considerable delay in the introduction of the new system would result on technical grounds alone. However, without such far-reaching changes in the basic legal framework it would be possible to abolish anonymity effectively for tax purposes, whilst retaining it for commercial purposes, by means of the following system:

(i) There should be a statutory requirement that the payment of interest and dividends by companies of all kinds should be rendered through the agency of a bank designated for the purpose. Each company resident in Mexico should designate for this purpose one particular bank from among a panel listed by the Ministry of Finance.

(ii) All securities relating to that company must be permanently deposited with the designated bank which automatically collects and surrenders the coupons to the company on receipt of the interest and dividend to be distributed among the bond and shareholders. The bank is responsible for deducting income tax, and issuing the tax deduction certificates to the income recipients.

(iii) The bank keeps a confidential register of the holders of bonds and shares in which all changes of ownership in the securities of the particular company are registered. This register is kept secret both from the public and the company (at least in the case of the Sociedad Anónima) but it is available for inspection under oath of secrecy by the officials of the tax department of the Ministry of Finance and the bank is obliged to submit periodic reports to the Ministry of Finance of all changes in ownership and of the prices at which the transactions were concluded as well as remitting to the Ministry copies of the tax deduction certificates issued.

(iv) The bank issues a deposit receipt with respect to each individual deposit of stocks and shares. These deposit receipts are not negotiable instruments themselves but they serve as proof of ownership; they must be surrendered to the buyer whenever the securities are sold. The buyer does not acquire title by the acquisition of the deposit receipt of the seller but only through the issue of a new deposit receipt made out in his own name. The same procedure should be followed with regard to mortgage certificates which should also be kept deposited with the bank which originally issued them.[1]

(v) The effective change, from the point of view of the shareholders will simply be that instead of holding the bearer securities deposited with their own bank, their own bank will hold the *deposit receipts* of the bearer securities issued by the designated

---

[1] In case of a partial sale of a holding the seller should instruct the bank to issue a certificate to the buyer on the number of shares transferred and to replace his old certificate which is now surrendered against a new one made out for his residual shares.

banks. The bearer securities themselves will be permanently held by the designated bank of each company. Effective transfer of titles in the ownership of securities which are so deposited will be, not by means of the *physical* handing over of bearer securities, but by means of the issue to the buyer of a deposit receipt for such securities, by the designated bank, and the cancellation of that of the seller.

In order that the designated banks should change the registration of the shares, the seller must fill up a prescribed form, indicating the number of shares sold, the price per share and his code number, and this, together with his deposit receipt is handed over to the buyer, who completes the rest of the form by adding his own name and code number, etc., and forwards it, together with the deposit certificate, to the bank which issues the new deposit certificate to the buyer.[1]

(vi) To facilitate the routing of all this information concerning interest and dividend payments and capital transactions, it would be convenient if each taxpayer were given a 3-tier code number (indicating income tax district/district category number/ category file number) by means of which the information could be processed and systematically routed to the file or card-index of each taxpayer. It would then also be possible to confine the information communicated by the designated banks to the tax authorities (both as regards dividend payments and capital transactions) to the *code number* of the parties to the transaction which would *ensure* that the identity of the parties remained concealed except to the particular office which handles the file of the taxpayer.

(vii) To ensure that this system—tax deduction at source and the reporting of capital transaction—applies equally to domestic and foreign securities it will be necessary to extend it to Mexican holders of foreign securities. This could be done by introducing a law obliging all Mexican citizens resident in Mexico to deposit their foreign securities with one of the designated banks, and in

[1] All these transactions would normally be handled as between the banks of the buyer and the seller, and the designated bank of the company. It would also be possible to devise a somewhat more complicated set of forms which would ensure that the identity of the buyer to the seller, and of the seller to the buyer, would remain hidden. But for the fact that the ownership and the transactions would no longer be hidden from the tax authorities, the present system of anonymity would thus be preserved intact.

the case of nominative securities to hold such securities in the name of one of these institutions and not in their own name.[1] A similar regulation was introduced in England during the last war and is still in force, and as far as I know, it works quite effectively. The British regulations require the deposit of all foreign securities with one of the designated banks and they only permit dealings in foreign securities on the London Stock Exchange in so far as these securities are registered in one of the "accepted marking names". The British nominee bank is obliged to deduct the British income tax from the foreign dividend and to issue a tax deduction voucher to the recipient. The problem in Mexico would no doubt be how far such an obligation would be effectively complied with. If heavy penalties were imposed on non-compliance, and if the co-operation of banks and brokers were enlisted, the system could probably be largely enforced, especially in view of the fact that the number of Mexican residents who operate on the New York Stock Exchange or other foreign stock exchanges in any magnitude must be rather limited.

III. AN ANNUAL TAX ON WEALTH

78. It is suggested that concurrently with the introduction of the comprehensive income tax there should also be introduced an annual tax on net wealth to be administered in close connection with the income tax. Such a tax forms part of the tax system of a number of European countries and has recently also been introduced in India and Ceylon. There is a strong case in favour of such a tax from the point of view of equity, from the point of view of its economic effects, and also from the point of view of improving the efficiency with which the whole system of personal taxation can be administered.

(i) From the point of view of equity a system of personal taxation based partly on income and partly on capital wealth is a much fairer approximation to taxation in accordance with

---

[1] In the case of dividends from abroad which have been subjected to a withholding tax (as in the case with U.S. dividends), the effective deduction on account of Mexican income tax would be confined to the difference between the foreign withholding rate and the Mexican rate.

taxable capacity than a tax based either on income alone or on capital wealth alone. The reason for this is that the possession of disposable wealth endows a man with economic power (or spending power) as such, quite apart from the money income which the wealth yields. A man who possesses a million pesos in forms that yield no money income (in gold for instance) is clearly much better off than another man who possesses neither wealth nor income, even though he is not as well off as a third man who possesses a million pesos *and* an annual income of, say, 1,000,000 a year in addition. If different individuals possessed disposable wealth and money income in the same proportion, it clearly would make no difference whether the taxes levied were expressed as a percentage of their wealth or as a percentage of their income. This is clearly not the case: some people earn an income but possess no disposable wealth, other people possess both in widely different proportions. Without a supplementary tax on wealth imposed alongside the tax on income it is impossible to do justice, not only as between wage and salary earners and property owners, but also as between different property owners. The tax system of some countries recognises the fact that income derived from property possesses a greater taxable capacity than income derived from work, and attempts to make an allowance for this by charging income from work (the so called "earned" income, as against the "unearned" income from property) at a lower rate. But precisely because the relationship between income and capital wealth varies so much, the taxable capacity which resides in the possession of wealth as such cannot adequately be taken in account by a differential levy based on income.

(ii) From the point of view of its economic effects the advantage of a tax on net wealth is that it discriminates against idle wealth in favour of the productive employment of capital, at least in comparison with the income tax. An income tax makes a charge on the different forms of employment of capital in strict proportion to the money income. But this ignores the fact that idle wealth which yields no money income possesses the advantage of liquidity, whereas wealth invested in productive enterprise yields an apparently high money return precisely because it is associated with risks of various kinds, and because, once funds are committed in a business venture, they cannot be easily withdrawn. With an annual tax on wealth, properties of equal value are taxed equally, irrespective of the money income which they yield.

(iii) From the point of view of administrative efficiency it has been the experience of many countries that an annual tax on wealth improves considerably the efficiency of income tax administration, just as the existence of an income tax improves the efficiency with which a tax on wealth can be administered. An examination of a man's wealth is bound to lead to the discovery of concealed income and, conversely, knowledge of a man's income is bound to lead to the discovery of concealed property. A tax on both provides, therefore, a better check on evasion and concealment than a tax on either one of them alone. Concealed profits in particular can generally only be detected by examining the individual's accretion of wealth over a period. The necessity to furnish an annual statement of net wealth, together with the requirement to account for any change in net wealth from one year to the next through a return of the purchases and sales of capital assets (which is necessary for the capital gains tax) by themselves go a long way in eliminating the possibility of concealing profits or income.

79. Unlike the property tax administered by the States, the suggested federal tax on net wealth should embrace assets of *all* kinds and not only real property, and should provide for the deduction of all liabilities so as to bring total *net wealth* into charge. Assets should comprise real property, tangible assets like vehicles and equipment above a certain value, intangible assets, securities of all kinds and bank deposits, jewellery above a certain value and cash. Household furniture, etc., and personal effects should be exempt and works of art included only if above a certain critical value. It is essential that the return of as many kinds of assets as possible should be controlled on the basis of independent information. Information on the ownership of real property is already obtainable through the cadastral register, and similar information on securities could be obtained through the registration of bearer securities through the banks in the manner suggested above.

80. It is recommended that individual items of property,

such as real property or stocks and shares, should be assessed to the net wealth tax at "book values", and not at "current market values". The book value of an asset is either its cost to the owner (plus the cost of improvements after acquisition) or its market value at the time when a taxpayer's capital account is first set up. When the tax is first introduced taxpayers should be asked to enter each item at its current market value (which thus becomes the "book value" for subsequent periods) on the understanding that the initially declared value of any particular property will remain unchanged for the purposes of the tax for each successive year,[1] until the item passes out of the taxpayer's account on the occasion of a sale, or transfer by way of gift or inheritance. The revision of capital values, in a manner analogous to the principles of business accounting, occurs only when a capital profit is brought into the account on the realisation of a capital gain. Otherwise the net wealth can only change from year to year as a result of saving or dis-saving out of income (the taxpayer's return on capital account would clearly show how much of the change in net wealth is the result of a transference to or from the income account and how much of the net capital gain or loss resulting from the capital transactions during the year).

81. The responsibility for the initial valuation of property should be left to the taxpayer who should be given to understand how the term "current market value" is to be interpreted in relation to assets of *various* categories. Thus in the case of real property, taxpayers may be advised (though not necessarily compelled) to call in the assistance of expert valuers. In the case of stocks and shares of corporations quoted on the Mexico Stock Exchange or on a foreign stock exchange the relevant value should be the official middle price on the "appointed day". In the case of the shares of private companies the correct principle is to take the net book value of the assets of the company at the last valuation prior to the "appointed day" but the taxpayer should be permitted, if he so desires, to put a valuation on the goodwill of a going concern by valuing the shares *above* the book value of the assets.

---

[1] A revision of the initial declared value should only be permitted in exceptional cases when the taxpayer can satisfy the income tax authorities that the initial valuation contained some unintended but definite error.

82. It should be made abundantly clear that the book value of the assets, as shown in the taxpayer's balance sheet on capital account, is in all cases the value on the basis of which the capital gain or loss is measured when an item passes out of the account through sale or other transfer, so that the taxpayer's initial valuation of his assets will determine not only his annual liability for the net wealth tax but also his future liability for the capital gain tax. Hence undervaluation of assets, whilst reducing the liability to the annual wealth tax, will enhance the taxpayer's liability to the capital gains tax, and *vice versa*.

83. It is not recommended that the wealth of family members should be aggregated for wealth tax purposes. Gifts of property between family members or bequests will be liable to the gift tax.

84. The wealth tax should in general only apply to individuals and not to companies whose main business consists of industrial or commercial activities. To prevent tax avoidance through the transfer of individually-owned assets into holding companies I recommend, however, that a net wealth tax be levied at the flat rate of one half per cent. on the property owned by holding or investment companies.

85. The proposed federal net wealth tax is a tax administered on different principles, and should not in any way be regarded as a substitute for the property tax administered by the States. However, the States might be encouraged to change their existing property taxes to something analogous to the net wealth tax and it is a matter for consideration whether (in a manner similar to the commercial receipts tax) the federal and state net wealth tax should not be administered jointly in the case of those States which opt in favour of this system in preference to their existing property tax. Since the basis of valuation of properties of most States (other than the Federal District) is very much out of date and since the new net wealth tax will encompass mobile as well as immobile property, there is little doubt that a change-over to this system will considerably increase the revenue of the States.

86. It is recommended that the rate schedule for the annual wealth tax should be rather low so as to secure (as far as possible), the cooperation of taxpayers in working the new system. The rates I suggest are as follows:

The first 500,000 pesos of net wealth   Exempt
The next 1,000,000 pesos of net wealth at $\frac{1}{4}$ per cent.
The next 1,000,000 pesos at $\frac{1}{2}$ per cent.
The next 1,000,000 at $\frac{3}{4}$ per cent.
The residue of net wealth at   1 per cent.

These rates should be doubled when the tax is levied as a combined federal and state tax.

IV. A UNIVERSAL GIFT TAX

87. The third component of the integrated structure of personal taxation recommended in this report is the gift tax. Mexico already possesses gift and inheritance taxes administered both by the Federation and by the various States, and considerable progress has been made in recent years in securing uniformity in rates and in methods of assessment. Considerations of administrative efficiency clearly require that these taxes should be administered in close connection with the taxes on income and net wealth. I would therefore suggest that the gift and inheritance taxes should be administered by the Federal Government on behalf of the individual States, at least in the so-called "co-ordinated States" (i.e. those which have adopted the uniform laws), and that the gift tax should replace the still extant federal taxes in the other States; that in the co-ordinated States the revenue should be divided among the Federal Government and the States in the present ratio, and that the rates of tax should be appropriately lower for the residents of the other States.

88. I recommend that tax should be levied on much the same principles as at present, i.e. that it should be a tax on the donee or the legatee, and not on the donor or the testator, but that the structure of these taxes should be considerably simplified through the following changes:

(a) Instead of two separate taxes on gift and inheritance, there should be a single universal gift tax encompassing both. The acquisition of property through bequest or inheritance is in every way analogous to the acquisition of property through gifts *inter vivos*; and there is no reason why the tax system should discriminate between the two. I suggest therefore that there should be only a single rate schedule applicable both to gifts *inter vivos* and gifts by way of bequest or inheritance and that the law relating to the two should be unified, though there would remain of course provisions (as e.g. those relating to the determination of the net share of a particular legatee in an estate) which are only relevant in the one case and not in the other.

(*b*) The present Mexican law discriminates between gifts to close relatives and those to relatives of the 2nd, 3rd and 4th degree (which includes non-relatives), with a separate rate schedule application to each category. There is little justification in equity for such distinctions that must complicate considerably the task of administration. I suggest therefore that there should be only a single rate schedule applicable to *all gifts* irrespective of the family relationship between the donor and the donee.

89. I would further recommend that the existing rate schedule should be considerably simplified, but that it should be made dependent, not on the size of the individual gift but on the total wealth of the recipient *including* the gift. Existing Mexican law provides that all gifts made by the same donor to the same donee within a period of 20 years should be added together and the tax computed on the cumulative total of the most recent and all preceding gifts. This is obviously a necessary pre-caution against the avoidance of the tax through the spreading of gifts over time. But it must aggravate the task of administration considerably, and I suggest that instead the tax on the gift should be applied at rates depending not only on the gift itself, but on the total net wealth of the recipient *including the gift*. As the recipient, if possessed of appreciable wealth, will in any case be subject to the wealth tax, this procedure appears to be far simpler than the existing procedure of aggregating gifts over a period of 20 years.

90. At the same time, there is a strong case for simplifying the rate schedule and for exempting small gifts altogether, if the recipients are not wealthy individuals. A good case can also be made out for a considerable reduction in the rates of the gift tax, at least in the middle ranges of properties gifted, in comparison with the present schedule. One reason suggested for the wide-spread evasion of the present gift and inheritance taxes is that

the rates of the tax are so heavy: they are comparable in magnitude (and on more distant relatives, considerably heavier) with the corresponding income tax rates, whereas it is strongly felt that a non-recurrent gift of capital ought to be taxed more leniently than a recurrent income of a corresponding amount.

91. I would therefore recommend that the first gift of 10,000 pesos from any single donor to a single donee be exempt and that further gifts under 20,000 pesos given to individuals who do not possess more than 50,000 pesos of net wealth should be exempt, and that the uniform rate schedule below should be applicable to *all gifts*.

92. In order to prevent tax avoidance through the creation of one-man companies, etc. I recommend that all gifts received by *companies* should be treated as taxable income in their hands.

93. Since the valuation of properties for gift tax purposes determines not only the charge on account of the gift tax but also the liability to capital gains tax on the donor (or the deceased) and the capital value for purposes of the annual wealth tax to the donee, the proper valuation of assets for gift tax purposes *constitutes an essential lynch pin of the whole system*. It is essential therefore that this valuation should be most carefully done by fully independent and reliable valuers. I am not in a position to say how far the detailed rules of the present Federal Law or its administration are adequate in this respect; I merely wish to emphasise the importance to the whole system of an independent appraisal on these occasions, particularly in the case of real property and of intangible property.

UNIFORM RATE SCHEDULE FOR UNIVERSAL GIFT TAX

Net wealth of donee, including gift (pesos)	Percentage rate on all gifts
50,000– 500,000	10
500,000–1,000,000	10, plus 20 on excess over 500,000
1,000,000–3,000,000	15, ,, 30 ,, ,, ,, 1,000,000
Over 3,000,000	25, ,, 40 ,, ,, ,, 3,000,000

V. THE QUESTION OF A PERSONAL EXPENDITURE TAX

94. A progressive tax on personal expenditure with a high exemption limit so as to confine the incidence of the tax to a

relatively narrow group of rich individuals is, I am convinced, a very important element in an integrated structure of progressive personal taxation. The experience with the introduction of this tax in India and Ceylon has led me to believe, however, that the opposition of the property-owning classes to the idea of such a tax is so violent that it would be unwise to attempt to impose it alongside a reform of income tax, and the introduction of a wealth tax, since it might jeopardise the success of the whole scheme. The strong resistance to this tax may seem unreasonable, since an expenditure tax is no different from an income tax with net savings exempted and net dis-savings brought into charge. However, the very idea that tax liability should vary with the taxpayer's own dispositions seems to be peculiarly repugnant to those who might be tempted or forced into a reduction of their living expenses; and there may be a feeling also that the scope for evading or avoiding taxes of all kinds is very much smaller when a taxpayer must declare what his personal expenditure is. A millionaire may easily manage his affairs so as to avoid having to admit more than a moderate amount of income. Through manipulations of various kinds his accounts (or the accounts of his companies) may easily succeed in showing a profit of say 50,000 pesos when the scale of his operations amounts to many millions. But he could not *declare* that he had spent 50,000 pesos when, in fact, his true living expenses were ten or twenty times that figure. Personal expenditure is externalised, and therefore tangible, which the abstract notion of a "business profit" is not.

95. The main advantage of a personal expenditure tax is that it enables an important additional element of progressiveness to be introduced into the tax system that cannot be accomplished (or not effectively) with taxes based on either capital or income. An income tax cannot function effectively when the marginal rate of taxation reaches up to two-thirds or more of the marginal income. In countries like Britain, to give an example, where the marginal rate of income tax goes up to 80–90 per cent. (or even more) these seemingly confiscatory rates of taxation are largely "on paper" since the tax system leaves numerous loop-holes by which wealthy taxpayers can avoid paying tax on this scale on their *true* income. Thus in all countries where the

marginal tax for income goes up to very high levels, capital gains
are left either untaxed or else (as in the United States or India)
are taxed at specially favourable rates. (In the U.S. the highest
rate on capital gains is 25 per cent; on dividend-income 86 per
cent.) At the same time the law leaves ample opportunities for
the wealthy property owner to make his true income accrue
largely in the shape of capital gains. If this were not so, and if a
genuine attempt were made to make the nominal rates truly
effective by closing the "loop-holes" in the tax system, it would
be necessary to reduce the progressiveness of the rate schedule
very considerably or else the whole system would break down.

96. For this reason low ceiling rates of taxation are an essential
feature of a well-functioning tax system and I regard the adoption
of the moderate ceiling rates recommended in this report (40
per cent. in the case of personal income and company profits;
1 per cent. per annum in the case of the annual tax on wealth) as
an essential part of the scheme. But this means that personal
taxation loses its progressive character at a relatively early
stage; income tax becomes a proportionate tax for income in
excess of around 1,000,000 pesos; as between two rich men, one
of whom has an income of 500,000, and the other of 5,000,000,
the difference in the *proportion* of income taken in taxation amounts
to very little. A progressive expenditure tax with an initial
exemption of say 200,000 pesos, would introduce this missing
element of progression without deleterious effects on economic
incentives, and without the grave administrative disadvantages
of high marginal rates of taxation on either income or capital.
The fact that the rich man can "avoid" this tax by living modestly
is not a defeat but a considerable merit; since it is a basic
objective of all taxation to restrain personal spending and thereby release resources for communal purposes. In contrast to taxes
on income or capital, action taken to avoid liability has beneficial
and not harmful effects on society.

97. Another important advantage of an expenditure tax as an
element in a combined system of personal taxation is that it
makes the whole system far more self-checking in character.
Whereas the wealth tax and the capital gains tax taken by
themselves provide an incentive to the taxpayer to conceal

his savings, an expenditure tax, on the contrary, provides a strong incentive to exhibit them since the tax is levied on the difference between the receipts of the year (on account of income and gifts) and of net savings or dis-savings as shown by the changes in the balance sheet. Similarly, the necessity to declare an amount of personal expenditure, which cannot be *too far* out of line with true expenditure, forces the taxpayer into a full disclosure of his taxable receipts, since it would be difficult for him to pretend to have financed his expenditure out of capital when his balance sheet does not show a corresponding reduction in his net assets. Just as it is easier for a man to conceal the ownership of property than to pretend to own property which he does not possess, so it is easier for him to conceal a reduction in his assets than to pretend to have lived on capital when he did not: both savings and dis-savings are more easily understated than overstated. A simultaneous levy on both income and on expenditure thus forces the disclosure of expenditure when the income (i.e. the receipts) is known; it forces the disclosure of income when the expenditure is known. To evade *either* of the two taxes a man must successfully conceal *both* his income and his expenditure.

98. However while the successful administration of an expenditure tax very largely depends on the existence of a comprehensive income tax and of a wealth tax (since the computation of expenditure requires the disclosure of income from all sources, and of the net change in the asset position from one year to the next) this is obviously not true (or not true in the same way) the other way round: a comprehensive income tax combined with a net wealth can be operated quite successfully, even without the expenditure tax. Hence the obvious course for Mexico at the present stage is to concentrate on the reform of the income tax and the gift tax, and on the introduction of an annual tax on net wealth, and to leave the question of the personal expenditure tax to a later stage when these taxes have been successfully established and have been in operation for a number of years.

99. In view of this I am not making any concrete recommendations in this report concerning the introduction of an expenditure tax in Mexico.

VI. PROBLEMS OF ADMINISTRATION

100. The adoption of the new system of taxation involves a considerable reorganisation of the system of administration. I understand that the existing administration is broadly divided into two parts. The taxation under the "business" schedules (Schedule I, II, III and V, and also the distributed profits tax which is *formally* under Schedule VI) is partly centralised and divided under the "Junta Califiondora" and partly decentralised and divided between the "Departamento Tecnico Califiondor" and the nine "Delegaciones". The taxation under the personal schedules (IV, VI and VII) is completely centralised and is under the "Departamento Administrativo".

101. Under the new system also the administration will have to be divided into two parts: first those organs dealing with business taxation (Schedules A and B) and second those dealing with personal taxation (mainly Schedules C and D as well as the cases of individuals who derive income from several schedules).

102. As far as the taxation of business income is concerned, no fundamentally new problems arise as a result of the proposals though in some respects the problems of assessment may be considerably simplified. The important problem here is to examine and audit the accounts submitted, and I understand that a new system was instituted a year ago which delegates the problem of verifying the accounts to a new organisation (Dirección de Auditoria Fiscal Federal) consisting of professional auditors employed by the Government, and that this has already led to the discovery of very considerable amounts of concealed profits.

103. The important new problems relate to personal taxation both under Schedule C and Schedule D. At the moment the taxation of salaries and wages is entirely in the hands of the employers: the tax administration has no knowledge of the individual taxpayers at all, and its only contact is with the employers who remit the tax deducted under this Schedule. Under Schedule D, the income tax department at present is only in contact with 12,000 individuals (largely those who receive non-exempt interest from several sources).

104. Under the new system it will be necessary for the tax department to keep track of the individual wage and salary earners, at least by keeping a report card on each. The employers will have to report on their individual employees and ask them to fill up a card giving their family circumstances, etc. as well as a declaration of whether they have income from other sources or not. On the basis of this card their taxation category will be determined by the tax department which informs the employer, who will be asked to deduct tax from their pay from tax tables which indicate how much is to be deducted for each income and for each taxation category. Claims as to allowances for wives or concubines and children will have to be supported initially by a birth or marriage certificate or some other document. The employer, who will receive from the income tax department a personal code number for each employee as well as an indication of his taxation category, must issue a tax deduction certificate once a year, or on the occasion of the termination of an employee's contract, of the total pay received and the total tax deducted for the last financial year. The employee should also receive at the same time a simple tax return form which he must fill out in case he wishes to make a claim for a refund of tax. He should also receive a printed table showing what the annual tax liability is for each tax category, from which he can easily find out by how much the actual tax deducted, based on monthly income, exceeded his true liability for the year; and it should be left to him to take the initiative to claim a refund by filling out the forms and passing them to the income tax department. All this will require a considerably expanded organisation for Schedule C (the present Schedule IV) as compared with the present system.

In the case of Schedule D the administrative problems will be more formidable since in these cases a new type of administration will be required to deal jointly with income tax on income from capital (and/or the income tax of those who derive their income from several schedules which have to be aggregated), income tax on capital gains, the annual tax on wealth and the tax on gifts.

105. The important new feature of the system is the institution

of a comprehensive return relating to the taxpayer's personal affairs which is analogous to the profit and loss account and the balance sheet which is now required in the case of businesses. This comprehensive return would, of course, only be required of those taxpayers whose income from rent, interest and dividends exceeds a certain amount (say 40,000 pesos p.a.) so that they can be presumed to possess net wealth which makes them liable to the wealth tax. The return would be in four parts, the first or the income account, consisting of the declaration of income from each source and an indication of the amount of income from which tax has already been deducted[1] and the amount of such deduction. The second part is the capital transaction account showing the purchases and sales of all capital assets (real property, stocks and shares, and the net change in bank accounts and savings deposits) during the year. The third is the capital account or balance sheet, containing the net wealth statement for the beginning and the end of the year, the statement for the close of one year being necessarily the same as the opening statement for the following year. Finally, the gift account showing all gifts received and all gifts made in the year in excess of, say 2,000 pesos in the case of any single gift. (Successive gifts to a single donee from the same donor being aggregated for the purpose.)

106. The statement of these various accounts must of course be consistent with one another: the transactions in capital assets as recorded in the capital transactions account being consistent with the changes in assets shown in the balance sheet. The capital transaction account and the balance sheet must clearly indicate how much of the change in net wealth resulted from the writing-up of the value of assets occasioned by the realisation of capital gains, and how much from an addition in assets resulting from an

---

[1] Under the system recommended here there will be tax deduction at source (at the full 40 per cent. rate, with minor exceptions that have already been specified) for income from all sources, Schedule A tax will be levied on the individual *business* at the profit tax rate, and individual owners will receive a tax deduction certificate with respect to the profits applicable to them. Taxes, etc. paid which fall under Schedule B (the present Schedule V) would be deducted at the rate of 20 per cent. And excepting for minor rents on houses, all rent, interest and dividend payments under Schedule D should be deducted at the full 40 per cent. rate. The only type of personal income for which tax will not be deducted at source is therefore capital gains, though, as explained below, large capital gains should be assessed in advance.

excess of the value of purchases over sales (or of assets acquired through gifts over assets disposed through donations) which must represent a transfer from income or from the gifts accounts, or both. On the basis of this return it should be possible for the same tax officer to determine the taxpayer's liability to income tax, capital gains tax, the net wealth tax and the gift tax simultaneously.

107. In the case of large transactions in real property (or in shares) involving a large amount of capital gains, say, in excess of 500,000 pesos I suggest that the tax department should assess the transaction as such to capital gains (without waiting for the completion of the annual return) and collect tax at the full 40 per cent. rate on it. It should issue a tax deduction certificate (in the same way as with other gains and income) which is credited against the taxpayer's annual liability, and should entitle him to a refund if applicable. Tne same procedure should be followed also with regard to the gift tax where large gifts are concerned *inter vivos* or by inheritance. It is essential however that preliminary assessment of individual transactions and collection of tax should not entitle the taxpayer to omit such items from his annual return. To ensure the proper functioning of the system, the tax-payer should be required by law to return all his income-receipts, all his capital transactions, and all the gifts received and made during the year, irrespective of whether tax has already been paid on individiual items or not.

108. Since much of the tax will be deducted at source, or on a provisional basis at the full rate before the taxpayer's final liability can be determined on the basis of his annual return, there will be very frequent cases of tax-refund, both under Schedules C and D and also on the personal income arising under the other Schedule. It is essential therefore that the machinery for remitting over-payment of tax should function smoothly and expeditiously. It has already been suggested that all refund should carry interest at 10 per cent. from the date the tax was withheld or collected until the date at which repayment is made. It will be also necessary however, to overhaul the existing regulations concerning tax repayment which are far too cumbrous and slow-moving. Under the present rules, I understand, repay-

ment cannot be on the decision of the income tax department or even the Federal Tax Directorate, but requires the approval of the Accountant General's Office (Contaduria). It will be necessary to change this rule so that repayment can be authorised by the income tax department alone and rendered through the income tax collecting offices.

109. The inspection and verification of such personal accounts will require much the same kind of qualifications as the inspection and verification of business accounts, and this could best be undertaken by an entirely new administrative unit manned by professional auditors who would be the best qualified to undertake this kind of work. The number of taxpayers liable to the wealth and the capital gains tax is not likely to be very large and a small proportion of them will probably account for a considerable part of the total income on wealth. It is very important, therefore, that the accounts of these taxpayers be carefully verified in the same way as with the large corporations. The administration of these taxes requires therefore highly paid personnel, carefully chosen for their ability as well as their integrity; it seems to me that the substantive work, if it is to be done efficiently, must be done by people who are paid at the rate of at least 5,000 to 6,000 pesos a month, and not at the rate of 500–1,000 pesos. This was already recognised when the "Dirección de Auditoria Fiscal Federal" was set up and the verification of business accounts allotted to the professional auditors. The introduction of the new tax system would require the extension of the same kind of administrative set-up to personal taxation under Schedule D.

110. Assuming that the administration of taxation can be given to highly-paid and highly-qualified personnel, there is much to be said for decentralising the administration as much as possible. Personal income tax cannot be efficiently administered if the administrators are far away from the taxpayers and have no knowledge of local conditions. There is much to be said therefore for this new administrative set-up having offices in each of the nine income tax districts from the beginning, and extending this later so that there would be at least a separate office in each of the major cities.

5

PROPOSALS FOR A REFORM OF TAXATION OF BRITISH GUIANA[1]

TABLE OF CONTENTS

[1]This report was prepared in Georgetown at the request of the Minister of Finance of British Guiana and presented on 30 December 1961. The letter of transmittal has been omitted.

INTRODUCTION

1. The proposals listed below serve both immediate needs and also the longer-term purpose of securing, through progressive taxation, a more equitable distribution of wealth and income. The *immediate needs* are concerned with the precarious state of British Guiana's international reserves, and the absence of financial reserves at the disposal of the Government; they are also concerned with the urgent need to increase the resources available to economic development. The *longer-term need* is to increase the effectiveness of the tax instrument in securing to the people of British Guiana a fair share of the surpluses generated by the economy; and to ensure that the wealthier individuals in the community contribute an appropriate share of the public burden.

2. More specifically the proposals are based on the following premises:

(i) Owing to the precarious state of British Guiana's international reserves (which have fallen by some $15 million in the last two years) it is necessary to impose some further restraint on imports. Since the most effective instrument for this purpose is an increase in import duties it was considered desirable, on balance of payments considerations, to increase the yield of these duties by some 20 per cent., or by some $5 million; and this in turn makes it desirable to increase excise duties in a corresponding proportion, yielding a further $1 million. (It should be pointed out that if the outflow of private capital were brought to a halt, the balance of payments could not in itself be regarded as unfavourable, since the inflow of foreign capital has so far exceeded the deficit on current account by a few million in recent years, and promises to

do so also in 1961. But British Guiana is so highly dependent on a few staple exports, exposed to the vagaries of the
world market, that it is highly desirable to generate a
temporary surplus for the sake of building up reserves, even
at the cost of current consumption). The concrete proposals
to this end are set out in Part III of this report.

(ii) The tight financial situation of the Government together
with a prospective deficit of the order of $4 million for 1962
(assuming that the Guillebaud proposals are substantially
implemented) makes it also desirable to raise taxation in
order to cover recurrent expenditure and to provide a
surplus on revenue account. Hence in addition to the
increase in import and excise duties various recommendations are made in relation to income tax for countering
avoidance and evasion, for accelerating the inflow of tax
receipts, and for reducing various allowances and exemptions (both in relation to business taxation and personal
taxation) and these are set out in detail in Part I of this
report. Whilst the immediate revenue effect of some of the
proposals cannot be estimated, their joint effect is likely to
amount to at least $1·5 million in the coming financial
year.

(iii) The urgent need to accelerate the rate of development
expenditure also calls for an increase in the flow of internal
savings (and a corresponding restraint on consumption)
and this purpose is served by the recommendation for a
new scheme of compulsory savings, which, when fully in
operation, is likely to yield some $5·5–$6 million a year.
Whilst for administrative reasons, this scheme could not be
immediately implemented, it might be possible to introduce it somewhere round the middle of 1962, if an early
decision were taken on its adoption. This scheme, which
calls for flat-rate contributions from both individuals and
companies, is set out in Part IV.

(iv) Finally there is the need to make the distribution of the
burden more equitable, and this is served by the proposed
new taxes on capital gains, the annual tax on net property
and a tax on gifts, set out in Part II, as well as the anti-

avoidance and tightening-up provisions concerning profits taxation in Part I. As suggested in Part II, the three new taxes on capital gains, net property and gifts should be integrated with the existing income tax to form a single system of comprehensive progressive taxation, the various parts of which support each other, and which jointly ensure a fair distribution on the burden of taxation.

3. Without taking any account of the revenue from the new taxes, with the exception of the $\frac{1}{2}$ per cent. wealth tax on companies, which may yield $1 million, the proposals thus imply an increase in taxation by $8·5 million, of which nearly $7 million will fall on residents, as well as compulsory savings of the order of $6 million, of which $2·5 million fall on residents. Excluding the savings scheme (which cannot of course be considered in the same way as taxation, since the amounts taken are fully repayable with accrued interest) the burden of taxation on *residents* is thus raised to some $40 million, or just over 17 per cent. of the net national income—a proportion which I would not regard as too heavy, at British Guiana's current stage of development, and in view of her real income per head. The compulsory savings on residents are best considered in relation to private consumption expenditure; their yield is the equivalent of 1·3 per cent. of national private consumption, though much greater of course in relation to the consumption expenditure of the actual contributors.

4. I feel that in view of the various tightening-up provisions, the restriction of initial allowances, the amendment of the tax holiday provisions, the 0·5 per cent. capital tax on companies which is recommended in Part II, and the prospective 10 per cent. levy on account of compulsory savings, no change should be made in the present rate of income taxation on companies.

5. If the Government decided to implement the recommendations made in Part I, as well as the three new taxes suggested in Part II, the best course would seem to be to incorporate these in the proposed Income Tax (Amendment) Bill, and thus put the whole scheme into a single piece of amending legislation. At a later stage, the whole of the Ordinance should be redrafted as a unified Inland Revenue Code which should incorporate also the proposed reform of Estate Duty legislation which already exists in

draft. The compulsory savings scheme would, of course, require a separate Bill.

PART I. INCOME TAX

A. RECOMMENDATIONS RELATING TO THE TAXATION OF BUSINESS PROFITS

The following are suggested additions to the present draft of the Income Tax (Amendment) Bill.

1. *Countering Possible Tax Avoidance by Foreign Companies*

It is well known that foreign companies which are merely branches or subsidiaries of companies resident abroad can under-state their true profits through the over-invoicing of imports or the under-invoicing of exports, in so far as their transactions are conducted with associated companies. Section 33, Subsection (3) of Chapter 299 already confers powers on the Commissioner to call for an examination of the profits of the foreign business partners of these companies and, where necessary, to raise an assessment on them through the medium of the resident company. It is however difficult for the Commissioner in many cases to establish what the appropriate prices for, say, bauxite, should have been, and to uphold a claim for adjusting the declared prices in the Courts. I suggest therefore that the existing provisions of Section 33 should be strengthened by the addition of the following new subsections at the end of the present section:

(8) Notwithstanding anything contained in this Ordinance the profits for the year of a company operating in British Guiana which is a branch establishment, a subsidiary or an associated company of a non-resident company, shall be deemed to be not less than that proportion of the total consolidated profit of the whole group of associated companies (including both resident and non-resident companies) which the turnover of that company, as shown in its accounts, bears to the consolidated turnover of the whole group of associated companies.

(9) Exemptions from the provisions of the above subsection shall be granted in those cases where the resident company can prove to the satisfaction of the Commissioner that no significant part of its business transactions (in the form of sales or purchases or any other form) was conducted with the non-resident associated companies of the same group.

(10) In the case of companies referred to in Subsection (8) of this Section, which have not been granted exemption under Subsection (9), the provisions of this Ordinance relating to the delivery of returns shall extend to the furnishing of returns of the consolidated profit and the consolidated turnover of the whole group of associated companies of which the resident subsidiary company or branch establishment forms a part.

This necessitates the following additional definitions to be inserted in Section 2 of the Ordinance:

"Subsidiary" means a company which is controlled by another company; a company is deemed to be controlled by another company if and so long as not less than 50 per cent. of its ordinary share capital is owned directly or indirectly by that other company.

"Associated companies" means two or more companies where one has control of the other or others, or any person has control of both or all of them; and where two or more companies share equally in the ownership of all the ordinary share capital of another company, all shall be treated as associated companies.

"Turnover" means in the case of a person carrying on a business, trade, profession or vocation, the total receipts in money or money's worth of the year from his activities, including all cash and credit sales, commissions and fees receivable, without any deductions whatsoever for expenses incurred, taxes or duties paid, etc.

"Consolidated profit" means the profits for the year of a whole group of subsidiary and associated companies, including that of the controlling company or companies, after the elimination of such income received by any of these companies which represents dividends paid by other companies of the group.

"Consolidated turnover" means the turnover for the year of a whole group of subsidiary and associated companies, including that of the controlling company or companies, after the elimination of all transactions between the various subsidiaries and associated companies, and between these and the controlling company or companies.

2. *Provisional Assessments of Business Profits and Professional Incomes*

I propose that the existing powers of the Commissioner under Section 48(3) should be strengthened by the replacement of the present Subsection (3) by the following:

> (3) Where a person has not delivered a return by the due date (including such returns as are prescribed by Section 33(10) of this Ordinance) the Commissioner shall make a provisional assessment within 3 months after the prescribed date based on a chargeable income of $7\frac{1}{2}$ per cent. of the turnover of the year previous to the year in respect of which the return is due; or, where the turnover for that year has not been ascertained, on such reasonable estimate of that turnover as the Commissioner to the best of his judgment may determine; but this assessment shall not affect any liability otherwise incurred by this person by reason of his refusal, failure or neglect to deliver a return.

> (3)(a) In the case of self-employed professional persons the provisional assessment prescribed in the above Subsection must be based on known average earnings of the particular profession concerned.

3. *Minimum Annual Contribution*

I suggest that, without prejudice to existing provisions which allow a business to absorb losses out of profits in future years, any person carrying on a business (excepting agriculture) in British Guiana should be required to make a minimum annual contribution to the Government based on the turnover of the business. Such a contribution would not increase the ultimate tax liability of a business in those cases where the losses are later recouped by profits; but it would ensure that no business would be able to carry on year after year without paying anything in tax, by showing continuing losses in its business accounts, and I would recommend that under Section 12 of the present Ordinance a new Section 12(a) be inserted:

> 12(a) Notwithstanding anything contained in this Ordinance a person carrying on a manufacturing, mining or mercantile business is liable with respect to any year of assessment, to a minimum chargeable income based on 2 per cent. of his turnover in the year preceding the year of assessment:
>
> Provided that where such person incurs a loss in the year preceding the year of assessment, this loss can be carried forward in accordance with Section 15 of this Ordinance:
>
> Provided further that where such a person makes a chargeable profit in the year preceding the year of assessment but which is less than 2 per cent. of his turnover, the difference can be carried forward in the same manner as if it were a loss.

This requires certain amendments to Section 15, which are given under 5 below.

4. *Methods of Assessment of Business Partnerships*

The existing Ordinance provides that the profits of a business partnership must be assessed and charged individually on each partner. This often creates difficulties, e.g. when a person resigns or goes abroad, etc. since a tax due cannot be recovered on the assets of the business as such. I suggest that the methods of assessing business partnerships should be assimilated to the methods in force in the case of companies: that is to say, the profits of the partnership should be assessed as such and a certificate be issued to each individual partner entitling him to a recovery of tax on his aliquot share of the profits in exactly the analogous manner to the tax deducted on the dividend of the shareholder. I therefore suggest that preceding the existing Section 45 there should be a new Section 44(a) as follows:

44(a) Where a trade, business, profession or vocation is carried
on by two or more persons jointly the whole of the
chargeable income of the partnership, shall be assessed in
exactly the same manner as if it were a company, but the
Commissioner shall issue a certificate to each partner
showing the amount of tax collected on his share of the
profits of the partnership and such tax shall be treated in
the same manner as a set-off of tax deducted from the
dividend under Section 30 of this Ordinance.

5. *Allowances of Trade Losses*

The existing Ordinance provides (as recently amended) that a
business loss can be set-off against income from other sources in
the same year and in so far as it cannot be so set-off, it should be
carried forward indefinitely, but *only* against future income from
the same source. I think these provisions are still open to a great
deal of abuse in that it is possible for a taxpayer to build up assets
by incurring continued losses in one business and financing it by a
saving in tax from his income from other sources. I therefore
recommend that the provisions should be further restricted by
allowing *only the indefinite carry forward of loss from the same source*, but
disallowing the set-off of loss against other income in the same
year. I regard such a restriction as particularly important in the
case of British Guiana since otherwise some of the businesses which
are now enjoying tax holidays (and which are bound to incur
losses for a number of years after the end of the tax holiday period
on account of their right to treat all capital expenditure incurred
during the tax holiday period as if it had been incurred in the year
preceding the first year of assessment) would be able to offset these
losses against other profits, with the result that revenue would be
further reduced when the tax holiday period comes to an end.
On the other hand I do not feel, in view of this change, that the
current restrictions which limit the set-off of past losses to one-half
of the tax liability in any year are justified in the case of those
enterprises which would be liable to the minimum annual contribution recommended above.

I therefore recommend that the existing Section 15 of the
Ordinance should be amended as follows:

(i) by the deletion of the words beginning with "is such" in line 4 up to the words "for the same year" in line 5 and beginning with the words "to the extent" in line 5 up to the words "for the same year" in line 7;

(ii) by the deletion of the words at the beginning of the present Subsection (d), starting with "in no case" and ending with the words "to an extent", and its replacement by the words "in the case of any agricultural business, the set-off shall not be allowed to an extent", with the rest of the subsection remaining as at present:

(iii) by the addition of a new Subsection (e) as follows:

(e) In the case of such businesses whose activities have been separated and in consequence of such separation some activities enjoy the privilege of tax holiday granted under Section 2 of Chapter 300, whereas other activities of this business are not so treated, the two kinds of activities must be deemed to be two separate businesses for the purposes of this section.

(iv) these changes also necessitate an amendment of the definition of "chargeable income" in Section 2 of the Ordinance on the following lines:

"Chargeable income" means the aggregate amount of the income of any person from the sources specified in Section 5 remaining after allowing the appropriate deductions and exemptions under this Ordinance pertaining to each source separately, and after allowing such appropriate exemptions and deductions as pertain to his aggregate income.

6. *Amendment of Tax Holiday Provisions*

I consider that the current tax holiday provisions for the encouragement of new enterprises are excessive and of doubtful efficacy in promoting the industrial development of British Guiana. These privileges not only allow a complete tax holiday for 5 years, but also allow all capital expenditure incurred during these five years to qualify both for initial and depreciation allowances after the tax holiday period comes to an end. My own feeling is that if foreign enterprises wish to come here they will do so when it is to their advantage—which means when the opportunities for making profits are sufficiently large as not to be seriously affected by questions of taxation. It must also be remembered that in a great many cases the benefits of these tax exemptions do not accrue to the companies or their shareholders but to foreign Governments who are thereby enabled to tax the profits originating in British Guiana without having to allow for double taxation relief. I therefore recommend that the whole of the existing Section 2 be withdrawn and replaced by a new provision according to which pioneering businesses which are primarily concerned with mining, manufacturing or processing activities should have the privilege of being allowed to write off 70 per cent. of any capital expenditure incurred during the first five years of their operation in British Guiana as a charge on their current profit. This would also mean (in view of the proposed amendment of Section 12 of the present Ordinance which is incorporated in the present Income Tax (Amendment) Bill, 1961) that any dividend paid by such companies would be taxable irrespective of whether the company as such is chargeable to tax or not. It will be necessary in this case to protect the existing privileges of companies which have already been granted tax holidays under this Section. I therefore recommend that the whole of Section 2 be rephrased accordingly and a new subsection be added on the following lines:

(8) Where prior to the commencement of this section as at present amended privileges have been granted to persons under this section these shall continue as if these provisions were still in force;

Provided that the provisions of Section 15 as amended will apply to such persons.

It may be desirable on the other hand to encourage agricultural settlements in new areas by tax concessions, and I would therefore recommend that for new agricultural businesses which are started in areas which at any time are designated as "pioneering areas" by the Government, the tax liability should be reduced to one-half of the normal liability for the first 10 years of operation.

7. *Reduction of Initial Allowance*

The existing provisions introduced in 1951 provide for an initial allowance of 40 per cent. which is in addition to the depreciation allowance (normally 10 per cent.) which is allowed in the first year. I consider these provisions as unduly generous and they involve a very serious loss of tax (particularly in the case of foreign companies) which averaged $500,000 in recent years. I suggest therefore that for at least an experimental period initial allowances for non-tax-holiday companies be reduced to 20 per cent. from the existing 40 per cent., yielding an additional revenue of $250,000.

8. *Restriction of Deductible Expenses*

I recommend that the powers of the Commissioner in disallowing deductions should in general be strengthened by the replacement of the words "wholly and exclusively" with the words "wholly, exclusively and necessarily" in Section 12(1) of the Ordinance.

I further recommend that entertainment expenditure should be explicitly disallowed under Section 14 of the Ordinance. I also suggest that expenditure on advertising should only be allowed as a business expense in so far as it relates to the sale of such goods and services which produce income for the year in question and not to general or "prestige" advertising. I therefore suggest that the following new Subsections should be added to Section 14 of the Ordinance:

(h) any expenditure on entertainment;

(i) any expenditure on advertising which does not primarily serve the sale of specific goods or services.

9. *Restriction of Directors' Emoluments*

I understand that the existing provisions are considerably abused in the case of private companies who frequently appoint family members as Directors with considerable emoluments so as to reduce the business liability to tax. I suggest therefore that in the case of private companies provisions analogous to the United Kingdom profits tax provisions be introduced restricting the total amount of emoluments of Directors of private companies which qualify as a deduction from the chargeable profit to a fixed sum or to a certain percentage of the gross profit or both.

10. *Deduction of Tax at Source in the Case of Company Directors*

Since it is frequently difficult to ascertain whether sums paid to Directors by companies represent chargeable income of the recipients (they may be dressed up as loan transactions of some kind) I recommend that the companies should be assessed on their profit without any deduction for payment made to Directors, but that the Directors should receive a corresponding tax deduction certificate which qualifies as a set-off for income tax liability, in the same manner as is suggested above in the case of the individual partners of partnerships. (In the United Kingdom and many other countries tax is already deducted at source from the emoluments of Directors.)

11. *Interest Allowance on Tax Refund*

Since the tax deduction scheme recommended for Directors and business partners will mean that considerable refunds will be due to such persons (as tax is deducted at the 45 per cent. rate on the *whole* of their income) I recommend that the Revenue should pay interest at the rate of 6 per cent. per annum for the period elapsing between the effective dates of deduction and the dates of repayment in all cases where the refund for any year exceeds $500. (The restriction to refunds in excess of $500 is purely for administrative reasons; with the introduction of P.A.Y.E., there will be many cases of small refunds, for which the calculation of interest would cause considerable complication and be of negligible benefit.)

B. INCOME TAX ON INDIVIDUALS

1. *Introduction of P.A.Y.E.*

I recommend that this should be introduced as soon as practicable (also in view of its being linked to a scheme for compulsory savings, dealt with below). I should also recommend that in order to simplify the task of the employers, the deductions should be on the non-cumulative principle, the adjustment to the annual liability being made subsequently as in the United States.

2. *Reduction of Allowances and Changes in the Rate Schedule*

The current level of *personal allowances* seem to me to be too high, with the result:

- (i) that only a minority of employees are liable to income tax, whereas, on general grounds, it is desirable in a democracy that a wide section of the population should be called upon to make some contribution to the common burden in the form of direct taxation;
- (ii) with the introduction of the P.A.Y.E. system, there is no longer the same need on administrative grounds for limiting the number of taxpayers; and
- (iii) with the present system of charging tax, the effect of a reduction in allowances in increasing the tax liability is all the greater the higher the income of the taxpayer, so that the burden of reduced allowances increases progressively with income; the burden thereby imposed on persons previously exempt is only a modest one.

I therefore recommend that

- (i) the personal allowance should be reduced from the current $900 to $750;
- (ii) the wife's allowance from the current $700 to $600;
- (iii) there should be a uniform child allowance of $300 per child, in place of the present three-tier system; and
- (iv) excepting the case of husband and wife, and the case of parents with respect to minor children, the number of persons with respect to whom allowances can be claimed should be limited to four.

I recommend also that the rate schedule should be smoothed out in accordance with the recommendations of the Nicholas report, by splitting the present 12 per cent. band into a 12 per cent. and an 18 per cent. band (of $1,200 each), and the present 24 per cent. band into a 24 per cent. and 30 per cent. (of $1,200 each). But for the recommendation of a property tax, I might have also suggested one additional category at a 70 per cent. rate, but there are very great advantages in not raising the ceiling rate of income tax beyond certain levels, and the same purpose is far better served by the introduction of a new tax, such as the property tax.

A very rough calculation suggests that these changes would increase the yield of the personal income tax by about $1 million, from the present $3·5 million to $4·5 million.

3. *Inclusion of Imputed Income on Owner-occupied Houses and Land*

It would be desirable, on grounds of equity, to levy the charge on the annual value (or full rental value) of owner-occupied houses and agricultural land, on the lines of the United Kingdom "Schedule A" tax. In view however of the great administrative problems of such a tax (valuation, where no up-to-date rateable values are available; allowance for maintenance expenses; machinery of assessment and collection) and also in view of the fact that the proposed property tax provides *some* remedy to the existing anomaly, I do not recommend this change for immediate consideration.

This question should however be kept under review and an examination made whether houses which are now outside municipal areas should not be made subject to a charge equivalent to the rates paid on houses within municipalities; and whether the tax now under consideration on land not in beneficial possession could not be made part of a more general scheme of taxing land and houses on the United Kingdom "Schedule A" lines.

C. MINOR RECOMMENDATIONS

1. *Taxation of Life Insurance Companies*

According to Section 27(2) of the Ordinance the tax upon the chargeable income of any Life Insurance Company is charged at 15 per cent. In view of the fact that in recent years Life Insurance Companies made very large profits as a result of the rise in interest rates (since it is now possible to invest premium income on much more favourable terms than those on which the original policies were issued) I think this is unjustifiably low in present circumstances, and I suggest that it should be raised to 30 per cent. This would yield additional revenue of some $130,000 per year.

2. *Deduction at Source on Government and Local Authority ̣Bonds and Provisions concerning Bearer Bonds*

I strongly recommend that the future issue of Bearer bonds should be prohibited by statute. With regard to the outstanding bonds there should be a provision—for reasons of enforcing income tax and property tax, and also in connection with exchange control —that all bearer bonds shall be deposited with an authorised depositary (in practice one of the two commercial banks) who are alone authorised to pay interest on the coupons of the bonds so deposited, after deducting income tax at the rate of, say, 30 per cent. Such deductions should qualify as a set-off against tax liability in the same way as the tax deducted on dividends. The necessary legislation must provide that the banks shall treat the name of the depositors as secret but shall communicate the list of the depositors, the value of bonds deposited, and the amount of tax periodically deducted, to the income tax authorities.

3. *Measures Consequent upon Exchange Control*

As provided in the existing Exchange Control Ordinance, businesses, financial institutions and private individuals should declare all assets owned abroad and should deposit all foreign securities etc. with an authorised depositary. They should be free to sell their securities and exchange them against other securities, provided the securities are held by, or registered in the name of, an authorised depositary. Financial institutions and insurance companies may be authorised to be their own depositaries provided that they declare their assets to the Exchange Control Authority. All foreign bank accounts must also be declared to the Exchange Control, and the accounts closed and the amount remitted to a local bank, unless the Exchange Control gives permission in each individual instance. Permission should normally be given in the case of businesses who need to keep balances abroad in connection with ordinary business.

It is reasonable that Life Insurance Companies should be asked to invest the greater part of their premium income, say 75 per cent. in British Guiana securities. In order to facilitate this the Government should offer to issue securities with a range of maturities to suit the financial needs of these companies. There is no need to recall the life funds which are actually invested abroad provided the holdings are declared to the Exchange Control.

4. *Interest on Loans Granted by the Government*

It is suggested that on any loan granted by Government (such as loans given to Civil Servants, members of the Government etc.) interest should be charged at roughly the same rates at which the Government is able to borrow.

PART II. NEW TAXES ON CAPITAL GAINS, PROPERTY AND GIFTS

By far the most important reform (at least from a long-run point of view) is to broaden the scope of direct taxation through introducing a tax on capital gains, an annual tax on net property, and a tax on gifts. These taxes, together with the existing income tax, would constitute a comprehensive and integrated system of progressive direct taxation which would ensure that the tax burden imposed on the different members of the community is in fair approximation to their true taxable capacity. All these taxes should be introduced jointly, as part of a single Code (which means that the necessary provisions should be incorporated into the existing Income Tax Ordinance, the title of which may have to be changed accordingly) and I am satisfied (after discussions with the Commissioner of Inland Revenue) that these reforms could be introduced in the coming Budget, and put into effect immediately, the necessary legislation being laid before the Legislature as soon as the drafting can be completed. (Since the reforms proposed are very close to the provisions of the new Ceylon legislation, the Ceylon Income Tax (Amendment) Act, 1959, and the Personal Tax Act, 1959, could serve as the basis for drafting the new clauses of the British Guiana Income Tax Ordinance.)

1. *The Case for the New Taxes*

Since the taxes proposed are strange to the British tax system (though they exist in varying forms in the tax systems of a number of western countries, particularly the Scandinavian countries, and have recently also been introduced in India and Ceylon) I feel that the fundamental case for these taxes needs to be briefly stated:

(i) Effective taxation of the so-called *capital profits* or *capital gains* is an essential feature of an equitable system of taxation, simply because capital profits increase spending power in exactly the same manner as other profits which are subject to tax; and because capital gains are a species of gain which accrues only to a particular class of taxpayer (the owners of businesses and real property) whose taxation therefore is necessarily deficient, in relation to other people who do not have the chance of making such capital profits. The taxation of capital gains is important also because when capital gains receive specially favourable treatment, or are altogether exempt, the way is opened to manipulations of numerous kinds by which a particular taxpayer can reduce his tax liability even further through the conversion of an operating profit into a capital profit, so that the basis for taxing operational or revenue profits themselves becomes arbitrary.

Most of the objections against the taxation for capital gains are without validity and they are discussed in detail in Chapter 2 of the minority report of the British Royal Commission on Taxation. One such argument is that since there is always some inflation, the increase in the value of capital in terms of money is not wholly a *true* gain. This argument ignores that the main purpose of personal taxation is to do justice between persons; if the gains of the gainers were excluded from charge on the ground that they are to some extent fictitious, it would be necessary to make a corresponding reduction from taxable income of all those whose position deteriorates on account of the rise in prices (the holders of bonds, saving deposits, insurance policies, etc.). In times of inflation those who only manage to preserve their real capital intact still gain relatively to those whose real wealth is reduced, and who do not get corresponding relief from the tax system on that account.

(ii) The fundamental argument in favour of an annual *tax on net property* (or net capital) owned, alongside a tax on income, is that such a dual system yields a much fairer approximation to taxation in accordance with taxable capacity than a tax based either on income alone or on capital wealth alone. The reason for this is that the possession of disposable property endows a man with spending power as such, quite apart from the money income which the property yields. A man who owns $100,000 for example, in gold and jewellery has clearly a much greater taxable capacity than a man who owns or earns nothing, even though in terms of income they are both in the same position. If different persons possessed disposable wealth and money incomes in the same proportions, it clearly would make no difference whether the tax levied were expressed as a percentage of their capital or as a percentage of their income. But this is not the case, and when different persons possess capital and income in varying proportions, taxes levied upon *both* produce much fairer results than a system which levies tax on either income alone or on capital alone. The tax system of some countries (but not of British Guiana) does recognise the fact that income derived from property possesses a greater taxable capacity than income which is not so derived, and attempts to make allowance for this by charging "earned" income at a lower rate than "unearned" income. But just because the relationship between income and capital varies so much (not only as between wage and salary earners and property owners, but also as between different property owners) the taxable capacity which resides in the possession of property as such cannot adequately be taken account of by a differential levy based on income.

From the point of view of its economic effects the advantage of a tax on net property is that it avoids the bias in favour of idle wealth and against the productive employment of capital, which is inherent in income tax. Idle wealth which yields no income, or only a small income, may possess great advantages of liquidity to the owner; whereas the high money return of capital employed in productive enterprise is partly a reflection of the risks associated with enterprise and of its relative illiquidity. In the case of a net property tax, properties of equal value are taxed equally, irrespective of the money income which

they yield; and this tends to counteract the bias produced
by income tax in favour of keeping wealth in idle (non-
income producing) forms.

(iii) The argument in favour of the *gift tax* is that the right of an
individual to pass on his property to his heirs and successors
must be limited by taxation if society wishes to avoid the ill
effects of an increasing concentration of wealth in the hands
of privileged families. This is necessary also to prevent an
increasing divorce between the ownership of capital and
managerial responsibilities, which is bound to occur if each
generation of *entrepreneurs* can pass on the fruits of their
accumulation unimpaired to a succession of *rentiers*. This
is recognised in the legislation of most countries which
impose progressive taxes of some kind on *inheritance*; which
is only one form (though normally the most important) in
which wealth is passed on by gratuituous transfers from one
generation to another. If the right to such transfers is
limited in the case of inheritance, logic requires that the
right to pass on property by gratuituous tranfers *inter vivos*
should be similarly limited; quite apart from the fact that
an inheritance tax can always be evaded in the absence of a
corresponding gift tax.

(iv) The case for these new taxes is very powerful also from the
point of view of the general efficacy of tax administration
and enforcement. The capital gains tax forces the compulsory disclosure of capital transactions and thereby
limits the scope of income tax evasion; the same purpose
is served by the annual property tax which forces a
disclosure of an individual person's balance sheet (assets
minus liabilities) each year, and which needs to be re-
conciled both with his profits for the year and with his
property transactions recorded for the purposes of the
capital gains tax. Thus concealment of income becomes
more difficult when the tax administration receives an
annual statement of the changes in a man's property;
concealment of property becomes more difficult whenever
the tax administration has independent sources of information on a man's income; the opposition of interest

between the buyers and sellers of property created by a capital gains tax makes it more difficult to conceal both income and capital transactions and makes it easier to ascertain the correct value of the properties transferred, both for the property tax and the capital gains tax. The taxation of gifts puts a limit to the evasion of estate duty and is of assistance also in the administration of the property tax and the capital gains tax (particularly since it makes it necessary to value the element of gift in property transactions).

From the point of view of both the simplicity and efficacy of administration it is desirable therefore that a taxpayer should furnish in a *single return* the information required for all these taxes, which would make it possible to keep the same check on the fullness and consistency of the accounts supplied as is already provided for by the legal provisions concerning company and business accounts.

2. *The Main Features of the New Taxes*
   (1) *Capital Gains*
      (a) Capital gains should be included as a separate category of gain in Section 5 of the Ordinance, and should subsequently be specified to arise in the following circumstances:
         (i) in connection with the change of ownership of property by way of sale, exchange, disposal by deed or gift, or will;
         (ii) from the surrender or relinquishment of any right to property, such as the right to the use or the exploitation of a property (the lease of a house or a mining concession, etc.);
         (iii) from the redemption of shares, debentures, or other obligations; and
         (iv) from the dissolution of a business and the formation, amalgamation or dissolution of companies.
      (b) The capital gain arising in connection with a change of ownership, to the person who was the owner immediately before such a change, is defined as the excess

of the value of the property at the time of the change of ownership over the value of the property when it was acquired. If both the original acquisition and the current change of ownership was the result of a sale for full consideration, the selling price in each case (i.e., the consideration given or received) is deemed to be the value of the property at the relevant date for the purpose of calculating the taxable gain. If the property was acquired by gift or inheritance subsequent to the introduction of the new tax system, the value of the property as ascertained for gift and inheritance tax purposes shall be deemed to be the value at the time of acquisition; in the same way, when the ownership is relinquished by deed of gift or will, the value at the time of the disposal of property shall be the value as ascertained by the public valuer for gift or inheritance tax purposes. Similarly capital gains arising from the redemption of shares are the excess of the money or other property received over the cost of acquisition of the shares, etc. and the capital gain arising from the dissolution of a business, or the liquidation of a company is the excess of the value of all the property received on such dissolution or liquidation over the cost of the share capital owned. Expenses incurred in improving the property (but not on repair or maintenance) subsequent to its acquisition, shall be added to the cost of acquisition.

(c) In the case of capital gains arising from the surrender, relinquishment or transfer of any right; or from the amalgamation or merger of two businesses or companies, the gain is simply the amount of money or other property received in connection with these events.

(d) The law should also recognise a *capital loss* arising from a change of ownership, redemption of any shares, etc. or on the dissolution of a business or liquidation of a company. Such capital losses should in the first place be offset against capital gains on other transactions in the same year, the amount to be brought into charge being

the net capital gain of the year, which is the excess of
capital gains over capital losses. If capital losses exceed
capital gains for any particular year, the unabsorbed
loss shall be carried forward for an indefinite period as
an offset against future capital gains, it should not be
allowed as an offset against a revenue profit, or other
kind of income. If a taxpayer's estate shows net unabsorbed losses at death, such losses should be carried
backwards and offset against past capital gains or other
income on which income tax was levied, up to five years
prior to the death.

(e) The kind of property on which capital gains and losses
are recognised should be limited to real property, to
businesses as going concerns, to fixed business assets
(in the case of fixed assets subject to a depreciation or
wear and tear allowance, the new conception merely
requires the removal of the limitation on balancing
charges in Section 18(4) of Chapter 300), to stocks and
securities, and titles to valuable rights, such as patents,
copyrights, or other "intangible" property. Gains from
the sale of furniture, jewellery, works of art, etc. should
be excluded below a certain minimum (in an analogous
manner to the provisions of the net property tax). On
account of the difficulty of enforcement, it may be
sensible also to exclude gambling winnings.

(f) Capital gains arising from the sale of a house which has
been effectively occupied by the owner should be exempt
from tax, provided the proceeds are wholly or at least
in greater part re-invested within twelve months in the
purchase of another house intended for occupation by
the owner. This concession should be limited to the
sale of the *principal residence* of the taxpayer, and should
not extend to the sale of summer residences, week-end
houses, etc.

(g) Net capital gains received from any of the transactions
specified should be treated as taxable income and
aggregated with the rest of the income, except that that
part of the income which is represented by capital gains

should not be liable to a charge higher than 45 per cent.
(In view of the fact that capital gains have so far been
entirely exempt, it would be undesirable if capital gains
were now taxed at the full ceiling rate of 60 per cent.)
When capital gains are brought into charge on properties which were held by the owners for more than
three years, it should be open to the taxpayer to spread
the gain over the period of ownership, but over not more
than the five most recent years of assessment.

(h) For the purposes of the initial introduction of the tax,
taxpayers shall return all properties owned on 1st
January, 1956 at the fair market price of the properties at that date, and shall also return the properties
acquired since that date at their actual cost of acquisition (plus cost of subsequent improvements, if any).
These initial values will thus serve both for the purposes
of the annual property tax and for the purposes of the
future charge on account of capital gains when the
ownership of the property changes.

(i) A capital gains tax on these lines makes no distinction
between short and long term gains; it ensures that no
gains are recognised until they are actually realised
through a transaction of some kind; and finally it also
ensures that over the taxpayer's whole life the net charge
on *realised* gains shall be the same as the net *accrued* gains
over his life-time.

(2) *The Property Tax*

This is primarily a tax on the net capital (assets minus
liabilities) owned by individuals, but in the special circumstances of British Guiana where so much of the national
wealth is foreign-owned, it is advisable to impose it on
companies as well. (This is also desirable to prevent
avoidance through the creation of holding companies for
the personal wealth of individuals). Analogous taxes are
already in operation in Sweden, Norway, Denmark,
Holland, India, Ceylon and perhaps a dozen other countries.

(a) Assets for the purposes of this tax shall comprise all real property, stocks and shares, valuable rights (such as mineral rights, patent rights, long term leases, etc.) insurance policies, bank deposits, cash over a certain amount, furniture and jewellery over certain amounts. Liabilities should include all debts.

(b) For the purposes of this tax it will be necessary to rule that all bearer securities and all foreign assets owned by residents shall be deposited with an authorised depositary (i.e., one of the two commercial banks) and a confidential list of such securities owned by residents shall be disclosed, under the usual conditions of secrecy, to the Inland Revenue Department.

(c) The assessment of tax each year should be on *book value* and not on current market value. The book value of an asset is either its actual cost to the owner (plus the cost of improvement since acquisition) or its market value at a time when the taxpayer's capital account is first set up. On the understanding that the initial declared value of any particular property will also serve as the basis for any future liability on account of capital gains, the taxpayer's own declaration of value can serve as the initial book value for the purpose of the net wealth tax. A revision of capital values, in an analogous manner to business accounting, only occurs when a capital profit is brought into account on the realisation of an asset. Otherwise the net capital can only change from year to year as a result of saving or dis-saving out of income, so that the taxpayer's return on capital account would clearly show how much of the change in net property is the result of transfers to or from the income account, and how much the result of the net capital gain or loss resulting from the capital transactions during the year.

(d) The responsibility for the initial valuation of property should be left to the taxpayer who should be warned that any under-valuation is likely to increase future tax liability on account of capital gains, and who should be given to understand how the term "current market value on the 1st January, 1956" is to be interpreted in relation to various categories of assets. Thus in the case of real property, taxpayers may be advised (though not compelled) to call in the assistance of expert valuers. In the case of foreign stocks or shares quoted on a recognised Stock Exchange, it should be the official middle market price, or the closing price, on the appointed day. In the case of the shares of private companies the correct principle is to take the net book value of the assets of the company at the last valuation prior to the appointed day, but the taxpayer should be permitted, if he so desires, to put some valuation on the goodwill of a concern by valuing the shares *above* the book value of the assets. Finally, where the market value of a property on 1st January, 1956 is difficult to ascertain, it should be open to the taxpayer to enter such properties at their estimated market value at the current date, provided that all properties acquired since 1st January, 1956 are entered at the actual cost of acquisition.

(e) The properties owned by family members need not be aggregated for property tax purposes, particularly when the gift of property between family members is liable to a gift tax. Aggregation could however be introduced later if it were found that wealth tends to be diffused between family members, which would also make the administration of the whole tax system more difficult.

(f) I recommend the following rate schedule for the net property tax:

the first $50,000 of net property. . Exempt
the next $150,000 of net property. . $\frac{1}{2}$% per annum
the next $300,000 of net property. . $\frac{3}{4}$% per annum
the next $500,000 of net property. . 1% per annum
the remainder   of net property. . $1\frac{1}{2}$% per annum

(g) The net assets of *companies* as indicated by the written down value of their book assets (but *excluding* any initial allowances granted for the purposes of calculating the written down value) should be taxed at a flat rate of $\frac{1}{2}$ per cent. (This tax could be levied on *all* companies, including those enjoying the tax holiday provisions).

(h) These rates are relatively modest; and in order to allay fears that the Government will raise them subsequently as a means of "expropriation", I recommend that the Minister of Finance should give an assurance in the Budget that the Government will not increase the currently recommended schedule of rates of the net property tax during the life-time of the present Legislature.

It is impossible to make an estimate of the revenue effect of these taxes in the first year of their operation. The capital gains tax will not attain its full yield for a number of years after its first introduction; the yield of the property tax on individuals will probably be a small one; only the property tax on companies is likely to yield a considerable sum immediately, and this may amount to $1 million a year.

3. *The Gift Tax*

The gift tax, as was stated earlier, is a necessary complement to an inheritance tax. Just as the inheritance tax can either be a tax on the estate of the deceased (as is the case with estate duty) or a tax on the heir or legatee (as is the case with a legacy or succession duty) so the gift tax can be conceived either as a tax on the donor or a tax on the donee; but in either case it is necessary that the gift tax should have the same character as its complement, the inheritance tax.

Looking at the matter strictly from the point of view of equity there could be little doubt that in the case of both taxes a tax charged on the recipient is more just in principle than a tax on the donor, since this relates the charge to benefit received. But a tax of this latter type is undoubtedly more difficult to administer; it gives wider opportunities for tax avoidance or evasion, and is bound to have (quite apart from avoidance or evasion) a smaller yield. We must also bear in mind that British Guiana already possesses an estate duty of the British type (which is a tax on the total estate of the deceased) and it would involve a great deal of administrative complication if a change were now made to an inheritance tax of the legacy duty type (as is in force e.g. in Mexico). For these reasons I suggest that the gift tax (which need be closely tethered to the provisions of the inheritance tax) should also be a tax on the donor (as in the case with the gift taxes already in force in the United States, Australia and a number of other countries).

The necessary features of such a tax, if it is to be effective, must include the following:

(a) The tax must be cumulative, i.e. the tax on any particular gift should be made to depend not on the size of the gift but on the total amount of gifts made (including the gift in question) since the inception of the tax. Cumulation must extend over the taxpayer's whole life-time, and for this reason a record must be kept by the Tax Administration of all the gifts previously made and the tax paid on them.

(b) The rate schedule must be an equivalent schedule to the actual rate schedule of estate duty and must relate to the cumulative total of gifts made. Thus if a man makes a gift of $10,000, having already made previous gifts of $50,000, the rate of tax applicable should be that stated in the schedule for the tranche $50,000–$60,000. For this purpose it is necessary that the rate schedule for the gift tax should be stated in terms of a succession of *marginal rates* (as is the case with the income tax schedule) and not in terms of *effective rates* (as is the case with the estate duty schedule). It must also be borne in mind that since the gift tax on the donor is necessarily a *net* tax (the tax on a gift actually made, and payable out of resources other than the gift), whereas the estate duty is a *gross* tax (it is a levy on the whole of the estate, and the duty is paid out of it), the rate schedule of the gift tax in terms of its effective rate equivalent, must exceed the corresponding rate schedule of the estate duty in the ratio of $t/1-t$ (where t is the *effective* rate of estate duty

on estates of a particular size) in order to provide full
equivalence between the two taxes. To obtain the
appropriate schedule of rates for a cumulative gift tax it is
necessary first

>   (i) to multiply the existing schedule of estate duty rates
>   by $t/1-t$;
>   (ii) to derive a corresponding schedule of marginal rates
>   by dividing the additional tax liability incurred
>   between one size-category and the next with the
>   additional value of the estate of that category.

(c) The introduction of a gift tax on these lines would necessitate
certain changes in the provisions for estate duty. Thus
provision must be made for inclusion in the dutiable estate
of *both* the cumulative total of the gifts made, and the
cumulative total of the gift tax paid on them (as well as all
gifts made five years prior to the introduction of the gift
tax), and estate duty must be calculated by reference to the
total estate after *adding back* these items; the total amount
paid in gift taxes must afterwards be deducted from the
gross liability so calculated. This method ensures that the
combined charge in gift taxes and estate duty on any
particular taxpayer is exactly the same, irrespective of
whether he makes gifts during his life-time, and how many,
or whether he maintains his property intact until his
decease.

(d) In principle only *gifts of a capital nature* should be subject to a
gift tax. But any such distinction is administratively un-
enforceable since when the gift is in the form of money, and
not an actual piece of property, it is impossible to distinguish between a capital gift and an income gift; if any
such distinction were made, the taxpayer could avoid the
gift tax by dressing up capital gifts as income gifts – as could
be conveniently done e.g. by borrowing money on a
property, giving the proceeds as gift to the donee, and the
donee purchasing the property from the donor with the
money and thereby extinguishing the loan. For this reason
in all countries where gift taxes are in operation the
exemptions introduced are stated in terms of a certain

annual total sum of gifts made, and when the total amount of gifts in any year exceeds the exemption limit, the rest is taxable, irrespective of the nature or character of the gifts. I suggest that if a gift tax were introduced in British Guiana the procedure would have to be the same, with gifts totalling say, $1,000 a year exempt and anything over and above that sum declared taxable and cumulated with the taxable gifts already made. It may be worthwhile to put the limit of exemption rather high (say $2,000 per year) and thereby allow for a certain amount of evasion, rather than face the strong protests that would be encountered if genuine income transfers (as e.g. annuity payments or remittances to needy relatives) were made subject to the gift tax.

(e) As the experience of Australia and other countries shows, even with this method there would be need for special anti-avoidance provisions to prevent the dressing-up of gifts as commercial transactions or loan transactions. One obvious form of such avoidance is when a minor (sometimes a newborn infant) borrows a large sum on the security of his parents and uses the proceeds to purchase property from the parents, the loan being gradually repaid out of income of the property during the child's minority.

(f) Though the liability for the gift tax is primarily on the donor, the legislation must provide powers to have recourse on the donee if for any reason it is impossible to collect the tax from the donor (otherwise the charge might be evaded by the donor giving his whole property away and becoming bankrupt).

(g) Although the gift tax is a complement to the Estate Duty, from an administrative point of view it should be jointly administered with the income tax and the property tax, gifts being included in the same comprehensive return which concerns income, capital transactions during the year and the net wealth statement—particularly as the income tax administration will in any case face the problem of separating the gift-element in all those cases where property is sold for less than full consideration.

PART III. CUSTOMS AND EXCISE DUTIES

Existing import duties yield $21·5 million which is 14 per cent. of the total value of imports and 18 per cent. of the value of dutiable imports. An increase of the order of $5 million would thus raise the average rate of duty on *dutiable* imports to 22·5 per cent., which, by international standards, is by no means excessively high.

In the detailed scheme worked out by Mr W. P. D'Andrade and Mr. H. O. E. Barker, the increase in duties was apread over all broad categories, but concentrated on such items as are not necessities, or which mainly affect middle-class, rather than working-class, consumption. This meant that of the $117·5 million of dutiable imports in 1960, the duties on over $80 million of imports were left unaffected, and the increase concentrated on $36 million of relatively inessential imports. On these the increase in duties will be just under 50 per cent., and it will increase the landed cost of these articles by 15 per cent.

The main items in this list are alcoholic beverages and tobacco, motor spirit, fabrics, and durable consumer goods of all kinds, including motor cars.

There is a parallel increase in excise duties on spirits (except local wines) and on beer which will increase the yield of these duties by 20 per cent., and the cost to the consumer by approximately 10 per cent. in the case of rum, and by 5 per cent. in the case of beer.

The total additional yield of these duties (on the basis of 1960 figures for imports and 1961 figures for excise duties) is an additional $5·4 million in import duties and $1·1 million in excise duties. Since, however, the increase in the duties may in itself cause some reduction in consumption, the net additional yield may be put at $5 million and $1 million respectively.

Since private consumption expenditure was estimated at some $190 million for 1961, the imposition of these duties may cause the average cost of living of all classes to rise by some 3 per cent. Since, however, only a few of these items enter into the working class budget in any quantity, the increase in the cost of living index (which is an index of the working class cost of living) will be very much less than this.

PART IV. A COMPULSORY SAVINGS SCHEME

In order to increase the flow of resources for purposes of economic development I suggest the introduction of a scheme of compulsory savings such as already exists in some Latin American countries (such as Brazil and Cuba) and which has recently been introduced in Ghana. I would recommend a scheme similar to the one introduced in Ghana this year, on the following lines:

(a) The scheme is administered in close relationship with the administration of income tax. Contributions are deducted monthly from the emoluments of employees and on all other persons (the self-employed, the business partnership and the companies). They are assessed and collected in the same manner as income tax.

(b) The rate of contribution should be 5 per cent. of the total income of wage and salary earners and 10 per cent. of all other incomes. Individuals whose total income is less than $1,000 a year should be exempt from the obligation to make a contribution, and in the case of the self-employed, the 10 per cent. rate should only be applicable to persons whose income is in excess of, say $5,000; in the range of $1,000 – $5,000 the rate should be 5 per cent., just as in the case of the employees.

(c) Contributors are given Government bonds which are registered in their names and are not transferable or negotiable but are repayable together with the accrued interest at the end of 7 years or at any time afterwards. Interest continues to accrue on the bonds until they are actually encashed. (In the scheme adopted in Ghana the bonds were made repayable at the end of 10 years but in the light of the Ghana experience I would prefer a shorter period of 7 years).

(d) Bonds are repayable when a person dies, or in the case of ex-patriate persons when they leave the country permanently; they are also repayable upon retirement, provided the holder has attained the age of 60, in five annual instalments. Interest accruing up to the date of repayment is payable in all such cases.

(e) It is possible to combine this with a lottery scheme which might make it more attractive to the majority of the holders who have a chance to win large cash prizes even before the bonds are due for repayment. The scheme originally envisaged for Ghana provided that the bonds should carry a simple interest of 2 per cent. per annum and that a further 2 per cent. of the value of the bonds outstanding in any year should be given away in prizes at not more than two drawings annually. Assuming a scheme of lottery prizes in which the great majority of the prizes are double the face value of the bonds, and with a few large prizes amounting to 10 or 100 times the face-value, it would be necessary to draw somewhat less than 1 per cent. of the bonds outstanding in any one year, and to make cash payments (including the repayment of the bonds drawn) of around 3 per cent. of the total value of the outstanding bonds.

(f) The lottery element of the scheme, introduced in the original Compulsory Savings Act of Ghana was later abandoned owing to its administrative complications, and even more owing to the opposition by the Churches and the Farmers' Organisation; and an amended scheme provided for straight bonds carrying a simple interest of 4 per cent. per annum which is paid when the bonds are encashed (similarly to the United Kingdom Savings Certificates). Ghana's experience is not necessarily relevant however to British Guiana, and the question of whether the bonds should be lottery bonds or straight interest bearing bonds, should be considered in the light of the question as to which scheme would prove more attractive to the majority.

It might be possible (without complicating the administration too much) to offer a choice to each contributor between a straight interest-bearing bond or a combined interest-and-lottery bond; except that businesses and companies should only be offered straight interest-bearing bonds.

(g) Simple interest was chosen to avoid the more complicated calculations involved when paying compound interest. In the case of British Guiana I feel such complications should not weigh too heavily, and I would recommend that interest should accrue at compound interest, since otherwise there is no inducement on holders to hold on to the bonds longer than they are obliged to. I would therefore recommend that straight interest-bearing bonds should be repayable at the end of 7 years from the date of issue at 130 per cent. of their face values—which corresponds to a tax-free compound rate of interest of approximately $3\frac{2}{3}$ per cent. a year—and should afterwards earn a tax-free interest of 4 per cent. compound for each further year they remain unencashed. Lottery bonds should be repayable at 110 per cent. of their face-value at the end of 7 years, but should participate in drawings in which 2 per cent. of the total face-value of such bonds outstanding is given away in each year (in addition to the redemption of the bonds drawn).

(h) In order to minimise administrative complications it is advisable that a *single bond* should be issued with respect to an individual's total contribution for each year (or at most for each quarter), the face value being inserted on the bond when it is issued, and interest calculated accordingly. In this case the lottery prizes must be stated, not in terms of fixed sums, but in terms of *multiples* of the face value of the bonds actually drawn.

(i) In the case of wage and salary earners contributions are collected monthly through the employers in the same way as is the case with P.A.Y.E. income tax. The experience of Ghana shows however that contributors are anxious to receive some evidence of their contribution simultaneously

L

with the deductions (otherwise they are afraid that they may
not get bonds at all, or not of equivalent value; also it may
be difficult to trace individuals if in the interval they change
their place of employment) and to avoid these difficulties
Ghana has now introduced a scheme by which employers
put stamps on a special savings card which is registered
in the name of each contributor (in an analogous manner
to insurance stamps which must be affixed to insurance
cards in the United Kingdom social insurance scheme) and
such cards, filled with stamps, are periodically returned to
the authority in charge of the whole scheme which issues
duly registered bonds in exchange. In Ghana the authority
is the Central Bank, in the case of British Guiana, until a
Central Bank is established, it would have to be a special
department of the Treasury. Ghana also issues a registered
Savings Book to each contributor, into which these bonds
are affixed, in the same manner as is the case with the
National Savings Certificate in the United Kingdom.

(j) A scheme on these lines might provide very considerable
internal resources for development—something like $3½
million from companies alone and around $2 million–$3
million from other persons. Owing however to the considerable amount of careful administrative preparation
which it requires (and also to the fact that the P.A.Y.E.
income tax scheme is not yet in force, and would probably
not be introduced until 1962) I cannot see that it can be
implemented in connection with the next budget. There is
no reason however why it should not be introduced some-
time later in the year, as the necessary administrative
preparations involved, e.g. the devising and printing of
forms, bonds etc., and the whole administrative machinery,
could be got ready in, say, six months' time. Also it may be
advisable to announce the scheme beforehand, and possibly
to leave the choice open whether the bonds should be
straight interest bearing bonds or combined interest and
lottery bonds, a matter on which the public preference
could be ascertained through various organisations. In
making the announcement the Government may also make

it clear that it is a simple alternative to a universal contributory pensions scheme, and that it may be transformed into a more elaborate pension scheme at a later date.

PART V. PROBLEMS OF ADMINISTRATION

1. *Organisation of the Inland Revenue Department*
   The adoption of the above reforms would throw a considerable burden on the Inland Revenue Department, and it is very important that the relatively high standards of efficiency of that Department should not suffer in consequence. I think that as soon as a decision is taken on its implementation the Commissioner of Inland Revenue should be invited to submit a scheme for the staffing requirements, and of such reforms in the organisation of the Department as he regards necessary for the efficient implementation of the scheme. Owing to the existing shortage of staff, and the need for additional staff, I regard it as particularly important that the proposals of the Guillebaud Report concerning the Inland Revenue Department be implemented.

Special problems will arise in connection with the compulsory savings scheme as regards the division of responsibilities between the Inland Revenue Department (who will be responsible for the assessment and collection of contributions) and the department of the Treasury responsible for the issue, registration etc. of the bonds and for operating the lottery scheme.

As the new taxes are to be administered jointly with the existing income tax, each Inspector of Taxes will have more work to do in connection with each file, and may require additional training in accountancy to evaluate the returns. It is inevitable of course that some years should elapse before the new taxes are fully and effectively implemented, and before they yield the full revenue that can be expected from them.

The proper administration of the new taxes will require the setting up of a *Valuation Section* within the Department for valuing properties in connection with the gift and inheritance taxes, as well as for checking the returns in connection with the capital gains tax.

Another urgent requirement is the creation of an *Investigation Section*, manned by properly trained auditors. (At a later stage it might be possible to introduce legislation which would compel companies to have their accounts audited by public auditors who would audit accounts from the point of view of their proper presentation to the Revenue, as well as from the point of view of their proper presentation to shareholders).

Finally, in the interest of general economic policy and planning as well as the efficient administration of taxes it is highly important that a *Statistics and Intelligence Section* be set up within the Inland Revenue Department, headed by a fully qualified economic statistician. The files of the Department are one of the most important sources of general economic intelligence available to planners and policy-makers; but in the absence of a separate Statistics and Intelligence Section it cannot be expected that the information obtained through the returns can be summarised and evaluated by the Department in the manner required for purposes of general economic intelligence. (This is additional to the need for setting up a Central Statistical Office of the Government.)

I suggest that the Government should make full use of technical assistance through the United Nations or friendly Governments in order to obtain the services of expert advisers in the setting up of these new Sections and that it should request friendly Governments with similar tax systems (such as the United Kingdom, Australia, New Zealand, Canada, India or Ceylon) to lend the services of at least two senior officials of their Income Tax Departments for periods of not less than a year in order to train additional Inspectors. It may also be advisable to call in the services of an expert to examine whether the existing system of record-keeping in the Department needs to be improved in view of the new system of taxation. (One such improvement which merits consideration is the setting up of a card index system where the main facts concerning the taxpayers' returns for each year (turnover, profits, capital allowances, etc.) are recorded in an easily accessible form.)

2. *Strengthening the Hands of the Revenue in the Courts*

I understand from the Commissioner of Inland Revenue that in regard to prosecutions for tax offences the Revenue in British Guiana is in a very weak position and is unable to take action except in a few cases owing to the impossibility of securing conviction in the Courts. This is partly due to the general inclination of judges to presume in favour of the taxpayer, partly because income tax offences come before the Magistracy Courts, and Magistrates are not always in a position to judge and evaluate complex issues that may be involved; partly because the wording of Section 77 makes it incumbent on the Revenue to prove that a person "knowingly" made a false statement or a false declaration and in general, it is impossible for the Revenue to give documentary proof of such "knowledge". I think the hands of the Revenue would be considerably strengthened if

    (a) prosecutions were brought before the High Court, instead of the Magistracy Courts;

    (b) if the Ordinance would indicate the circumstances in which such knowledge must be presumed.

I therefore recommend

    (i) that in Sections 76 and 77 the words "shall be liable upon conviction by the High Court" be substituted for the words "shall be liable on summary conviction"; and

    (ii) that a new subsection (3) be added to Section 77 on the following lines:

        77(3) For the purposes of this Section, a false statement or false declaration must be presumed to have been knowingly made whenever

            (a) it reveals a degree of negligence on behalf of a person that is inconsistent with his obligation to make a full, true and correct return, statement, declaration, or account; and

            (b) a person fails to notify the Commissioner without unreasonable delay of any error or omission in a return, statement, declaration or account submitted by him.

6

REPORT ON THE TURKISH
TAX SYSTEM[1]

I. FISCAL ASPECTS OF DEVELOPMENT POLICY

Problems of taxation, in connection with economic development, are generally discussed from two different points of view, which involve very different, and often conflicting, considerations: the point of view of *incentives* and the point of view of *resources*. Those who believe that it is the lack of adequate incentives which is mainly responsible for insufficient growth and investment are mainly concerned to improve the tax system from an incentive point of view through the granting of additional concessions of various kinds, with less regard to the unfavourable effects on the public revenue. Those who believe that insufficient growth and investment is mainly a consequence of a lack of resources, are chiefly concerned with increasing the resources available for investment through additional taxation even at the cost of worsening its disincentive effects.

In my opinion it is the limitation of resources, not of incentives, which governs the pace of economic development, and except in cases where added incentives may in themselves lead to additional resources (in the case of tax concessions granted to foreigners which may increase capital inflow from abroad) a great deal of the prevailing concern with incentives is misplaced. In consequence the present memorandum will chiefly be concerned with questions of taxation from the resources aspect.

In the case of Turkey, the present revenue from taxation is insufficient to meet current needs—as witnessed by the fact that about 9 per cent. of current requirements are financed by

---

[1] Written at the invitation of the State Planning Organisation of the Government of Turkey in Ankara, Turkey, in April 1962. Letter of transmittal omitted.

foreign aid (counterpart funds) and a further 5 per cent. by straight deficit financing; in relation to the national income it is low in comparison with other countries at Turkey's stage of development; and it is quite inadequate if the current level of economic activity is to be expanded as part of the process of accelerated investment and also as a means of stimulating growth. As will be argued below, such an expansionary policy, contrary to wide-spread view, requires *more* revenue being raised in taxation and also revenue of the kind that contributes to the attainment of a better balance in the economy. In terms of a taxation target, I think Turkey should aim at raising her total tax revenue to at least TL 10,000 millions by 1963, an increase of TL 3,500 millions over 1961. It may be assumed that the increase in the yield of existing taxation would provide TL 2,000 million of this, but without taking into account the various reforms in income and corporation taxes, which are now to come before the legislature, and which might reduce the actual revenue by as much as TL 500 million. It thus appears that the Government ought to aim at no less than an additional TL 2,000 million in taxation.

Reallocation of Resources

The main objective of national policy is to secure a higher rate of economic development that would allow an appreciable improvement in living standards, as well as provide for the 3 per cent. annual growth in the population. In view of this the annual growth target has been set at 7 per cent., which in turn requires that at least 18 per cent. of the national product should be devoted to investment. To achieve this it is necessary to reduce the proportion of current income consumed by at least 3 per cent. of the gross national product; this can be done—and can only be done—through additional taxation or other compulsory levies.

Consideration of justice and equity suggest that the needed resources should mainly be provided through a reduction of unnecessary, or luxury, consumption—i.e., the consumption of the well-to-do classes—and to the extent that it is possible to do so by fiscal means (it could also be promoted by other means—

e.g., import controls or building licensing) measures designed to reduce luxury consumption should certainly have priority. There is however a fundamental reason why additional taxes on the well-to-do cannot, by themselves, be sufficient to provide the needed resources. Increased investment entails increased employment, and this in turn requires increased availabilities of "wage-goods"—the kind of goods that wage and salary earners consume. The foremost among these is food, which probably takes up two-thirds or more of the average worker's expenditure, but which is only a small proportion of the consumption of the higher income groups.

Moreover, since economic development invariably entails that a steadily growing proportion of the population is employed outside agriculture—in the so-called "secondary" and "tertiary" sectors—balanced (or non-inflationary) development is not conceivable unless the "agricultural surplus" (the excess of agricultural production over the food consumption of the agricultural sectors) steadily expands as well. Such an expansion cannot be relied on to occur automatically, as part of the overall process of growth in the economy. Economic incentives do not operate in the same way in agriculture as in the case of industry and commerce; a shortage of food is not likely to call forth increased production—a rise in the price of basic foodstuffs may even lead to a *decrease* in marketable supplies, since it will tend to increase the farmers own consumption of foodstuffs, and/or reduce their incentive to work. But, since on account of the nature of food as a primary necessity, the price of foodstuffs can never rise very much in relation to other commodities (any such a tendency merely creates general inflation) it is the supply of foodstuffs which limits the demand for the products of the other sectors of the economy. Hence it is the growth of the demand for labour outside agriculture which is ultimately limited by the growth in the farmers' sales of agricultural products, and not the other way round.

II. THE TAXATION OF AGRICULTURE

These considerations argue that any economic plan aiming at rapid industrialisation must give the highest priority to measures of raising the productivity of agriculture, since the latter is a pre-condition of the former. They also suggest that the taxation of agriculture (by one means or another) has a critical role to play in the acceleration of economic development, since it is only the *imposition of compulsory levies on the agricultural sector itself* which enlarges the supply of "savings" for economic development, in the required sense. Countries as different in their social institutions or economic circumstances as Japan or Soviet Russia have been similar in their heavy dependence on agricultural taxation (in the case of Japan through a land tax, in the case of Soviet Russia through the system of compulsory deliveries at low prices) for financing their economic development.

In the Ottoman Empire agriculture had to carry almost the whole burden of public expenditure. The relief of this burden, and the amelioration in the lot of peasantry, was one of the great achievements of the Revolution. In the last 20 years, however, more as a by-product of the war and the inflation than of any deliberate and thought-out policy, the situation seems to have swung to the other extreme, and the agricultural sector now appears hardly to be taxed at all. Although the net income of the agricultural sector (according to the estimates of the State Planning Organisation) at TL 17·6 billions, accounted for 42·5 per cent. of the net domestic product of TL 41·3 billions, agriculture contributed 0·8 per cent. of all direct taxation, and (owing to the high ratio of income which is directly consumed and not bought through the market) a less than proportionate share of all indirect taxation. Although it is not possible to allocate the incidence of indirect taxation with any precision, the proportion of these taxes falling on the agricultural sector could hardly exceed 20–25 per cent. Therefore, taking into account both direct and indirect taxation, the contribution of agriculture could not have amounted to more than one-tenth or, at most, one-eighth, of the total tax revenue of the State. In terms of percentage of income contributed in taxation of all kinds the burden on the agricultural sector may thus be put at 4–5 per cent., while the burden of taxation on the remaining sectors—industry, commerce, services, etc.—is 20 to 25 per cent.[1]

This situation will be improved, though not greatly altered, when the new agricultural income tax comes into force. Even if one accepted the forecast of revenue of TL 150 million (which many regard as far too optimistic), this would only increase agriculture's share by 5 per cent. of direct taxation and less than $2\frac{1}{2}$ per cent. of total taxation.

In my view income tax is a clumsy and inefficient instrument for the taxation of agriculture, particularly in a country like Turkey. Even the most developed Western countries, such as the U.K., the U.S.A. or France, have never succeeded in imposing a successful income tax on the farming community; and the farmers greatly resent it, because it forces them into vexatious bookkeeping and into following concepts of accounting which are alien to them. Indeed one of the fundamental difficulties seems to be that modern accounting techniques have never succeeded, in the case of agriculture, in separating current expenses from increases in capital in the manner in which commercial or industrial accounting has succeeded in doing. As a result, the farmer's accounts may show continuing losses even though both the production and the value of the farm is continually rising. It is well known in the U.K. and the U.S. that it "pays" successful men engaged in commercial activities to acquire a farm as well, so as to be able to escape taxation in their

---

[1] The low share of agricultural taxation at present is partly due to the fact that the land tax has been largely eroded, owing to the absence of any reassessment of land values since 1936. The following table shows the comparative value of various kinds of land (1) according to the 1936 cadastral valuation, (2) according to a recent sample survey, relating to 1960, by the University of Ankara:

Type of Land	1936	1960	Province
Kiraç	3·00	287	—
Sulu	30·00	1081·6	—
Bahçe	15·00	2400	Izmir
Kiraç	2·00	136	Diyarbakir
Sulu	27·00	1044	Konya

This shows the average increase in land values, for various kinds of land and in various parts of the country, to have been around 50 fold between 1936 and 1960. As against that the revenue from land taxation in 1961 was TL 24·2 million or only 2·7 times the 1936 figure. In 1936 the land tax contributed 4 per cent. to the total tax revenue of the Government, and in 1960 its contribution was only 0·3 per cent.

commercial business (in stockbroking for example) by the "losses" incurred in their farming activities.

The Case for a New Land Tax

For these reasons, it seems to me that the yield of a new agricultural income tax may fall well below current expectations. But even if the current forecasts were fulfilled the direct taxation of agriculture would still amount to only just over one per cent. of the net income of agriculture—a figure which is far too low in the light of the considerations advanced earlier. If agriculture is to make a genuine contribution to economic development, which would make it possible to expand investment and industrial production without creating inflation, and if the official estimates of the net product of agriculture are anywhere near correct, *its contribution to direct taxation should be nearer to TL 1,000 million than to TL 100 million.* Even at TL 1,000 million, the burden of direct taxation on agriculture would only amount to 5·7 per cent. of net agricultural incomes, whereas the burden of *direct* taxation on all other incomes—on wages and salaries, and on the profits of the self-employed and businesses of all kinds works out at 12·5 per cent., on the basis of the official estimates.

I fully realise that a levy of this sort, moderate though it may be, might require substantial education of public opinion. But sooner or later public opinion would have to be brought round to the view of the necessity of such an imposition if Turkey's development plans which, in view of her continuing large increase in population is not a matter of choice but of necessity, are to be realised. A levy yielding a revenue of the order of TL 1,000 million could only be imposed by some form of a revised land tax. The type of land tax which I would favour would differ from either the tithes of the Ottoman era or the land tax of the Republic period in two main respects:

1. It would be based on the average net product of agriculture, of each particular region and each particular type of land, *as defined for purposes of national accounting*, and not on the market value of the land (as is the case with the present land tax) or on the *gross* produce of the land (as was the case with the ancient tithes system).

2. It would be a progressive tax, taking into account the size of the landholdings of the individual farmer, and not just a tax on the land itself, irrespective of the wealth of the owner.

The tax would be akin, however, to these earlier taxes in that it would be a tax on the "potential output" rather than on the actual output of any piece of land, meaning by "potential output" the *output which the land would yield if it were managed with average efficiency*. Thus the inefficient farmer whose production is less than the average for the region and for the type of land concerned would be penalised, whereas the efficient farmer would be correspondingly encouraged. Such a tax on potential output is far superior in its economic consequences to any tax based on actual income or profit; and it is technically feasible to impose it in the case of agriculture (where land provides a measurable yardstick) in a way which is not feasible for other types of economic activity. It would thus give the maximum incentive for efficient farmers to improve their land and expand their output; it should also greatly encourage the transfer of land ownership from inefficient to efficient hands, and thereby raise the average productivity of land nearer to that obtained by the best-managed farms. The procedure that I would suggest for imposing such a tax as follows:

1. An estimate be made of the net output of agriculture as defined for the purpose of national accounting (but excluding animal husbandry and dairy farming which should be taxed differently) for each of the 67 provinces of the country (or rather the existing estimate for the country as a whole divided on the basis of the best available sources of information among the 67 provinces), where necessary sub-dividing the provinces into several regions. The estimate of net output should be based on the *average of the last five years*, not on any single year.

2. An estimate be made of the number of hectares in each province which are either actually producing crops or could be brought into cultivation without any large capital outlays; and the net product for each region should be divided by the number of "cultivable" hectares so as to give a "basic value" of land per hectare for each particular province.

3. Officials of the land revenue administration, appointed for this purpose and acting as a Commission should then proceed to determine in each province what the relation of any particular hectare of land in the province should be in relation to the "basic value" for the province, but in such a way that the *average* of these individual values should not deviate from the "basic value". This determination should take into account all the usual factors—i.e., the percentage of wet land and dry land in the country, the quality of the soil, etc.—but should take no account of the value of the crops or the type of crop actually produced, except in the case of horticulture and viniculture, where the land should be valued on the basis of the crop. If, in the course of this determination, the number of "cultivable" hectares turns out to be different from the original estimate, the "basic value" per hectare is to be adjusted correspondingly. The determination of the actual value in relation to the "basic value" should be based on principles specified in detail in the legislation, so as to minimise the scope for disputes and arbitrary assessments. The work of the Commission should in fact proceed on the so-called "points system"— —i.e. by adding or subtracting legally defined percentages on the basis of a number of measures of "quality", such as average annual rainfall, irrigation, slope or inclination of the land, porousness and other qualities of the soil (it is a matter for consideration whether the physical distance and accessibility to a recognised market should also be included).

4. The novel feature in this approach is that each region is thus given a certain "target" to fulfil—not in terms of tax revenue, but in terms of the net product of the land on which taxes will be levied at varying rates—and its task will thus be to allocate the net product among the different lands of the region in due relationship to their potential output, as specified in the legislation.

5. Until the assessments in terms of actual values are completed for a province, the tax should be levied on the basis of the "basic value".

6. The important advantage of this system is that the assessment of each hectare of land in relation to its provincial or regional average, and which is based on permanent attributes, will only have to be done once, and will result in each land having a (more or less) permanent percentage of the average quality of land in the province attributed to it. On the other hand, the "basic values" to which these percentages relate could be revised annually as a moving average of the net value of the output of the province in the last five years. Hence the system could be kept up to date both with variations in the output and variations in the average level of prices of agricultural products of each region, without the need for re-assessment of individual pieces of land.

7. The actual schedule of rates should then be imposed on a progressive scale, depending on the total size of the landholding of the family (i.e., comprising the head of the household, and his wife and children, as under the present income tax), this schedule of rates being fixed in such a way as to yield a national average of approximately 6 per cent. of the net product. For purposes of illustration, the following schedule might be suggested:

Size of family holding	Rate of tax per hectare as per cent. value per hectare	Per cent. of total families[1]	Percentage of total land owned[1]	Percentage of National Agricultural product paid in tax
0– 2	Exempt	30·5	4·2	0
3–10	5	53·0	34·4	1·7
11–50	10	14·3	31·0	3·1
Over 50	15	1·5	21·8	3·3
			TOTAL	8·1

[1] Distribution of holdings, according to agricultural census, 1960.

It thus appears from the distribution of the number of families by the size of their landholdings that 30·5 per cent. of the land-owning families would be altogether exempt from the taxation, whilst tax on the remaining categories would average 8·1 per cent. of the net value of total agricultural output. This assumes that the average quality of the land does not vary with the size of land-holdings. In actual fact the larger land-owners are more likely to possess the best quality land. It would thus be possible to collect TL 1,000 million, or 6 per cent. of the net product, by taxing only families owning more than 10 hectares of land and thereby exempt 83·5 per cent. of agricultural families from the operation of the tax altogether, and confine the tax to the 16·5 per cent. of families who are relatively large landholders; even on them, the tax would never exceed 15 per cent. of the net product of the land. A land tax which is thus confined to the more wealthy sector of the agricultural population may prove politically far more acceptable. It would be necessary, however, for the operation of this tax, to value every hectare irrespective of whether the owner is an exempt land-owner or not.

In the above example, the rate of progression was made to depend on the number of hectares, irrespective of the value or quality of the land in question. However, a proper system of progressive land taxation would relate the scale of progression not just to the number of hectares, but also to the value of the land per hectare; otherwise a man who owns irrigated land for example, might be greatly undertaxed in relation to the man who owns the same number of hectares of dry land.

The simplest way to give effect to this would be to fix a national average annual value for agricultural land and translate our criterion based on the size of family holdings in terms of hectares to size of family holdings in terms of a certain total annual value of the land possessed, the totals being calculated with the aid of this national average. Thus if we assume that the national average annual net product per hectare is TL 750 (this is based on an estimate of TL 17·5 billions for the net national product of agriculture and on the assumption of 24 million hectares of cultivable land) the above rate schedule would be restated as follows:

Total Annual Value of Family Holding	*Rate of tax per cent.*
under TL 1,500	Exempt
under TL 7,500	5 per cent.
under TL 37,500	10 per cent.
above TL 37,500	15 per cent.

Thus for a family whose land has an assessed value corresponding to the national average, the rate schedule comes to exactly the same as that stated earlier in terms of hectares; but when the actual value of land is below the average, both the exemption limit and the steps of graduation refer to larger areas, and if it is above that average, to smaller areas.

Another important advantage of a tax on these lines is that it would also operate as a most potent instrument of land reform; and its efficacy in this respect could be enhanced to almost any degree by adding further "tiers" of tax-rates for the owners of the really large estates, as e.g. a 20 per cent. rate for those owning more than 200 hectares, a 30 per cent rate for those owning more than 500 hectares, etc. But even without the introduction of such "penal" rates, there will be a strong inducement on many owners to sell part of their land, *so long as the tax schedule is expressed in terms of effective rates, and not marginal rates.* Thus for a man who owns 55 hectares, it will certainly be worth while to sell 5 hectares and thus bring himself to the under 50 category, since the tax on his last five hectares will work out at $15 + 250/5 = 65$ per cent. Even the man who owns 75 hectares might be tempted to sell 25 hectares rather than carry the tax of 25 per cent. per hectare ($= 15 + 250/25$) on his last 25 hectares. In this way far more land will come into the market, the land-market will become much more fluid, and the able and energetic farmer will be able to get hold of more land. The progressive tax in itself will make the distribution of land-ownership far more equal.

It would be necessary of course to make the most reliable and detailed statistical estimate of the agricultural net product of each province, since the whole operation of the system, and its equity, depends on this. For this purpose I would recommend that Turkey should make use of the services of some high-grade experts on agricultural and national income statistics (the U.S. Department of Agriculture and the Bureau of Business Economics of the U.S. Department of Commerce contain among them probably the best experts in this field).

III. TAXATION OF BUSINESS PROFITS AND OF CAPITAL

Inadequate taxation of business profits and of the benefits derived from capital is the other major defect of the Turkish tax system.

It is evident from a comparison of the income tax revenues from wages and salaries with the income and corporation tax revenues on business and on persons in the professions that the taxation of businesses and property income is very considerably evaded. Of the TL 24,000 million non-agricultural net income, wages and salaries could hardly account for more than 55–60 per cent., or TL 13–14 thousand million.[1] Yet wage and salary earners (whose effective tax liabilities should be much lower owing to their relatively low per caput incomes) were responsible for 60 per cent. of the total income tax collections and 45 per cent. of the total revenue from income and corporation taxes. An even more glaring example of tax evasion and avoidance is the collections from inheritance taxes, which amount to only some TL 12 million annually. On the basis of rough estimates of the national capital, the value of estates passing annually from one generation to another must amount to TL 3,000 million; and, if one takes the average rate of duty at only 10 per cent., this would yield TL 300 million, or 25 times the actual revenue.[2] The fact that the income of persons in the professions and of small traders cannot be brought effectively within the income tax net is not peculiar to Turkey; it is common to almost all countries which operate an income tax. It is idle to

---

[1] The annual emoluments of 400,000 civil servants only amount to TL 1,500 million, and there are 1·8 million wage earners of all kinds whose average daily wage is TL 15, hence the total annual wage bill amounts to TL 10,000 million.
[2] The total amount of private wealth cannot be less than TL 100,000 million, of which three-quarters must be owned by families liable to an inheritance tax. One-twenty-fifth of this sum—the length of a generation being 25 years—is a reasonable estimate for the amount passing annually through death or *inter vivos* gifts.

expect that the large-scale tax evasion could be effectively countered within a short space of time, but there are a number of measures which could be taken to improve the situation:

1. A certain improvement can be expected to follow when the *wealth declaration* introduced last year becomes available for inspection by the Revenue authorities in 1964. It is not known, of course, to what extent these wealth declarations represent full disclosures of wealth. However, through collecting more comprehensive information on capital transactions (either through the existing system of stamp duties or through a new capital gains tax), it might be possible in time to verify such declarations.

2. As regards the taxation of the *small trader*, an annual tax based on the net value of his property (including real estate, business assets, stock-in-trade, etc.) and deducting all debts would seem to me a far more promising method of extending the tax net to this class of taxpayer than the system proposed in recent legislation which is based on gross receipts (turnover) and a fixed deduction for expenses. In my opinion, without an extensive administrative apparatus that pays frequent visits to shops or small industrial undertakings and inspects their books, etc., business turnover is not much easier to ascertain than business profits. On the other hand, the property of the trader (whether in the form of business assets, or real estate) is not something that can easily be concealed. For small traders, therefore, an annual tax based on property seems a more promising method of direct taxation than a tax based on income.

3. An *annual tax on net property* (or net capital owned) such as is operated in Sweden and the Scandinavian countries, some Continental countries and in India and Ceylon, has great advantages as a supplement to income and profits taxation, both from the point of view of equity and from the point of view of administrative efficacy of the tax system. From the point of view of equity, it is more just than a system of taxation based on income alone, simply because a man of property who possesses disposable assets has a greater spending power than a man who has an equivalent

income from work but no disposable assets. This is best shown by the fact that the free disposal of property is of considerable value to the owner quite apart from the income which it yields: a man who owns, say, TL 1,000,000 and derives an income of TL 100,000 from it is in every sense better off than another man who has only an income of TL 100,000. From the point of view of administrative efficiency, the two taxes complement each other in that the necessity to reconcile declarations of incomes with changes of net wealth makes the concealment of income more difficult. It is true that the same purpose is served by an annual wealth declaration, but it remains to be seen whether the compulsory requirement to make such a declaration can be upheld if no tax is associated with it. I realise, however, that the fact that wealth declarations have been introduced without the introduction of any tax on wealth (and with promises not to use these declarations as a basis for any future taxation on wealth) makes the introduction of a net wealth tax extending to all classes of property owners rather difficult at the present time.

4. There is no reason however why the taxation of *capital gains* should not be extended. From the point of view of spending power and taxable capacity, there is no difference between a capital profit and the revenue profit, and the tax exemption of capital profits constitutes a very serious discrimination in favour of property owners as against wage and salary earners: the more so since it is generally open to a man of business to convert, by various devices, revenue profits into capital profits and so escape tax even on the restricted definition of income on which he is taxable. From the point of view of administrative enforcement, a universal capital gains tax would provide information on all capital transactions (on the purchases and sales of capital assets) and this provides an important check both on the declarations of profits and of wealth. Under the present law, only short-term transactions in real estate are taxable under schedule 7 of the Income Tax Law. Until recently this tax related only to assets realised within two years of ac-

quisition, but this has now been extended to four years subject to an exemption of TL 10,000 in each case.[1] There is no reason in equity why any such limit should be set, or why a sum as high as TL 10,000 should be exempted when the ordinary exemption limits in income tax (for a married couple) are only TL 1,600. The equitable procedure would be to treat capital gains as income quite irrespective of the period for which an asset was held. I recognise, however, that any such measure would be regarded as far too drastic and the adoption of a wider and more equitable notion of "income" would have to be undertaken in stages. I would recommend therefore, that for the time being the gains made on the sale of real estate should be taxed fully if the realisation is within 4 years, but that afterwards the taxable gain should be reduced by 10 per cent. for each further year for which an asset was held, so that an asset that was held, say, for eight years and then sold would only be taxed on 60 per cent. of the total gain and if it was held for more than 14 years it would escape taxation altogether. (The extension of the tax to cover gains from the sale of stocks and shares does not seem necessary in Turkey's present stage of development, since I understand that portfolio investment in shares is relatively rare).

5. With regard to the *income from professions*, there are two different methods by which the position could be improved (both of which have been used by some countries), though it is a matter of doubt whether it is worthwhile to introduce either of them. One is a straight tax on the professions in the form of an operating licence on doctors, lawyers, accountants, engineers, etc., who work on their own account and are not employees. The other is to make some estimate of what the true average earnings of doctors, lawyers, etc., are and then levy a certain total assessment on the profession as such and charge the professional organisations concerned with dividing the levy among their members

[1] On the views of the Taxation Commission on this point reference will be made below.

according to their own investigation of their relative earnings. Both methods may be efficacious in raising additional
revenue but I am doubtful whether it is justified to take
such strict measures for one particular class of taxpayer
as long as there is such large-scale tax avoidance and tax
evasion on the profits of business or on the income and
gains derived from property.

IV. FURTHER SUGGESTIONS FOR RAISING REVENUE

There are, however, a number of directions in which it seems
to me that, without any major alteration in the framework of the
existing tax system, further revenue could be raised, and the
system improved at the same time. These suggestions are as
follows:

1. *Corporation Tax and Income Tax*

   (a) The rate of corporation tax in Turkey, only recently
   raised from 10 per cent., still seems to me extremely low
   in comparison with other countries, developed or under-
   developed. The rate of this tax is 52 per cent. in the
   United States, 58 per cent. in Israel, 50 per cent. in
   France and 45 per cent. in Ceylon. In all these cases,
   these corporation taxes are imposed apart from any
   income tax liability on the personal income of shareholders. It seems to me that a rate as low as 20 per cent.
   is quite unjustified—particularly in view of the important
   new concessions proposed in the form of the 20 per cent.
   investment allowance, the adoption of the degressive
   method of depreciation and the suspension of any charge
   on the profit of the sale of capital assets so long as the
   money is re-invested within three years. Since these concessions mean in any case a substantial loss of revenue, it
   seems reasonable to balance these tax reductions by increasing the rate of the corporation tax to 40 per cent.,
   which would still be low by international standards.

   (b) On the other hand, it seems to me that the existing system
   of withholding income tax which deducts this tax from

the *whole of* the profit and not only from the actual dividends, is an unfair one which needlessly penalises the ploughing back of profits of business. The reason given for this provision is that in Turkey most of the corporations are closely held family concerns and there are innumerable ways of distributing profits to "inside" shareholders other than through a formal dividend payment. This may well be true, but since most corporations *do* require to plough back a considerable share of their profits for purposes of economic expansion, I think the dangers of tax evasion would be adequately met if the minimum withholding tax were limited to a proportion, say one-third, of the profits earned; and there ought to be a provision for reducing this charge still further in all those cases where a company can show that their capital expenditure for the year was greater than the sum of the allowances for depreciation and of two-thirds of the profits, after charging corporation tax and after deducting any new long-term borrowing.

On the other hand, the rate of withholding tax on distributed profits seems to be unduly low and represents another form of concealed discrimination against the wage and salary earner. On the present schedule of income tax rates, an effective rate of 20 per cent. is reached at an annual income of a little over TL 20,000, which is surely far below the typical or average income of a shareholder in a Turkish corporation. Since the average income of corporations appears to have been TL 400,000, even if one assumed that ownership of the typical corporation was divided between three families and that only one-third of the profit was distributed, the average income appears more likely to be TL 45,000, on which the effective tax charge is over 30 per cent. I would recommend, therefore, that *the rate of withholding tax should be raised to 33⅓ per cent. and confined to the actual dividend payments or to one-third of the profits available for distribution, whichever is greater.* Once this system is adopted, any justification for the present discrimination between the rate of corporation tax for private and public corporations disappears (at present the corporation tax is 35 per cent. on public, as against 20 per cent. on privately owned corporations) and I would recommend that the uniform rate of 40 per cent. be applied to *all* corporations.[1]

2. Inheritance Tax and Transfer Tax

The very low yield of this tax is partly due to low rates, partly to the peculiar rules for the valuation of estates, and partly to evasion. In order to counter evasion, it seems to me that the present system of an inheritance tax (which is a charge on the recipient of a gift or legacy) should be supplemented by an estate duty which is a charge on the total *estate* of an individual on his decease. It has been the experience of many Western countries that an inheritance tax or legacy duty is ineffective in the absence of an estate duty; an estate duty cannot be easily avoided simply because measures can be taken to prevent the inheritors from taking possession, or acquiring title to properties, until the proper duty is paid. In view of the very low rates of the existing inheritance tax, I would suggest that an estate duty varying at progressive rates from, say, 2 per cent. on estates of TL 5–20,000 to a maximum of 30 per cent. on the excess of estates over TL 1,000,000 could be introduced on top of the existing inheritance tax; this would still leave the combined burden of the death duties far lower than in most countries in Western Europe.

But the most important defect of the present system—which must surely be unique—is that it values real estate which is *not* part of a busines enterprise, not at the current value but at the values of the cadastral valuation of 1936—which, as we have seen, are around one-fiftieth of their current level in the case of agricultural land. On the other hand, all business estates, whether tangible or intangible, are valued for purposes of inheritance and gift tax at their current market value. This is not only unjust, but it represents an economically most harmful discrimination against the productive employment of capital

---

[1] The question of extending income tax to agriculture and to the small trader has already been dealt with earlier in this memorandum, and the proposed revision of the rate schedules of income tax recommended by the Tax Reform Commission will be referred to below.

and in favour of keeping wealth in idle forms. For anyone who takes the question of incentives for risk-taking at all seriously, the abolition of this particular discrimination against productive enterprise should have a very high priority.

3. *Taxation of the Road User*

It appears that despite the very heavy expenditure, past or contemplated, on the road system, the taxation of road vehicles either in the form of licences or of taxes on fuel consumption are very light and do not cover the up-keep of the roads, let alone yield a return on the sums invested in constructing the roads. From the point of view of the optimal allocation of resources, this represents a serious defect in that road transport appears to be heavily subsidised as against transport by rail. There is therefore a strong economic case for putting heavier taxes on the road user, quite apart from the need for greater revenue.

There are two ways of doing this, either through annual licence fees for road vehicles, or through duties on petrol and fuel oil. The disadvantage of putting too much tax on fuel oil consumption is that it penalises equally other users of oil (in industry or in households) where the use of oil ought to be encouraged (particularly for purposes of heating and cookery in the villages). It seems to me therefore that a licence fee for commercial vehicles (lorries and buses) which would supplement the existing licence fees for passenger motor cars and would be on a progressive scale, varying with the total weight of the vehicle or its passenger carrying or freight carrying capacity, is preferable to the taxation of fuel oil; or if the licence fee alone would not be sufficient for revenue purposes without making the charge appear exorbitantly high, the tax revenue required from road users should be divided between these two forms of taxation. There appears to be a strong case in any event for putting an additional duty on motor spirit (as distinct from heavy oils).

4. *The Building Tax*

The building tax, similarly to the land tax, has also been greatly eroded as a result of the inflation and of the 10-year exemption granted to new buildings, and I would recommend that there should be a general re-valuation of all buildings serving residential, industrial or commercial purposes as soon as possible. I do not think that the existence of rent control should be regarded as an obstacle to a revaluation of all properties in accordance with their current (uncontrolled) letting value; in the case of rent-controlled houses, a special provision should be made authorising the landlord to recover the increased tax from the tenants until such time as rent control is removed; and there is a strong case for removing rent control (which is only partially effective) in any case.

On the other hand, I do not think that the current 10-year exemption for residential building is generally justified, and I propose that the *restriction should be confined to three years (as in the case of other buildings), with the exception of tenement houses for the lower income groups,* where a 10-year exemption might be retained provided that none of the dwelling units contained therein exceeds a certain maximum floor space. On the other hand, the *10-year exemption might be extended to the building of new hotels,* which is a form of export promotion that is likely to bring foreign money both for the construction of hotels and through increased tourism.

5. *Fees Charged for Import Licences*

Since the importation of many consumer goods is at present severely restricted for balance of payments reasons and it is not likely that these restrictions will be lifted in the near future, it seems to me wrong that the Government should allow the large profit resulting from licensed imports (which is due to the gap between the landed cost of imported goods including duties, and the domestic selling price) to go to the private importer. There are many ways in which the special profits arising from import restrictions can be channelled to the Government; and the system which seems to me most appropriate is one which imposes a fee for issuing an import licence that is approximately equal to the difference between the actual selling price of the imported goods and the price that would have ruled in the absence of import restrictions. This is approximately measured by the price at which import licences are sold among traders. In the case of commodities where the market value of such licences cannot be readily ascertained, I recommend that the Government should introduce a licence fee at the same ad valorem rate as in the case of the other licence fees; and then be prepared to adjust the rate in successive stages until a situation is reached where the number of applications for licensing any particular article no longer exceeds the import quotas that have been decided on.

6. *Pricing Policy of State Enterprises*

It appears that the problem of inflation in earlier years was considerably aggravated by the then prevailing Government policy of holding down the prices of the products of State-owned enterprises, which must have had a considerable effect in increasing the demand generated by productive activities, and thus the inflationary pressure on the economy. In the absence of such price controls, prices tend to find a level at which effective demand no longer exceeds available supplies; and this means that the share of profits of enterprises (the excess of prices over the prime costs of production) will tend to be such that, for the economy as a whole, the savings generated by the profits balance the investment expenditures undertaken. When, however, in an important sector of the economy prices are held down artificially in relation to costs, the savings–investment balance can only be secured through inordinate increases in profits in the other sectors of the economy; and this in turn entails a much greater increase in uncontrolled prices with the consequential upward pressure on all prices caused by the distortions in the price system. It also means that the profits which the Government forgoes through fixing low prices for the products of the Government enterprises will tend to reappear in additional profits in the private sector. It is thus really a method of transferring profits from public to private enterprise.

Quite apart, however, from the question of the avoidance of inflation, considerations of economic efficiency argue *for the same principles of pricing to be applied in the publicly-owned enterprises as are applied in the private sector.* It is a mistake to think that publicly-owned enterprises provide a service to the community by charging lower prices than they would have done on purely commercial considerations; from the point of view of the best allocation of resources, the opposite is the case. I think therefore that it should be laid down *as a definite principle that publicly-owned enterprises should charge the most profitable price and not the cost price*— i.e. the price which is most likely to maximise profits in the long run.

In so far as the products of State enterprises are sold to the final consumer, the effect of charging a price lower than the most profitable price is the same as if indirect taxation had been reduced. In so far as the products of the State enterprises are sold to private enterprises, the effect is a concealed subsidy to private enterprise and in this respect is analogous to an open tax concession, but far more capricious and arbitrary in its incidence.

I therefore recommend that price fixing for all State-owned enterprises by the Ministry of Industry should be abolished, except in those cases where the State enterprise is in a monopoly position providing an essential service (in the case of the so-called public utilities). This would make a substantial addition to State revenues.

V. OBSERVATIONS ON THE REPORT OF THE TAX REFORM COMMISSION

I have only seen the 30-page summary in the German language of the Commission's Report concerning the Income Tax and the Corporation Tax. I cannot, however, refrain from expressing the view that this Commission seems to have been actuated almost entirely by the desire to secure fresh concessions to taxpayers—and particularly to the *large* taxpayers—to the exclusion of almost every other consideration. Although the Commission do not appear to have been given any definite terms of reference, the Commission mentions the following as its fundamental guiding principles: to secure the "optimum yield" of the taxes; to develop the taxes in such a way that they should fulfil their social and economic functions; to secure the simplification and rationalisation of the tax laws; and, finally, to develop tax legislation on democratic principles so as to secure the rights of the taxpayers. There is no mention of consideration of equity in the allocation of the tax burden between different social and economic groups; or of the urgent requirement of the State to secure a higher proportion of the national product in tax revenue; or of the need to improve the efficiency of the existing system and to counter tax evasion and avoidance.

The recommendations of the Commission consist, apart from the extension of income tax to agriculture and to the small traders, of a long series of new concessions, without any regard either to the direct revenue loss resulting from their recommendations or to the indirect revenue loss due to the additional scope for manipulations of various kinds which the adoption of the Commission's recommendations would make possible. In my opinion if the Commission's ideas were adopted as a whole this would be more likely to lead to a serious deterioration, and not to any net improvement, of the existing income and corporation tax system of Turkey.

Most of the large concessions recommended are argued on the grounds of their effect on economic development and the acceleration of economic growth—as if Turkey had large untapped resources at her disposal whose activation was only a matter of providing adequate incentives to business circles. The fact, on the contrary, is that inflation can only be kept at bay by an extremely restrictive monetary and credit policy, which makes official interest rates 10–12 per cent. per annum and the unofficial rates as much as 25 per cent. If the Commissions's basic conception were sound, and investment were only held up by lack of financial resources or incentives in the hands of firms, surely the right thing to do would be to loosen the reins of monetary policy long before any special tax concessions are given. The members of the Commission would not I think deny the serious inflationary risks of an easier credit policy in the present situation. But they seem to be completely oblivious of the fact that the adoption of their recommendations as regards investment allowances and depreciation would be equally inflationary, at least in the absence of countervailing increases in other taxation. The Commission makes no attempt whatever to estimate the revenue loss resulting from any of their recommendations and makes no proposal as to how these revenue losses should be met.

No doubt there is something to be said for subsidies on new investment and for the declining balance method of depreciation, as stimulants to new investments. But there is no indication in the Report that the original recommendations, which provide for a 60 per cent. investment allowance for corporations and 30 per cent. for individuals, might have reduced the amount of taxable profits by as much as TL 500,000,000 even after allowance is made for the restriction of the concession to investment in excess of TL 250,000. The form in which the recommendations were finally approved and codified halved the above rates; but even so the tax loss resulting from the investment allowance might be anything between TL 150–200,000,000, whilst the introduction of the degressive system of depreciation—which doubles the existing rates—would mean a further loss of some TL 100,000,000.

There seems to be no justification for a restriction of the investment allowance to investments of over TL 250,000—a measure which discriminates in favour of the large business in a manner that is both anti-social and unsound from an economic point of view. There is no reason for supposing that in Turkey's present stage of development large enterprises or large investments are necessarily more efficient. As far as the stimulation of economic growth is concerned, investment allowances given to smaller business seem to me on the contrary more efficacious, since it is the fast-growing but small business which is likely to be hampered in its growth by lack of finance; and it is mainly the expansion of those businesses which are limited by financial difficulties which would be effectively promoted by the kind of investment allowance proposed by the Commission.[1]

---

[1] The Commission's Report refers to the fact that investment allowances of this type were recently introduced in the United States. There is, however, a basic difference in the situation of the two countries which the Commission ignores. In the United States there is no shortage of genuine savings and the rate of investment does appear to be limited by lack of profitable investment opportunities. In Turkey, there does not seem to be any lack of profitable investment opportunities (otherwise unofficial interest rates could not possibly be so high), but there is a shortage of investable funds which confines investment to inadequate levels if inflation is to be avoided. The augmentation of savings which would alone enable an increase in the rate of investment requires on the other hand that consumption be reduced, and this requires an increase in taxation and not a reduction of taxation.

The same kind of criticism can be made with regard to their recommendation for reducing rates of income tax. There may be a good case for reducing the rates of income tax on salary earners in the ranges of an annual income of TL 5,000–20,000, where the effective rates of taxation in Turkey are very high by any international standard. But precisely in these income brackets the Commission's concessions amount to very little—at TL 5,000 the reduction in the effective rate of taxation is only from 8·5 to 7·8 per cent., at TL 10,000 from 14·2 to 13·2 per cent., and at TL 20,000 from 21·3 to 18·7 per cent. As against that, the reductions in the high income ranges (where the present rates are relatively low by international standards) are much more substantial; at TL 75,000 from 36·5 to 29·5 per cent., at TL 300,000 from 52·9 to 44·7 per cent., and at TL 500,000 from 59·8 to 49·3 per cent. On the other hand, in the draft law in which the Commission's recommendations have been codified, the personal allowances for income tax have been halved (in relation to the scale envisaged in the previous law). Yet even those rates were far too low (far lower, in fact, than in any other country known to me). As against the scales laid down in the earlier law, the allowance is cut from TL 1,800 to TL 810 in the case of the allowances for a single person, from TL 1,080 to TL 540 in the case of the wife, and in the case of children from an annual TL 720 to an annual TL 144. To show how low these allowances are, it should be sufficient to point out that in the United Kingdom the single man gets TL 3,000, his wife a further TL 3,000, and each child an allowance of TL 2,500 per year. The cost of the changes in income tax rates proposed by the Commission is officially estimated at TL 280 millions in relation to the rate schedule now in force.

I should only like to refer to two other recommendations of the Commission which I understand have not yet been approved and codified. One concerns their suggestion concerning the time limit for transactions in real estate which are liable to tax. This has recently been increased to 4 years, when the tax free allowance was also raised to TL 10,000. The Commission does not object to the TL 10,000 tax-free allowance, but wishes the time limit to be reduced again to 2 years. The need, from the point of view of both equity and the efficacy of the tax system, is on the contrary to increase the time limit and lower the exemption and ultimately to abolish it altogether.

The second refers to the recommendation of the Commission in connection with family aggregation. Under the present law, which was taken over from the prevailing provisions of the German law, the income of husband and wife and minor children are aggregated for tax purposes. This seems to me the only just principle, because a family invariably pools its economic resources and allocates them amongst its members on the principle of need. Family aggregation is also very important in the case of business income or property income, because any other system opens the door widely to manipulations of various kinds which enable such taxpayers to reduce their liability by dividing income between themselves and their children in a way which is not open to those taxpayers who derive their income from work. The Commission now recommends that aggregation should be completely abolished and the income of both the wife and of the minor children should be treated separately. It argues in favour of this "reform" by reference to the principle of human rights enshrined in the new Constitution.[1] This would only be correct if the conception of human rights embodied in the Constitution included the right to evade the payment of taxes by the wealthy taxpayer—which is hardly a permissible interpretation.

---

[1] It also adduces (here and elsewhere) recent changes in tax legislation of some Western countries (such as the U.S. or Germany) in support of their case. But it is a mistake to assume that in Western countries changes in the tax laws are only introduced when they represent a genuine improvement. Vested interests exert a continuous pressure for "loosening" the tax laws in Western countries just as much as in other countries.

7

ECONOMIC AND TAXATION PROBLEMS IN IRAN[1]

I was invited to Iran to advise on how best the suggestion that the consumption effect of increases in the pay of Civil Servants might be deferred could be implemented; and also to give my views on issues of economic and taxation policy. In the short time available I held discussions with Ministers and officials in the Plan Organization, the Ministry of Finance and the Ministry of Economy. I also had discussions with the Governor and Deputy Governor of the Bank of Iran. From all these I received help and cooperation in preparing the report which follows. It is divided into three sections corresponding to the three matters referred to above.

I A PLAN FOR DEFERRED CONSUMPTION BY CIVIL SERVANTS

1. The first question was whether it would be possible and practicable to sterilise the additional purchasing power resulting from increases in the pay of civil servants (and possibly of other categories of employees) for a certain period, in order to avoid undue pressure on the demand for consumer goods as a result. It is envisaged that the increase in pay should be in some form that would prevent the employee from utilising it for purposes of immediate consumption.

2. I shall assume that the Government desires to grant some general increase in the pay of civil servants (to compensate for the rising prices in the last few years), as well as to give some specific increases in particular cases where promotion has, for financial reasons, been deferred. In the nature of the case it is easier to devise a scheme for offsetting the effects of a general increase,

---

[1] Report on specific issues, written in Teheran at the request of the Prime Minister of Iran, in June 1966.

which can therefore be applied impartially to everybody, than to devise a scheme which would offset the rise in *specific* salaries. In the latter case, it would be necessary either to confine the scheme to those individuals who have benefited from up-grading, or else to reduce the actual cash pay of all the others; and neither of these suggestions seems to me to be practicable. I shall assume that any scheme introduced will apply equally to all civil servants, or at any rate to all civil servants above a certain grade.

3. I do not think that the objectives aimed at could be achieved by paying some proportion of Civil Service salaries in a paying medium with a "restricted franchise"—for example, in a special kind of money which can only be used for specific purposes, such as the purchase of services provided by Government affiliated organisations or the purchase of investment goods, like buildings, plant or machinery. The reason for this is that unless the "franchise" was so severely restricted as to make the possession of the medium almost valueless, the recipient could always convert his medium into ordinary money by exchanging it—at some discount —with people who need to make payments for the kind of goods and services for which the "franchise" applies.

4. The only practical method of achieving the desired result is some form of compulsory saving, whereby some percentage of the current pay is deducted at source and accumulated to the credit of the employee, to be repaid, together with interest, at some future date. Such schemes of compulsory saving have been, or are, in force in some countries, such as Brazil and Turkey; they have also been introduced in other countries for emergency periods, for example in the United Kingdom during the War. They have been tried, and subsequently abandoned, in some other countries (for example, in Ghana and British Guiana).

5. Schemes of compulsory saving can take three different forms:
  (i) Deferment for a fixed period, let us say, 10 years. This is equivalent to the compulsory purchase of non-negotiable savings certificates, which are repayable together with the accumulated interest at the end of a pre-determined number of years after the actual date of purchase.
  (ii) Deferment for an indefinite period, i.e., a compulsory deduction repayable at some future date to be determined

M

subsequently. (This was the case with the scheme of "post-war credits" in the United Kingdom).

(iii) Deferment until retiring age. Here, the actual period of deferment would vary with the age of the employee at the time when the contributions are made.

6. The last method is analogous to a compulsory endowment policy in favour of the employees, which could, in principle, be combined with an element of life insurance; for example, it would be possible to provide that when an employee dies before reaching the age (say 60 or 65) at which he is entitled to get his past contributions repaid, his widow or other dependents would be entitled to receive the same cash payment which he would have received with respect to his actual contributions, had he survived until that age.

7. As compared with the other types of compulsory saving, I think a scheme of this latter type has distinct advantages both from the point of view of its general popularity and acceptability, and also of its economic and financial effects. Compulsory savings for fixed periods of years or for indefinite periods are likely to be unpopular, partly because they are never wholly believed in: the employees who are asked to make these contributions will feel no certainty of getting their money, since they will feel that it is always open to the Government to alter the terms and conditions of repayment by subsequent legislation. This is much more difficult to do with a scheme which promises everybody a certain cash sum on reaching a certain age or on death; since some people are bound to be near retiring age, and others die, some repayments will begin soon after the scheme is introduced; and this will generate confidence in the scheme itself. From a presentational point of view the introduction of a compulsory scheme of retirement benefits would strike the public as something desirable in itself, and not just an instrument of financial expediency.

8. From the point of view of the Government, the very fact that the flow of repayments will be spread over time avoids the problems of "bunching" that would arise if the contributions of any one year had all to be repaid, together with accumulated interest, at some pre-determined future year. Moreover a *continuing* scheme of this sort is likely to be more than self-financing—

permanently, and not just temporarily. In effect, the scheme involves the setting up of a Provident Fund for all Government employees. A certain percentage of the current pay of the employees is deducted and paid over to the Fund, and the repayments of the accumulated credits are paid out of the Fund. Since only a proportion of employees will be entitled to repayment in any one year, the repayments will, in the initial years, represent only a small proportion of the current contributions. With the passage of time, the repayments will increase both absolutely and relatively to the contributions; but so long as the total wage and salary bill is rising (on account of the increase in the number of employees, as well as increases in the average pay), the payments *out* of the Fund will always lag behind the payments *into* the Fund; the size of the Fund is thus likely to increase indefinitely. In consequence, there is an element of *permanent* deferment in consumption inherent in the scheme.

9. A scheme of this kind may be regarded as something additional to the existing retirement benefits to which State employees are entitled. I understand that existing Governmental pension schemes are inadequate, mainly because they are paid by reference to the basic pay of the employee in the year before retirement, which is often only a small fraction of his actual earnings. However, there are cases of civil servants who already make contributions to a Superannuation Fund; (this, I understand, is the case with the employees of the Plan Organisation) and it would be possible to exempt these from the scheme if it were thought that it would merely duplicate an existing scheme.

10. The basic idea of this scheme is capable of a large number of variations. Thus it would be possible to have a scheme with contributions both from employees and from the Government (this would make it more analogous to social security schemes or superannuation), or it could be limited to contributions by the employees only (which could be justified on the ground that the scheme would be something additional to existing retirement benefits). Equally, the element of life insurance could be varied— e.g. it would be possible for each person to be entitled to a fixed sum in the case of death, irrespective of the extent of his previous contributions; or only be entitled to the accumulated value (up to

retiring age) of the contributions which he actually made during his lifetime. The rate of interest could be varied; to ensure popular acceptance, it would be sensible to offer a reasonable rate of interest, such as a compound rate of 5 per cent. a year.

11. The possible details of the scheme could best be illustrated in terms of an example. Let us suppose that the Government decides to increase the *aggregate pay* of its existing employees by 10 per cent.; 5 per cent. of which would be used for a general increase in pay, and the remaining 5 per cent. for up-grading particular civil servants whose promotion is overdue. In that case, I do not think it would be possible to match the *whole* increase in disbursements by compulsory savings. It would be possible to make the scale of contributions somewhat higher than the general increase in pay—say 6 per cent. instead of 5 per cent.—which would leave some employees *slightly* worse off in terms of cash pay (i.e. by 1 per cent. in this example), while others would remain better off. Actual cash disbursements would then increase by 4 per cent., while the nominal disbursements increased by 10 per cent.

12. Contributions equivalent to 6 per cent. of the current salaries of employees, even if accumulated throughout the working life, would not alone be sufficient to secure a sum on retirement which would give a reasonable pension in terms of its annuity-equivalent. (I think from the point of view of the attractiveness of this scheme it is important that the employee should be entitled to draw his accumulated credit on retirement in cash and not just in terms of a life annuity; or at least that he should have the option to do so; from the point of view of Government finances, it will make very little difference in the long run whether the contributions are repaid in cash or in terms of life-annuities).

13. If it were desired, on grounds of presentation or on other grounds, to make equal contributions from the employer as well as the employee, the same financial effect could be achieved by making both the nominal increase in pay and the employees' contribution smaller, and making up the difference through the contribution of the Government. For example, it would be possible to make the general increase in pay $2\frac{1}{2}$ per cent. instead of 5 per cent. in the above example; and to introduce a scheme with a

contribution of 3 per cent. each from the employee and from the Government.

14. If an employee were to leave the Government service before the statutory retirement age, he should remain entitled to the cash payment with respect to his past contributions upon retiring age (or upon death), but not earlier. He should be free, however, (if this proves administratively feasible) to continue his contributions up to retiring age.

15. In principle, there is much to be said for extending the scope of the scheme to employees of private firms, and not only to public employees. This may raise serious administrative difficulties initially; but the possibility of extending the scheme to the whole of the employed population subsequently could be kept in view.

16. Even with a scheme restricted to State employees, the setting up of a large new administrative apparatus which maintains a running account for each individual employee is unavoidable. The main reason for this is that the repayment of the contributions cannot be made dependent on the possession of an instrument on behalf of the holder if the Government wishes to ensure that the sums annually set aside are really witheld from current consumption.

17. It would no doubt be administratively simpler if the employee received some document—a "savings certificate"—with respect to his annual contributions, the presentation of which in the prescribed eventualities (on death or retirement) would constitute his title for drawing the cash benefits. But even if such securities were made formally non-negotiable, there is nothing to prevent the holder from using them as a collateral against a loan; a man could borrow against them, since the physical possession of the certificate would provide security to the lender.

18. Under the alternative method the Government Department administering the scheme (the Provident Fund) would issue periodic notices to the employee (say once a year) showing the amount standing to his credit. Such notices could not be used as collateral for loans if the payment of the retirement benefit is not made dependent upon their presentation. In that case, however, it is necessary that the Provident Fund should keep a careful record

of each individual's contributions and the interest accumulated on them. This is necessary also to calculate the amount of the benefit to which the dependents of any individual would be entitled in the case of death.

19. It would be necessary to set up a quasi-autonomous public organisation to administer the Fund, which would maintain its own account with the Central Bank. The assets of this Fund would thus be invested by the Central Bank in the same way as other deposits: this means in practice that they may be invested in gold foreign exchange reserves, or in Government securities. But the Government would not be able to utilise the accumulations of this Fund directly; it could do so only indirectly, insofar as the accumulations in the Provident Fund made it possible for the Central Bank to extend credit to the Government more liberally than they would have done otherwise.

20. The accumulation of contributions in the hands of the Provident Fund takes on a different aspect from the point of view of availability of real resources and from the point of view of Government finances. From the point of view of the use of resources (i.e. the effect of the scheme on current consumption and saving) the past accumulations in the Fund are not really relevant: it is the *current* inflow of new contributions each year which really "finances" the current drawings on the Fund on account of retirement or death benefits. The net effect on consumption and savings is thus to be measured by the net excess of the current inflow over the outflow. Since, for the reasons given above, such an excess is likely to continue indefinitely, the scheme represents a permanent addition to savings, and not just a temporary addition; or looked at in another way, it secures some permanent deferment of the consumption generated by incomes currently earned.

21. From the point of view of governmental finances, however, there is no net advantage resulting from the scheme as such, since money will still have to be raised by other means (i.e. through taxation or borrowing) in order to finance the increased pay of the civil servants. If such an increase in pay were decided upon and were financed out of additional taxation, the effect of the increased pay would be balanced by the reduced purchasing power of the community resulting from additional taxation. In these circum-

stances the introduction of the scheme would represent a genuine addition to the investible resources of the community. If, on the other hand, the Government were to raise the pay in the Civil Service without increasing taxes, the introduction of a compulsory savings scheme would make it possible for it to incur deficit financing without inflationary consequences; but for that very reason the scheme would not secure any net addition to current savings.

22. The balance of the above argument can be summed up as follows:

(i) The introduction of a compulsory savings scheme which takes the form of cash benefits on death and retirement can definitely be recommended as a scheme that is beneficial to employees and at the same time increases the investible resources of the community.

(ii) It follows from this that the wider the coverage of the scheme (the more it extends to private as well as public employees), the greater the benefits to be derived from it.

(iii) If the present low level of earnings in the Civil Service makes it impossible to introduce such a scheme by itself, it could be combined with the introduction of improvements in the gross pay of public employees. (The case for such a combined operation is probably strengthened by the fact that civil servants are about to become liable to income tax under the provisions of the new Income Tax Bill.)

(iv) Assuming such a combined operation, the introduction of the compulsory savings scheme will only secure a net addition to national savings if the increased pay is covered by increased taxation. If it is financed by an increased budgetary deficit, the merit of the scheme consists only in avoiding the inflationary consequences (or at least some of the inflationary consequences) of the increased deficit.

(v) The main disadvantage of the scheme is that it entails the creation of a new administrative apparatus, involving careful record-keeping in respect of many thousands of contributors. This, in my view, cannot be avoided. There is no way in which it would be possible to pay civil servants in some medium other than money which is "not convertible into immediate consumption", if that medium represents a future claim or title to money (or a current claim on a restricted range of goods and services). Non-convertibility into current consumption can only be ensured by *not* issuing a "medium" of any kind; in the latter case, however, an organisation with careful record-keeping is essential.

23. My own view is that some such scheme as suggested here is worth serious consideration, particularly if the "combined operation" could be accomplished without increasing the budgetary deficit. The actuarial aspects of the scheme, and the likely rate of net accumulation in the Provident Fund will require careful examination, as will the administrative apparatus required. But it would be a mistake to look upon this scheme as an alternative to more taxation; it provides such an alternative only in the restricted sense explained above.

II. THE NATURE OF IRAN'S ECONOMIC PROBLEMS

1. With the accomplishment of Land Reform, Iran has taken the decisive step to ensure its progress towards a developed, high-income society. Land Reform has been an essential pre-requisite of this, because, without it, it would not have been possible to create a progressive system of agriculture capable of generating a steadily rising surplus of food production over rural self-consumption. The latter provides the means for the progressive transfer of labour from agriculture to manufacturing and services which is the essential feature of economic development. The rate at which non-agricultural employment can be created is mainly governed by the rise in productivity (in terms of yields per hectare as well as yields per man) in agricultural production. This is not only because food is the commodity on which the greater part of wages is spent, it is mainly because the supply of food, unlike the supply of manufactured goods or of housing, does not increase in direct response to rising demand.

2. Hence the problem of maintaining a steady pace of development, and of avoiding major inflations, is essentially nothing else

than that of keeping the proper balance between the rise in the demand for food—which is governed by rate of increase in urban employment—and the rise in the marketable supplies of food. Countries in a high stage of development are in a position to supplement their domestic food supplies with imports from abroad; but this pre-supposes an ability to procure the foreign exchange through industrial exports; such exports can only be secured in appreciable volume in the more mature stages of industrial development, and not in the earlier stages. Iran is in a fortunate position in having large foreign exchange revenues through oil, but these will be needed for the purchase of equipment of various kinds, and of manufactured goods; if they were to be used to an increasing extent for the purchase of food this would merely mean that the "bottleneck" limiting development was transferred to another sector, not that it would be eliminated.

3. In order to attain a rate of growth of 6 per cent. or more it is not of course necessary that agricultural production should rise by an identical percentage, since only a small part (perhaps 1/8th or 1/10th at the present time) of the total food production is marketed in urban areas and a relatively small rate of increase in total production may be sufficient to secure an adequate increase in the marketed part of the food supplies. My guess is—without having examined the matter in any detail—that an annual rise in agricultural production of the order of 3 to 4 per cent. would suffice to take care of the needs of the growing population in the rural areas, and also to secure an annual increase of, say, 6 to 8 per cent. in the market supplies reaching the urban areas.

4. It follows from these considerations that at the present stage of Iran's development first priority in economic planning should be given to the complex of measures and policies that are necessary to make Land Reform a success. The nature of these measures is well-known and does not require detailed enumeration. I would, however, particularly wish to draw attention to the importance of the *extension of credit* to farmers; to the better organisation of *marketing*—either through public purchasing boards or co-operatives; to the creation of an efficient *agricultural extension service* for the training of farmers and the introduction of improved seeds, veterinary services, etc.; to rural education and the elimi-

nation of illiteracy; to new irrigation schemes and the extension of the cultivated areas; and finally, to the improvement of communications to outlying areas through the creation of an extensive system of *feeder roads*. It is not often realised how much costs of transport limit the depth of the rural areas from which urban food supplies can be drawn.

5. I am convinced that the above objectives should claim the major part of the financial and organisational resources of the country, and should have priority over industrial projects for the next 5 to 10 years. The major reasons for this is that with the increase of marketable food supplies an increase in industrial activities will follow almost automatically, whereas this is not true the other way round. If priority were given to the creation of industrial capacity it might well happen that much of this capacity would remain under-utilised for lack of demand, or else would lead to inflation and balance of payment difficulties, which would sooner or later cause stagnation.

6. Whilst progress requires a certain balance between an increase in agricultural production and an increase in industrial production, the expansion of these two sectors does not proceed under symmetrical impulses. While industrial enterprises tend to expand through the profit motive in response to increases in the *demand* for industrial products (which fundamentally is nothing else than an increase in the *supply* of agricultural products), an increase in the *demand* for food resulting from an increased *supply* of industrial products does not, in itself, evoke a rise in food supplies. For this reason, the best way to promote industrialisation is to invest in agricultural development.

7. Industrialisation and urbanisation necessarily increase the demand for imported materials and components as well as of manufactured goods. For this reason, it is essential that industrialisation should, as far as possible, be export-orientated in order to provide the means for purchasing the additional imports which the process generates. From this point of view, projects of industrialisation based on local materials and intended largely for export (as in the case of a petro-chemical industry) seem to be far more promising than the kind of industrialisation which aims at import substitution. This is because industrialisation increases the

level of the incomes and will therefore increase the total import requirements, even when it succeeds in reducing the proportion of imports in relation to consumption.

8. The fact that the improvement in marketable food supplies is the essential pre-condition for a fast rate of growth on the "resources" side does not obviate the need for a steady increase in public revenues on the financial side. Economic growth is bound to increase the scale of public expenditures very considerably. The need for publicly provided services in education, health and a host of other things increases more than in proportion to the rise in the national income during the intermediate stages of economic development. This means that the proportion of national income represented by public revenues will have to be raised quite considerably. I do not think that oil revenues can be expected to expand rapidly enough to fill this need; nor would it be safe to rely on them as the main source over long periods. When an increasing proportion of public expenditures comes to be financed by budgetary deficits this is bound to lead to trouble in the balance of payments. An increasing deficit necessarily means that the incomes generated by the public and private expenditure will exceed the value of goods and services produced in a growing proportion; the excess is bound to spill over into imports and generate a rising gap between imports and exports.

9. I do not think that the present system of taxation will prove adequate for providing the necessary revenue, and I think it will be necessary, in the longer terms, to look for the creation of new sources of revenue. The present yield of taxation of all kinds is only about 8 % of the gross national product, and of this no more than a quarter (or 2 % of the G.N.P.) comes from direct taxes of all kinds. The specific issues connected with taxation will be discussed in the concluding section.

III. ISSUES CONNECTED WITH TAXATION

(i) *Income tax*

1. I was asked for my views on the new Income Tax Bill which is now before Parliament. I have read it in the English translation.

I cannot say that I have understood it fully—this may be the fault of the translation, but it may also be due to lack of precision in the draft itself.

2. Subject to this uncertainty, my general view is that this is a most unsatisfactory piece of legislation that seems quite unsuited to Iran; indeed, it would be unsuited to any country, however developed in matters of tax administration, accountancy practices and tax morality. It may well be true that the new Bill incorporates significant improvements in relation to the existing system, and may even achieve a certain amount of simplification. But this does not seem to me an adequate justification for introducing a comprehensive new law which is not well thought out or reasonable in itself. There is everything to be said for proceeding cautiously in introducing major reforms in a tax system, as usually frequent changes in the law are themselves a major source of uncertainty and lack of confidence. My suggestion must therefore be that there is very much to be said for delaying the passage of the present Bill, so as to give opportunity for a more careful and thorough examination of its basic principles and of the best ways of giving effect to them; even if this involved the postponement of desirable improvements.

3. Income tax is a most complicated tax to administer. The main *raison d'être* for its introduction is to secure fairness in the tax system between persons in differing circumstances— between rich and poor, and between those who derive their income from work and those who derive it from property and business activities. The case for *having* an income tax is to make the tax system fairer than it would be if revenue were collected only through tax on commodities and on transactions. An income tax which cannot be effectively and impartially administered between taxpayers in different circumstances is quite capable of producing the opposite result—of making the tax system *less* fair than a system which relied on simpler and cruder methods.

4. Most under-developed countries have introduced highly complicated income tax laws which are not effectively implemented, particularly as regards incomes derived from capital or business activities, whilst they may operate harshly on the wage

and salary earners. The income tax statistics show that in under-developed countries the bulk of the tax is paid by people in moderate circumstances who derive their income from work; whereas the basic intention of the tax is to collect a proportionately larger amount from the wealthy sector of the community.

5. This is illustrated by relating the current yield of income tax in Iran on various types of income to the total of incomes arising under the different categories. Thus, according to the national income estimates of the Ministry of Economy, total wages and salaries paid in the non-agricultural sectors of the economy (excluding Government services) amounted to Rials 55 billion in 1341—or say, Rials 65 billion in 1344.[1] The taxes collected on salaries and wages in 1344 amounted to Rials 2.5 billion which is 4 per cent. of this total. Since a considerable part of the total wage and salary bill (perhaps half) must relate to workers earning less than Rials 48,000 per annum and therefore exempt, the effective rate of taxation on *taxable* salaries and wages is around 7 to 8 per cent.

6. In comparison with this, the total yield of the tax on commercial enterprises, tradesmen and corporations was Rials 2.9 billion in 1344, whilst the national income estimates show the total income under these categories was Rials 212 billion in 1341. This includes oil and agriculture; and if these were deducted, the residue is 104 billion in 1341, or say, 125 billion in 1344. Of the Rials 2.9 billion, only Rials 500 million was collected from unincorporated enterprises, whilst of the 2.4 billion of taxes collected on corporations no less than Rials 1.1 billion represented the tax paid by State enterprises: the total taxable profits of which were around Rials 6 billion in 1344. Hence deducting both the profits and the taxes paid by State enterprises, and attributing the residual revenue entirely to non-agricultural activities, the effective rate of tax on incomes derived from property and of corporate and unincorporated enterprises comes out at 1.8 billion on 119 billion—that is to say, $1\frac{1}{2}$ per cent. as against 7–8 per cent. on wages and salaries, and an effective rate of 16 per cent. on the profits of State enterprises. As far as I can judge, there is

---

[1] Hejira lunar years date from the Muslim flight from Mecca in 622 AD. These dates, 1341–1344, correspond approximately to the years 1962–1965 AD.

nothing in the new Bill that could secure a fundamental improvement in this situation.

7. There can be little doubt, in the light of these figures, that broadly based taxes on expenditure would secure much fairer results in the distribution of the burden of taxation than the tax on income. A man who earns Rials 500,000 is bound to spend much more, even if not proportionately more, than a man earning, say, Rials 100,000, and would therefore pay far more in indirect taxes than the other man. This is by no means certain with income tax.

8. My main objections to the new Income Tax Bill can be summarised as follows:

(i) The provisions as regards business income (and particularly as regards corporate enterprises) are extremely complicated and much of the information required to establish the true liability according to the law would be very difficult to obtain, even by the most *bona fide* taxpayer. Indeed, it would require a pretty arduous study of the law to establish what the true liability is in individual cases.

(ii) It follows that assessments are bound to be arbitrary; inspectors are armed with wide discretionary powers to assess a business to tax. The assessor is free to reject evidence submitted by the taxpayer and to assess on the basis of a number of presumptive criteria, from which he is free to select according to his judgment.

(iii) There is an unpredecented variety of exemptions introduced for "incentive" reasons, which cannot be properly circumscribed or defined with any precision. Indeed, they may often depend upon criteria which can not be measured or ascertained from books and accounts (see, for example, Clause 108 and subsequent Clauses, which depend on an attribution of profits derived from different parts of an enterprise). This is bound to give wide discretionary powers to the inspector in operating such exemptions.

(iv) The combination of these—wide discretionary powers in assessment and, in effect, a wide range of administrative discretion in operating the numerous and far-reaching exemptions—is bound to lead to a highly unsatisfactory situation in administering the tax. It almost inevitably gives rise to a great deal of vexation to the taxpayer and presents opportunities for petty tyranny by the bureaucracy. The system provides so many ways in which a person can be made liable, and so many other ways in which he can nevertheless be exempt, that there must necessarily be opportunities and temptations to bribery and corruption. This is inherent in any system in which the provisions of the law do not yield clear and unambiguous results. Adam Smith's famous canons of taxation laid down that taxes must be certain, impartial in operation, and imposed with a minimum of vexation to the taxpayer. On all these principles, the present Bill comes out very badly.

9. I do not question that many of the Bill's most unsatisfactory features are due to the desire to give the maximum incentive to growth and development. Indeed, the Bill seems to be animated by a belief in the almost magic powers of taxation to promote these objectives. However, the incentive effect of any particular exemption depends on the taxes being effectively charged in its absence. When the exemptions are so wide and numerous that almost any business can be brought under them in one way or another, the incentive effect may be non-existent.

10. It has been suggested in this connection that the lenient treatment accorded to corporations as against unincorporated businesses will provide an incentive to withdraw capital from small businesses and to form large corporations which are economically more efficient. There are two observations to make on this. First, taxes on unincorporated businesses are very largely on paper; the very fact that they yield so little revenue shows that it is administratively impossible to bring them effectively within the tax net (even developed countries find it very difficult to bring the profits of small enterprises effectively within the tax net). Low rates of taxation on corporate enterprises cannot provide an advantage if the higher taxation of unincorporated enterprises is not effectively enforced. The second, and more important point, is that the formation of corporations is by no means the same thing as the promotion of large-scale business enterprise. I

understand that the great majority of corporations in Iran (perhaps over 90 per cent.) consists of closely-held family businesses,
where the corporate form has been adopted for commercial or
tax reasons, but where in the nature of the case incorporation has
not involved any change in the manner or in the scale in which the
businesses are conducted.

11. My feeling is that the tax system in Iran would be enor-
mously improved if the whole of the income tax system were
scrapped, and replaced by a broad, flat rate tax on the incomes
generated in economic activities. Such a tax is a non-selective "value
added tax", assessed on enterprises on the difference between
sales receipts and the purchase of materials, fuel and equipment.
This difference is in fact nothing else than the sum of profits,
interest, rent, salaries, and wages generated by the activities of an
enterprise. Taxing the "value added" at, say, 5 per cent. (or, say,
10 per cent.) is the same thing as imposing a collective tax of 5 or
10 per cent. on all these forms of income. I am not suggesting that
such a radical reform should be considered for immediate adoption
—it clearly requires very careful consideration. But it seems certain
that, if the present income tax were replaced by a tax of this kind
far more revenue would be collected at a fraction of the administrative effort, vexation and annoyance now involved in administering a complicated income tax. And despite the fact that it
would be a flat rate tax and not a progressive tax, it would be
much fairer in its incidence than the present income tax could
possibly be. I am equally certain that its incentive effects in
promoting investment and expansion would be *more* favourable
than the present tax with all its uncertainties and exemptions.
The most important consideration for promoting growth is to give
business confidence. This is far better promoted by a relatively
simple tax. What the businessman wants to know is exactly what
he will be asked to pay, without too much uncertainty, vexation or
argument.

12. In other words, it would be far better to tax *all* incomes at a
moderate flat rate, than to have numerous progressive rate
schedules which can be only very partially effective. A value
added tax may have to be supplemented by an income tax on civil
servants (since the Government cannot be made subject to a

"value added tax") and possibly by a progressive surtax on high incomes derived from all sources) operating with a high exemption limit that would severely limit the number of taxpayers liable to such a charge. I am doubtful whether such a "global surtax" could be made very effective in present circumstances; but assuming that the bulk of the revenue is secured by the flat rate tax, there would be no harm in introducing a supplementary progressive tax provided the rate schedule is kept moderate. The rate schedules in the present Bill appear to me to be much too high for securing confidence. Taxpayers' cooperation and voluntary compliance—which are essential for any really success-ful income tax—are tender plants which grow slowly and might not develop at all if taxpayers felt that they were too harshly treated.

(2) *Other sources of revenue*

13. If the present income tax could really be replaced by a "value added tax" on the lines suggested above and if such a tax could be successfully established and administered, I am con-vinced that it would provide a sufficient source of revenue to make the introduction of further taxes unnecessary at the present stage.

14. However, in the absence of such a radical change, I think there is a strong case for strengthening the tax system by the introduction of at least two new taxes:

(i) a production tax;
(ii) an annual tax on the value of urban properties.

The introduction of both of these is supported by a number of Iranian economists. I have not been able, in the time available, to consider either of them in detail, nor am I in a position to make an estimate of the likely revenue which they would yield. How-ever, I should like to offer the following brief comments in support of them.

15. (i) *Production tax:* This is the name given to what is really a sales tax levied at the factory stage on a wide range of goods manufactured in Iran and destined for personal consumption. The case for introducing this tax (apart from the need for ad-ditional revenue) is that it would reduce the present excessive

protection given to domestic industries, many of which could operate profitably (and possibly more efficiently) with a lower range of import duties. The margin could, of course, be reduced by reducing the level of duties on imports. But given the need for revenue, the introduction of a production tax would achieve the same effect. I would suggest that a tax be levied on the range of commodities selected at a uniform ad valorem rate, or as near a uniform rate as possible. This would tend to reduce the degree of *differential* protection now accorded to different commodities; it would hit more severely commodities whose domestic production is relatively inefficient (as compared with the cost of the imported article) and benefit those commodities whose domestic costs are relatively lower. I feel that while the protection of domestic production by means of import duties is essential in the early stages of industrialisation, efficient industrialisation requires that the degree of effective protection as between one commodity or another should not vary too much.

16. (ii) *An annual tax on urban properties*: This is probably the simplest and most effective method of levying tax on property owners. The main objection to its introduction is the difficulty of valuation. If valuation is left to the fiscal authorities, it creates a very serious burden, given the lack of expert valuers. My suggestion is that it would be possible to make use of the market mechanism to obtain a reasonably accurate valuation of properties. The basic principle of this suggestion is that of "self-assessment"; the property owners should be asked to declare the current market value of their properties and the tax would be levied as a small annual percentage (say, 2 to 3 per cent.) of such values. To prevent under-valuation, the declared values of the properties in each local area would be publicly posted, and it would be open to anyone to make a bid for them at, say, 25 per cent. or more above the declared values. The owner is then left with the choice either of selling his property or of re-valuing it at the bid price for tax purposes. If the bid is thus frustrated, the person making the bid would be entitled to a commission for his services (this commission could take the form of a year's extra revenue resulting from the re-valuation). The particular property should only be open for such "bidding" for a limited period—say, three months, such

periods being "staggered" as between districts—and at the end of that period the values established should stand for, say, five years.

17. A system of this kind has frequently been canvassed by academic economists, but has not, as far as I know, been adopted yet in any country. Its adoption undoubtedly raises a number of difficulties; for example, special provisions might well be necessary for owner-occupiers. I was asked to discuss this suggestion in more detail with officials of the Ministry of Finance and I am hoping to do so before I leave.

OBSERVATIONS ON THE FISCAL REFORM IN VENEZUELA[1]

1. The main purposes of the reform are stated to be (*a*) the modernisation of the fiscal system so as to make it into a more efficient instrument for collecting revenue; (*b*) to reduce the inequities arising from widespread tax evasion and tax avoidance; (*c*) to secure a more equitable distribution of income through progressive taxation; (*d*) to introduce three new taxes for specific purposes (partly for equity, partly for economic and partly for revenue reasons); (*e*) to augment Government revenue from domestic sources so as to increase total revenue, and reduce the present large dependence on petroleum exports for financing current expenditures; (*f*) to provide additional incentives to investment in connection with Venezuela's development plan.

2. Many of these are long-term objectives which are only expected to bear fruit gradually over a period of years. This is also true of the revenue aspect since little additional revenue can be expected from the proposed changes in the schedules of income tax rates or of the revised manner of levying alcohol and tobacco taxes and customs duties.

3. The first question to be considered is does Venezuela need more revenue in the next few years? For the moment the budget is in a small surplus even if all capital expenditures are included. The balance of payments on current account is also in surplus and is expected to remain in surplus for the period of the V Plan to a cumulative total of US$9 thousand million of 1975 purchasing power (see Plan, Table II–10). There is, therefore, no apparent need to raise additional revenue. It is true that the Plan envisages

---

[1] Written, at the invitation of the Minister for Economic Coordination and Planning of the Government of Venezuela, in Caracas in December 1976 and printed in Spanish in the official publication of the Ministry of Finance in March 1977.

that there will be a cumulative gap of Bs. 37 milliard in the Central Government Budget of which only Bs. 20 milliard is envisaged to be financed by the Venezuelan Investment Fund, leaving Bs. 17 milliard (or including the debt service, Bs. 23.7 milliard) to be financed through further borrowing. But since a deficit of this order appears to be consistent with a continued surplus in the balance of payments, there is no obvious reason why this purely financial gap (as shown in Table II–13) should require additional taxation.

4. In the peculiar circumstances of Venezuela the question of the amount of taxation to be raised cannot be decided by the financial requirements of the Government. Nor could it be asserted that the very existence of a budget deficit would generate inflationary pressures that would frustrate the Government's economic objectives.

5. It is far from certain (in my view) whether this would be the case, or whether the reduction or elimination of the fiscal deficit through additional taxation would enhance Venezuela's rate of economic growth rather than reduce it. If the plans had been consistently drawn up, the additional demand generated by the fiscal deficit would lead to higher domestic demand which in turn would be satisfied by additional imports; but these imports would not be so large as to imbalance the current balance of payments. This means that as far as *traded* goods are concerned, the additional demand could be satisfied by additional imports and could not, therefore, lead to inflation. Inflation could arise, however, as a result of a shortage of non-traded goods (mainly in the form of a shortage of housing accommodation and various other services).

6. The important political question is, therefore, how far such inflationary pressures should be allowed to occur for the sake of higher growth. There is a trade-off between growth and inflation and the question to be decided is where the optimum combination is to be found.

7. Everyone is agreed that the present situation provides a unique opportunity for Venezuela to become a "developed" nation in terms of living standards, material and cultural, and in terms of full employment—an opportunity which must on no account be missed. At the moment, the organised "developed"

sector of the economy probably absorbs little more than half of
the labour force which is estimated to grow, on account of high
natural rate of increase, at 4.4 per cent. per annum, in the next
five years. On the calculation of the World Bank it would require
an increase in manufacturing output of about 8 per cent. a year
just in order to prevent the situation from getting worse: in
other words, to provide enough additional employment in the
"developed" sector to prevent unemployment and underemploy-
ment from rising faster than the working force. The new Plan
provides annual increases in manufacturing output of 13.2 per cent.
over the Plan period which, according to the Plan, would imply
a 5.8 per cent. increase in manufacturing employment or 1.4 per
cent. more than the natural increase in the labour force. So, even
if the high targets of the Plan were fully realised, the absorption
of the large reserve of labour which is unemployed or underem-
ployed at present, would proceed only very slowly.

8. And it must be emphasised that an annual increase in manufacturing output of 13.2 per cent. over a five years period is an
extremely ambitious target which should be compared with the
attained increase of 8·3 per cent. in the period 1970–75, 8·8 per
cent in the period 1971–75 and 9·0 per cent. in 1972–75. Clearly it
would require conditions of very high demand pressure to step
up the rate of growth to 13·2 per cent.; indeed it would be impossible to do so unless demand is kept in excess of supply and
grows at a faster rate than supply so as to give maximum push to
higher production and expansion of capacity.

9. The physical factors which will limit the attainable rate of
growth do not lie in either labour as such, or capital as such, but
in the scarcity of managerial and skilled labour, and in the
inevitable time-lags in the preparation of detailed blue-prints,
etc., for the installation of new factories. It is doubtful whether the
resources released through any reduction in consumption secured
by higher taxation would ease these bottlenecks. For such reductions are not likely to release labour, of the required kind, nor
to shorten the gestation period involved in the creation of new
capacity.

10. It follows that, to secure maximum growth, specific
measures of physical control are required over the allocation of

scarce resources rather than financial measures operating on *overall* consumption demand. There may be a case for releasing building labour now engaged in the construction of luxury apartment houses, or office buildings, or even roads, so as to make more labour available for the building of factories, schools and hospitals, and working class houses, but these objectives could not be attained by higher taxation as such. There is no reason to expect that the growth of consumption and investment in the private sector is negatively correlated. It is more likely to be true that the two are positively correlated, so that restraints in consumption achieved by budgetary measures would have an adverse effect on private investment with unfavourable consequences on the rate of growth.

11. The above analysis relates to the situation which is likely to obtain in the next five to ten years. In the further future the situation might become quite a different one, and large increases in taxation, and particularly of progressive taxation, may well be needed to secure a sustainable balance of the economy and to create a balanced society.

12. For this reason the emphasis given to the structural character of the fiscal reform (found, for example, in Dr Hurtado's speech on the 24th November) strikes the right note in my opinion —even though one might doubt whether the actual reforms proposed are adequate from the point of view of the long-run objectives. This is partly because it is difficult to spell out the precise nature of the changes in administrative procedures, and in the whole system of administration, which is the centre-piece of the proposed reform. The changes in the structure of income tax do not seem to me to go very far and I would not invariably regard them as improvements.

13. In the case of *personal income tax*, it is, of course, a commendable feature of the Venezuelan tax system that a relatively large number of steps secure a smooth rate of progression; and also that the rates of the individual steps are very low—thereby securing an important, unexploited revenue potential for the future. I see no justification, however, for the provision that 30 per cent. of taxable income should be exempt from tax irrespective of the size of income; indeed I know of no other country the

income tax of which contains any such provision. It is unfortunate
that the opportunity was not taken to abolish the 30 per cent
exemption in connection with the present scheme of reform. (It
is of course far easier to abolish an anomalous provision of this
kind while the schedule of rates remains very low.) There is also
a total exemption limit of Bs. 24,000 (which, as I understand,
could mount up to Bs. 38,000 according to the taxpayer's family
circumstances) which operates incongruently in conjunction with
the 30 per cent exemption on incomes above this: thus a single
man earning, say, Bs. 25,000 pays tax on 70 per cent of Bs. 25,000
—meaning he pays a tax on Bs. 17,500, when in any other country
he would only pay tax on Bs. 1,000, i.e., on the *excess* of his taxable
income over the exemption limit.

14. I can see the justification for making the maximum rate
applicable to incomes in excess of Bs. 2 million because there must
be very few incomes that are above this figure, and it is somewhat
ludicrous to have the rate of progression continued to an even
higher level. But I can see no justification for the *moderate* increase
in rates which, even in their original form, would only have added
Bs. 220 million to income tax revenue; after the President's recent
intervention which limits the increase in taxation to incomes in
excess of Bs. 200,000, the net additional revenue becomes quite
insignificant. According to the Ministry of Finance there were only
3,700 such persons in Venezuela in 1975 with incomes in excess of
Bs. 200,000 and total tax collected from them was rather less than
Bs. 300 million. Since this measure creates a considerable kink
in an otherwise smooth tax curve, I cannot see any point in making
this change. It is not likely to satisfy the desires of the masses of
voters who want greater justice in taxation; at the same time it
exposes the Government to the charge, however unjustified, of
raising the tax burden on the business community (who alone are
capable of earning incomes of this size) at a time when the
Government is relying on them to secure maximum savings and
investment for expansion.

15. On the other hand, I regard the idea of taxing business
people, etc., on *presumed incomes* as a potentially good one, provided
one can rely on an honest tax administration and provided that
detailed criteria for the determination of presumed income are

spelled out in the legislation and not left to administrative discretion. To make any such system effective would require that the law should lay down something like a "point-system" which accords so many units of presumed income to different categories of personal expenditure—for example, the type, location and size of habitation, the number of servants kept, motor cars and yachts owned and the frequency of journeys abroad for non-business purposes. It would also be required that the taxpayer should make a declaration of total personal expenditure on a detailed form provided, and that he should make a signed declaration on oath that, to the best of his knowledge and belief, the above compilation agrees with his total expenditure in the previous year. In this way, the income tax in the highest ranges of income could in effect be made into an *expenditure tax*, which gives much stronger inducements to a reduction in unnecessary luxury spending—a far more powerful inducement than would be provided by a graduated indirect tax which taxed luxury goods at relatively high rates. (The reason why an expenditure tax of this kind is a much more powerful incentive to reduce spending and increase saving, is partly because the implicit rates of taxation at the margin would be very much higher than the likely rates of a sales tax on luxury goods; and mainly because it would discourage *all* forms of expenditure at the margin and not only expenditure on commodities which are subject to luxury tax.)

16. With regard to the reform of company taxation, I have two main points to make. One is that the new marginal rate of 55 per cent is too high for a country like Venezuela and its height could hardly be justified by reference to the fact that owing to various avoidance devices which the law permits, very few firms would effectively be taxed at that rate. The second point is that while reducing the number of steps from 8 to 4, the reform maintains the principle of a progressive schedule of rates which has no justification in the case of company taxation. Indeed, as the formal submission to Congress says in the Introducción de la Reforma Fiscal 1976, "Un sistema global puro debería contemplar una tarifa proporcional para las compañías de capital, con lo que se podrá evitar las distorsiones en la asignación de recursos que implica una multiplicidad de tarifas para este tipo de contri-

buyentes". The main reason, which is not explicitly stated, is that it discriminates against companies *merely* on account of their size, which, from an economic point of view should, if anything, be favoured, because the large firms are likely to be the more efficient producers on account of economies of large-scale production. The justification given in the report for the maintenance of these steps is "la co-existencia en Venezuela de sectores económicos con diferentes grados de desarrollo". This does not seem to me an effective argument for maintaining a differentiated system.

17. I would propose, therefore,—unless of course it is too late for the Government to introduce such changes in their reform plan —that there should only be a *single* rate on companies; but at a much lower level—say 35 or 40 per cent.—than 55 per cent.[1] And this rate should apply irrespective of the amount of income of companies.

18. The problem of *small* companies could best be dealt with by introducing an option whereby Sociedad Anónimos and other collective societies could opt to be taxed under the schedule applicable to personal taxation (with adjustments according to the share of individual partners), rather than on the company tax rate, provided that total income of the Associedad is less than, say, Bs. 150,000.

19. I regard the other major item of reform, the removal of the 40 per cent. credit on dividends, as a good thing which discourages consumption, encourages the retention of profits and also provides an additional justification for reducing the rates of company taxation below the present level. I also approve of the specific provision described in Article 62 of the projected income tax law, whereby retained profits become subject to a 10 per cent. surcharge if they are not invested in fixed or working capital of the enterprise (or of other enterprises referred to in Article 70) after three years.

20. On the other hand, where the reform fails, in my opinion, in terms of its own "structural" objectives, is in maintaining the

---

[1] I presume the 55 per cent emerged because the Government intended to have a schedule of rates that is 5 per cent above the existing level, and the present 50 per cent top rate is a survival from the days when the levy of income tax was the preferred method of profit sharing for private companies in the oil industry. Now that companies are nationalised, I cannot see any reason for keeping up with this high company tax rate.

existing system of "exoneraciones" and indeed in adding to the existing list eight new ones. This whole system of exonerations could be criticized on the ground that it gives far too much discretionary power to the tax administrator and must therefore be a rich source of tax avoidance as well as of fraudulent evasion. It is these exonerations which must largely account for the fact that the total revenue from company taxation in 1975 amounted to Bs. 1,244 million[1], which was only 4·6 per cent. of the total of profits and rents earned in that years according to the National Accounts.

21. In my view, the actual effect of all the various exonerations is very questionable and tends to be the less the more widespread these exonerations are. I think it would be very much better, assuming it is politically feasible, to abolish all exonerations and use instead the instrument of a direct subsidy on investment (like the "investment grants" introduced in 1965 in the United Kingdom), combined perhaps with a licensing system for building permits both in order to stimulate new investment and to direct it to the desired channels. Subsidies are much preferable to "exonerations" from taxation for various reasons—the most important being that they are paid promptly and without regard to the tax position of the recipient. Exonerations only benefit firms insofar as their tax liability is effectively reduced in consequence. For firms who have no current tax liabilities—because they are new firms or because they do not make sufficient profits in the year in question—exonerations may be of no value at all. Subsidies on investment by means of "exonerations" tend to discriminate in favour of large and well established firms as against newcomers.

22. But an even more important reason is that they make tax evasion so much easier, since the Government's administrative machinery is not in a position to verify systematically whether particular exonerations claimed are justified or not. It appears, in fact, that lack of facilities for cross-checking or verifying taxpayers' returns is one of the most important causes of the high degree of tax evasion in Venezuela.

23. The other main cause of tax evasion is direct bribery and corruption. By the very nature of this type of activity it is im-

---

[1] Estimate given to me by the Ministry of Finance.

possible to get any solid evidence as to how widespread corruption is and how much tax is lost thereby. I am convinced that in most underdeveloped countries corruption must be very widespread, mainly on account of the fact that the tax officials are grossly underpaid especially when account is taken of the amount of money they "handle" i.e., of the gains that taxpayers are able to make according to whether the tax official admits some particular claim or not. The temptations to which tax officials are exposed cannot be effectively countered by any system of administrative supervision; they can only be countered by creating a *corps d'élite* of revenue officers—something akin to France's "Inspecteurs des Finances"—and paying them on a scale at which they are able to live at a comfortable middle class standard without depending on bribery; and which enables them not to feel inferior to the wealthy businessmen with whose affairs they have to deal.

24. Of course, the creation of such a *corps d'élite* could not be done overnight; it is not just a matter of money, but a matter of education from early childhood. Improvement in standards of education seems to be the most important problem of countries like Venezuela, not just from this particular aspect but also from many others.

25. In the short time available I have not been able to study the provisions of the new reform in any great details; but in answer to the main question put to me, whether the reform itself is likely to promote the objectives of the V Plan of the Nation or, on the contrary, likely to be in conflict with it, it seems to me pretty clear that it is going to do neither. Unless the new system is used as an instrument to raise excessive amounts of taxation prematurely—and there is no danger of this whatsoever because the changes in the income tax laws and in the laws regulating indirect taxation will yield very little extra revenue and, in some cases, are not intended to bring in any net additional revenue at all— I cannot see that they could have any substantial effect on the Plan. I do not believe that the *threat* of additional taxation would be sufficient to deter people from undertaking activities that they find profitable especially when the threat (as in the present case) is so ill-founded.

26. On the other hand, the economic effects of the two new

taxes on land are bound to be favourable, particularly that of the tax on unutilized land—though here again, for purely admini- strative reasons, the beneficial effects are hardly likely to be effective within the period of the V Plan.

27. The Special Contribution is a variant of the old idea of a tax on the betterment value of land, resulting from expenditure by the State, on roads, railways, canalisation systems, etc., which should be used to finance (in part or in whole) the public expendi- ture which gives rise to it. The variant suggested in the present reform law does not make use of the "betterment" concept— which would require a tax on the *increase* in value resulting from public works. Instead it allocates 80 per cent. of the cost of a particular public improvement among the surrounding land- owners on an aliquot-share basis, subject to maximum levy from each contributor of 30 per cent. of the pre-betterment value of the land. I regard this as an inferior method from an equity point of view; but presumably it is administratively easier since it does not require a post-betterment valuation of the land as well as a pre- betterment valuation.

28. Finally, there is the tax on gross sales (or turnover) im- posed on enterprises at all stages of production and distribution (presumably including retailing) for the finance of a Special Fund for scientific and technical research and education. The curious feature of this provision is that there are *three* rates proposed for this levy depending on the size of the enterprise—$\frac{1}{2}$ per cent., 1 per cent. and $1\frac{1}{2}$ per cent. This makes it probable that the amount effectively passed on to the final buyer will be the charge levied on the price-*leaders*, who are likely to be the largest firms, paying at the highest rate. Hence the cost to the consumer is likely to exceed the revenue to the Fund; the difference being an addition to the profit of the firms who are paying at the lower rates. It would have been much better to have a single-stage tax levied at the wholesale stage, than a multi-stage general sales tax; and given the latter, it would have been much better to make the charge uniform at, say, 1 per cent—which might have yielded Bs. 1–2 milliards annually, thus making a handsome contribution to the development of technical education which is very badly needed.